Learning Library Science Series

Learn
Library Classification

Anil K. Dhiman
Yashoda Rani

Ess Ess Publications

4837/24, Ansari Road, Darya Ganj,
New Delhi-110002
✆ : 23260807
Fax : 23274173
E-mail: info@essessreference.com
url:http://www.essessreference.com

First Published 2005

ISBN : 81-7000-452-7

Price : 325/-

Published by :

Ess Ess Publications

4837/24, Ansari Road, Darya Ganj,
New Delhi - 110 002
Phone : 23260807
Fax : 23274173
E-mail: info@essessreference.com
url:http://www.essessreference.com

Printed at :

Printline, New Delhi

Contents

Learning Library Science Series

Each book in this series has been written to provide in-depth knowledge of the basics of Library and Information Science and is in accordance with the B.Lib.Sc. syllabus of major Indian universities imparting the said course. To make this work series more comprehensible for the students, the books under this series have been written in Question-Answer format and the language used is very simple, easy and understandable. This series has been divided into six parts, each of which is dedicated to one basic aspect of library and information science.

The present series consists of six books in all, its first part deals with Learn Library and Society, second is Learn Library Management, third is Learn Library Classification (Theory), fourth being Learn Library Classification (Theory), fifth, Learn Reference Services, Information Services and Their Sources and the last and sixth book is Learn Computer Basics and its Application in Libraries. This gives a comprehensive and complete coverage to almost all the syllabi of most of the Indian universities imparting Bachelors' Degree in Library and Information Science (B.Lib.Sc.).

Although this book has primarily been written, keeping in mind the students making an attempt at the above mentioned Degree course, but it is hoped that this book shall find its place with anyone who is interested to know and learn more about the basics of library and information science. Not only the students, but the teachers of library and information science can derive equal benefit from this series. The books are equally suited to librarianship, library science students and library staff seeking to upgrade their skills.

Authors

Acknowledgements

It is indeed difficult to write one book and writing such a series of books is naturally much more difficult but this series could finally see the light of the day, but this could never have been possible without those innumerous books which have been consulted at every step and we are grateful to the authors of all those books, naming all of whom would not be humanly possible. We are thankful to Mrs. Sheel Sethi and Mr. Sumit Sethi, the owners of Ess Ess Publications for giving us an opportunity to present this voluminous work to the readers. We would also like to record our thanks to our friend, Mr. Sushil Kumar of IIT, Roorkee for his kind help. We feel indebted to Sh. Ram Lal Dhiman, Smt. Kamla Devi and Ms. Alka Rani who helped us at various steps. Last but not the least, we are thankful to our son Aman who could not get much of our attention while we were working on this work.

Anil. K. Dhiman
Yashoda Rani

1

Library Classification : Its Need and Purposes

Q. : What is Library Classification? Discuss the need and purposes of classification in a library.

Or

Explain the purpose of book classification stating the difference between knowledge or classification and book classification.

Or

'Classification has been devised to bring a system out of confusion of things'. Comment on this and explain the need and purpose of classification in a library.

Or

'Without classification no Librarian can build up a systematic library'. Comment on this and explain the need and purpose of classification in a library.

Or

Why do you mean by library classification? Explain in detail.

Or

Discuss the need and purpose of classification in a library.

Ans. Classification lies at the root of all human activities. Our daily life is very much dependent on the process of classification, however, elementary this process may appear. You can surely recall a number of activities around you where classification plays its part. For example, take the arrangement of contents in a railway time table, the display of goods in a grocery shop, the arrangement of modules in a departmental store to facilitate the selection of goods by customers, the seating arrangement in a theatre or stadium, the assignment of registration numbers to various motor vehicles by a state transport authority, or the sorting of letters by postmen first by the city, then by the street and lastly by the house numbers for quick delivery of post. These are simple examples of how we use classification in our activities.

The word classification was derived from the Latin word *classes* which means order or rank of mobility in Roman society based upon birth and wealth. Classification is a mental process by which we group or separate things on the basis of common characteristics.

The term classification is used and defined in almost every sphere of knowledge by various philosophers, social thinkers and scientists. L.M.Harrod in his *Librarian's Glossary* has defined the term pin-pointedly –"The arrangement of things in logical order according to their degree of likeness. Especially the assignment of books to there proper places in a scheme of book classification. A scheme for the arrangement of books and other material in a logical sequence according to subject or form." According to W.C. Berwick Sayers –" classification is a process of the mind by which things are arranged according to their degrees of likeness and separated according to their degrees of unlikeness." Arthur Maltby also defined the term as –" the systematic arrangement of books and other material on shelves or of catalogue and index entries in the manner which is most useful to those who read or who seek a definite piece of information". Margaret Mann has also given a similar definition –"the arranging of things according to likeness and unlikeness". According to a Wolf "Classification is a mode of knowledge, a way of grasping the unity of certain things and the relation between various kinds of things". In simple terms, classification is a method for systematic grouping of things or objects on the basis of their shared or variant characteristics. S.R.Ranganathan, in *Prolegomena to Library Classification (1967),* elaborately discusses the meaning of classification. In the case of physical objects, division and assortment are the two results of classification. According to him, while division implies sorting objects into two or more groups, assortment additionally denotes arrangement of these groups in a predetermined sequence. Further, in library classification, the sequence of objects, i.e., documents, is so mechanised by the use of notation that it is reflected in the notation when a document is withdrawn or added.

Thus, one can see that the term 'classification' is a homonym. Ranganathan, therefore, tried to resolve the homonym by examining the various ways in which the term has been used:

Classification in Sense 1 is DIVISION.

Classification in Sense 2 is ASSORTMENT.

Classification in Sense 3 is CLASSIFICATION IN SENSE 2 *plus* representing each entity by an ordinal number taken out of a system of ordinal numbers, designed to mechanise the maintenance of the sequence.

Classification in Sense 4 is CLASSIFICATION IN SENSE 3 when complete assortment is made of an amplified universe – that is when the entities and the pseudo-entities arising in the process of successive assortment stand arranged in one filatory sequence.

Classification in Sense 5 is CLASSIFICATION IN SENSE 4 with all the entities removed but only the pseudo-entities or classes retained.

It is classification in Sense 5 that is used:

(i) either when the universe classified is infinite.

(ii) When some of the entities are unknown and unknowable at any moment, even though the universe classified, is finite.

It is classification in Sense 5 that is practiced by the library profession.

The primary concern of libraries is to establish the most helpful arrangement of documents. Library classification, therefore, presupposes the use of notation, i.e., a brief symbol for the names of subjects.

Library Classification

The term library classification has been defined by various library and information scientists. Few such definitions are as follows:

S.R.Ranganathan: 'It is the translation of the name of the subject of a book into a preferred artificial language of ordinal numbers, and the individualisation of the several books dealing with the same specific subject by means of further set of ordinal numbers which represent some features of the book other than their thought content'.

H.E. Bills: 'Classification is a series or system of classes arranged in some order according to some principle or conception, purpose or interest or some combination of such'.

W.C.Berwick Sayers : The arrangement of books on shelves, or description of them, in the manner which is most useful to those who read'.

Margaret Mann: "Classification is the arranging of things according to likeness and unlikeness. It is the sorting and grouping of things, but in addition, classification of books is a knowledge classification with adjustments made necessary by the physical form of books".

It may, therefore, be said that classification is a key to knowledge, it is a logical process for grouping documents in a library.

Need and Purpose of Library Classification

The information explosion has created problems for the libraries in arranging and disseminating the information to their users. In some libraries, where the books are arranged by author, title or accession numbers, it becomes very difficult to provide the documents if required on a particular subject at a time, because the documents on that subject will be found scattered throughout the collection. Hence, the library authorities devised the schemes of classification so as to arrange the collection by subject. With the help of classification schemes the closely related subjects can be arranged in filatory sequence.

In short, the need and purpose of library classification may be discussed as under:

(i) Library classification helps to arrange documents in a systematic order, which is most convenient to the reader and the library staff. It brings related subjects in close proximity, called collocation by Henry Bliss.

(ii) Library classification helps the identification and location of a document on a given subject wanted by a reader whatever may be the size of the library collection. Documents can be quickly retrieved from and replaced to their original positions. The location, lending and replacement of documents are completed mechanically in libraries.

(iii) Library classification helps to arrange documents into organised groups, like pigeonholes; and when a new document is added to the collection, classification finds an appropriate place for the newly added documents among the other documents on the same subject.

(iv) The universe of knowledge is dynamic, continuous, infinite and ever growing. New areas or subjects are being continuously added to the sum total of human knowledge. When the first document on a new subject is added to the library collection, it finds itself at the appropriate place among the already existing related subjects, i.e., among its kith and kin and according to the level of its relationship to them. The functions stated in (ii), (iii), and (iv) are also known as mechanisation of the arrangement.

(v) The Classification helps to organise book displays and exhibitions. It facilitates withdrawal of certain documents from the main collection for special purposes and occasions such as book talks, seminars, symposia, conferences and special exhibitions, on a given topic.

(vi) Library classification helps in recording the daily issue and return of documents on various subjects at the circulation counter of a library. This facilitates the compilation of statistics on issues, which reflect the pattern of use and demand of documents on different subjects. The feedback helps in the allocation of funds to various subjects and guides the book selection policy of the library. The statistics so collected can be included in the annual report of the library.

(vii) Stock verification is a very important aspect of library administration. Library classification, through the medium of shelf lists, facilitates an efficient and thorough stock verification of the library's holdings.

(viii) Library classification helps in the compilation of reading lists. This facilitates facet analysis of the reference queries on various aspects and indirectly helps in an efficient reference service.

(ix) The classification helps in the compilation of subject union catalogues and bibliographies of books and other reading material. The union catalogues are very important tools for resource sharing and cooperation among libraries.

(x) Classified catalogues are only possible with a classification scheme. In a research library, classified catalogues are preferred over dictionary catalogues.

(xi) Library classification assists in systematically deriving subject entries. It also aids the cataloguer to use the alphabetical list of subject headings for deriving specific subject headings through class numbers, i.e., by the chain procedure.

(xii) Classification principles are used in subject headings and thesaurus construction.

(xiii) The classification also helps the library staff, especially the classifiers, to be aware of and comprehend the complexities in the development of the universe of knowledge, which is the basis for a systematic arrangement of documents in libraries.

(xiv) Nowadays classification finds immense uses in OPACs (i.e., online public access catalogues). In a computerised catalogue, the class number field can be used in combination with other fields such as language date or even subject heading and can be used with logical operators such as AND/OR/NOT or the Boolean logical operators. Class numbers can be used to broaden or narrow the searches. Class number searches in combination with other fields increase the efficiency of the information retrieval system, of which classification is a tool.

(xv) Overall, it is the basis for the organisation of knowledge embodied in documents for maximum use. It is the basis for efficient bibliographic control and retrieval of documents. It is a great time saving device for the reader and the library staff.

Knowledge Classification and Document Classification

When we classify the books in the library, we classify the knowledge and not the books. The order in which the classification takes place, has been found most convenient in the consensus opinion of scientists, intellectual workers and great scholars. The documents have their own physical form and serve distinctive purpose. The document classification, therefore differs from knowledge classification because of the forms, their composite character, shape etc. which distinguish them from subjects. For this reason, the schemes of classification provided special artificial classes and piece of apparatus which discriminate documents as documents.

Knowledge is not static, it always advances, changes comes forth in accordance with the progress of thought.

When the documents are classified in the library, it becomes necessary for the classifier to individualize each and every document otherwise disorder will prevail on the shelves. It often happens that a number of documents on a particular subjects are received and classified. Then are classified in accordance with the knowledge classification.

But this sort of classification does not provide the technique to individualize the documents and hence he has to take up the physical features or other attributes of these documents such as author, year of publication, volume number, copy number etc. Here is thus evident that only knowledge classification may not individualize the documents. The library classification therefore differs a bit from the knowledge classification.

As we know that one requirement of classification is to reveal the relations between books and that natural relation appears to be their thought contents or subject matter. Therefore the documents are arranged in exactly the same order that the subjects they contain.

As stated earlier, Dr. Ranganathan has advocated that the library classification (or document classification) is a combination of three areas of classification known as Class Number represents *Knowledge Classification,* Book Number i.e., *Book Classification* and the Collection Number for *Sequence Classification.*

According to Sayers a classification of books is a classification of knowledge with adjustment conditioned by the physical form of books. He explained the above statement by saying that a book-classification is not a current statement of classification of pure knowledge, it is an adaptation of as perfect a statement of knowledge as the classification maker can find when he modes his classification and it is preserved in use by its additional apparatus in the shape of notation, index and other auxiliaries. Such an adjustment is necessary being the book a complex affair. To make it more clear we take an example of separate and definable subject Botany. A book relating to Botany may be a history, a periodical, a dictionary etc. On the basis of their physical form we have to provide means of discriminating them in the most useful way.

So, we may say that when we classify the documents we take help from knowledge classification. We assign them a class number first which implicitly represents the knowledge classification. On a particular subject a number of documents come into the library and all such documents bear the same class number. But then a question arises as to how we could given them a helpful sequence. It means the documents bearing one and the same class number still need individualization. We have to further assign them book number, copy number etc. Such type of adjustment is necessary. This is library classification which may not be helpful or convenient if the documents are classified only in accordance with knowledge classification. When we classify knowledge contained in the documents and we put together them which contain like division of knowledge and separate which have unlike divisions of knowledge. This process is called subject classification. When we classify the documents in accordance with their physical form we simply say book classification. The latter type of classification cannot be done in the libraries.

Comparison between Knowledge Classification and Document Classification

(i) Knowledge classification is a classification of pure knowledge whereas the book classification is of applied knowledge.

(ii) The knowledge classification is based on the thoughts of logicians or epistemologists and that it may not be of much use libraries.

(iii) In knowledge classification, the nature of books is ignored but in the library classification the nature of books remains upper hand. Sayers has also emphasized: "In order to make a classification scheme a practical instrument for the arranging of books the nature of books themselves must be considered".

(iv) In book classification, to consider the nature of books, each field of knowledge is broken into main classes, sub-classes and the notation is provided to them but in knowledge classification it is not needed.

(v) Both book classification as well as knowledge classification represent mental process by which the ideas are classified. In the former, the division and subdivision of each tract of knowledge continues until such division becomes impossible or unnecessary but in the later such division is not required.

(vi) In book classification, the process of division must be exhaustive. Sayers says, 'each subject must be divided, step by step' as minutely as is possible, and again, that the sum of all the divisions, sub-divisions and sections shall be as complete as analytical statement of the meaning and content of the class term as is possible. But in the knowledge classification, the division comes out as logical statement without class term.

(vii) Books themselves are not subject. They are statements of subjects. In other words, a book is a written account of the ideas and notions. In book classification, the thought contents for the place of the document in accordance with the strata arranged. But in the knowledge classification, the thought contents may not fix up the place of the document.

(viii) In knowledge classification, the classification is done by the philosophers for their self satisfaction, compatible to their own requirement. But in book classification, the classification is done keeping in view the mass-interest and usefulness.

(ix) The knowledge classification is more abstract in nature whereas the book classification is more concrete in nature.

(x) The knowledge classification is natural but the book classification is artificial.

(xi) The arrangement of thoughts is based on the practical experiences of the self in the knowledge classification, but in the book classification the sequence is fixed.

(xii) In the absence of notation there is unlimited comprehensiveness in the knowledge classification whereas the provision of notation in the book classification confines the comprehensiveness in array and chain.

(xiii) Sayers explains the basic difference, "the book classification must also differ from the knowledge classification because of the forms of books, their composite characters, shapes, and other qualities which distinguish them from subjects. To differentiate these the classification-maker adds to his scheme special artificial classes and pieces of apparatus which discriminate books as books". On the other hand Mills also expressed the same difference: "that library classification is a classification of knowledge with certain adjustments necessitated by the physical nature of books. This also has been the view held in varying degrees by Richardson, Cutter, Bliss, Sayers and others."

(xiv) Knowledge classification is philosophical classification which is relatively broad and neglects the principles of subject analysis on which fool proof library classification resets.

(xv) The Knowledge classification gives importance to the

evolutionary sequence but the book classification does not follow such a sequence.

(xvi) There is no physical structure embodying subject in the knowledge classification but on the other hand in book classification, physical structure of the document having units of knowledge is required.

(xvii) Index is not required in the knowledge classification whereas in book classification, it is must.

(xviii) In knowledge classification, the books on one and on the same subject cannot be individualized whereas in book classification such books can easily be individualized with the physical features.

(xix) Sayers represents the knowledge like a tree with a main stem, representing the principle of division selected, which throws of branches which are the main divisions of knowledge, and these branches in turn throw off smaller branches, which in turn throw off their own even smaller ones; and the process is continued to any extent. But we cannot usefully make a working classification in the likeness of a tree we must reduce it merely to words or terms, arrays or chains. This view evidently expresses that the knowledge like a tree may not be able to provide the range of things or ideas and hence we may not divide them so as to proceed from terms of greater extension and smaller intension to terms of great intension and small extension which is the basic need of book classification. Extension of a thing is all the things it cover and intension is all the qualities of those things.

Concluding, it can be said that though the book classification, to a greater extent, is based on the knowledge classification, yet differs basically and purposefully from it. The knowledge classification has been improvised with some adjustments to suit the library requirements. Sayers has rightly pointed out: "A book classification is not a current statement of the classification of pure knowledge; it is an adaptation of as perfect a statement of knowledge as the classification-maker can find when he makes his classification, and it is preserved in use by its additional apparatus in the shape of notation, index and other auxiliaries."

Q. : What are the fundamental Laws of Library Science? Discuss their implications with regards to Library Classification.

Ans. The Five Laws of Library Science were formulated by Ranganathan in 1928 and published in 1931. The book describes the essence of librarianship within the ambit of five laws. These Laws are:

- Books are for use
- Every reader his book
- Every book its reader
- Save the time of reader
- Library is a growing organism

These five laws are capable of resolving any problem arising in library science, library service and library practice.

In the discipline of library classification, the laws of library science help in resolving the conflict between Canons and/or Principles. If a problem in classifying exceeds the capacity of the Canons and Principles, the Five Laws provide the solution. The five Laws are like the Head of the State, whose authority is to be accepted as final and binding.

1. First Law : Books are for use

In 1957 the term 'Books' has been replaced by 'Documents'. The first law is actually the creation of Edward, B. Ross who was Ranganathan's Professor of Mathematics in Madras. Seeing Ranganathan's persistent struggle to formulate some norms which may help in organizing Madras Library one day he said "you mean, 'Books are for use'; you mean that is your first Law." After this Ranganathan took only three hours to formulate all the remaining Laws.

The demand of the First Law is that the arrangement of documents and the main entries should primarily be based on the characteristics of the subjects embodied in the documents. The study of these characteristics is, therefore, essential for the efficient classification, search, and retrieval of subjects and service to the readers.

Further, the criterion for "use" assumes significance. Therefore, it may be helpful to examine the differences, if any in the respective purposes of the reader. Certain affinities and dissimilarities among the subjects will then be recognized.

2. Second Law: Every Reader his Book

To fulfill the demand of this Law it is necessary for a classifier to satisfy all types of users:

(i) users, who are unable to pinpoint the specific subject and usually approach by broader subject;

(ii) users, who may pinpoint the exact subject but what they want is more specialized subject than their request suggest.

Thus, the Second Law suggests that:

(a) the arrangement provided by the class numbers should be such that all books on one subject are arranged together;

(b) the sequence of the subject should be from broad to specific;

(c) the books on different subjects should be arranged according to their degree of filiations. In other words, the shelf arrangement should display the full field of user's interest, unexpressed or expressed.

3. Third Law : Every Book its Reader

The third law "Every book its reader" implies that the time of retrieval no document relevant to the interest of the reader at the moment should be missed, irrespective of his approach.

To fulfill the demand of this Law, it is necessary that each document should get its user. The probability for getting proper users for every document would be higher if subjects are arranged among themselves in the degree of mutual relationship.

4. Fourth Law : Save the Time of the Reader

The fifth law "Library is a growing organism" implies that the Universe of subjects is ever growing and, therefore, library science is ever growing. Hence, the arrangement of documents should not be such which may consume and waste the precious time of the users. However, the demand of the Fourth Law is inherent in the demand of Second and Third Laws. That is, the arrangement of documents should be according to the degree of mutual relationship of subjects; within each subject documents should be arranged first by languages in which these are written; then by year of their publication; that the alphabetical arrangement would be unhelpful, as it is not capable to provide filiatory sequence and therefore, would be time consuming.

5. Fifth Law : Library is a growing Organism

There is direct impact of the scientific and technological developments on the growth of documents, users and manpower *vis-à-vis* the infrastructure of the library. The documents in a library should be arranged to facilitate the pin-pointed, exhaustive and expeditious service to the users, irrespective of its growth in size, number of documents or emergence of new subject. This is the demand of Fifth Law.

So, in relation to classification, these Laws fulfill the library objectives in real sense.

2

Species of Classification

Q. : Describe the enumerative and analytico-synthetic classification.

Or

Enumerate the different species of library classification. Make a comparative study of the enumerative and the faceted classification with the help of suitable examples.

Ans. The classification is the backbone of the library and it is very interesting to note how the schemes of classification have developed in the past. They took a long time in their proper development.

Rangnathan has recognized three distinct periods in the growth and development of library classification during the past hundred years. These are : 1. Pre-facet period 1876-1896, 2. Transition-to-facet period 1897-1932, and 3. Facet period 1933 to date. In the pre-facet period Melvil Dewey's Decimal classification (1876) and C A Cutter's Expansive classification (1893) were published. In the Transition to Facet period (1897-1932), UDC (1897) LC (1901) and SC (1906) were published. The Facet period (1933) has been the publication of CC (1933), BC (1935) BBK (1960), RIC (1961) and IC (1970).

On the basis of certain characteristics such as mapping of the universe of subjects, type of notation, length of schedules, provision of schedules of common isolates and special isolates, capacity for resilience and the structure of class number, the existing library classification schemes may be categorized under six types or species. They are :

A. Enumerative classification scheme

1. Purely enumerative scheme
2. Almost enumerative scheme

B. Faceted classification scheme

3. Almost faceted scheme

4. Rigidly faceted scheme
5. Almost freely faceted scheme
6. Freely faceted scheme

A. ENUMERATIVE CLASSIFICATION SCHEME

An Enumerative Classification Scheme enumerates all the possible classes of the past, present and anticipated in the future. It attempts to encompass the whole universe of knowledge in its schedules. It divides, sub-divides and arranges them in an order which may display their hierarchical relationship along with readymade class numbers for them.

According to Ranganathan 'A scheme of classification is enumerative, if it enumerates all possible specific subjects in a preferred helpful order along with their respective class numbers. An enumerative scheme has the following advatitages :

(i) It consists of a single schedule which enumerates simple and composite classes along with readymade class numbers for them;

(ii) It tries to encompass the whole universe of knowledge in its schedules;

(iii) The schedule in an enumerative classification may be termed as a dictionary of sentences;

(iv) It lacks connecting symbols to indicate even main facets of a subject;

(v) Its popularity among the libraries is because of the Relative Index, which is the basis of its purposive use and handling.

But there are certain demerits also, which are :

(i) The enumerative schemes are unguided schemes as these do not conform to an established set of postulates and principles, but enumerate virtually all classes;

(ii) The design of enumerative schemes depend solely on the flair and intuition of each individual classification;

(iii) As it lacks provisions to provide hospitality to new subjects, it becomes the cause of considerable time-lag in the organization of knowledge and the documents embodying them;

(iv) Its schedule loses its slimness as it attempts to provide class numbers for all specific subjects which are either known to exist or can be anticipated to appear in future;

(v) It lacks provisions to indicate various kinds of relationship that may appear among basic classes, facets or isolate ideas;

(vi) The process of analysis and synthesis is alien to enumerative classification.

1. Purely Enumerative Classification

'An Purely Enumerative schemes for classification consists essentially of a single schedule enumerating all subjects- of past, present and the anticipatable future/. When a scheme lists all the subject of the past, present and future with no provision of synthesis of numbers, will naturally have to be longer. Such schemes generally leave gaps in between the consecutive numbers for accommodating the new subjects. But such gaps may soon be filled up. Thus making the scheme incapable of receiving other new subjects. Hence each new subject may not find its filiatory position among the existing one. The class numbers so constructed consist of a block of closely written digits, but they are not separated by any punctuation marks etc.

The following demerits are found in enumerative schemes of classification :

(i). Schedules will be long.

(ii). It is difficult to accommodate newly emerging subjects in a filiatory sequence within the existing subjects.

(iii). Class number of such schemes often consists of a succession of semantically rich digits not separated into meaning facets.

Examples : Library of Congress Classification (LC) and Rider's International Classification (RIC)are good examples of the enumerative schemes of classification.

LC is a long schedule of 11300 pages in 45 volumes. There is no provision for synthesis of numbers. For example, in LC:

HA	Statistics	HB	Economic theory
HA1	Statistics periodicals	HB9	Periodicals
HA9	Statistics conferences	HB21	Conferences

Another member Rider's International Classification (RIC) (1961), is a long schedule and enumerates about 18000 subjects each represented by three digits namely, Roman Capital Alphabets. There is no possibility of number building here.

Consequently, it is not possible to represent new subjects. Hence, one is forced to give the same Class-Number for several subjects. This is liable to produce "Chaos-in-Little" among the books carrying that single number for representing several subjects. Therefore, the resilience of RIC is very limited.

2. Almost-Enumerative Classification

An almost-enumerative scheme for classification consists of a large schedule enumerating most of the subjects of the past, the present and the foreseeable future, and in addition, a few schedules of common isolates. This type of scheme enumerates all subjects of the past, present and future. It has a few schedules of Common isolates that can be used to construct class numbers for compound subjects. The schedule of such a scheme is lengthy. Such schemes can not keep pace with the growing universe of subjects. The class numbers consist of digits of a single block.

Examples : Subject classification (1906) of J.D. Brown is a clear example of Almost Enumerative Scheme.

It consists of a main schedule of subjects, mainly compound subjects denoted by alphabets further divided by numerals. Brown also appended a table of commonly used subdivisions, which he called Categorical Table. It lists forms and other divisions used with any class in the schedules, thus providing a limited notational synthesis. These are:

.0	Generallia
.00	Catalogues, Lists
.1	Bibliography
.2	Encyclopedia
.10	History

Main and supplementary schedules are fairly long though not as long as those of LC or RIC.

Dewey's Decimal Classification (DDC) is another good example of an almost enumerative classification scheme. It has a large schedule of enumerated subjects. There is a provision of table for standard sub divisions and geographical subdivisions which have shortened the class numbers of the compound subjects. The first edition of the DDC was published in 1876 in 44 pages. It has used Arabic numbers for its notation. This scheme was criticized by the librarians of that time. Melvil Dewey published the second edition in 1885 in 314 pages. It has a revision policy and so far its 21 editions have been published. Since 1930 DC numbers have been printed on Library of Congress printed cards. The features of the DC are laid down as under :

(i) It is an hierarchical scheme which proceeds from general to specific.

(ii) It has divided the whole universe of knowledge into ten main classes as:

(0) Generalities
(1) Philosophy
(2) Religion
(3) Social sciences
(4) Languages
(5) Pure sciences
(6) Technology (Applied Sciences)
(7) Fine Arts
(8) Literature
(9) General Geography and History

(iii) The DC has used the Decimal principle for the sub divisions of knowledge. So in practice each class number in DC is a decimal fraction and consists of three digits. The decimal is used only after three digits. In this way full notation for the main classes are shown as under:

000 Generalities
100 Philosophy
200 Religion
300 Social sciences
400 Languages
500 Pure sciences
600 Applied Sciences
700 Fine Arts
800 Literature
900 Geography & History

Thus, each of the main class has been divided into ten sub-divisions. So 100 divisions are known as second summary. The digit 0 (zero) is used for the general works. For example 500 is pure science.

510 Mathematics

520 Astronomy

530 Physics

540 Chemistry and so on.

The second division is further divided into 10 sections making 1000 sections of the main classes. This is known as third summary.

330 Economics

331 Labor Economics

332 Financial Economics

333 Land Economics

334 Cooperation

335 Socialism

336 Public Finance

337 International Economics

338 Production

339 Macro Economics

Similarly, the process of division is continued to any required subject. A decimal point is used after three digits such as :

336	Public Finance
336.1	Non Tax Revenues
336.2	Taxation
336.241	Income Tax
336.242	Personal Income Tax

The other special features of this scheme are:

(i) This scheme is an almost enumerative scheme of classification.

(ii) Its classes reflect all the areas of specialized knowledge developed in the modern society. As it has been translated in other languages of the world, so it has become a universal scheme.

(iii) Melvil Dewey introduced the idea of relative location against to fixed location. Due to this a new document on a given subject may be put in between the existing sequence at the required position.

(iv) Melvil Dewey used decimal fraction notation for arrangement of knowledge on the shelves. Indo- Arabic numerals 0-9 are used for the purpose.

(v) This scheme has a provision & useful for Minute classification.

(vi) The other important feature of DC is mnemonics which are aid to memory. There are various tables such as Area Table, Language Table, Standard Division tables etc. which are used to achieve subject synthesis.

The 21st edition of DC is in 4 volumes.

Vol.1 : Introduction, Tables

Vol.2 : Schedules 000-599

Vol.3 : Schedules 600-999

Vol.4 : Relative Index

Besides, the DDC has a provision of add to device which helps in construction of class numbers for compound subjects.

B. FACETED SCHEME

A Faceted Scheme for classification consists of schedules of Basic classes, Common isolates, and Special isolates only. The class numbers for compound subjects are constructed with the help of Basic Subjects, special isolates and the common auxiliary tables.

The quality of syntheses is, therefore, inherent in a faceted scheme, which helps in recognizing different facets and sub-facets presented by the subject of the document and then combining these facets and sub-facets with the help of some connecting symbols. The synthesized class number thereby presents a vivid picture of the thought content of the document.

According to Vickery, A faceted classification is a schedule of standard terms to be used in the subject description of documents. The terms are first of all grouped into homogeneous subject fields and... within each subject field the terms are divided into groups known as facets and within each facet they may be arranged hierarchically. The facets are listed in the schedule in a prescribed order which is usually the order in which terms are to be combined to form compound subjects.

By means of this combination order the relations between terms are displayed. A good faceted scheme has following features.

- It provides autonomy to classifier;
- It provides co-extensive class numbers to micro-subjects.
- It provides hospitality to new emerging subjects and isolates both in array and chain.

3. Almost Faceted Classification :

'An Almost-Faceted Scheme for Classification consists of a large schedule enumerating most of the subjects of the past, the present and the anticipated future and in addition a few schedules of common isolates and also some schedules of special isolates'.

In such a scheme, the schedule of subjects is lengthy because it lists basic as well as compound subjects. The class numbers of many more compound subjects can be constructed with the combination of common isolates and special isolates. In such compound subjects different type of connecting digits are used and the class number is divided into many blocks.

Examples: Universal Decimal classification (UDC) is a good example of Almost Faceted Classification Scheme. This scheme is peculiar in the sense that it consists of a combination of both enumerative and faceted character of the schemes. The UDC is basically derived from Dewey's Decimal Classification. It is called universal in the sense that encompasses the whole field of knowledge. It is essentially a practical system that any item once coded and filed correctly can be readily found from whatever angle it is sought. This is achieved by the notational device that permit the linking of simple main numbers either with other main numbers or with auxiliaries denoting place, time and similar commonly recurring categories. It is a feature which adds to its universal character.

This scheme was initiated by International Institute of Bibliography (now International Federation of Documentation or FID in 1905 and first edition was brought out by Paul Outlet and S H La Fountain in French language. It used the outline of decimal classification in a modified manner. The scheme has been published in many languages and has proved useful in large and specialized libraries. It is useful for organizing scientific literature. The most important feature of this scheme is the provision of synthesis device.

The development and maintenance of UDC is achieved by FID through its central classification committee. The revision takes place in three different ways.

(i) Extension of topics by more detailed sub divisions.

(ii) Minor changes in existing class numbers of sub divisions.

(iii) Starvation Policy introduced donker duyvis.

UDC is a analytic synthetic scheme meant for shelf arrangement and arranging entries in the catalogues and bibliographies. It has two parts.

Part one: Systematic tables and part two: Index.

Its connecting symbols are +,/,:, (), =, "..." (Double quotation marks), (hyphen). Some examples are as under:

Plant Biology and Filed Crops 581 + 633

America's North and South (taken to /) (7/8)

Arbitration Disputes between India and USSR 327 (540:47)

Libraries and Education 02:37

And so on...

As in DDC, the theme of knowledge in UDC is derived from into the following classes:

0. Generalities, Science and Knowledge
1. Philosophy, Psychology
3. Social Sciences-Law, Government etc,
4. Vacant
5. Mathematics & Natural Sciences
6. Applied Sciences, Medicine, Technology
7. The Arts, Recreation, Entertainment, Sport
8. Languages, Linguistics and Literature
9. Geography, Biography and History

Each of the above classes are divided to form narrower classes.

The second part of UDC is an alphabetical subject index published in 1988.

Another example is Bibliographic Classification (1940-53) or (BC) of Bliss. He introduced the concept of composite specification in his Bibliographic classification. He made provision of two kinds of systematic schedules – (i) the common systematic schedules the class numbers of which could be used commonly with all the classes of the main schedules, and (ii) special systematic schedules which could be applied to specific subjects for which these were designed using the indicator, (comma). This synthetic element enabled BC to achieve to a limited extent a faceted quality in its notation, and so it has been designated as Almost-Faceted Scheme

4. Rigidly – Faceted scheme

In a Rigidly-Faceted scheme of classification, the facets and their sequences are pre-determined for all the subjects going with a basic class. But in this scheme, each basic subject is divided on the basis of facets. The sequence of these facets are predetermined. Each one of the facets prescribed by the facet formula should find a place in any compound subject of a document to be classified but this does not warrant such a use of all the facets of a basic subject. This brings in rigidity in the facets formula of a basic class and also ideas to the "clustering" of connecting digits.

Example : The colon classification editions from 1-3 (1933-1950) is an example of Rigidly Faceted classification. Its 1st edition consists of the following features :

(i) The universe of knowledge was divided on a mixed base of Arabic numerals, roman capitals and small roman. Smalls were used along with (:) colon as a connecting symbol.

(ii) Roman capitals were used for basic classes and chronological device and Roman smalls for common isolates, Arabic numerals for some main divisions; also for representing isolates listed under each main class. Colon (:) was the separating device for the facets.

(iii) Each main class had a definite order of Facets.

(iv) Foci in each facet were enumerated.

(v) Common subdivisions, geographical divisions and language divisions are given separately.

(vi) Octave notation was used to increase the capacity of the notational system.

(vii) Geographical device, chronological device, subject device, alphabetical device, bias device and classic device were used.

(viii) Rules for constructing class numbers were given.

(ix) Techniques for constructing book numbers were also given.

In the second edition (1939), the following changes were made.

(i) It has following 4 parts.

Part I – Rules of Classification

Part II – Schedules of Classification

Part III – Index of Schedules

Part IV – Examples of Class Numbers

(ii) Main class mysticism was introduced and represented by a Greek letter – Δ (Delta).

(iii) The subject of Anthropology was shifted from History to Sociology.

(iv) The schedules for Jainism. Buddhism and some others were revised.

(v) Schedules for classic device were enlarged.

In the edition 3 (1950) of the colon classification, the following important features were noteworthy.

(i) The new terminology of foci, facet and phase was adopted and the rules part was accordingly changed.

(ii) Different kinds of phase relations with specific connecting symbol were introduced.

(iii) The following four devices were introduced.

(a) Evolutionary Device

(b) Mnemonic Device

(c) Octave Device

(d) Auto-Bias Device

Thus, colon classification edition 1-3 (1950) is an example of Rigidly Faceted Classification. It consists of short schedules of Basic subjects, common isolates and large number of special isolates listed under different basic subjects. Compound subjects are not listed in any type of faceted classification scheme. In the Rigidly Faceted classification, each basic class has a facet formula which is to be strictly followed in constructing the class numbers of the compound subjects. Thus the facet formula determines the facets and their sequence for all the subjects. For this reason, Edition 1-3 of colon classification are recognized as rigidly faceted classification scheme.

5. Almost-Freely faceted scheme

As mentioned above, in a rigidly-faceted scheme of classification "the facets and their sequence are predetermined for all subjects going with a basic class." This leads to a great deal of rigidity. A scheme becomes almost freely faceted "because the use of different indicator digits for diverse kinds of facets and the concept of rounds and levels removed severe rigidity in the number and the sequence of facets that can occur in a compound subject. However, some rigidity lurked in respect of levels of facet within a round". Therefore, we can see that such a scheme does have some rigidity, because of which it cannot be freely faceted in full measure. As a result, it cannot be referred to as freely faceted classification.

Examples : Edition 4 (1952), edition 5 (1957), edition 6 (1960) and edition 6 with annexure (1963) of CC are regarded as colon classification version 2. These are almost-freely faceted schemes for classification. In the 4th edition published in 1952, the following features were incorporated.

(1) In the rules part examples of class umbers were given under each main class.

(2) The common sub divisions were grouped as under :

  (a) Anteriorising Common Subdivisions

  (b) Posteriorising Common Subdivisions

  (c) Form Part of Book Number

(3) The main class of Generalia represented in the 3rd edition by Arabic numerals was represented by 'Z' in the 4th edition.

(4) Arabic numerals were used for a number of preliminary main classes.

(5) Five fundamental categories along with separate connecting symbols, were used for facet analysis in place of colon (:) which was used in the earlier edition.

(6) In the schedule of main classes, partially comprehence main classes were introduced by Greek letters such as:

β	Mathematical Science
γ	Physical Science
ψ	Humanities
Σ	Social Sciences

(7) Another important feature of this edition was the alphabetical Index to the Schedules of geographical divisions, Botany, Agriculture and Zoology.

In Edition 5 (1957), the following changes were introduced:

(1) As the constituent states in India were reorganized, a brief alternative schedule of divisions was given at the end of the old one in chapter 4.

(2) A new schedule giving details for phase and inter facet relations was given. The concept of Intra facet relations was given which provided some economy in the length of class numbers.

(3) The divisions of Fine Art (N) were revised. Capital Roman letters were used in place of numerals to denote them, such as :

CC.4	CC.5
N1	NA
N2	ND
N4	NM
N5	NQ

(4) The schedules for Management and Labor in Economics revised.

(5) A new class for mining was included a Greek letter etah.

(6) Some additions were made in the schedule for Z law.

In the 6th edition of CC published in 1960, a few changes that were made are given below :

(1) It gave a selection from schedules for second level of time, space and common energy isolates.

(2) The subject facet was brought over from second level to the first level in the second round of the main class Education viz:

Audiovisual Method teaching Algebra in Elementary schools

The class no, by CC 5th edition = T15:31 (B2)

Class no, by CC 6th edition = T15:3 (B2), 1

(3) In view of the literary warrant, the partially comprehensive main class NZ, Language and Literature was introduced.

(4) Greek letters of some main classes were by roman capitals certain other changes brought out by CC edition 6 were repoled in the Annexure of reprints.

Hence, the severe rigidity in number and the sequence of facets in a compound subject is greatly represented by various indicator, digits for different kind of facets and the concept of round and levels of facets within a round. It is for this reason, the scheme is called an almost Freely Faceted Scheme.

6. Freely Faceted Classification

A Freely Faceted Classification is based on postulates and principles and "there is no rigid, pre-determined facet formula for the compound subjects going with a Basic Subject". Since such a scheme is based on analysis and synthesis, so each subject determines its own facet formula. The facet formula is open. Since the work involves analysis and synthesis of facets and the sequence of facets is guided by postulates and principles, another name for this kind of classification is Analytico-Synthetic Classification.

Example : CC (1987), the Version 3 of Colon Classification incorporates all the findings of the dynamic theory of library classification developed by a research team in DRTC from 1962 to 1986. The rigidity found in the predetermined facet formula was removed, thereby CC7 became a freely faceted scheme for classification.

The present volume of CC7 is comprised of 5 parts as below :

1. Part A – Introduction
2. Part B – Guidance to Beginner
3. Part C – General Rules
4. Part D – General Divisions and Common Isolates
5. Part E – Special Isolates

Part A is further divided into 6 chapters. It describes the genesis and development of the colon classification as well as theory of the library classification.

Part B gives the guidance to the beginner "how to use CC7, how to classify a simple subject or the compound subject by the eight steps laid down by Dr. S.R. Ranganathan."

Part C consists of 24 chapters dealing with General Rules. After explaining the methods of construction, call number. and collection numbers, it deals with the work of idea plane, verbal plane and the notational plane together with the terminology for the three planes.

Part D deals with general divisions and common isolates in 14 chapters.

Part E Special Isolates gives the schedules for different main subjects from Z laws.

This edition has made many changes viz :-

(1) The indexes provided for Geographical Divisions, I Botany, K Zoology and a General Index are not given.

(2) Schedules for many subjects like universe of subjects, book science and journalism for which only main class number were provided in CC 6th edition have been included in this edition.

(3) Many new canonical subjects have been included to "B" mathematics, G Biology, H Geology, M Useful Arts and F Fine Arts.

Thus, the rigidity in the number of levels of facets of their sequence within a round which was presented in CC6, has been nearly removed. Further the rigidity is broken by recognizing facets belong to compound subjects not to Basic subjects.

Comparative Study of Enumerative and Faceted Classifications

The enumerative pattern is as old as the concept of classification of documents. Freely-faceted or Analytico-synthetic pattern has developed out of the enumerative pattern, when the latter pattern developed cracks and gradually become out-moded. Two features of the universe of knowledge, i.e., its infinite nature and the dynamic continuum, ultimately succeeded in breaking the back of the enumerative pattern. This was unfortunate because the enumerative pattern was simple in its structure, while the analytico-synthetic pattern is comparatively not so simple. The difference between the simplicity of these two patterns can be compared with the difference in the simplicity between the Medieval Era man and his knowledge, and the Space-Age man and his knowledge. In other words, the modern man is less simple and so also is his knowledge, as compared to the man in distant past and his knowledge at that time. There are several factors which outmode the enumerative pattern, they are :

(i) By the turn of the last century the documents dealing with micro-thought, became enormous.

(ii) The manifestation of specific subjects started towards specialization.

(iii) Facets like organs and problems of a class got more inter-related in their exposition and became the topics of greater interest.

(iv) In the exposition of the subjects reference to space and time facets became more general.

(v) Multi-dimensional progress of knowledge started.

(vi) Number of periodical reached numerous which made documentation a necessity. The tool required was the depth classification instead of superficial classification.

(vii) Various types of relations – started appearing among classes and the isolates of classes.

Due to these factors the enumerative pattern found itself helpless and therefore become out of date. These factors troubled the thinkers in the field and as the necessity is the mother of invention, the thinkers like Henri La Fountain, Paul Outlet, Rangnathan, and Cordonnier, were able to show the new way. This new way is the freely faceted or analytico-synthetic pattern of classification. A comparative study of the distinctive features, their advantages and disadvantages is often made as under :

	Enumerative Scheme	*Faceted Scheme*
1.	It is more or less a systematic list of basic, compound and a few complex subjects of the past, present and foreseeable future, it means all the class numbers are available readymade.	No class number is available readymade for compound and complex subjects, it is a list of basic subjects and their special isolates and a few schedules of common isolates.
2.	It is the first species of classification in the line of evolution. Library of Congress Classification is the best prototype of this species.	It is the latest stage in the evolution of classification systems. Ranganathan's Colon Classification is the best example of this species.
3.	It is a classification of the past	It is a classification of the

	Enumerative Scheme	*Faceted Scheme*
	and is unable to meet the challenges of the present revolution in information processing and organization. Class numbers are not co-extensive.	present and of the near future and is fully equipped to meet the challenges of information revolution. Their class numbers are co-extensive.
4.	Enumerative systems usually do not have any explicit theory and guiding norms. Therefore, they are not able to accommodate new subjects. The structure is rigid, and soon becomes outmoded and outdated.	These are based on a explicit theory guided by postulates and principles. By virtue of these guiding principles these are able to accommodate new subjects. These are very resilient, and, thus, enduring and can be easily kept up-to-date.
5.	Notation is simple, class numbers are monolithic.	Notation is mixed and seems complex at times. Class numbers are polylithic.
6.	Schedules are lengthy; system is difficult to design but easy to use.	Schedules are short, so easy to design, comparatively complex to use.
7.	Index is indispensable.	Schedules being slim. The index is less used.

3
Theories of Library Classification

Q. : Write an essay on general theory of library Classification.

Or

What different types of library Classification's theories have been put forward? Discuss them with examples.

Ans. The multidimensional, infinite and continuous growth of knowledge is directly affecting the field of library Classification. Library Classification is a process through which multidimensional subjects are arranged in a single linear manner. It helps in arranging the documents in a systematic and helpful way so that the users can use the sources of information effectively. The library classification should bring more closely related subjects together, by grouping documents on the basis of thought content. Thus, library classification is a technique which helps in the systematic and helpful organisation of documents as well as effective retrieval of documents in quickest possible time.

Today, a number of subjects are arising as a result of inter-disciplinary research. Many micro-subjects are also coming into existence. Any branch of a subject may take an independent status. Today, there is a need of depth classification to face the challenges of multidirectional growth of knowledge. Thus, the theory of library classification has become necessary today. According to Sayers, "the foundation of the library is the book; the foundation of librarianship is classification". Among all the library techniques, classification is at the pivotal position which helps in providing a comprehensive view of the literature of subjects.

The theory of library classification refers to an organised body of principles, which provides guidance to the classifier. The theory of classification provides a scientific basis and also enables the classifier to solve their day-to day problems regarding classification.

The theory of library classification has undergone two stages of evolution. The first stage resulted in the formulation of Descriptive Theory which is the sum total of past practices in designing the work. The second stage is the formulating of Dynamic Theory for guiding desiring work.

TYPES OF CLASSIFICATION THEORY

As stated above, there are two types of theories established for library classification. These are :

1. Descriptive theory
2. Dynamic theory

1. Descriptive Theory

The descriptive theory was the first stage in the development of library classification. This theory was able to meet the requirements of the universe of subjects, as it existed at that time. The descriptive theory was based on the practices in vogue based on different schemes of classification then available.

In early fifties, the development of Universe of Subject was not as fast as it is today, so the descriptive theory served its purposes well. During this period, the theory followed practices. Thus, the theory was manipulated to fit into practice as the theory had little power to influence practice. There was lack of scientific approach. The normative principles provided in the theories were not well defined and lacking objectivity.

The period between 1898 and 1937 witnessed the genesis and development of this theory. The development of the descriptive theory is attributed to several stalwarts like Brown, Richardson, Hulme, Sayers, Bliss and Ranganathan.

The contributions of the personalities and the principles formulated, are briefly outlined in the following sub-sections:

(i) J.D. Brown (1862-1914) : J.D. Brown was an English librarian, who brought out three different schemes of classification. The first of these three was developed in 1894 jointly with J.H. Quinn and was known as Quinn-Brown Scheme. This scheme did not make much impact. Three years later, in 1897, Brown independently brought out another scheme and called it Adjustable Classification. This scheme also proved inadequate even in those days. In the year 1906, Brown published the first edition of his Subject Classification, the scheme for which he is mostly known. Its second edition was brought out in 1914 and the third, edited by J.D. Stewart, in 1939.

Brown's Subject Classification was founded on the principle that *every science and art spring from some definite source.*

In addition to the above principle, Brown also advocated two other principles. The first of these two was his one place theory. According to this principle, each subject has only one place in the scheme irrespective of its aspects and numerous manifestations. The other principle advocated by Brown was the science and its applications theory. According to this principle, he places each subject as nearer as possible to the science from which it has sprung. He faithfully followed these principles in his Subject Classification.

(ii) E.C. Richardson (1860-1939) : E.C. Richardson, the first Librarian of Hartford Theological Seminary, USA, is regarded as the first classificationist to have made a systematic attempt to set down a theory of library classification. In 1910, he published his book *Classification, Theoretical and Practical.* It was the first textbook on classification, which later influenced W.C.B. Sayers. He enumerated basic laws and principles meant to guide the work of designing a scheme of classification, which are called as Criteria of Classification. Classification should follow the order of things; classes should be arranged in historical sequence. These are as follows:

(1) Division of classes should be minute.

(2) Arrange things according to likeness and unlikeness.

(3) Books are collected for use; they are administered for use, and hence, it is the use, which is the motive behind classification.

(4) A scheme of classification should be provided with a notation. The notation should be amenable to indefinite subdivisions preferable using a mixed symbol with decimal base and with mnemonic features.

Richardson asserted that "things in nature are already classified and man has to trace only the order of the classification and record it".

(iii) E.W. Hulme (1859-1954) : Hulme 1911-1912, published his book *Principles of Book Classification* in the *Library Association Record.* His principals influenced the later theories of book classification. In the words of W.C.B. Sayers, the contribution of Hulme was "a valuable leadup to the more complete and satisfactory theories today". According to Hulme, all classifications could be arranged into two groups (categories), viz,.

(a) Mechanical and

(b) Philosophical

According to above categorisation, book classification is mechanical. Hulme's principles of book classification are as follows:

(1) Book Classification is the plotting of areas pre-existing in literature, and coincidence with a philosophical order is no guarantee of accuracy.

(2) Book classification is mechanical assembly of material into classes.

(3) The division and coordination of classes in literature is determined mainly upon formal and non-philosophical lines.

(4) Classification should be based on literary warrant.

His mechanical classifications are left uncoordinated but the theory of literary warrant attracted the attention of later Classificationists. The Library of Congress Classification scheme is greatly inthenced by this principle.

Literary warrant simply means that a subject cannot be listed in the scheme unless some literature has already appeared on it. Or, the existing literature on a subject only justifies the inclusion of the subject in the scheme.

(iv) W.C.B. Sayers (1881-1960) : William Charles Berwick Sayers, is referred to as the first Grammarian of library classification. He is responsible for interpreting and systematising the ideas of other theoreticians. He never designed any classification scheme, though, through his theory he has shown the way for others in the designing of classification schemes. His theory of book classification first appeared in 1915 under the title "*Canons of Classification*". He expanded the outline of the theory contained in his book in three other books, viz., Grammar of Classification (Ed.2, 1915; Ed.4, 1935), Introduction to Library Classification (Ed.1,1918;Ed.9,1958) and Manual of Library Classification (Ed.1, 1926; Ed.3, 1955; Ed.4, 1967 and Ed.5, 1975, revised by Arthur Maltby). It has now been revised by Rita Marcella and Robert Newton in 1994.

Sayers simplified his theory of classification by stating 29 principles. viz., 7 Canons of divisons; 4 Canons of terms; 4 Canons of book classification; 5 Canons of notation; 6 Canons of definition; and 3 Canons of book classification schemes. He called them canons, meaning rules, regulations, standard tests or criteria of classification.

(v) **H.E. Bliss (1970-1955) :** Henry Evelyn Bliss devoted his entire active life to the intensive study of the art and science of classification. In his first work titled, Organisation of Knowledge and the System of Science (1929), he formulated scientific, philosophical and logical grounds for the study of bibliographic classification. This work is regarded as one of the basic texts on the theory of organisation of knowledge. He laid down the foundation for a relatively stable, scientifically acceptable and consistent scheme of classification. He also published another basic work on the theory of library classification titled, Organisation of Knowledge in Libraries and the Subject Approach to Books (1933, 2nd ed. 1939). His work helped in establishing librarianship as a scholarly discipline.

These two basic works convey to us the fundamental principles of classification which Bliss later tried to apply in his System of Bibliographic Classification (BC), whose outline was first published in 1935.

(iv) **S.R. Ranganathan (1992-1972) :** S.R. Ranganathan had been developing his theory of library classification since 1924. In the first edition of *Prolegomena to Library Classification* (1937), he provided an integrated theory, mainly descriptive and comparative, of the practices in classification then in vogue.

Ranganathan went ahead of those classificationists, mentioned in the preceding sub-sections, by extending the principles put forward by them. He also provided the largest list of normative principles named by him as Fundamental Laws, Postulates, Principles and Canons and evolved a special terminology, which is evident from the first edition of Prolegomena. These rightly belong to stage-2 in the development of the General Theory of Library Classification. His theory is now synonymous with the General Theory of Library Classification.

(2) Dynamic Theory

The second stage in the development of classification theory is termed as Dynamic Theory. During this stage number of developments took place in the field of library classification. According to R.S. Parkhi, it is "a theory of library classification capable of carving out a methodology for the design of a scheme for library classification".

The Dynamic theory of library classification, developed by Ranganathan between 1948 and 1955, was presented for the first time in the second edition of his *Prolegomena to Library Classification* published in 1957. A more advanced version of this theory appeared in 1967 in the shape of the third edition of the *Prolegomena.* This theory has provided sound methodology for designing a classification scheme. This theory enables one to accommodate already existing subjects as well as the future developments of universe of subjects in a helpful sequence.

The dynamic theory started developing ahead of practice and provided guidelines in the form of guiding principles. These guiding principles help the designers of schemes for classification to develop such a library classification scheme which can meet the demands of ever changing universe of knowledge. The dynamic theory has provided a methodology for designing classification scheme on the basis of scientific methods. This theory divided the work of design into three planes i.e. idea, verbal and notational plane. A large number of postulates principles and canons have been formulated in the field of library classification in consistence with the normative principles of library science. These principles made the work of classifications as well as classifier systematic and objective.

By 1963, the dynamic theory was refined further and some of the new additions included the following:

(i) Identification of Property isolates as manifestations of Matter along with Matter-Material isolates with the result that some of the isolates forcedly included in earlier years in the 'Problems Schedules' but later named forcedly "Energy Schedules ", were in reality Matter-Property isolates.

(ii) Prescription that the indicator digit, (,) 'should be inserted before the first Personality isolate number.

(iii) Capacity of an array in the Notational Plane was increased by divesting Roman small letters of anteriorising quality and by restoring to digit (0) 'zero', its natural ordinal value lying between the digits. 'z' and '1'.

(iv) Postulation of digits T to Z as Emptying Digits which facilitates interpolating at any point in the array.

(v) The theory in the Idea Plane formulated 18 principles of helpful sequence and the powerful Wall-Picture Principle for helpful sequence of facets and of isolates.

These findings of the deeper and more dynamic theory of classification consciously developed, have been incorporated in Colon Classification Version 3 (Edition 7), making it a truly Freely Faceted Analytico-Synthetic Scheme for Classification.

Thus, the basic laws, canons and principles enunciated by Ranganathan have greatly contributed to the evolution of the dynamic theory. His laws, canons and principles of library classification have been presented in his Prolegomena to Library Classification. This is regarded as one of the seminal works on the Theory of Library Classification.

The problem of transforming the multi-dimensional universe of knowledge into a uni-dimensional one was the fundamental and perennial problem faced by the classificationsts in the design of schemes of classification. To meet this problem squarely, formulated the General Theory of Classification, which was guided by Basic Laws, Laws of Library Science, Canons, Principles and postulates. With the help of these laws, canons and principles, the mapping of the universe of knowledge in a scheme of classification could be successfully represented. These laws are summarised below.

Basic Laws: Ranganathan formulated six basic laws, viz.,

1. Law of Interpretation
2. Law of Impartiality
3. Law of Symmetry
4. Law of Parsimony
5. Law of Local Variation
6. Law of Osmosis

These basic laws govern the thinking process in general. These may be invoked when two or more Laws of Library Science or Canons for Classification lead to conflicting or equally valid different decisions.

Laws of Library Science: Ranganathan's Five Laws of Library Science are:

1. Books are for use.
2. Every reader his/her book.
3. Every book its reader.
4. Save the time of the reader.
5. A library is a growing organism.

These were formulated in 1928 and were first published in the book *The Five Laws of Library Science* (1931). These laws have an impact on library functions and are invoked when two or more canons or principles of classification lead to confecting or equally valid alternate decisions. These are useful in every branch of library and information science.

Postulates for Facets: The most significant contribution to the Theory of Classification is the enunciation of postulates dealing with the concept of facet analysis and fundamental categories.

Fundamental Categories: A subject may manifest itself in anyone or all of the fundamental categories. He postulated that "there are five and only five fundamental categories, namely Time, Space, Energy, Matter and Personality", PMEST; for short.

Facet Sequence: The five fundamental categories form the following sequence when they are arranged according to their decreasing concreteness - PMEST.

Rounds of 'Energy': Ranganathan also postulated that "the fundamental category Energy may manifest itself in one and the same subject more than once. These manifestations of energy are called rounds of manifestations. Similarly, the fundamental categories Personality and Matter may manifest themselves in Round 1 Round 2 and so on.

Levels: He further postulated that the fundamental categories Personality and Matter may manifest themselves more than once in one and the same round within a subject. The first manifestation of a fundamental category within a round is said to be its level – I facet in that round.

Space and **Time** manifest themselves in the last round.

Principles of Facet Sequence: Ranganathan formulated four principles of Facet Sequence, viz.,

1. Wall-picture Principle
2. Whole-Organ Principle

3. Cow-Calf Principle
4. Act and Action-Tool Principle

These principles guide us in deciding the sequence of facets, which may appear in a compound subject.

Principles of Helpful Sequence: *To achieve a helpful sequence* of entities in an array, Ranganathan formulated eight Principles of Helpful Sequence. These are :

1. Principle of Later-in-Time
2. Principle of Later-in-Evolution
3. Principle of Spatial Contiguity
    - 3.1 Principles for Entities along a Vertical Line:
        - 3.1.1 Principle of Bottom Upwards
        - 3.1.2 Principle of Top downwards
    - 3.2 Principles for Entities along a Horizontal Line:
        - 3.2.1 Principle of Left to Right
        - 3.2.2 Principle of Right to Left
    - 3.3 Principles of Entitles along a Circular Line:
        - 3.3.1 Principle of Clockwise Direction
        - 3.3.2 Principle of Counter-clockwise Direction
    - 3.4 Principles for Entities along a Radial Line:
        - 3.4.1 Principle of Centre to Periphery
        - 3.4.2 Principle of Periphery to Centre
    - 3.5 Principle of Away-from-Position
4. Principles for Quantitative Measure
    - 4.1 Principle of Increasing Quantity
    - 4.2 Principle of Decreasing Quantity
5. Principle of Increasing Complexity
6. Principle of Canonical Sequence
7. Principle of Literary Warrant
8. Principle of Alphabetical Sequence

Canons of Classification: Ranganathan provided a completely new direction to the concept of classification originally formulated by

Sayers. Ranganathan formulated 43 canons and grouped them into three planes of work.

(i) Canons for Idea Plane (15).

(ii) Canons for Verbal Plane (4).

(iii) Canons for Notational Plane (24).

These are in total conformity with his Basic Laws and Laws of Library Science. These are normally invoked in the design of a scheme of library classification. These three groups of canons are :

Canons for Idea Plane (15) : The fifteen canons for Idea Plane are further grouped into :

(i)	Canons for Characteristics	-	4
(ii)	Canons for Succession of Characteristics	-	3
(iii)	Canons for Array	-	4
(iv)	Canons for Chain	-	2
(v)	Canons for Fillatory Sequence	-	2

The four Canons for characteristics deal with the process of division of knowledge. The characteristics selected for division should be easily differentiated, ascertainable, relevant and permanent. The three canons for succession of characteristics in the process of division of knowledge deal with the application of more than one characteristic and the sequence in which these characteristics are to be applied. The four canons for array (coordinate classes) state that the classes in an array should be collectively exhaustive and mutually exclusive, and the sequence among them should be helpful and consistent. The two canons for chain (subordinate classes) deal with the process of division of knowledge which should proceed from general to specific and it should be properly regulated. The two canons for filiatory sequence state that a scheme of library classification should clearly identify both coordinate and subordinate classes and they should be arranged among themselves according to their mutual affiliation.

Canons for Verbal Plane (4): The four canons for Verbal Plane deal with the language and terminology aspects in a scheme of classification. The terminology used in the scheme should clearly indicate the context in which a particular term has been used and what aspects it comprehends. The terms used to denote concepts should be current and non-critical.

The four canons are:

(i) Canon of Context

(ii) Ganon of Enumeration

(iii) Canon of Currency

(iv) Canon of Reticence

Canons for Notational Plane (24): These have been further grouped into:

(i)	Basic Canons	-	12
(ii)	Mnemonics	-	5
(iii)	Growing Universe	-	4
(iv)	Book Classification	-	3

Notation means a system of ordinal symbols representing classes in a scheme of library classification. The basic canons, which are twelve in number, deal with the need for the removal of homonyms and synonyms in class numbers. The notation, according to these canons, should reflect hierarchy of classes. The base of the notation may be mixed or pure. However, the basic canons discuss the relative capacity of each of these two types. The notation may be faceted or non-faceted. The canons nevertheless deal with the relative advantages of both kinds. The class number should be co-extensive or non-co-extensive. The implications of these two varieties are also explained through these canons.

The five canons for mnemonics deal with the need for different types of mnemonic devices, namely.

- alphabetical,
- scheduled,
- systematic, and
- seminal.

The four canons for Growing Universe deal with the capacity of a notational system for admission of newly emerging classes into the fold of a scheme of classification.

Ranganathan called this capacity of a notational system by the terms hospitality in array and hospitality in chain. The Notational system should be capable of admitting emerging new classes at the beginning, or at the end, or in the middle of an array or a chain. This is also known as extrapolation (at the beginning or end) and interpolation (in the middle) in an array.

The three canons for Book Classification deal with the provision of a system for construction of book numbers and collection numbers in a scheme of classification, and the sequence of these three elements - class number, book number and collection number-making up a Call Number.

Role of Postulates, Canons and Principles: The postulates lay down the process of work in the idea plane. The canons lay down the rhythm of classification. The principles deal with the details of the arrangement of the isolates in the schedules.

The laws, postulates, canons and principles listed above laid down a sound foundation for the Dynamic Theory of Library Classification. The application of the principles has amply been demonstrated in Colon Classification scheme. From the fourth edition, published in 1952, Colon Classification has been a freely faceted scheme of classification based on the laws, postulates, canons and principles discussed above. Prior to the fourth edition, Colon Classification was a rigidly faceted scheme.

Today, the universe of knowledge is developing at such a faster rate that as soon as a library classification scheme is designed it becomes outdated. Thus, the present-day theory of library classification should be truly dynamic and be constantly improved.

4 A
Work of Classification in Three Planes

Q. : Discuss in brief the concept of work of classification in three different planes.

Ans. In designing a scheme for classification, the classificationist has to deal with dynamic, infinite and multidimensional universe of knowledge which need to be clearly and thoroughly analysed, thereafter it is required to be transformed into an artificial language for smooth and convenient use of the scheme as well as systematic and helpful arrangement of documents. To make this complicated procedure systematic and smooth, Ranganathan separated the work of classification in three planes, which provide the guidance in the goals to be achieved.

These three are as follows:

- Idea Plane
- Verbal Plane
- Notational Plane

1. IDEA PLANE

An idea is "a mental image, concept, notion; the mental image of or picture of something previously seen or known, and recalled by the memory; a notion or anything conceived by mind; any product of mental apprehension or activity, existing in the mind as an object of knowledge or thought" etc. Thus an idea is a notion, a presumption or a guess about an object or a thing or a concept. In the Idea Plane, all aspects of the Universe of Knowledge are analysed-its structure, dimension, qualities, characteristics, kinds of relationship and the bond of strength among classification-actual grouping and arranging the isolate ideas, determining the correct places for ever emerging new subjects in the existing subjects without disturbing their sequence. So the work in Idea Plane is Paramount.

2. VERBAL PLANE

The ideas which come up in the 'Idea Plane' are expressed in the words and sentences. These ideas are given names in the languages used in the world. A thing may be called differently in different language. For example in Hindi, we call Surya/Suraj to Sun in English, Sonne in German and Aftab in Persian etc. But it does not matter. Though a term may whatsoever be denoted yet the entity will be the same in the Idea Plane. The work in the Verbal Plane is to decide the type of terminology to be used in the scheme for classification. The objective of the Idea Plane is to clear the thinking, analyses and arrange the Universe of isolate ideas. It is for the Verbal Plane to give name to a class or ranked isolate. In the words of Sayers 'a classification is a map of things which cannot be drawn graphically, but is set down in words. The task is to provide for the field of knowledge, or part of it, as comprehensive and clear a statement as the cartographer is able to make of a territory of earth.' However, there are various inherent problems in the use of natural language for enumerating classes or isolate ideas in a scheme for classification. These are as follow :

(i) **Vagueness in the Meaning of Ordinary Words :** The language of conversation in general is vague and imperfect. This vagueness is also visible in carefully written documents, even in the technical treatises. It is, therefore necessary for a classificationist to keep this aspect in view while allotting names to the classes and isolate ideas.

(ii) **Creation of New Terms:** With technological and scientific developments the simultaneous result is also the growth of new documents written on new ideas and subjects using new terminology in place of old one, making the old terminology obsolete; or creation of totally new terms or words indicating new concepts of ideas. For example, the use of the term physics in place of Natural Philosophy, and Library Science in place of Librarianship/Library Economy and the current term being the Information Science. There are innumerable new subjects like Computer Science with new names which are appearing incessantly as a result of new technologies.

(iii) **Incidence of Homonym:** The another problem relates to etymology and semasiology in terms of homonym. Homonym means one, two or more words having the same sound and often the same spelling but different in meaning. A word which has the same name but is used to designate different classes is termed as homonymous word. For example the word 'subject' represents different meaning when used with different disciplines or classes. For example:

1. One who is a subject to a monarch or a ruler, and is governed by his law;
2. One who or that which is subjected to any operation or process;
3. An organised body of knowledge, as Chemistry, Algebra or Botany forming a study;
4. In Grammar - the word or word-group denoting that of which anything is affirmed or predicated.

(iv) **Incidence of Synonyms:** In natural language, there may be many words denoting one and the same meaning. The different aspects of terminology create confusion and problems to the classificationist and the classifier in interpreting the terms in the schedules. For example the terms thorax and chest are often taken as synonyms.

3. NOTATIONAL PLANE

The Notational Plane has the responsibility of implementing the findings of the Idea Plane. While designing the scheme for classification, the Idea Plane decides the necessary characteristics to be used for the arrangement of the universe of subjects in a filiatroy sequence. The Notational Plane, therefore, has to provide the mechanism in the form of notational system for the helpful and systematic arrangement for existing as well as for future unknown subjects in a scheme for classification.

It transforms the natural language into classificatory language of ordinal numbers, so that it is possible to provide uniqueness to the idea presented in the Verbal Plane by translating it in the form of a symbol having a fix place in the sequence of ordinal numbers. It also helps in eliminating the problem of homonyms and synonyms created at Verbal Plane by providing distinct symbol to every idea or subject representing different connotations.

4 B
Canons for Idea Plane

Q. : State the meaning and purpose of Canons of Classification. Explain with examples different canons for characteristics.

Or

What is the difference between attribute and characteristics? Explain with examples the Canon of Differentiation and Canon of Concomitance.

Or

What are the Canons of Characteristics? Explain in detail any two of them.

Ans. : The Canons for the Idea Plane regulate the work of classificationists in picking and applying the characteristics, formation of coordinate and subordinate classes and arranging them in a filiatory sequence in a scheme for classification.

A scheme for classification implies the prior concept of scheme of classes and involves the following five inherent concepts which belong essentially to the Idea Plane.

1. Canons for Characteristics
2. Canons for Succession of Characteristics
3. Canons for Array Classes
4. Canons for Chain of Classes
5. Canons for Filiatory Sequence

1. CANON FOR CHARACTERISTICS

The word 'characteristics' simply means as attribute by which the concepts are assembled or divided in the classification.

Though Richardson, Sayers and Bliss have also provided canons or principles for characteristics, however, the four Canons for characteristics of Ranganathan are quite specific and make it clear that no scheme for classification should violate the canons. They are:

(i) Canon of Differentiation;

(ii) Canon of Relevance;

(iii) Canon of Ascertainability; and

(iv) Canon of Permanence

(i) Canon of Differentiation

This Canon directs that 'A characteristic used as the basis for the classification of a universe should differentiate some of its entities- that is, it should give rise at least to two classes or ranked isolates'.

The demand of this Canon is quite simple-that is the characteristics used to divide the classes should be able to produce at least two different classes, e.g, like and unlike, otherwise it should not be used.

For example, there are twenty students in a class. Each has face, neck, eyes, ears and legs etc. Such characteristics are common and on the basis of them we cannot differentiate the students. However, the characteristic of height can be able to differentiate them. Some other characteristics such as sex, complexion etc. may also be taken for differentiation. Dr. Ranganathan emphasized that it should give rise at least to two classes or ranked isolates. So, in library classification the related material is kept together but are differentiated on the basis of characteristics.

Sayers and Bliss have used the term likeness-to arrange according to the degree of likeness.

(ii) Canon of Relevance

Dr. Ranganathan defines it - "A characteristic used as the basis for the classification of universe should be relevant to the purpose of the classification. Sayers recognises it as "Essential Characteristic". He says characteristic chosen as the basis of division should be the most useful for the purpose of the scheme.

The Canon demands that among several characteristics possessed by the universe of entities, only those characteristics should be chosen which are relevant for the purpose of classification. For example, for dividing the Universe of Professors the relevant characteristics may be their specific discipline, area of specialisation and academic qualification. For them the height, colour and physical strength are irrelevant characteristics.

(iii) Canon of Ascertainability

This Canon demands that "A characteristic used as the basis for classification of a universe should be definite and ascertainable. A universe of entities may have many relevant characteristics. But all of them may not be ascertainable. This Canon emphasises that only the characteristic which are ascertainable should be chosen. This can be understood by an example. Suppose there are many poets and we divide them as 'major poets', minor poets' These characteristics, no doubt, are relevant but are not ascertainable because some of the minor poets may become major poets after sometime. If we take the year of death of each poet to differentiate, this process will not include the living poets. Dr. ranganathan has therefore, has taken the year of birth and not the year of death to represent author facet in Literature. This is because, the year of birth is definite and ascertainable and may be used as the basis for classification.

(iv) Canon of Permanence

The Canon directs that 'A characteristic used as the basis for the classification of a universe should continue to be unchanged so long as there is no change in the purpose of classification.

In other words we may say that one must select only those characteristics which are of stable nature. We take an example to show the application of this canon. Suppose we have to classify periodicals and we put them in two different orders (i) Periodicals published by the learned societies and (ii) Periodicals not published by the learned societies. But such a characteristic is likely to be changed. The periodicals which are not being published by learned societies may be published by learned societies in due course of time. Dr. Ranganathan therefore devised this canon and for the classification of periodical the stable characteristic has been determined as the year in which it was first published. i.e. epoch of origin which is to be obtained form the Chronological Division.

2. CANONS FOR SUCCESSION OF CHARACTERISTIC

A set of three canons has been devised by Dr. Ranganathan to make a logical and helpful sequence between the characteristics selected for classification. The three canon are as under–:

(i) Canon of Concomitance

(ii) Canon of Relevant Succession; and

(iii) Canon of Consistent Succession

(i) Canon of Concomitance

This Canon directs that 'No two characteristics in the associated scheme of characteristics should be concomitant-that is, they should not give rise to the same array of subjects of isolate ideas'.

For example, in classifying the universe of men, the concomitant characteristics like age and year of birth should not be used in succession, as both the characteristics would produce the same array of classes. However, the characteristics height and age when used in succession would produce two different array of classes.

(ii) Canon of Relevant Succession

The Canon directs that "The succession of the characteristics in the associated scheme of characteristics should be relevant to the purpose of classification".

The cannon has been devised to fix the sequence of characteristics when they are more than two. For example, when we classify a work on literature we have to face a group of four characteristics (personalities) i.e. language, form, author and work. This cannon gives a relevant succession to these characteristics. In DC, the sequence is of language, form and period which, of course, is relevant and serves the purpose of the readers.

(iii) Canon of Consistent Succession

Consistency means to have a regular pattern or a state of keeping to the same course of action. The Canon directs that 'The succession of the characteristics in the associated scheme of characteristics should be consistently adhered to, so long as there is no change in the purpose of classification".

The demand of this canon is quite simple, but useful to avoid confusion and chaos. It states that the succession of characteristics chosen for the purpose of classifying a specific universe of subject, should be followed consistently.

Dr. Ranganathan has explained it "when the same categories occur explicitly or implicitly in different places, they must be arranged in the same order in all the places." The lack of it will bring confusion, haphazardness and consequently the purpose of classification will forget. Fox example, if we are using DC and dealing with Main Class 'History', two characteristics i.e. geographical and period in succession are to be applied. But in case of CC four characteristics i.e. community, organ of state, attribute or organ and the period are to be chosen consistently.

3. CANON FOR ARRAY

An Array is a class derived from a universe on the basis of a single characteristic in its sub-division of a subject and arranged in a preferred sequence. In other words, an array is a set of coordinate classes or sub-division.

For example, if the universe of animals is divided on the basis of a single characteristic, say, presence of the vertebral column, it would yield two classes, viz. Invertebrates and Vertebrates which are coordinate (equal) in status. The class vertebrates, in its turn, can be sub- divided into an array of sub-classes like prochordates, fishes, amphibia, reptiles, aves, and mammals by using the characteristic of evolutionary stage. These sub-classes formed by the application of a single characteristic is an array.

Dr. Ranganathan has prescribed four canons for array which are as follows;

(i) Canon of Exhaustiveness;

(ii) Canon of Exclusiveness;

(iii) Canon of Helpful sequence;

(iv) Canon of Consistent sequence.

(i) Canon of Exhaustiveness

This canon directs that "the classes in any array of classes and the ranked isolates should be totally exhaustive of their respective common immediate universe." In other words, we may say that it is necessary to exhaust on characteristic before the introduction of another.

The Canon demands that in the process of classification, the immediate universe under classification should be totally exhausted. Keeping in view the dynamic and infinite universe of subjects provisions should also be made, so that on the emergence of any new class or isolate idea in an array, may be extrapolated or interpolated in its proper place among the already enumerated classes.

The Colon Classification has provisions of various notational techniques which help in fulfilling the demands of this Canon, and through which any number of classes may be enumerated in an array.

For example, take the first order array of the personality facet of the basic subject L Medicine in CC (7th Edn.)

Human body

Regional organs	Degestive system	Circulatory system	Respiratory system	Genito-Uninary system	Endocrine system	Nervous system	Other system

These eight classes are coordinate in status and are derived from the universe *human body* on the basis of a single characteristic : system. You may observe that any of the entities of the universe can be assigned to any of the classes of the first order array. For example, the isolate ideas mouth, heart, lung, kidney, thyroid, brain and skin can be assigned respectively to regional organs, degestive system, circulatory system, respiratory system, genito-urinary system, endocrine system, nervous system and other systems respectively. Together, the various regional and functional systems belonging to the first order array exhaust the universe human body.

In DDC, the rigidity in the notational system has been partly removed by recognising the 'Other Device', with the help of which eight 91-98 coordinate classes may be created. For example:

290 Comparative religion and religions other than Christianity.

The class numbers 291-298 are used for this purpose.

(ii) Canon of Exclusiveness

The Canon directs that "The classes in an array of classes and the ranked isolates in an array of ranked isolates should be mutually exclusive".

According to this canon, an entity in a universe can belong to only one class in the array derived from that universe. The meaning is, it is mandatory that no two classes of the array can overlap or have an entity in common. This is ensured by deriving the classes of an array from its immediate universe on the basis of one and only one characteristic. The main purpose of this canon is to prevent cross classification of entities.

This is possible only if the classes of an array are derived from its immediate universe on the basis of one and only one characteristic. For example we may divide the universe of students using the characteristic subject into the array comprising the classes-students of

Fine Arts, Students of History, Students of Economics and Students of Sociology etc., We may also use another characteristics-their rhetorical ability, to form the set of classes-dull students, mediocre students and brilliant students. Accordingly, each student would be arranged in two different classes of array so formed and thus the canon of exclusiveness would be violated.

However, it is possible to arrange the students by using these two characteristics in succession. For example:

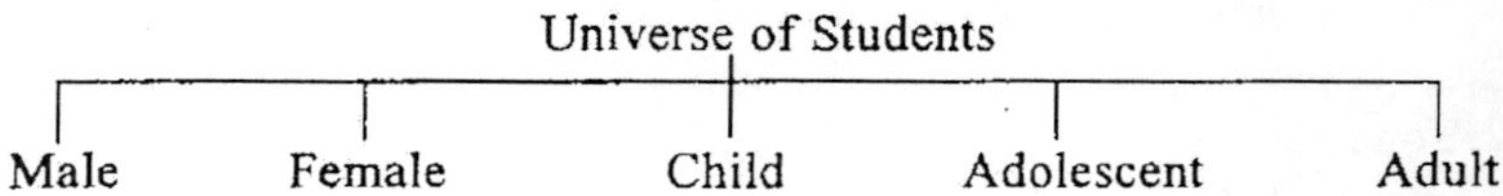

The simultaneous application of two characteristics age and sex created the possibility of a member falling at once in two divisions. For example, a student can be male and also an adult, or a female and also an adolescent. Such a situation is undesirable as it would result in cross classification (an entity simultaneously belonging to two classes) Hence, the canon of exclusiveness is violated.

It is however, possible to arrange the universe of students by using two characteristics in succession as shown below:

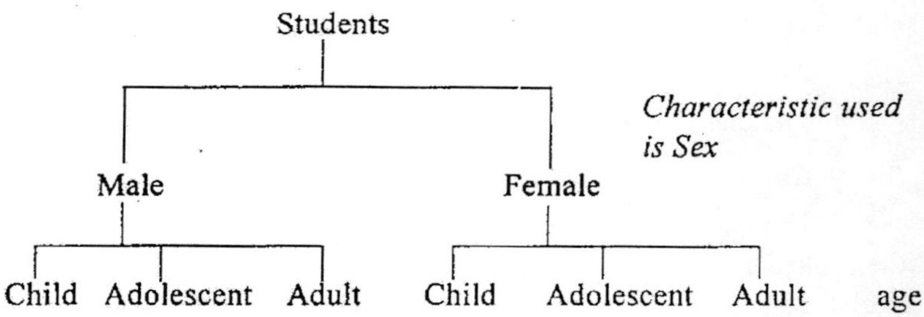

If necessary, it is possible to form a single array by resorting the coalescene of the arrays in the example above. The coalesced array and the original universe may be represented as as follows:

Students
- Child students
- Adolescent students
- Adult students
- Male students
- Male Child students
- Male adolescent students
- Male adult students
- Female students
- Female child students
- Female adolescent students
- Female adult students

This canon of exclusiveness is generally observed by all classification schemes.

(iii) Canon of Helpful Sequence

The Canon directs that "The sequence of the classes in an array of classes, and of the ranked isolates in an array of ranked isolates, should be helpful to the purpose for whom it is intended."

The helpful sequence may vary as per need and purpose of the users of the scheme. A sequence which may be helpful to one category of users may not be helpful to another category of users. Ranganathan, therefore, suggests that the sequence which is helpful to the majority of users may be followed. The helpfulness of the sequence, in its turn, can be achieved by the application of the following principles of helpful sequence:

- Principle of later-in-time
- Principle of later-in-evolution
- Principle of spatial contiguity
    - Principles for entities along a vertical line:
        - Principle of bottom-upwards
        - Principle of top-downwards
    - Principles for entities along a horizontal line:
        - Principle of left to right
        - Principle of right to left

- Principles for entitles along a circular line:
  - Principle of clockwise direction
  - Principle of counter-clockwise direction
- Principles for entities along a radial line
  - Principle of periphery to centre
  - Principle of centre to periphery
- Principle of away-from-position

— Principles for quantitative measure
- Principle of increasing quantity
- Principle of decreasing quantity

— Principle of increasing complexity

— Principle of canonical sequence

— Principle of literary warrant

— Principle of alphabetical sequence

Principle of Later-in-Time: If the subjects in an array of subjects or the isolates in an array of isolates have originated in different times, they should be arranged in a parallel progressive time sequence, except when any other overwhelming consideration rules it out.

In designing the schedule of Religions in CC (7th Edn.), the various religions are arranged in the parallel progressive time sequence of their origin. This can be seen from an example taken from CC:

Q1 Vedic Hinduism

Q2 Post-Vedic Hinduism

Q3 Jainism

Q4 Buddhism

Q5 Judaism

Q6 Christianity

Q7 Islam

Principle of Later-in-Evolution: If the subjects in an array of subjects or the isolates in an array of isolates belong to different stages in evolution, they should be arranged in a sequence parallel to the evolutionary sequence, except when an overwhelming consideration rules it out.

In Zoology, the animal groups are arranged in the following evolutionary sequence in CC and DDC:

Protozoa	Porifera	Coelenterata
Echinodermata	Pisces	Amphibia
Reptilia	Aves	Mammalia

Principles of Spatial Contiguity: The meaning is that if the subjects in an array of subjects or the isolates in an array of isolates occur contiguously in space, roughly along a unidirectional line or a radial line or a circle, they should be arranged in a parallel spatial sequence, except when any other overwhelming consideration rules it out.

Among the nine principles listed, eight occur as antithetic pairs, the only exception being the principle of away-from-position. This may result in a dilemma in the choice between the antithetic pair. Fortunately, in most situations, the dilemma does not surface as the choice is rendered obvious due to the context. However, at time, a peculiar situation may arise when both the alternatives in an antithetic pair yield a helpful sequence.

Principles for entities along a vertical line: There are two principles for entities along a vertical line : bottom-upwards and top-downwards.

Principle of bottom-upward: If the subjects in an array of subjects or the isolates in an array of isolates can be conveniently taken to occur along a vertical line, they may be arranged from bottom upwards, if it is helpful.

In the enumeration of the regional organs of the human body, CC conforms to this principle by adopting the sequence.

L,13	Lower extremity	L, 16	Upper extremity
L,13T	Pelvic region	L,17	Neck
L,14	Abdomen	L,18	Head
L,15	Thorax		

Principle of top-downwards: If the subjects in an array of subjects or the isolates in array of isolates can be conveniently taken to occur along a vertical line, they may be arranged from top downward, if it is helpful.

Unlike CC, DDC and UDC prefer this principle in the enumeration of regional organs of the human body:

611.91	Head	711.95	Abdomen
611.92	Face	611.96	Pelvic and Perineal region
611.93	Neck	611.97	Upper extremities
611.94	Thorax	611.98	Lower extremities

Principles for entities along a horizontal line: There are two principles for entities along a horizontal line : left-to-right and right-to-left.

Principle of left-to-right: If the subjects in an array of subjects or the isolates in an array of isolates can be conveniently taken to occur along a horizontal line, they may be arranged from left-to-right, if it is helpful.

The following is a helpful left-to-right sequence of the lanes and other items in a highway in India.

(Left) Pedestrian way, Path for slow moving vehicles (bicycles, carts), Path for heavy motor vehicles, motor cars (Right).

Principle of right-to-left: If the subjects in an array of subjects or the isolates in an array of isolates can be conveniently taken to occur along a horizontal line, they may be arranged from right-to-left.

Principles for entities along a circular line : There are two principles for entities along a circular line: clockwise direction and counter-clockwise direction.

Principle of clockwise direction : If the subjects in an array of subjects or the isolates in an array of isolates can be conveniently taken to occur along a circular line, they may be arranged in the clockwise direction, if it is helpful.

Principle of counter-clockwise direction: If the subjects in an array of subjects or the isolates in an array of isolates can be conveniently taken to occur along a circular line. They may be arranged in the counter-clockwise direction, if it is helpful.

An example of arrangement of entities along a circular line can be seen in the following sequence of the twelve zodiacal signs:

1. Aries	4. Cancer	7. Libra	10. Capricorn
2. Taurus	5. Leo	8. Scorpio	11. Aquarius
3. Gemini	6. Virgo	9. Sagittarius	12. Pisces

Principles for entities along a radial line: There are two principles for entities along a radial line : periphery to centre, centre to periphery.

Principle of periphery to center : If the subjects in an array of subjects or the isolates in an array of isolates can be conveniently taken to occur along a radial line of a circle or a cylinder, they may be arranged from periphery to centre, if is helpful.

Principle of centre to periphery: If the subjects in an array of subjects or the isolates in an array of isolates can be conveniently taken to occur along a radial line of a circle or a cylinder, they may be arranged from centre to periphery, if it is helpful.

A good example of conformity with this principle can be seen in the following numbers taken from the personality facet of the basic subject L Medicine of CC (7th Edn.).

L,82	Bone
L,83	Muscle
L,86	Connective tissue
L,87	Skin

Principle of away from position: If the subjects in an array of subjects or the isolates in an array of isolates can be conveniently taken to start from a certain point and diverge away from it roughly along a line, they may be arranged from the starting point along the diverging line, if it is helpful.

Principles for quantitative measure: There are two principles for quantitative measure: increasing quantity and decreasing quantity.

Principle of increasing quantity: If the subjects in an array of subjects or the isolates in an array of isolates admit of quantitative distinction, they may be arranged according to their increasing quantity, if it is helpful.

In classifying the universe geometry on the basis of the characteristic number of dimensions, CC (7th End.), arranged the resulting sequence of isolates in the order of Line, Plane, Three dimensions, Four dimensions, Five dimensions, n dimensions.

Principle of decrasing quantity: If the subjects in an array of subjects or the isolates in an array of isolates admit of quantitative distinction, they may be arranged according to their decreasing quantity, if it is helpful.

Principle of increasing complexity: If the subjects in an array of subjects or the isolates in an array of isolates show different degrees of complexity, they should be arranged parallel to the sequence of increasing complexity except when any other overwhelming consideration rules it out.

In classifying the universe optical instruments, the principle of increasing complexity would suggest the following sequence:

Optical instruments
Microscope
Dissection microscope
Compound microscope
Phase-contrast microscope
Electron microscope

Principle of decreasing complexity: If the subjects in an array of subjects or the isolates in an array of isolates show different degrees of complexity, they may be arranged parallel to the decreasing complexity. For example.

Transport vehicle Space-craft Motor car Motor cycle Cycle	decreasing complexity in the design of the vehicle.

Principle of canonical sequence: If the subjects in an array of subjects or the isolates in an array of isolates are traditionally referred to in a specific sequence, though there is no underlying principle behind it, it will be convenient to conform to this traditional sequence.

In DDC, the classes in the following arrays are in canonical sequence: The fruits in agriculture, namely, Palmaceous fruits, Store fruits, Citrus fruits, Minor fruits, Nut fruits, Palmaceous fruits and Small fruits. Similarly, the subjects of law, namely, International Law, Constitutional Law, Criminal Law, Martial Law, Private Law and Church Law.

Principle of Literary Warrant : The subjects in an array of subjects or the isolates in an array of isolates may be arranged in the sequence of decreasing quantity of the documents published or anticipated to be published on them, except when any other overwhelming consideration rules it out.

Principle of Alphabetical Sequence: When no other sequence of the subjects in an array of subjects or the isolates in an array of isolates is more helpful, they may be arranged alphabetically by their names current in international usage.

In CC (7th Edn.), alphabetical sequence has been used in the enumeration of programming languages and manufacturing companies in the subjects electronic calculator. Thus,

Programming language

- APL
- BASIC
- COBAL
- FORTRAN

Manufacturing company

- Hewlet Packard
- Sinclair Scientific

(iv) Canon of Consistent Sequence

This Canon directs that whenever similar classes or ranked isolates occur in different arrays, their sequence should be parallel in all such arrays, whenever insistence on such a parallelism does not run counter to other more important requirements.

The demand of this canon is quite simple, that is (i) in a scheme for classification proper attention should be given while arranging similar classes and isolates when occurring in different arrays; (ii) the sequence of all such similar classes and isolates should be parallel in all such arrays. The advantage of this being; (i) economy of time and mental energy; (ii) would minimise the load on the memory of both for classifier and the user.

Two methods have been adopted for securing consistent sequence by different schemes of classification:

(a) Automatic conformity by using one and the same schedule to form an array in isolates or by other devices.

(b) Maintenance of parallel sequence.

(a) **Automatic conformity:** In DDC, automatic conformity is secured by providing

* Table of standard subdivisions giving a schedule of certain common isolates.
* Area tables giving schedules of geographic isolates.
* Add-to instructions.

It also adopts a parallel sequence in different arrays by the applications of principles for helpful sequence. For example:

In Medicine	*In Psychology*
Eye	Vision
Ear	Hearing
Organs of smell	Smell
Organs of taste	Taste
Organs of touch	Touch

On the other hand, automatic conformity is secured in CC by

* Schedules of common isolates such as anteriorising common isolates, time isolates, space isolates, language isolates, common energy isolates, common property isolates and common personality isolates.
* Use of device such as chronological device, geographical device, subject device, alphabetical device, enumeration device, and also facet, phase and superimposition devices.

(b) **Maintenance of Parallel Sequence :** The parallel sequence in different arrays may be obtained with the help of principles for helpful Sequence. However, it is only CC which has specifically provided Principles for Helpful Sequence to obtain parallel sequences of subjects and of isolates. The sequences of classes and isolates of other schemes, although conform to these principles, but it is not clear whether parallel sequences are the results of conscious application of such principles or are achieved uncosciously. For example:

CC7

Psychology	*Social Phycology*	*Education*
Child	Infant	Infant
Infant	Child	Children
Pre Adoplescent	Preadolescent	Adolescents
Adult	Adolescent	Adults
Middle age	Adult	
Old age	Middle age	
	Old age	

In CC, principles for helpful Sequence are applied consciously, therefore, innumerable such examples are available.

4. CANON FOR CHAIN OF CLASSES

A Chain can be defined as a sequence of classes made up of any given class and its universe of Remove 1, Remove 2, Remove 3. etc. carried backward to any point desired. Thus, any sequence of subordinate classes generated by successive sub-divisions is a chain. Each class of a chain is termed as Link. For example

World
↓
America
↓
United States
↓
Washington

There are two canons, of which each chain of classes or of ranked isolates in a scheme of classification should satisfy. They are:

(i) Canons of decreasing extension

(ii) Canon of modulating

These canons are applicable to the classification of any universe of entities, be it a universe of basic subjects (Main classes), of isolate ideas, of compound subjects, or of complex subjects.

(i) Canons of Decreasing extension

The Canon directs that while moving down in a chain from its first link to its last link, the extension of the classes or of the ranked isolates, as the case may be, should decrease and the intension should increase at each step.

The two terms extension and intension need to be explained. The extension is measured by the number of entities or the range comprising the class, intension is measured by the number of characteristics used in deriving it (class) from the original universe. This measure is the same as the order of the class or of the ranked isolate. In other words, while extension can be considered a quantitative measure, intension should be considered an qualitative measure. This can be diagrammatically shown as follows:

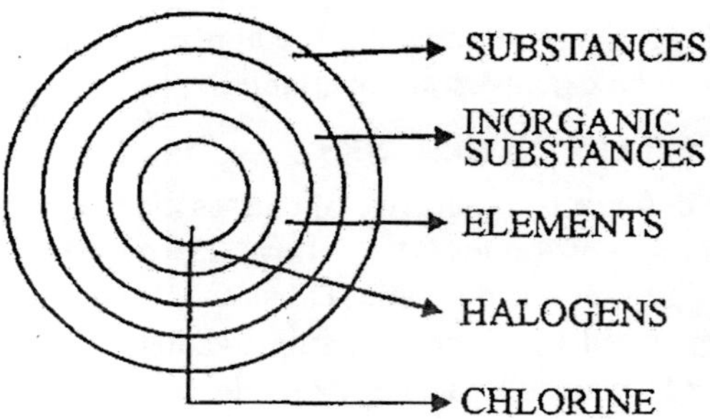

The number of entities comprising each ranked isolate decreases and the number of characteristics used to derive it from the original universe **Substances** increases as one goes down the chain and reach the ranked isolate **Chlorine**.

In library classification, term intension indicate the number of characteristics used in deriving the class or isolate idea from its original universe. If the class is of small range the numbers of characteristics that can be predicted would increase. This means extension is quantitative measure of a class and intension is qualitative measure of it.

The Canon of Decreasing Extension is, therefore, applied to a chain of classes or of ranked isolates in one and the same chain having lineal kinship. A family presents a good example of the lineal kinship of decreasing extension—from grandfather to great grandson. Similarly the whole world consists of many continents, countries, and each country may be divided to the smaller geographical units.

World

↓

Continents (Asia) One Characteristic

↓

Countries (India) Two characteristics

↓

State (Rajasthan) Three characteristic

↓

Jaipur (City) Four characteristic

↓

Sanganer (Town) Five characteristic, and so on.

(ii) Canon of Modulation

The canon of modulation states that "a chain of classes or of ranked isolates should comprise one class or one rankec isolates, as the case may be, of each and every order that lies between the orders of the first link and the last link of the chain.

In other words, the implication of this canon would be that each and every link starting from the first to the last in a chain of classes or ranked isolates should be identified and provided for in a scheme of classification, without missing any of them. For instance, in the example from chemistry given above, the first link is substance and last link is chlorine, the intermediary links being inorganic substances, elements and halogens, If any one of the intermediary links is omitted, then the canon of modulation is said to be violated.

Generally, schemes of classification like DDC, UDC and CC are in conformity with this canon. There are, however, instances when this canon has been ignored. Upto and including the 14th edition of DDC, there was no class number to represent the class Christianity. In the 19th edition, Christian religion is represented by a span of numbers 220-280, but there is no specific number for Christianity. Thus/the canon of modulation is violated.

5. CANON FOR FILIATORY SEQUENCE

The Canon for Filiatory Sequence demands that the classes of universe of subjects in a scheme for classification should be arranged according to their degree of mutual relationship. There are two Canons for this purpose.

(i) Canon of Subordinate Classes

(ii) Canon of Coordinate Classes

(i) Canon of Subordinate Classes

The Canon directs that in a coalesced array, if A1, A2, A3, etc. are sub-classes of any order whatever of Class A, originated in one or another of the chains originating from class A, the classes A1, A2, A3, etc. should immediately follow the class A in succession without being separated from it or among themselves by any class.

For example : The sons are arranged along with their sons as subordinate classes.

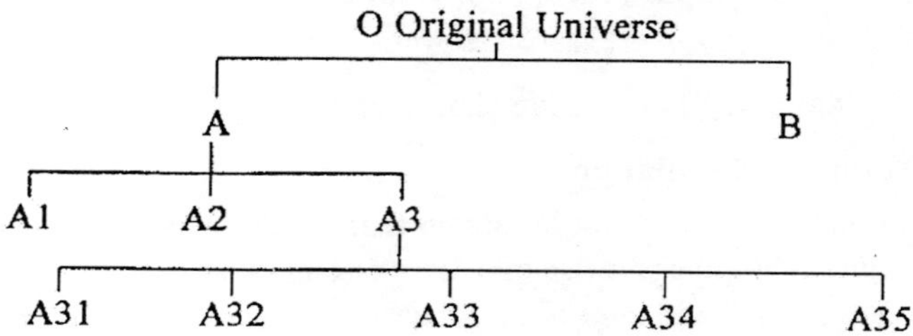

O original Universe

A

A1

A2

A3

A31

A32

A33

A34

A35

(ii) Canon of Coordinate Classes

The Canon directs that in a coalesced array, if class B had originated in one and the same array and had been consecutive in it, they should not be separated from each other by any other than the classes, A1, A2, A3, etc. as their common immediate universe.

This canon helps while arranging the coordinate classes in an array. While dividing the original universe the coordinate classes should be arranged in fillatory sequence that is representing class affinity.

For example :

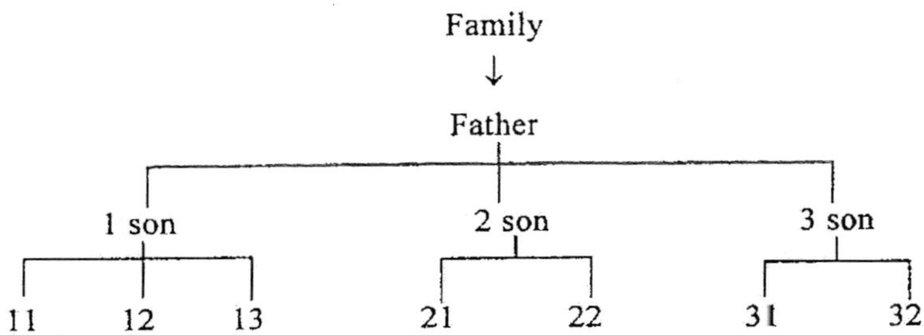

In this example, in the first order Array, the three sons should be arranged as 1, 2, 3 no cousin brother should come in between them, Again the family of these brother divided, and the subordinate classes i.e. the sons of each brother would be arranged with them.

Canon of Subordinate Classes			*Canon of Cordinate classes*
1	2	3	1
11	21	31	2
12	22	32	3
13	23		

4 C
Canons for Verbal Plane

Q. : What are the canon in verbal planes? Discuss them in brief with examples.

Or

What do you mean by canon of verbal planes? Describe in brief various types of them giving examples.

Ans. Ranganathan has formulated the following four canons for work in Verbal Plane, which may helpful classificationist and the classifier in the correct interpretation of terms. The purpose of the terms is to represent current and non-critical meanings of different orders of classes or ranked isolates. The documents embody knowledge which can be translated into a language to represent the entities. The schedule is not graphic but verbal which consist words or names and these words are the terms of the classification. A term may be a single word or sentence which stands for an idea or for a part of field. The schemes of classification use this artificial language of terms. The knowledge that documents have in the form of subjects is transcribed through these terms. In doing so, the classifier has to jump from Idea Plane to Language Plane i.e. Verbal Plan in order to represent the ideas, gathered in the Idea Plane, by these terms. Sayers has also explained this process, "A schedule of a classification is written statement of a classification which has already been formed in the mind of its maker. It is, as it were, in the first place a mental map of the whole of knowledge or of some part of it, and this map is transcribed in words or terms". Dr. Ranganathan assigns the works in the plane i.e. getting transformed title from the analysed title. This transformation amounts to re-arranging the Kernel. Terms to suit the syntax of the classificatory language. These canons are:

1. Canon of context
2. Canon of Enumeration
3. Canon of Currency

4. Canon of Reticence

1. CANON OF CONTEXT

The Canon Directs that "the denotation of a term in a scheme for classification should be determined in the light of the different classes or ranked isolates of lower order (upper links) belonging to the same primary chain as the class or the ranked isolate denoted by the term in question". This statement clearly indicate that before classifying a document we must ensure the context in which the term is used, because the denotation of the term sometime be different.

For example, the books on Morphology should be classified keeping in view the context as these may belong to different main subjects. e.g.:

CC6	*CC7*	*Main Subject*
G:2	G;2	Morphology (Biology)
I:2	I;2	Morphology (Botany)
KX:2	KX;2	Morphology (Husbandry)
L:2	L;2	Morphology (Medicine)
P:2	P;2	Morphology (Linguistics)

But sometimes, this canon is violated in different schemes. As for example, in UDC Med. Edition 1985

368.4 Social insurance, social security generally

.41 Social accident insurance

.42 Social insurance against occupational illness

.43 Social old age insurance.

.44 Social unemployment insurance

.45 Social insurance of surviving dependent

Here, the terms social and insurance have been repeated in the lower links also when it is already denoted in the upper link. This is the violation of Canon of Context.

2. CANON OF ENUMERATION

This canon demands that "the denotation of a term in a scheme for classification should be determined and should be left to be determined in the light of or through the sub-classes or ranked isolates (lower links) enumerated in the various chains having the class or ranked isolate, as the case may be, denoted by the term in question as their common link." As it is not possible to have a general agreement or uniformity in the denotation of terms, we usually find difference.

The classifier, therefore, should determine the meaning and scope of each term in the light of subordinate classes or ranked isolates of lower links while using a scheme for classification. The following example makes this more clear.

DDC 19 and 20		CC6	CC7
513	Arithmetic	B1	B1, Arithmetic
.1	Arithmetic Combined with other branches	B11	B1,1 Lower Arithmetic
.2	Arithmetic operations	B12	B1,2 Concept of numbers
.4	Arithmetic and geometric progression	B13	B1,3 Integers (Theory of Numbers)
.5	Numeration systems	B14	B1,4 Imaginary Numbers
.6	Non weighted systems	B15	B1,5 Algebraic Numbers
.7	Special purpose Arithmetic (Rapid	B16	B1,6 Complex and hyper complex numbers
	Calculations, shortcuts)	B18	B1,8 Transcendental Number

It may be noted that in DDC, the enumeration of the subclasses of the class denoted by the term Arithmetic indicates that it comprehended only 'Lower Arithmetic' and B13 theory of number (as in CC), otherwise known as 'High Arithmetic' as not enumerated under Arithmetic.

3. CANON OF CURRENCY

The Canon directs that "the term used to denote a class or a ranked isolate in a scheme for classification should be the one current among those specializing in the subject field covered by the scheme." "The scope of the canon given by Dr. Ranganathan states that the term included in the schedule should accord with their current usage and the terms which have become obsolete should be changed with the current ones. So, it is imperative for the scheme to keep pace with current terminology and revise constantly the scheme and replace the obsolete terms by current terms. For example:

In Space Isolate

Old Names	*New Names*
Burma	Myanmar
Ceylon	Sri Lanka

The new name Sri Lanka has replaced the old name Ceylon in the new editions of DDC, CC and UDC, but none of the scheme has used the new name for Burma, which is a violation of Canon of Currency.

4. CANON OF RETICENCE

The dictionary meaning of the word 'Reticent' is 'silent' and 'reticence' means a state of less speaking. The Canon directs that "the terms used to denote a class or a ranked isolate in a scheme for classification should not be critical—that is, express any opinion of the classificationist".

Up to DDC 14, the term 'Minor Author' was used by DDC in main class Literature. Regarding this arbitrary distinction Ranganathan then observed 'How can anybody assert who is minor and who is major writer? At any rate, classificationist has no business to parade his own opinion about the relative values of authors in the schedules of his scheme. The offensive term 'minor writers' can easily be replaced by the colourless, but perfectly description one 'Other writers. To get rid of this situation Dr. Ranganathan prescribed the year of birth as individualizing element. This critical work however, was dropped from DDC 15 onwards.

In DDC16, the term 'Humbug' was used as a subdivision of 'occultism'. The term Humbug mean-deception, hoax or a person who attempts to trick or deceive. The use of such a term is also the violation of the Canon of Reticence. The term was replaced by 'Frauds' in Occultism in DDC17.

4 D
Canons for Notational Plane

Q. : What are the different canons of work in Notational plane? Discuss them by giving examples.

Or

Describe the different devices adopted in CC, DDC and UDC to accommodate new subjects.

Ans. The classificationist has to make provisions in his scheme to accommodate the continuously growing universe of subjects and isolates. Therefore, together with making all necessary provisions to accommodate them, the notational system of the scheme should also be such that it may withstand the ever growing pressure of this unpredictable universe of subjects and isolates. A classificationist who keeps this important aspect in view while deciding the notational system of his scheme may be capable to provide hospitality to new subjects and isolates at any point in Array and Chain.

The term hospitality may, therefore, be defined as quality of the notational system which adds new life to a scheme by making it flexible in order to keep pace with ever growing universe of subjects. It may, therefore, be said that hospitality is such a pre-eminent, quality without which any modern library classification scheme can not survive. The hospitality accommodating new subjects and isolates, according to Dr. Ranganathan may be demanded in two places-in array and in chain.

Accordingly he formulated Canons for Hospitality, which help in understanding the demands of the Idea Plane and assist the Notational Plane in implementing the demands of Idea Plane.

(A) CANONS FOR HOSPITALITY IN ARRAY

An Array contains sequence or coordinate numbers. So in an array the new subjects may demand placing at the end or beginning of an array (extrapolation), or between two existing consecutive numbers in an array (interpolation). Accordingly Ranganathan has provided the following two Canon for Hospitality in Array:

- Canon of Extrapolation in Array
- Canon of Interpolation in Array

(1) Canon of extrapolation in array

The Canon directs that 'An array of class numbers or of isolate numbers should admit of any number of new coordinate numbers being added at the beginning and at the end of the array'.

To satisfy the demands of the Canon of Extrapolation different schemes for library classification have been using the following notational techniques:

(i) Gap Device
(ii) Mixed Base
(iii) Sectorising Digits

(i) Gap Device : As its name indicates, the classificationist leaves certain numbers unused at both ends of any array to accommodate new subjects as and when necessary. This method facilitates extrapolation only to a certain extent as the unused digits may all be used up at some point of time. After this stage, further extrapolation in the array would become impossible. Such gap devices facilitating extrapolation are present in different schemes of classification, e.g., DDC, CC and UDC. These gaps may be purely accidental, though at times they have been resorted to deliberately.

In the schedule of 1P1 isolates of 1 Universe of Subjects in CC (7th Edition), the digits 7 and 8 are left unused as gap devices. Thus,

1. Science	3. Social Science	5. Religion
2. Natural science	4. Philosophy	6. Fine arts and literature

Extrapolation to a pure base such as Indo-Arabic numerals is also possible by using other kinds of symbols like Roman smalls and Roman capitals to extend the array at either end. In effect, this too will prove to be equivalent to the method of leaving digits unused.

(ii) Mixed Base : A scheme with pure notation may also satisfy the demands of the Canon of extrapolation in array if the scheme starts using other kinds of species of digits also. This may provide some flexibility to its notational system. Even CC with mixed base has been constantly adding new species of digits to increase the capacity of its notational system. For example in 1933, CC1 had base of Indo-Arabic Numerals and Roman capitals only with few connecting symbols. In 1939, the hyphen as indicator and 9 as semantically empty digit was used to extrapolate new subjects and coordinate classes at the end of an array. In 1952, many new Greek alphabets were used to represent comprehensive main classes. This process is continuing till today. With the result the CC7 has capacity of 66 sectors in an array.

(iii) Sectorising Digit : Another method to satisfy the demands of this Canon is to use sectorising digits, by postulating the first and last digits to be empty. It is a device used for increasing the capacity of an array with the aid of an Empty digit. This method is adopted to satisfy the canon of extrapolation as it facilitates extrapolation at the beginning and at the end respectively of the array.

For example, if Indo-Arabic numerals 1 to 9 are used, one can accommodate only nine classes in an array. But, if more classes are to be accommodated, problems arise. To overcome such a problematic situation, CC has postulated 9 to be an empty digit. The result is a set of coordinate numbers in one sequence as under:

1 2 3 4 5 6 7 8 91 92 93 94 95 96 97 98 991 992.....998

This process can be extended to any length giving rise to a fresh set of coordinate numbers. It may appear not logical or funny to say that the numbers 1 and 998 are coordinate. But, this is true since 9 has been postulated to be an empty digit with an ordinal value but no semantic value. In other words, the digit-pairs 91,92...98 and the digit-triads 991-998 are treated as if each of them is single digit. In CC, the first and the last digits of Indo-Arabic numeral and 9; and the last digits of Roman smalls and Roman capitals-digits z and Z are postulated as Empty digits.

digit	9	in	1937 used in 1939
digit	0	in	1965 used in 1970
digit	z	in	1959 used in 1960

These digits are empty digits because these themselves do not represent any specific subject or isolate. These rather help in the extrapolation of new subjects in array at both ends.

Both DDC and UDC have provisions of open arrays. The digits 0 and 9 are used as sectorising digits which may permit extrapolation only to some extent. Ranganathan in Prolegomena, has cited certain examples from DDC 16 and 17 to demonstrate to which extent the digits 0 and 9 may admit extrapolation.

(2) Canon of interpolation in array

The Canon directs that 'An array of class numbers of isolate numbers should admit of the interpolation of any numbers at any point in an array'. In order to satisfy this canon, following different approaches have been adopted by different schemes of classification, namely.

- Gap Device,
- Mixed Base,
- Introduction of new species of digits,
- Emptying digits,
- Empty and Emptying digits,
- New Empty and Emptying digit

(i) Gap Device : While allocating isolate numbers in an array, the classification leaves certain unused numbers between two enumerated numbers to accommodate new classes or isolates as and when these emerge in future. However, this device has been found inadequate and insufficient to accommodate ever growing new subjects and isolates. The unused numbers once fully exhausted, then such an array would be treated as closed array for future arrivals. This is because the new arrivals requiring the numbers in this closed array would not be accommodated in their correct places.

For example, in the schedule of 1P1 isolates of U Geography in CC (7th Edition), the digits 4,5,6, 8 and 91 to 97 are left unused as a gap device to facilitate interpolation. Thus,

1 Map	7 Marine map
2 Map projection	98 Topographical survey
3 Globe	

In DDC Edition 20

094 Printed books

.2 Early printed books

.4 Special editions

094. 1 and 3, and 5-9 are left unused. There are several examples like this in DDC.

UDC 1961 Ed.	*UDC Med. Ed. 1985*	
312	312	Demography
312.2	312.3	Marriage...
312.4 unused	312.4	Celibacy...
312.5 unused	312.5	Household...
312.6 unused	312.6	Statistics of...
312.7 unused	312.7	Statistics of...

(ii) Mixed Base : When the notation used is of a mixed base variety, extrapolation to a zero or a sector, other than the first and the last ones, may also be looked upon as a case of interpolation. Only CC has mixed base of Roman smalls, Indo-Arabic numerals and Roman capitals, which are used to represent main subjects and in which new numbers may be incorporated as and when necessary. For example:

Sectors

(Z-a)	za-zy	(Z-1)	91-98	(Z-A)
a-y	za-zy	1-8	91-98	A-Y

(iii) Introduction of New Species of Digits : Interpolation of new subjects and isolates in an array is also possible by introducing new species of digits, if such digits are postulated with defined ordinal value. For example, in CC (6th Edition), the digit representing Spiritual Experience and Mysticism is interpolated between M Useful Arts and N Fine Arts.

(iv) Emptying Digits : Another method used for interpolation in an array is the Emptying Digits Device. The emptying digit is defined as a digit with its usual ordinal value and also semantic value, and having the power to deprive the preceding rich digit of its power of representing an idea. In other words, the emptying digits are postulated to the semantic value of the preceding digit but allow it to retain its ordinal value. Thus, T, V and X have been postulated as emptying digits. Thus, the digit-pairs JX and KX are coordinate in status with the digits J and K respectively.

In CC (7th Edition), in the schedule of basic subjects, JX forestry has been interpolated between *J Agriculture and* K *Zoology*. KX Animal husbandry has been interpolated between K Zoology and L Medicine.

Two emptying digits may also be used successively to make further interpolations.

Examples

Main Subjects

B	Mathematics
BT	Statistical calculus
BTT	Operational research
BTV	Informational Theory
GT	Cytology
GTX	Histology

Space Isolates

44T	Nepal
44TT	Sikkim
44TV	Bhutan
44VT	Maladive Islands

In these examples the first emptying digit T empties the semantic value of its preceding digit B, G and 44; whereas the second emptying digits-T, V and X empty the preceding digit T of its semantic value.

(v) **Empty-Emptying Digits :** The digits U, W and Y have been postulated as empty-emptying digits. These digits are both empty and emptying. In other words, these digits have an ordinal value but without a semantic value and also have the power of emptying the digit preceding them in a number of its semantic value while allowing it to retain its ordinal value. Therefore, when U, W and Y are used to represent basic subject numbers or isolate numbers, they have to be followed always by a rich substantive digit.

In CC (7th Edition), interpolation of more basic subects has bee possible by such digit-traids. Thus,

L	Medicine
LUD	Medical technology
LU5	Public health

LYX	Medical jurisprudence
LY1	Nursing
LU6*Z	Hospital and sanatorium
M	Useful arts

(vi) **New Empty and Emptying Digits** : Since 1966 the improvisation of 'A' (inverted V) as a new Empty and Emptying digit has been under consideration, so that the digits T to Y may be released for normal use as an array isolates. It was also thought that this new species of digit might be improvised for use in interpolation in Personality and Matter Facets only, in which the need for interpolation would be a rarity. However, in CC7 it is stated that 'For interpolation in an array of isolates, other than space isolates, the new digit 'A' (inverted V) may have to be improvised as an Empty-Emptying Digit. Its ordinal value will be greater than that of 'C' (starter bracket). The need for the use of this new digit will rarely arise. But it is suggested by way of abundant caution.

(B) CANONS FOR HOSPITALITY IN CHAIN

A chain of classes represent the subordinate ideas. The chain, therefore, contain a chain of subordinate numbers beginning with the numbers for whole universe of entities. The first link being the whole universe, as it is both natural and logical that nothing new may emerge before that. Therefore, in a chain of numbers the new ideas may demand hospitality either at the end of the chain or between any two consecutive succession of subordinate numbers. Accordingly the following two Canons have been formulated.

- Canon of Extrapolation
- Canon of Interpolation

1. Canon of Extrapolation in Chain

The Canon directs that 'A' chain of class numbers or isolate numbers should admit of the extrapolation of any number of successive links at its end. In other words, the notational system should admit of the chain ending with any number, being lengthened to any extent found necessary'.

The importance of this canon becomes obvious when one considers the implementation of the canon of decreasing extension in the case of a growing universe. Therefore, the notational system used by a scheme of classification should be versatile and resilient enough with the necessary devices to comply with this canon. Some of the devices that have been used for securing hospitality in chain are :

- Gap Device
- Decimal Fraction Device
- Agglomeration Device

(i) **Gap Device :** In Gap Device, some numbers are left unused after a particular number in an array, to accommodate a new sub-division, although it may or may not be a sub-division of that specific number. The Gap Device has following drawbacks:

(a) If the new subdivision which has been accommodated in the gap is not a subdivision of that specific number then, it violates the Canon of Hierarchy and Canon of Expressiveness.

(b) No one can foresee either the place or number of subjects or isolates that would emerge in future. So Gap Device can never cope the demands of growing universe of subjects.

(c) If one and the same number is left unused to accommodate both coordinate and subordinate classes, this would further limit the possibilities of accommodating the new subjects and isolates.

(ii) Decimal Fraction Device : The Decimal Fraction Device consists of treating each class number as a pure decimal fraction. Accordingly a new class may be created in a chain by subdividing the class forming its last link on the basis of a new additional characteristic. This process may continue *ad infinitum*. For every successive link of a chain, a digit is added in the class number-thus satisfying the Canons of Hierarchy and Expressiveness. The decimal fraction device may create a distinct helpful number for each new class or isolate without disturbing the ordinal value of the existing class numbers.

DDC, UDC and CC use this device to provide for infinite extrapolation in the chain. Thus,

Subjects	*CC*	*DDC*	*UDC*
Mammalia	K,97	599	599
Marsupialia	K,972	599.2	599.2
Diprotodontia	K,9721	599.2	599.22

(iii) Agglomeration Device : Agglomeration has been defined as 'the process of collecting together of entities into larger masses without cohesion among the components'. Attempts have been made to use agglomerates for extrapolation of a link in the beginning of the chain, if and when need arise. For example a new link may be created in the following manner:

Space Isolates

4442 * Z Haryana and Punjab

4442 Haryana

4443 Punjab

2. Canon of Interpolation

The Canon directs that 'A chain of class numbers or of isolate numbers should admit of the interpolation of any number of links between any two consecutive links in the chain.'

This Canon demands the interpolation of any number of links between any two consecutive links in a chain, whereas the Canon of Modulation prescribes that there should be no missing link in a chain. Normally all the schemes for classification conform to the demand of the Canon of Modulation. So the ruling of the Canon of Interpolation in Chain becomes automatically imperative. However, the emergence of new classes or isolate ideas in a universe of subjects is unpredictable. For example, the universe of political and administrative areas in Space isolates are such classes which are constantly changing.

In such a situation interpolation of a class or isolate between two consecutive links of a chain may become imperative. As yet no notational device has been formulated to solve this situation.

Examples: There are few examples in DDC, wherein DDC has used-(dash) or /(stroke) for interpolation in chain.

220/280	Christianity (Ed.16)
280-280	Christianity (Ed.17)

However, no such number is used from DDC 18 onwards.

Though CC (7th Edition) generally is in conformity with the canon of modulation, it has provided for certain devices/procedure to facilitate interpolation in a chain, if necessary. For example, it is possible to interpolate between any two consecutive links in the chain by using the connecting digit asterisk (*) or the plus sign (+) which has an anteriorising value. For example, if an interpolation is necessary between L,37A external carotid artery and L,37A1 thyroid artery, it is possible by using the connecting digit asterisk and synthesizing the number. The synthesized number would be L,37A1*. Thus, the chain would be as follows:

	L,37A	External carotid artery
INTERPOLATION-L37A1*		
	L,37A1	Thyroid artery

In UDC also, the use of extension and plus signs (/and +) can be used for interpolation between successive links, if necessary.

4 E
Notation, its Canons and Mnemonics

Q. : Describe the qualities of a good notation from the point of view of classification. Which among these do you think to be the most important and why?

Or

Define the term 'Notation' in library classification. Discuss its use in Colon Classification.

Or

What is notation? State its importance and also discuss Ranganathan's Canons of Notation.

Ans. The term notation denotes the artificial language of signs and symbols which is used in a scheme for classification for translating the words, terms and classes of natural language enumerated on the basis of the work of Verbal Plane. The term notation has been defined by different library scientists in the following manner:

(i) E.C. Richardson: notation is a 'shorthand sign.'

(ii) W.C. Berwick Sayers: A book notation is a series of signs or symbols standing for the names of terms and forming a convenient means of reference to the arrangement of our classification.

(iii) Palmer and Wells: Notation is a device for mechanizing arrangement and must be composed of written symbols whose order is defined.

(iv) H.E. Bliss: A notation is a system of marks or symbols in some order, denoting terms of a members of a series of system of things. For a classification a notation serves to denote the classes and their order, without naming or defining them; but it is not as has erroneously been said, a 'shorthand' writing of names.

(v) S.R. Ranganathan: A system of ordinal numbers used to represent the classes in a scheme for classification.

Need for Notation

The primary objective of the schemes for classification is to provide a mechanism to libraries on the basis of which the documents may be arranged in a helpful filiatory sequence. Secondly, it is also imperative that for maximum and expeditious utilization of documents all documents of related subjects are kept in juxtaposition. The terms, words and sentences used to describe the thought contents and physical features of documents can not be reproduced on catalogue cards, or on documents for arranging them on shelves as these would not provide helpful, filiatory and systematic arrangement of documents which is necessary for their smooth and expeditious use. It is in this context, a scheme for classification is used to mechanize the process of sorting and arranging the documents in helpful sequence whereby all related documents are placed on shelves depending upon their proximity with each other. As a result utilization of documents is maximized. A notation therefore assumes indispensable preposition in classifying documents and arranging them on shelves.

A Notation may be divided in Faceted and Non-Faceted Notation.

(i) Faceted Notation : When the digits for constructing the class numbers are segmented into blocks with the help of indicators, this constitutes a multi-partite notation. However when this multi-partite notation is constructed with the help of meaningful indicators, indicating the distinct character of the succeeding digits, it is termed as Faceted Notation.

Example

J, 371; 43:55.4447 'N95

Measures used for the control of Parasites in Apple in Himachal Pradesh in 1995.

J	Agriculture	First Facet [BF]
,371	Apple	Personality Facet [P]
'43	Parasites	Matter Property Facet [MP]
.55	Control measures	Energy Facet [E]
.4447	Himachal Pradesh	Space Facet [S].

.N95 1995 Time Facet [T].

Each indicator in this example is a meaningful indicator, specifically pinpointing the type of facet represented by the succeeding digit.

(ii) Non-Faceted Notation

A non-faceted notation is one in which the digits used for constructing the class number forms one block only. This type of notation is also termed as Unipartite Notation.

Examples form LC and BC

LC	RC372	Epilepsy in Medicine
	NA2940	Structural Frame in a building
BC	BQW	Impact and Reactions of Liquids
	K35	Classification of Sociology

TYPES OF NOTATION

Notation may be of two types:

– Pure Notation

– Mixed Notation

(i) Pure Notation

A notational system in which no class number contains more than one species of digit is a called a pure notational system. In other words, use of only one set of symbols or digits in a scheme for classification is termed as pure notation.

Examples:

Arabic numerals 0-9

Roman capitals A-Z

Roman small a-z etc.

Melvil Dewey made decimal use of Arabic numeral 0-9, as for him pure notation was ideal notation.

(ii) Mixed Notation

A notational system in which a class number may have two or more species of digits is called mixed notational system.

It was E.C. Richardson who for the first time advocated for mixed notation, provided a principle of mixed notation and said that every practical scheme sooner or later will have to adopt mixed notation. Bliss also suggested that 'notation for library classification should... combine letters and figures'. Sayers, although has given Canon of Pure Notation, but he has also advocated for mixed notation. However, it was Ranganathan who made the best use of mixed notation in making his scheme Colon Classification freely faceted scheme, capable of keeping pace with growing knowledge. In Colon Classification, the following species of digits are used:

Species of digits 6

Roman Capitals A-Z

Roman smalls a-z except i, l, o

Indo Arabic numerals 0-9

Greek letter Δ (delta)

Fourteen indicator digits

Qualities of Notation

The notation which ultimately serves the users must possess certain basic qualities. It is on these qualities that the efficiency, viability and use of a scheme for classification depends. The qualities of notation may be described as follows:

(1) Simplicity : Simplicity of notation means that it should be easy to read, write and remember. They should convey order or sequence clearly and should be acceptable to users. Indo-Arabic numerals and Roman Capitals are such numbers with which the user is not only familiar but is also conversant with the ordinal sequence provided by these numbers and alphabets. However if other unknown symbols are used, their ordinal value must be predetermined. This was the main reason why pure notation was once rated superior to mixed notation. Besides, the notation should be easy to read, write and pronounce. For this it is necessary to divide in blocks a class number with long string of digits, the classification should keep in view that numbers like 0 and alphabet O may create confusion, as both these are identical on Typewriters and unknown letters like Greek alphabets in CC are not easy to read, write or pronounce.

(2) Brevity: The library staff is required to record class number at various places. It simplify the work if numbers are brief. Thus, brevity is a desirable quality of a notation. It depends on the length of the base of a notational system of a scheme for classification. Longer the base shorter would be the notation. For example DDC and UDC have a base of 10 digits and CC using mixed base has a capacity of 60 digits.

Example:

Subject	*DDC*	*UDC*	*CC*
Sociology	301	30	Y
Hindi Language	491.43	491.43	P152

Brevity of notation has many advantages. It is easy to read, write and pronounce, may be written easily on different parts of documents or on catalogue cards, etc. However, brevity of notation should not be at the cost of either systematic order of documents or service to readers. In a special library brevity of notation has no meaning as it has to provide specialist information service based on micro literature, which require co-extensive class numbers.

(3) Hospitality : The knowledge being dynamic, grows with an unabated pace. As a result all classification schemes require to accommodate newly emerging subjects at appropriate places within the existing classes. So, the notation should have the quality to accommodate new subjects or classes in their correct places within already enumerated classes in a scheme for classification. This is the only quality which makes the scheme to keep pace with ever growing knowledge.

For example, If 1 represents 'Fiction' and 2 'Poetry' then further expansion is possible in this manner:

1. Fiction
11. Historical fiction
12. Romantic fiction
13. Science fiction
2. Poetry
21. Lyric poetry

The insertion of new coordinate subjects is more difficult but it could be provided for by leaving gaps, for example:

1. Construction
4. Testing
7. Maintenance

But the gaps may not be in appropriate places and therefore could interfere with the required order.

(4) Expressiveness : The expressiveness precisely means that a class number should represent relevant and essential characteristics of the subject being classified. The notation that expresses the structure of the scheme is known as expressive., hierarchical or structural. For example :

I Military ordnance

II Artillery

III Field artillery

Though expressiveness sometimes considered helpful yet it is not essential. It results in longer classification numbers and limits hospitality.

Colon classification is the best example of this kind. See the way in which the structure of the scheme is reflected in the notation.

X	Economics
X7	Public finance
X72	Tax
X724	Income tax
X7244	– on salary

(5) Mnemonics : A good notation should also possess mnemonic quality which is of great value to classifier. The mnemonic quality in the notation is obtained by using consistently one and the same digit or digits for one and the same concept or concepts wherever it occurs in the schemes for classification. For example in classification schemes-CC, DDC and UDC the mnemonic quality in their notational system has been obtained through the schedules for space isolates, language isolates and common isolates as well as by other devices and methods.

Using one and same digit for the same concept consistently both the classifier and users become gradually conversant with it and remember such class numbers.

Q. : What do you mean by Canon of Notation? Discuss them in brief.

Ans. In order to make the notation simple, flexible, feasible, brief, expressive, and hospitable, Dr. Ranganathan has devised Canons for Notational Plane. He has devised two sets of Canons, which are as under:

- Canon of Synonym
- Canon of Homonym

The second set consists of ten other canons. These fall into five pairs and each pair consists of one canon and of its negation. These are as under:

- Canon of Relativity and Canon of Uniformity
- Canon of Hierarchy and Canon of Non-Hierarchy
- Canon of Mixed Notation and Canon of Pure Notation
- Canon of Faceted Notation and Canon of Non-Faceted Notation
- Canon of Co-Extensiveness and Canon of Under-Extensiveness

1. Canon of Synonym

This canon demands that "each subject should be represented by one and only one Class Number. No subject should be represented by two or more Class Numbers. Similarly, each isolate idea should be represented by one and only one isolate number." This canon helps to avoid the scattering of documents.

2. Canon of Homonym

While defining this canon, Dr. Ranganathan says, "the subject represented by a class number if a system of class numbers and the isolate idea represented by an isolate number in a system of isolate numbers, should be unique. It implies that each class number should represent one and only one subject. No class number should represent two or more subjects. Similarly, each isolate number should represent one and only one isolate idea." In other words, the canon demands that there should be only one class number for one subject.

(i) Canon of Relativity as Canon of Uniformity : It is a pair of two negative canons. The *Canon of Relativity* prescribes that the number of digit (including digit-groups treated as single digit) in a class number or in an isolate number should be the same as the order of the subject or the isolate idea, as the case may be, represented by it. This means that there should be exact representation of a subject in a class number. This, canon further demands that the order in the number of digits and the order of the subject should be the same. In other words, a class of greater extension should be assigned lesser number of digits and a class of lesser extension should be individualized by greater number of digits. We see that the classification steps starts from higher class and proceeds towards lower class. We take an example:

Education	T	1. digit
Secondary Education	T2	2. digits
Secondary Teaching Technique	T2:3	4. digits (includes connecting Symbol)

The *Canon of Uniformity,* as negation to the above Canon, demands that the number of digits in a class number or in an isolate number should be constant whatever be the order of the subject or the isolate, as the case may be, represented by it. This canon insists upon that the digits should be constant whatever the order be. So it attaches more importance to the constancy of the digits.

(ii) Canon of Hierarchy vs. Canon of Non-Hierarchy : The *Canon of Hierarchy* states that in a class number or in an isolate number, there should be a digit to represent each of the characteristics used in constructing the class number or the isolate number, as the case may be. On the other hand the *Canon of Non-Hierarchy* opposes it that there need not be a digit to represent each of the characteristics used in constructing the class number or isolate number.

For example if we take Geographical Division in which digit 1 represents 'World', 4 represents Asia, 5 represents Europe etc. World is a class of order 1 and the rest of the divisions are in order 2. Thus, continents are sub-ordinate to World in the Idea Plane but on the other hand they will appear as coordinate class in Notational Plane.

(iii) Canon of Mixed Base Us. Canon of Pure Base : The *Canon of Mixed Base* emphasizes that the "Base of the Notational System of a scheme for classification should use two or more species of digits."

The Canon of Pure Base demands that the "Base of the Notational System of a scheme for classification should use one and only one species of digits."

Dr. Ranganathan has made the inferences in respect of both the bases. He says that if the number of subjects is less than 600 thousands, a Pure Base of Indo-Arabic numbers can be chosen: and if the number of subjects is less than 200 millions, a Pure Base of Roman Capitals can be chosen. But the mixed base notation is more useful because a mixed notation of Indo-Arabic numerals, Roman capitals, and Roman smalls, we can give distinctive class number to 30,000 millions subjects.

(iv) Canon of Faceted vs Non-Faceted Notation : The faceted notation, as Mills stated, is that notation which allows simultaneous specification of any required number of facets in the correct sequence. Dr. Ranganathan prescribed two conditions for each of the above canons. *The faceted notational system* should be used when the (a) length of the base of the notation is about 10 and the universe is likely to contain more than a million or more entities or subject; and (b) length of the base is about 56 and the universe is likely to contain 1,000 millions or more entities or subjects.

(v) Canon of Co-extensiveness vs. Canon of Under-Extensiveness The *Canon of Co-extensiveness* demands that the digits should be added successively so that even the last characteristic in the succession of characteristics may represent the measure of incidence.

On the other hand the *Canon of Under-Extensiveness* states that it is not essential that the digits should be continued so as to represent the measure of incidence of the latter characteristics in the succession of characteristics.

Q. : Give definition of the mnemonics. How are systematic mnemonics used in CC?

Or

What do you mean by mnemonics? State their kinds and canons and use in various classification schemes.

Ans. The term mnemonics originates from a Greek word mnemonics which means 'to remember'. In dictionary, it is defined as 'aiding or intending to aid the memory; a device, as a formula or rhyme, used as an aid in remembering'. Consciously or unconscioly every human being uses this devise in numerous ways. Notation used in modern classification possesses a very general quality, referred to as *mnemonic quality*. Artificial language of signs and symbols used in library classification does not possess mnemonic quality by itself. Mnemonic quality is rather created in a scheme of library classification by classificationist while designing the scheme to assist the memory of the classifier and to reduce the work of reference librarian. Sayers has rightly stated that there is a very general quality in modern classification, notation which is ingenious and within limits of great value to the classifier. This is its mnemonic quality; its power of assisting the memory and of reducing the work of reference to tablets and indexed to the minimum".

Ranganathan propounded a general canon of mnemonics which explains the exact meaning of the term mnemonic as 'The digit or digit-group used to represent a specific concept in a class number (or any of its constituents) should be the same in all class numbers having that concept represented in them, provided that insistence on such consistent representation does not violate more important requirements'.

Kinds of Mnemonics

According to Ranganathan, the following four kinds of mnemonics are possible in notation:

1. Alphabetical (Verbal) Mnemonics;
2. Scheduled Mnemonics;
3. Systematic Mnemonics;
4. Seminal Mnemonics.

(1) Alphabetical Mnemonics

The use of verbal mnemonics is quite common in everyday life. This is also known as alphabetical mnemonics. Using alphabetical mnemonics, classification is called an alphabetical device. In Alphabetical Mnemonics, the insistence is on the consistent use of alphabets for one and the same name or concept wherever it occurs. These are to be preferred only when arrangement on the basis of any other characteristic is not more helpful than alphabetical arrangement and if an international nomenclature exists in the field to which it is applied.

For example, in CC alphabetical arrangement is preferred for subdividing various brands of machines and strains of agriculture crops in the following manner:

CC6

Brands of Motor Car

D 5133	Motor Car
D 5133A	Ambassador Car
D 5133F	Fiat Car

Different species of *Mango*

J I351	Mango
J I351B	Banarasi Mango

J	I351C	Chausa Mango
J	I351F	Fuzli Mango

In DDC 20, the names of programming languages, names of specific computers or processors are used for subdividing programming languages or computers etc., as these are internationally recognized names, and may be used consistently wherever, these are used in library classification. For example:

005.2 Programming for specific types of computers

005.262 In specific programming language

005.262 FORTRAN

But one of the objectives of classificatory language of ordinal numbers is intended to work as an international language to facilitate international communication. It is, therefore, necessary that internationally accepted terminology is available in every discipline and subject. But in reality even today, such internationally accepted terminology does not exist in several fields. The Canon of Alphabetical Mnemonics, therefore, directs that 'Alphabetical mnemonics should be rejected without any hesitation, if a sequence more helpful to readers or more filiatory than alphabetical sequence exists. Alphabetical mnemonics should be preferred if the alphabetical sequence is as helpful as any other sequence and if an international nomenclature exists in the field to which it is applied'.

(2) Scheduled Mnemonics

The Canon of Scheduled Mnemonics directs that 'A scheme for classification should use one and the same digit or digit-group, as the case may be, to represent an isolate idea or an array isolate idea, in whatever subject it may occur'.

If the direction of Canon is compiled it would automatically conform to the Canon of Consistent Sequence; and would also satisfy the Law of Parsimony by reducing the length of the schedules of classification.

CC makes extensive use of parallel schedule by giving appropriate instructions in the schedule.

Basic Subject	*Facet*	*Parallel Schedule*
2	M	Same as Foci in [P] for general bibliography

L	[E] cum [2P]	522 animals. To be subdivided as in 'K2' Animal husbandry
NA	[P3]	22 Library Building to be divided as the [P] Of "2 Library Science".

In DDC, provisions of 'Special Add Tables' is made to avoid repeated enumeration of one and the same class number in different places in the schedules.

Example

582-58 Specific plants and groups of plants.

Add to each subdivision identified by * as follows:

Such Special Add Tables are provided for different subjects and disciplines. In place of enumeration, DDC now prefers these 'Special Add Tables' and thereby fulfilling the demand of the Canon of Scheduled Mnemonics.

(3) Systematic Mnemonics

According to the canon of systematic mnemonics "in a scheme of classification, the digits used to represent the array isolate ideas in an array should run parallel to the sequence in which the principles for helpful sequence would arrange the array isolate ideas".

Ranganathan has provided eight canons for helpful sequences.

(i) Time sequence

(ii) Evolutionary sequence

(iii) Spatial contiguity sequence

(iv) Quantitative sequence

(v) Complexity sequence

(vi) Canonical sequence

(vii) Literary warrant sequence

(viii) Alphabetical sequence

Following are the examples of some sequence followed in CC, DDC & UDC.

(i) Time Sequence

Subject	*CC6*	*DDC 19+20*	*UDC*
Religion	Q	200	2
Vedic	Q,1	—	294.11
Post Vedic	Q,2	294.5 (Hinduism)	294.2
Jainism	Q,3	294.4	294.35
Buddhism	Q,4	294.3	294.3
Judaism	Q,5	296	296
Christianity	Q,6	220/280	22/28
Islam	Q,7	297	297

(ii) Evolutionary Sequence

Subject	*CC6*	*DDC 19+20*	*UDC*
Botany	I	581	58
Thallophyta	I2	589	582.22
Bryophyta	I3	588	582.32
Pteridophyta	I4	587	582.35
Gymnosperm	I6	585	582.42
Monocotyledon	I7	584	582.61
Dicotyledon	I8	583	

All the scheme conform to the Canon of Systematic Mnemonics.

(iii) Spatial Contiguity Sequence

Subject	*CC6*	*DDC 19+20*	*UDC*
Botany	(IP2)	581	580
Root	I,13	581.498	581.43
Stem	I,14	581.495	581.44
Leaf	I,15	581.497	581.45
Flower	I,16	—	581.46
Fruit	I,17	—	581.47
Seed	I,178	—	581.48

The principal of bottom upwards seems to be followed by all the three schemes and thereby, conform to the Canon of Systematic Mnemonics.

(iv) Quantitative Sequence

Subject	*CC6(P3)*	*DDC 19+20*	*UDC*
Town Planning	NB	781	711.43
Village	NB,1		711.437
Town	NB, 3		711.434
City	NB, 5		711.433
Metropolis	NB, 7		711.432

CC follows the Principle of Increasing Quantity and the sequence of UDC conforms to the Principle of Decreasing Quantity.

(v) Complexity Sequence

Subject	*CC6*	*DDC 19+20*	*UDC*
Psychology	S	150	159.9
Perception	S:2	152.1	159.93
Consciousness	S:3	152.3	—
Cognition	S:4	153	159.95
Emotion	S:5	152.4	159.942
Conation	S:6	153.8	159.943
Personality	S:7	153.9	—
Metapsychology	S:8	154	159.96

The Principle of Complexity as enunciated by Ranganathan is followed in CC. But the complexity of human psychology can not be measured in a uniform manner. The other two schemes have, therefore, followed their own sequence of increasing complexity in this regard.

(4) Seminal Mnemonics

According to seminal mnemonics canon "A scheme of classification should use on and the same digit to denote seminally equivalent concepts in whatever subject they may occur". This clearly states that seminally equivalent concepts are to be represented by the same number irrespective of subjects where these may occur. According to Ranganathan, the concept of seminal mnemonic is found in ancient traditions, when he writes, 'In the mystic tradition of Chelsea and India, many such equivalences are believed to have been recognized. I have not yet been able to get hold of that tradition. It gives seminal mnemonic significance to letters as well as numerals. A correct knowledge of it will make use of digits conform with seminal mnemonic. The forgotten tradition needs to be re-captured'.

For example digit 3 is used for three dimensional, space, cubics, analysis, function, physiology etc. Likewise digit 4 represents Pathology, disease. Hence any entity which can be regarded as analogous to such concepts will get the same digit. For example, I:4 is Plant pathology in Botany and J4 is Disease in Agriculture; Y:4 is Social pathology, etc. These concepts are apparently seminally equivalent but they do not possess the same terms in the different subjects.

5
Principles of Helpful Sequence

Q. : Discuss the principles of Helpful Sequence with examples from CC, UDC and DDC.

Or

State the Principles of Helpful Sequence. Explain any three of them.

Ans. It isneccessary that the sequence of the classes in an array should be helpful. It should be according to some convenient principles and not arbitrary, whenever insistence on only one principle does not violate other more important requirements. This is the pre-requisite of the Canon of Helpful Sequence.

The Canon of Helpful Sequence has been enunciated by Dr. Ranganathan with a view to arrange classes in the array. He has provided following guiding principles for implementing the demands of the Canon of Helpful Sequence:

1. Based on Time Sequence

    11. Principle of Later-in-Time

    12. Principle of Earlier-in-Time

2. Based on Evolutionary Sequence

    21. Principle of Later-in-Evolution

    22. Principle of Earlier-in-Evolution

3. Based on Spatial Contiguity Sequence

    31. Principle of Spatial Contiguity

4. Based on Quantitative Measure Sequence

    41.Principle of Increasing Quantity

    42.Principle of Decreasing Quantity

5. Based on Complexity Sequence
   51. Principle of Increasing Complexity
   52. Principle of Decreasing Complexity
6. Based on Traditional Sequence
   61. Principle of Canonical Sequence
7. Based on Literary Warrant Sequence
   71. Principle of Literary Warrant
8. Based on Alphabetical Sequence
   81. Principle of Alphabetical Sequence

1. TIME SEQUENCE

11. Principle of Later - in-time

The Principle directs that 'If the subjects in an array of subjects or the isolates in an array of isolates have originated in different times, they should be arranged in a parallel progressive time sequence, except when any other overwhelming consideration rules it out'.

In Colon Classification, the use of this principle can been seen in the systems as given below:

Ayurveda LB	Experimental Psychology SM
Siddha LC	Psycho-Analysis SM9
Unani LD	Gestalt SN

Other schemes have violated this principle while arranging the classes in main class religion, as is indicated in the following table:

Subject	*CC6*	*CC7*	*DDC 19-20*	*UDC Ab 1961*	*UDC Med. Ed. 1985*
Religion	Q	Q	200	2	—
Vedic	Q,1	Q,1	—	294.11	294.11
Post Vedic	Q,2	Q,2	294.5	294.2	294.2,294.5
Jainism	Q,3	Q,3	294.4	294.35	294
Buddhism	Q,4	Q,4	294.3	294.3	294.3
Judaism	Q,5	Q,5	296	296	296
Christianity	Q,6	Q,6	220/289	21/28	21/28
Islam	Q,7	Q,7	297	297	297

12. Principle of Earlier-in-time

This principle directs that 'If the subjects in an array of subjects or the isolates in an array of isolates have originated in different time sequence, they may be arranged in an Earlier-in-Time Sequence. For example, religions of above table may be arranged in a reverse order, if it is more helpful.

2. EVOLUTIONARY SEQUENCE

21 Principle of later-in-evolution

This principle directs that 'It the subjects in an array of subjects or the isolates in an array of isolates belong to different stages of evolution, they should be arranged parallel to the evolutionary sequence, except when any other overwhelming consideration rules it out.'

The application of this principle can be seen in the Schedule of Psychology:

1 Child

11 New born

12 Toddler

13 Infant

14 Pre-adolescent

22 Principle of earlier-in-envolution

The evolution of a subject is gradual, and consistent. This evolutionary sequence of subjects or isolates may be based on either the Principle of Later-in-Evolution-first place to subject or isolate which is first in evolutionary sequence; or Principle of Earlier-in-Evolution-to give first place to subject which is last in order of evolution. *i.e.* the reverse process. However, preference is usually given to the Principle of Later-in-Evolution as it indicates the evolution from first stage onwards. This is clear from the following example:

Subject	*CC6*	*CC7*	*DDC 1920*	*UDC*
Botany	I	I	581	58
Thallophytic	I 2	I, 2	589	582.22
Bryophyta	I 3	I, 3	588	582.32
Pteriodophyta	I 4	I, 4	587	582.35

Gymnosperm	I 6	I, 6	585	582.42
Mononocotyledon	I 7	I, 7	584	582.52
Dicotyledon	I 8	I, 8	583	582.61

Both the principles have been applied in this example. It may be said that the sequences of CC and UDC are based on principle of Later-in-Evolution and of DDC on Principle of Later-in-Evolution.

3. SPATIAL CONTIGUITY SEQUENCE

31 Principle of Spatial Contiguity

The term 'Spatial Contiguity' means the state of being adjacent to each other along an unidirectional line or a radial line or a circle. The principle directs that 'It the subject in an array of subjects or the isolates in an array of isolate occur contiguously in space-roughly along a unidirectional line or a radial line, or a circle, they should be arranged in a parallel spatial sequence, except when any other overwhelming consideration rules it out.' This principle is a bundle of principles which may be shown as under:

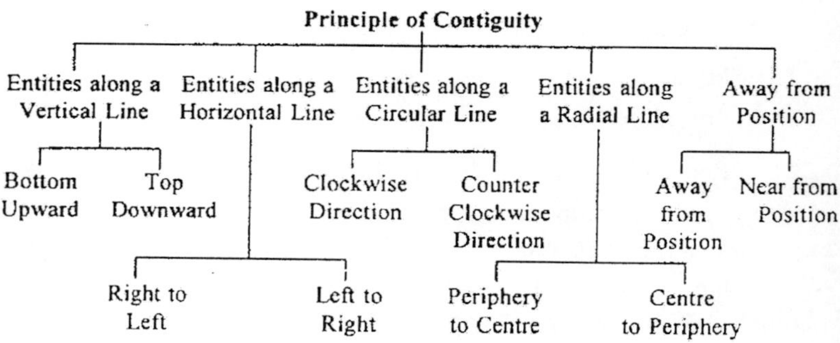

31.1 Entities along a Vertical Line

31.1 (i) Principle of Bottom Upwards: The principle directs that 'If the subjects in an array of subjects or isolates in an array of isolates can be conveniently taken to occur along a vertical line, they may be arranged from bottom upwards, if it is helpful.'

For example, regional organs in Botany may be arranged on the basis of this principle.

Subject	*CC6*	*CC7*	*DDC 19 and 20*
Botany	I	I	581
Root	I 13	I,13	581.498
Stem	I 14	I,14	581.498
Leaf	I 15	I,15	591.497
Flower	I 16	I,16	
Fruit	I 17	I,17	
Seed	I 18	I,18	

31.1 (ii) Principle of Top Downwards: The principle directs that 'If the subjects in an array of subjects or isolates in an array of isolates can be conveniently taken to occur along a vertical line, they may be arranged from top downwards, if it is helpful'.

Example : Medicine, Regional Organs

Subject	*CC6*	*CC7*	*DDC A+20*	
Medicine	L	L	610	61
Head	L 18	L,18	611.91	611.91
Neck	L 17	L,17	611.93	611.93
Thorax	L 15	L,15	611.94	611.94
Abdoman	L 14	L,14	611.95	611.95
Pelvic region	—	—	611.96	611.957/958
Upper extremities	L16	L,16	611.97	611.97
Lower extremities	L13	L,13	611.98	611.98

It may be said that DDC and UDC have followed the Principle of Top Downwards and CC Principle of Bottom Upwards.

31.2 Entitities along a Horizontal Line

31.2 (i) Principle of Left-To-Right : The principle directs that 'If the subjects in an array of subjects or isolates in an array of isolates can be conveniently taken to occur along a horizontal line, they may be arranged from left-to-right, if it is helpful.'

31.2 (ii) Principle of Right-To-Left: The principle directs that 'If the subjects in an array of subjects or isolates in an array of isolates can be conveniently taken to occur along a horizontal line, they may be arranged right to left, if it is helpful.'

Example : Different lanes and other items on the highway can be arranged by either of the two principles:

1. Motor Cars 2. Heavy Vehicles 3. Bicycle 4. Cart; and 5. Pedestrain	or	1. Pedestrain 2. Cart 3. Bicycle 4. Heavy Vehicles 5. Motor Cars

31.2 (iii) Principle of Front-To-Back: The principle directs that 'If the subjects in an array of subjects or isolates in an array of isolates can be conveniently taken to occur along a horizontal line, they may be arranged from front to back, if it is helpful'.

31.2 (iv) Principle Back-to-Front: The principle directs that 'If the subjects in an array of subjects or isolates in an array of isolates can be conveniently taken to occur along a horizontal line, they may be arranged from back to front, if it is helpful.'

Example: The regional organs of fish may be arranged either front-to-back or back-to-front.

1. Pectoral 2. Dorsal 3. Ventral 4. Pelvic 5. Candal	or	1. Candal 2. Pelvic 3. Ventral 4. Dorsal 5. Pectoral

31.3 Entities along a Circular Line

31.3 (i) Principle of Clockwise Direction: The principle directs that 'If the subjects in an array of subjects or isolates in an array of isolates can be conveniently taken to occur along a circular line, they may be arranged in the clockwise direction, if it is helpful.'

31.3 (ii) Principle of Counter-Clockwise Direction: The principle directs that 'If the subjects in an array of subjects or isolates in an array of isolates can be conveniently taken to occur along a circular line, they may be arranged in a anti–clockwise direction, if it is helpful.'

Example: 1. The zodiacal divisions may be arranged in the clockwise direction or anti-clockwise direction:

1. Aries		1. Pisces
2. Taurus		2. Aquarius
3. Gemini		3. Capricornus
4. Cancer		4. Sagittarius
5. Leo		5. Scorpic
6. Virgo	or	6. Libra
7. Libra		7. Virgo
8. Scorpio		8. Leo
91.Sagittarius		9. Cancer
92.Capricornus		10.Gemini
93.Aquarius		11.Tarurus
94.Pisces		12. Aries

Example: 2. In CC, the space isolates are arranged according to the principle of clockwise direction:

4 Asia; 41 China; 42 Japan; 43 Vietnam; 44 India; 45 Iran; 46 Arabian Peninsula; 47 Turkey (Asia); 48 USSR (Asia)

31.4 Entities along a Radial Line

31.4 (i) Principle of Periphery to Centre: The principle directs that 'If the subjects in an array of subjects or isolates in an array of isolates can be conveniently taken to occur along a radial line of circle or a cylinder they may be arranged periphery to center, if it is helpful.'

31.4 (ii) Principle of Centre to Periphery: The principle directs that 'If the subjects in an array of subjects or isolates in an array of isolates can be conveniently taken to occur along a radial line, they may be arranged from center to periphery, if it is helpful'.

Example: In CC, DDC and UDC, the principle of centre to periphery is used to arrange the following organs in Medicine:

Bone (center), Muscle, Connective tissue, Skin and Hair (periphery).

31.5 Entities Occurring Away from Position

31.5 (i) Principle of Away-from-position: The principle directs that 'If the subjects in an array of subjects or the isolates in an array of isolates can be conveniently taken to start from a certain point and diverge away from it roughly along a line, they may be arranged from the starting point along the diverging line, if it is helpful.'

31.5 (ii) Principle of Near-From-Position: The principle directs that 'If the subjects in an array of subjects or the isolates in an array of isolates can be conveniently taken to start from a certain point and diverge away from it roughly along a line, they may be arranged from the terminating point, if it is helpful'.

Example: In CC, DDC and UDC, the principle of away-from-position, seems to have been followed in arranging the following isolates in Astronomy:

Mercury, Venus, Mars, Asteroid, Jupiter, Saturn, Uranus, Neptune, and Pluto.

4. QUANTITATIVE SEQUENCE

41. Principle of Increasing Quantity

The principle directs that 'If the subjects in an array of subjects or the isolates in an array of isolates admit of quantitative distinction, they may be arranged according to their increasing quantity, if it is helpful'.

Example : CC arranges the isolates in (1P1) *Geometry* in the following sequence:

Subject	*CC6*	*CC7*
Geometry	B6	B6
Line	B61	B6,1
Plane	B62	B6,2
Three dimensions	B63	B6,3
Four dimensions	B64	B6,4
Five dimensions	B65	B6,5
n dimensions	B67	B6,7

42. Principle of Decreasing Quantity

The Principle directs that 'If the subjects in an array of subjects or the isolates in an array of isolates admit of quantitative distinction, they may be arranged according to their decreasing quantity, if it is helpful.'

Example: In CC, the different kinds of libraries are arranged to the decreasing quantity i.e., area or the size of the population served.

Subject	*CC6*	*CC7*
Library Science	2	2
World Library	211	2,A
National Library	213	2,B
Regional Library	214	—
State Library	215	2,C
District Library	216	2,D
City Library System	—	2,E
Rural Library System	—	2,F

5. COMPLEXITY SEQUENCE

51. Principle of Increasing Complexity

This principle states: "If the subjects in an array of subject on the isolates in an array of isolates show different degrees of complexity, they should be arranged parallel to the sequence of increasing complexity except when any other overwhelming consideration rules it out." This means that if one of the two related classes deals with a lesser degree of complexity than the other one must have precedence over the other.

Example: 1. On the basis of the characteristic "Subject of Study", CC arranges subjects in Geography in the sequence of increasing complexity:

Subject	*CC6*	*CC7*
Geography	U	U
Mathematical geography	U1	U1
Physical geography	U42	U2
Biogeography	U23	U3
Anthropogeography	U4	U5
Political geography	U5	U6
Economic geography	U6	U7

Example: 2. On the basis of the characteristic 'Element', CC arranges the subjects in Linguistics according to the principle of increasing complexity.

Subject	*CC6*
Linguistics	P
Isolated sound	P,1
Syllable	P,2
Word	P,3
Phrase	P,4
Clause	P,5
Sentence	P,6
Pieces of composition	P,7

52. Principle of Decreasing Complexity

The principle directs that 'If the subjects in an array of subjects or the isolates in an array of isolates show different degrees of complexity, they may be arranged parallel to the decreasing complexity'.

Example: The different transport vehicles may be arranged in the sequence of decreasing complexity on the basis the design of vehicles, as Spacecraft; Aircraft; Motor car; Motor cycle and Cycle.

6. TRADITIONAL SEQUENCE OR CANONICAL SEQUENCE

61. Principle of Canonical Sequence

This principle prescribes that if the subjects in array of subjects or the isolates in an array of isolates are traditionally referred to in a specific sequence, although no underlying principle is discoverable, it will be convenient to conform to this traditional sequence. Dr. Ranganathan further says that when no other principle is available to exist in fixing a helpful sequence among a set of given classes, any traditional of conventional or canonical sequence may be adopted. Mills seems to be doubtful when he expresses that "It is doubtful whether such order, if they indeed exist, are sufficiently well known or accepted as to constitute a helpful order in their own right." We may simply say that the Canonical divisions are no other but only the recognized divisions on the basis of characteristics.

Example : In CC the basic divisions of Mathematics, Physics, Geology, etc. are arranged in Canonical sequence e.g.

Subject	*CC6*		*CC7*
Mathematics	B		B
Arithmetic	B1		B1
Algebra	B2		B2
Analysis	B3		B3
Other Methods	B4		B4
Trigonometry	B5		B5
Geometry	B6	Topology	B6T
Mechanics	B7	Statistical Calculus	B7
Physics-Mathematics	B8	Operational research Cybernetics	BTT
Astronomy	B9		BV

7. LITERARY WARRANT SEQUENCE

71. Principle of Decreasing Literary Warrant

The principle directs that 'If subject in an array of subjects or the isolates in an array of isolates may be arranged in the sequence of the decreasing quantity of the documents published or anticipated to be published on them, except when any other overwhelming consideration rules it out'.

The term 'Literary warrant' was first introduced by E. Wyndham Hulme, while writing series of articles entitled 'Principles of Book Classification published during 1911-12 in Library Association Record. Ranganathan, however, was the first to recognize the concept; which he applied in his scheme CCI in the main class Agriculture for arranging Food Plants. He then termed this principle as 'Principle of Favoured Category.' The principle should be applied without any bias to the country of origin of the scheme.

Example: In CC, the Food Plants in Agriculture are arranged according to the principle of decreasing literary warrant:

Seed as Food, Rice, Wheat, Oat, Rye, Corn, Barley, and Millet.

J Agriculture   Seed as food J38

Rice   381

Wheat	382
Oat	383
Rye	384 etc.

The other two schemes DDC and UDC, also conform to this principle except for Rice which is enumerated in the last: Seed as Food, Wheat, Oat, Rye, Corn, Barley, Millet and Rice.

72. Principle of Increasing Literary Warrant

The principle directs that 'If the subjects in an array of subjects or the isolates in an array of isolates may be arranged in the sequence of the increasing quantity of documents published or anticipated to be published on them, if it is helpful'.

Example: The isolates of Food Plants in Agriculture may be arranged on the basis of this principle, if it is more helpful-Millet, Barley, Corn, Rye, Oat, Wheat and Rice.

8. ALPHABETICAL SEQUENCE

81. Principle of Alphabetical Sequence

When the subjects/isolates in an array may not be arranged then as a last assort the principle of alphabetical sequence is recommended to follow. Dr. Ranganathan says. "When no other sequence of the subjects in an array of subjects or of the isolates in an array of isolates is more helpful, they may be arranged alphabetically by their names current in international usage. Almost all the existing schemes for classification are using this principle:

Examples:

CC6: The use of alphabets was a rare phenomena up to CC6.

(i) O Literature for Author Facet, AD may be used only when year of birth of the author may not be found;

(ii) Subdividing classes on which books are rarely written:

Agriculture: Genus or species number

J381	Rice
J381B	Basmati Rice
J381P	Parmal

Engineering: Brands of machines

D5133 Motor car

D5133F Fiat

D5133M Maruti

CC7: However in CC7, the principle gets more favour and the classifier is given full freedom to use alphabets. As it states 'The (AD) can be used without any restriction in any array of order 1...'

Examples:

(i) Geographical Isolates

44511 = OB Ballia

561 = OC Cambridge

73 = ON + Y New York City

(ii) Language Isolates

6 B Bantu language

6 BU Bushman language

DDC: To give local emphasis, the libraries are allowed to arrange serial publications, encyclopaedias, languages and literature etc. alphabetically i.e., using the first alphabet of the language etc.

05H Hindi language

40H Hindi language

80H Hindi Literature

UDC: UDC prescribes the use of alphabets first through its common auxiliary and second through special instruction to use alphabets given under different classes in main table.

6
Five Fundamental Categories, Facet Analysis and Facet Sequence

Q. : Explain five fundamental categories as propounded by Dr. Ranganathan with examples. Can all actions be treated as manifestation of Energy Fundamental Category? Give reasons for your answer.

Or

Explain the five fundamental categories of classification. Illustrate you answer with examples.

Or

Enumerate and explain the fundamental categories of classification as enunciated by Dr. Ranganathan.

Or

What are five fundamental categories? Explain them with the help of suitable examples.

Or

Explain with the help of examples the concept of 'Rounds' and 'Levels' in the Colon Classification.

Or

Explain the five fundamental categories and their use in classification.

Ans. When Rangnathan started designing Colon classification in November 1924, he had little knowledge of the users needs. He was made aware by E C Richardson that Reference Service was the *summum bonus* of library service. He, therefore, spent nearly six hours a day in helping users in Madras University. This enabled him to know the varying purposes and approaches of the users. In mapping the universe of subjects, Ranganathan adopted a systematic procedure based on certain assumptions which are called Postulates. The process of division that Ranganathan followed recognises that every subject has a basic facet, i.e., the first context-specifying facet and represented by the concept/term called basic subject (BS), to which one or more isolate ideas may be attached. He postulated these fundamental ideas by the term 'Fundamental Categories'.

The concept of Fundamental Categories as a basis of classification came in to vogue, with the publication of 'Library Classification-Fundamental and Procedure' in 1944. There are five and only five fundamental categories-viz., Time, Space, Energy, Matter and Personality." Explaining these, Ranganathan emphasises that these terms and the ideas denoted by them belong strictly to the context of the discipline concerned. Their significance, in our context, can be seen only in the context of the discipline concerned. This set of FC is, for, brevity, denoted by the antonym PMEST.

The scholars of library science discipline opined differently. Some praising this unique concept and some criticising it on various different grounds. Some such opinions are as follows:

B.I. Palmer : The concept of PMEST formula has facilitated the teaching of classification to a remarkable degree'. PMEST provides a frame for the initial laying out of a new scheme of classification.

A.C.Foskett : Analysis into Ranganathan's fundamental categories is often useful in establishing the correct citation order for subjects in other schemes.

Norman Roberts : These categories were introduced having their existence without proof.

Derek Austin : His fundamental categories operate within the separate main classes as per their respective contexts-essentially a discipline-centered or traditional approach, which has broken down under the strain of modern information requirements; and as such they are unsuited to a new general scheme of classification which needs categories applicable directly to the whole field of knowledge.

JEL Farradane : For a classification to be fully relational and logical we must define true relations and the logic involved therein-and that philosophic, non-experimental or intuitive methods of approach to knowledge offer no conviction of truth.

Ranganathan, however, made it quite clear that 'there is nothing sacred or metaphysical either about their number or about them individually. They are only postulated entities which do the work for us. The moment they fail to do the work satisfactorily we may retire them, or add to them and thereby reinforce them'... 'It is open to any one to bring forth another set of postulates and do all the work necessary to make them do library classification with efficiency, meeting all the challenges thrown out by the documents'. Each fundamental category is represented by a distinct symbol and connecting symbol representing it. These are given below:

Fundamental Category	*Symbol*	*Connecting Symbol*
Personality	[P]	' (Comma)
Matter	[M]	; (Semicolon)
Energy	[E]	: (Colon)
Space	[S]	. (Dot)
Time	[T]	' (Inverted Comma)

These five fundamental categories are arranged in the sequence of decreasing concreteness and are indicated by the initiation PMEST.

1. Personality

Personality is the most concrete category and is the axis of the specific subject. It is inherent in every subject. It forms the basis as well as the locus of all other fundamental categories. Any manifestation having a distinctive, character is likely to be one of the personality. Without personality there can be no organ, constituent, attribute or reaction in space and time. It is very difficult to recognise Personality. This fundamental category is identified on the basis of the method of residue. It means in case a given manifestation is not one of the fundamental categories of time, space, energy, and matter, then it should be considered as the manifestation of fundamental category 'Personality'.

However, this method was later reversed to identify first the Personality Category and then the remaining categories.

Personality can manifest itself in Round 1, Round 2, and so on. It can also manifest more than once in the same round within a subject. The rounds of personality are represented by [2P], [3P] and so on, and the levels of personality are represented by [P2], [P3] and so on. *Crops* in agriculture, *natural groups* of plants in botany, *animals* in zoology, the *community of people* in history, *substances* in chemistry, and *social groups* in sociology are some of the best examples to understand and comprehend the FC *Personality.*

2. Matter

This category deals with the entities existing physically in space and time. In theoretical disciplines such as Literature, Language, Education etc., this category is absent. Its manifestations are taken to be of two kinds-*Matter-Material* and *Matter-Property*. Viewed from the angle of Classification, *Matter-Material* ranges from chemical elements or raw materials from one end to finished products at the other end. There is a series of intermediate stages, connecting these two ends. For example, *cotton* is a raw material in the context of *garment manufacture* which is a finished product. *Cotton* fabric is at the intermediate stage. *Cotton,* however, is the ultimate crop product in the context of agriculture.

According to Ranganathan's school of thought, properties of things, persons, etc., are also deemed to be manifestations of *Matter.* Isolates such as variance, intensity, wave length, height, weight, volume, etc., are regarded as manifestations of *Matter.* The (FC) Matter may manifest itself more than once in one and the same Round within a subject e.g.,

[1M1]-Round 1 Level 1 Matter Facet

[1M2]-Round 1 Level 2 Matter Facet

The (FC) Matter may manifest itself in Round 1 or Round 2 and so on-be it Matter-Property, or Matter-Material. For example:

- *Density* of solid
- Ink *quality* in printing
- Rubber *quality* in the manufacture of mattresses
- *Electric current resistance* of superconductors; are some examples of titles displaying Matter Isolates. Here, Density, quality, and electric current resistance represent the matter category.

3. Energy

The manifestations of *Energy* are generally actions. They connote dynamic actions, such as, "doing", "changing", "evaluating", "determining", "forecasting", "analysis", etc. the action may be among and by all kinds of entities-inanimate, animate, conceptual, intellectual, and intuitive. The identification of the FC *"Energy"* is a little more difficult than that of "Time" or "Space". As matter of fact, the distinction between the manifestation of "Energy" isolate and "Matter–Property" isolate poses problems mainly due to action-associated ideas. The fundamental category 'Energy' has been used by Ranganathan strictly in the classificatory discipline and its manifestation is action, interaction or mutual action of one kind or another.

- 'Energy' can occur only once within a round, thus, there are no levels in this fundamental category. But, 'Energy' may manifest itself in one and the same subject more than once to, giving rise to different rounds of energy. The different manifestation of 'energy' can be represented as [1E] [2E] and so on. For example :

- Powers and functions of the Prime Minister of India.
- Ecology of Indian Animals.
- Documentation in Engineering Libraries of U.S.A.
- Optical surgery, are the examples.

In above examples, Functions, Ecology, Documentation and Surgery represent the fundamental category 'Energy'.

4. Space

This fundamental category represents the physiographic feature of the earth. It can be regarded as the conventional division of the surface of earth such as Continents, Countries, States, Districts, Town, Village etc. It also represents other political or general administration division, oceans, rivers, valley, island, desert, plateau, mountain etc. This category represents inside or outside of the earth. This category occurs in every subject forming a local description or local history of any subject. This category can be identified easily.

The fundamental category 'Space' does not manifest itself more than once in one and the same subject so there are no round of space, but this category may manifest itself more than once within a round and thus there may be more than one level of space. In classification, special schedules have been provided to represent the physiographic features of the surface of earth as second level of space isolate.

Second Level SI

1	Geosphere	16	Valley
124	Forest	2	Mountain
137	Delta	3	City (Town, Village)
14	Island	5	Hydrosphere
		6	River

A . (dot) is to be inserted as the connecting symbol between (S1) and (S2). When warranted any isolate in (S2) may be individualised by the Alphabetical Device e.g.,

D885.594.3Z Street cleaning in Zurich

K:12.44.2V Fauna of Vindhya Mountains

Whereas the divisions of the first level Space Facet may be used to represent political and administrative divisions of space, the second level space facet represents physiographic features of the surface of the earth.

The following are examples of titles wherein Space Isolates are present.

- Prospecting of Diamonds in Madhya Pradesh.
- Birds of the desert region.
- Fauna and Flora of Western Rajasthan - an ecological study.
- Computer application in libraries in Western Countries.
- Comparative study of Hindu Culture in South-East Asia.

In these examples, Madhya Pradesh, Desert region, Western Rajasthan, Western Countries, South-East Asia, represent the fundamental category space.

5. Time

The FC *"Time"* gives the least difficulty in identification. It is used in accordance with what we commonly understand by the term. The usual Time isolate ideas such as millennium, century, decade, year and so on are its manifestations. Time isolates of another kind-such as, day and night, seasons such as summer and winter, and time with meteorological quality such as wet, dry, snowy, stormy, etc., are also taken as a manifestation of the FC "*Time*". Ordinarily, any of the fundamental categories Space and Time may manifest itself only in the last of the Rounds in a subject. i.e., the (FC) [S] and [T] can not be placed between two rounds. The only place of their occurrence is the last round. Some examples of titles presenting the Time element are given below:

- Production of eggs in Northern Denmark - Annual Statistics of 1993.
- Medical facilities for semiskilled labor in steel industry during 20th century.
- History of World War 1914-19
- Automation of Libraries in the new Millennium.

In these examples 1993, 20th century, 1914-19, and Millennium represents the fundamental category time.

Q. : What is facet analysis? Discuss it with relation to CC and DDC.

Or

What do you mean by facet analysis? Compare facet analysis in DDC and UDC.

Ans. In the process of classification, the various subjects or disciplines are represented by various main classes. When universe of knowledge is divided, main classes appears and when main classes are divided, the concept of facet appears. The generic term Facet used to denote any component-be it a basic subject or an isolate-of a compound subject, and also its respective ranked forms, terms and numbers.'

Thus, dividing a subject into different groups on the basis of a single train of characteristics, such a group of sub-classes is termed as a Facet. A main class is divided into various facets to cover all possible aspects in which a subject can be divided. On the basis of characteristics, the main classes are divided into facets. All possible entitles of a class are grouped under each division or facet. According to need and future developments each facet or division may be further divided into possible sub-divisions are known as isolates or foci. Thus, universe of knowledge is divided into various main classes. Each main class in divided into facet to cover all possible aspects of it, and a facet covers the totality of subdivision of a basic class divided according to a single characteristics.

The process through which the facets of a subject are determined is known as facet analysis. Thus, facet analysis deals with the analysis of a subject into its aspects obtained on the basis of a systematic application of a set of characteristics. Facet analysis of a subject results in the formation of groups of classes. According to Ranganathan, facet analysis is the mental process by which possible trains of characteristics which can form the basis of classification of a subject are enumerated and the exact measure in which the attributes concerned are incident in the subject are determined. To Palmer and Wells, Facet Analysis simply means the analysis of a specific subject into the facets produced by the application of different characteristics.'

The earlier schemes of classification were enumerative in nature and the entire universe of subjects was systematically divided into classes and sub-classes and resulted in readymade class numbers. In contrast a classification scheme which consists of schedules of Basic Classes, Common Isolates and Special Isolates only is called a faceted scheme for classification. In a Faceted Classification, there will be no schedule enumerating Compound subjects. The Colon classification is a fully faceted classification in which all the main classes or basic subjects have been analysed into its facets, thus there is no need for enumerating any compound subject. The Universal Decimal Classification is almost faceted classification having many compound subjects in the schedules.

The analysis of any compound subject reveals that it has a basic class or basic subject. This basic subject may be explicit i.e., stated in the terms or it may be implicit i.e., not stated in the terms. For example, Studies in Rural Economics' has explicitly the basic subject 'Economics', while 'Rubber Technology' has implicitly the basic subject 'Agriculture'.

When two or more concepts are added to a basic subject, then it becomes a compound subject. The concepts are represented by isolates. On analysis of a subject, all possible isolates or concepts may be viewed as groups of related isolates. Thus, a facet is the sum total of isolates related by a common characteristics. The process of analysing a subject into its facets is called *Facet Analysis of a subject*. The entire process of determining the facets of a subject is Facet Analysis. While the facet analysis approach is adopted by the classifications in designing classification schemes, the classifier adopts it for classifying documents.

1. Facet Analysis in Colon Classification (CC)

It is in Colon Classification where we see the explicit application of facet analysis in full measure. Ranganathan developed his postulate of Fundamental Categories from the rigorous analysis of subjects into their facets. In fact, in the first three editions of Colon Classification, the Fundamental Categories of PMEST had not featured. Table-I Matrix of Basic Subjects and their corresponding facets illustrates the analysis of subjects into their facets. After carefully studying the kinds of facets in different subjects, Ranganathan was able to establish that they could be accommodated in Five Fundamental Categories, despite their apparent surface differences. In subsequent editions of CC, the Postulate of Fundamental Categories has been used to design schedules for every basic subject. CC is regarded as a *Freely Faceted Classification System* because it is the nature of subjects that determines their facets which are fitted into the frame work of postulates and not based on any predetermined facet structure. The enumeration of isolates for each class, the common isolates, the space and time isolates, the language isolates, etc.,-all these have emerged using the Principle of Facet Analysis.

Applying the postulate of Fundamental Categories of Ranganathan to the subject 'Toy Manufacture' we may regard :

Toys as a manifestation of Personality

Materials as a manifestation of Matter

Space and Time can be added when warranted

If the title "Treatment of Lung Disease in India in 1997", is analysed, it results in the following facets:

Basic Subject	:	Medicine
Personality	:	Lung
Matter	:	Disease
Energy	:	Treatment
Space	:	India
Time	:	1997

2. Facet Analysis in Dewey Decimal Classification (DDC)

In Dewey Decimal Classification, there is clear indication of the implicit use of Facet Analysis for the design of the classification system. In the Editor's Introduction to the 19th edition of DDC, it is stated, "In all classes (002-029, 069, 079.1-9,090,100-700, 900) unless a different sequence is prescribed, arrangement is first by most specific discipline and most specific subject under it, then by area of specification, then by time specification if the schedules permit then by form of presentation. For example, a work on the *Native Snakes of Texas* is classified as follows:

Discipline	Science	5
	Zoology	9
	Cold-blooded Vertebrates	7
	Reptiles	9
	Snakes	6
Area	(Sign of Geographic concept to follow	09
	North America	7
	South Central U.S	6
	Texas	4

Thus, 597.960 976.4

Work of Shakespeare is classified as follows:

Discipline	Literature	8
Language	English	2
Form	Drama	2
Period	Elizabethan period 1558-1625	3
Works	Shakespeare's Works	3

Thus, 822.33

In the first example given above, the facets that divide the work *Native Snakes of Texas*, are "Discipline", Zoology is one of the divisions of this facet; "Subject" representing a natural group of animals, snakes being a member of this facet; "Area" is the Space Facet, Texas being a member of this facet. In the second example, the facets are "Discipline "Language", "Form", "Period" and "Works".

Although DDC does not indicate explicitly the method of basic analysis in the schedules, it should be clear from these two examples that the method of facet analysis has been the basis of its design. It should be noted that DDC does not enumerate in its schedules "Facet Isolates" as is done by CC, but display combinations of "Facet Isolates" representing a compound subject. The standard subdivisions, the area table, the time schedules applicable to certain subjects, etc., are given separately which can be added to any class when needed.

In addition, throughout its Schedules, DDC had given copious notes to divide a particular class, by a set of divisions given elsewhere in its schedule, indicating thereby that the principle of facet analysis could be applied to any subject when required. For example:

1. Jews in India : This is analysed into the following facets: Social Stratification (305.6), Religions groups, Jews, under social startification by Religious Groups (305.6), the following note is given.

Add to Base Number 305.6, the numbers following 2 in "Persons" notation 21-29 from Table 7.

The number for Jews in Table 7 is 296. The final class number is 305.696

2. Migration of Birds : This is analysed into the following facets: Bird, Migration

Under a note given at 598.21-28 (General Principles) at Birds, the instructions are given to "Add to base number 598.2 the numbers following 591 in 591.1-591.8" and the number for migration is 591.525. The final class number is 598.2525

3. Sacred Places of Jainism : This is analysed into the following facets: Jainism, Sacred places.

The Note given at 294.41-48 "Add to base number 294.4, the numbers following 291 in 291.1-219.8" and the number for sacred places is 291.35. The final class number is 294.35

These are examples where there is a clear indication of facet analysis and synthesis.

3. Facet Analysis in Universal Decimal Classification (UDC)

The Universal Decimal Classification (UDC) has adopted the basic structure of DDC but has developed on its own philosophy, policies and principles. The facet structure of UDC is much more explicit than it is in DDC. Some of its faceted features are given below:

(i) Common auxiliaries of Place, Race and Nationality, Time, Points of View, etc.;

(ii) Facet indicators Colon (:) Square Brackets [ ] Double Colon (::) to combine two or more facets;

(iii) Special auxiliaries to introduce facets peculiar to a given basic class with specific facet indicators;

(iv) Availability of a facet division for application to any class which warrants such division. This is somewhat similar to the provisions in DDC.

Some examples of the application of Common auxiliaries and Special auxiliaries are give below (The words in italics fonts represent the respective common auxiliary):

Place, Race & Nationality	Coal mining in *India.* The sociological importance of kinship among the *Jews.*
Time	Superconductivity Research in the *1980s.*
Points of View	Nuclear reactors for power production from the *environment point of view.*
Special Auxiliaries	Reciprocating valve gear in Electric *switch mechanisms.*

Q. : What do you understand by Facet sequence? Discuss it with relation to CC, DDC and UDC with examples.

Or

What is facet sequence? Discuss the various principles of facet sequence.

Ans. : In classification, once the facets are determined, the next step is to identify the definite sequence among these facets. The postulates for facet sequence of a compound subject are helpful in determining sequence of isolate ideas in a compound subject where each isolate idea is a manifestation of a different fundamental category.

Indeed facet analysis and facet synthesis are the two sides of the same coin, the one has no purpose without the other.

The question now arises is what should be the sequence of facets? Is there any single order by which to sequence of facets could be established which is most helpful for the purpose of document storage and retrieval?

In the example "Toy Manufacture", we identified three facets'. viz., Toys (A), Materials (B) and Process (C). The following are the six ways of arranging these three facets:

(i)	Toys, Materials, Process	ABC
(ii)	Toys, Process, Materials	ACB

(iii) Materials, Toys, Process BAC

(iv) Materials, Process, Toys BCA

(v) Process, Toys, Materials CAB

(vi) Process, Materials, Toys CBA

If there are only two facets, there are two ways of arranging them viz., AB or BA. If there are three facets, as we have seen above, there are six ways of arranging them. If there are four facets, there are 24 ways of arranging them. If there are five facets, there, are 120 ways of arranging them. Obviously we have to choose only one among the various choices available, as we cannot have all of them. There are given some postulates by Dr. Ranganathan for facet sequence, which are used in his classification scheme i.e., CC.

1. FACET SEQUENCE IN COLON CLASSIFICATION (CC)

Ranganathan has expound the following postulates to determine the consistent order of different facets for all subjects:

(i) Postulate of First Facet

(ii) Postulate of Concreteness

(iii) Postulate of Facet Sequence within a Round

(iv) Postulate of Facet Sequence with the Last Round

(v) Postulate of Level-Cluster

Each of above is discussed below:

(i) Postulate of First Facet

In a compound subject, the basic facet should be the first facet. So, the basic facet should be given the first position among the facets of a compound subject.

For example : Treatment of Lung Cancer. In this example, the basic facet is implicit, i.e., Medicine. The other isolate facets of the compound subjects are:

Treatment (E) Lung (P) Cancer (M)

As per the above mentioned postulate, the sequence of facets should be:

Medicine (BF), Lung [P], Cancer [M], Treatment [E]

At this juncture, it may be worthwhile mentioning that the indication of the basic facet in the title of document may be either explicit or implicit or absent. In the absence of any indication, the information professional would do well to read the contents page and/or the whole document.

(ii) Postulate of Concreteness

The postulate states that the five fundamental categories fall into the following sequence when arranged according to their decreasing concreteness: P, M, E, S, T.

This sequence of the FCs according to their relative concreteness conforms to the approach of the majority of readers.

Consider the following titles:

(a) Library Science in the 1980s: *BS* (Basic Subject) and *T* (Time) are specified.

(b) Library Science in India in the 1980s: *BS, T,* and *S* (Space) are specified.

(c) Classification in India in the 1980s: *BS, T, S, E* (Energy) are specified.

(d) Classification of microforms in India in the 1980s: *BS, T, S, E* and *M* (Matter) are specified.

(e) Classification of microforms in special libraries in India in the 1980s: *BS, P* (Personality), *M, E, S* and *T* are specified.

In the above titles, we can see a clear indication that the different aspects discussed move from the general to the specific. All aspects of *library science in the 1980s* are discussed in item (a) Item (e) however, discusses a very specific area, viz., *Classification of microforms in special libraries in India in the 1980s.* In other words, as we run down from (a) to (e), the contents are becoming increasingly concrete and move in the ascending order of concreteness. This is obtained by fixing a sequence for the Fundamental Categories which is in decreasing concreteness if we move from *P* and *T*, or in increasing concreteness if we move from *T* to *P*. The intellectual organisation of subjects would command this arrangement of moving from the general to the specific and would be acceptable to the majority of users.

(iii) Postulate of Face Sequence within a Round

In any Round of facets of a compound subject in which each or any of the Fundamental Categories - Personality, Matter, Energy- occur only once, their sequence should be: Personality Facet, Matter Facet, and Energy Facet.

	Subject	Facet Sequence
–	Prevention of Diseases in Rice Plant	Agriculture [BF]
		Rice Plant [1P1]
		Disease [1M1]
		Prevention [1E]
–	Treatment of Lung Cancer	Medicine [BF]
		Lung [1P1]
		Cancer [1M1]
		Treatment [1E]

(iv) Postulate of Facet Sequence within the Last Round

In the last Round of facets of a compound subject, in which each of the fundamental categories other than Energy may occur and occurs only once, the sequence of facet should be Personality Facet, Matter Facet, Space Facet and Time Facet.

Example: Assessment of ultra-violet treatment of bone cancer in Karnataka in 1997.

An analysis of the title using the Postulate of Basic Facet, Fundamental Categories, Rounds, etc., gives rise to the following facet sequence:

Medicine [BF]; Bone [1P]; Cancer [1M]; Treatment [1E]; Ultra-violet Ray [2P]; Assessment [2E]; Karnataka [S]; 1997 [T].

Note : While the FC "Personality" occurs twice as [1P] and [2P], "Matter" occurs as [1M], and "Energy" twice as [1E] and [2E], "Space" and "Time" occur once as [S] and [T]. It may be observed that [S] and [T] occur only in the last Round of the compound subject. It may be appropriate to mention that with the introduction of the concept of specter in the General Theory of Classification, speculation of the FC "Energy" was allowed. This has resulted generally, in the elimination of the concept of Rounds as far as the FCs "Personality and Matter" were concerned. Consequently, [2P], [2M], [3P], [3M] and so on have become specters to the FC "Energy" depending on whether it is [1E], [2E], etc. However, in some special cases they may occur. For example, the concept of "side effects" of treatment may occur as [2M].

(v) Postulate of Level-Cluster

This postulate states that Facets of different levels of the same Fundamental Category within a Round of facets in a compound subject should be kept together. It can be understood by the following titles:

(a) Criticism of Shakespeare's Hamlet.

(b) Hindu law of property.

(c) Diseases of leaves of flowering plants and their treatment bychemical spray.

(d) Quality of cotton fabrics for designing shirts.

In the above examples, we can see a cluster of isolates that can be deemed as manifestations of the FC Personality. In the first title, *English, Drama, Shakespeare* and *Hamlet* are deemed to be manifestations of *Ps* and *criticism* is an energy isolate. The sequencing of the personality isolates is to be on the basis of Wall-Picture Principle. The sequence of facets, according to the Well-Picture principle would be *language, form, author* and *work*. In the second example. *Hindu law* is followed by *property*, both being *Ps*. In the third example, the sequence of the FC Personality in the first round would be *flowering plants* and then *leaves*. In the fourth example, the terms *quality* and *cotton fabrics* can be regarded as manifestations of M and the sequence would be cotton fabrics preceding quality.

"Classification of documents according to their contents should be done with the help of facet analysis and synthesis. One must bear in mind that we must be sensitive to the postulates and principles that would help us in arriving at a sequence of helpful and logical terms for storage and retrieval". It must be remembered that the FCs will operate only after the basic class is identified. All facet terms will follow the basic class in their respective order of arrangement.

Principles for Facet Sequence

Accordingly, the following Principles for Facet Sequence were postulated for determining the helpful sequence of the various facets occurring in a compound subject.

1. Wall–Picture Principle
2. Whole-organ Principle
3. Cow-calf Principle
4. Act and-Action-Actor-Tool Principle

1. Wall-Picture Principle

According to this principle 'If the two facets A and B of a subject are such that the concept behind B will not be operative unless the concept behind A is conceded, even as a mural picture is not possible unless the wall exists to draw upon, then the facet A should precede the facet B.'

The Wall–Picture Principle has been termed as 'master principle' and all other principles for facet sequence as its corollaries. Although the Wall–Picture Principle was specifically formulated to derive a helpful sequence among facets, it has also been found helpful in determining helpful Sequence among Array Isolates, Quasi Isolates and groups of Quasi Isolates. It has also been found that when both, the Postulate for Facet sequence as well as Wall Picture Principle are applied, parallel sequence is derived. In such cases the help of Wall–Picture Principle is not taken. But the postulate is not sufficient when any fundamental category manifests itself in a compound subject more than once, then the Wall Picture Principle and its corollaries need to applied.

Examples :

(i) Diagnosis of Disease

The concept behind the term "Diagnosis' is not operative unless the concept behind the term "disease' is conceded. Therefore, sequence of these two facets would be Disease, Diagnosis-L, 4:3.

(ii) Gitanjali by Rabindranath Tagore, the Bengali poet

The concept behind "Gitanjali' is not operative, unless the concept behind the term Rabindranath Tagore is conceded. Again the concept behind the term Rabindranath Tagore is not operative unless the concept behind the term 'Poetry' is conceded. So also, the concept behind the term Poetry is not operative unless the concept behind the term 'Bengali' is conceded. Therefore, while arranging facets the sequence would be:

Bengali, Poetry, Rabindranath Togore, Gitanjali.

Class No: 0,157,1M61,1

2. Whole-Organ Principle

According to this principle 'If, in a subject, facet B is an organ of facet A, then A should precede B.'

The principle is based on the analogy of the body of living beings-man, animal, the whole human body and its parts or organs. As the existence of the regional parts, or organs depend upon the whole body therefore, while arranging the whole body would precede the organs.

Example:

(i) Governor of Rajasthan

Here both the isolates-Governor and Rajasthan belong to [P] Facet. But the isolate Governor exists because the state of Rajasthan exists. The isolate 'Governor' is an organ of the whole state Rajasthan. Therefore, the whole Rajasthan should precede the organ Governor. Accordingly, the sequence of these two facets would be:

History [BF], Rajasthan [P1]

Governor [P2}

Class.No. V, 4437.12

3. Cow-Calf Principle

According to this principle 'If a facet A and another facet B belonging to the same subject are not to be separated though they are distinct from each other and thus separable, A and B should be kept together in the same Round, even as a milch cow and its unwind calf are not separately sold out though they are distinct entities and thus separable, but are kept together in possession of the same owner.'

This Principle helps in determining the sequence of [P] and [M] as well as [S] and [T] if the successive levels relate to last round. The Facet [E] is not concerned with this Principle as it ends a Round and starts a new Round.

Example :

Design of Electric Lifts

There are four facets in this title including the Basic Facet. These are:

Design, Electrical Engineering, Lift, Engineering.

The facet design belong to [E] facet so it is not concerned with the Cow-Calf Principle. The facets Electrical Engineering and Lift are two distinct facets, but both are inseparable facets, and so these have to be kept together in the same round. So the sequence would be:

Engineering [BF], Electrical

Engineering [P1], Lift [P2], Design [E]

Class.No: (CC6) D66.71:4

4. Act and–Action–Actor-Tool Princple

According to this principle 'If in a subject, facet denotes action on facet A, by facet C with D as tool, then the four facets should be arranged in sequence A,B,C,D.'

Example :

Spinning of Cotton by Girls with Charkha

Here Action is spinning: Actinide is Cotton; the Actor is girls; and the tool is charkha. Therefore the sequence would be:

Cotton, Spinning, Girls, Charkha

On the basis of the research carried out in DRTC, the principle of Commodity-Raw Material Transformation seems to have been modified in the following manner:

Result-Act and-Action-Actor-Tool Principle

According to this principle 'If in a subject, facet C denotes action on facet E, which is actand by facet D as actor with facet E as the tool, and the facet A is the commodity or result of the action, the five facets should be arranged in the sequence, A,B,C,D, E.'

Example :

Spinning of Cotton with Charkha by Girls for producing Yarn. Here Yarn is commodity (A); Cotton is Actand (B); Spinning is action (C); Girls is actor (D); and Charkha is tool (E). The sequence of facets would be

Yarn, Cotton, Spinning, Girls, Charkha

2. FACET SEQUENCE IN DEWEY DECIMAL CLASSIFICATION (DDC)

DDC does not specify any facet sequence in its schedules of compound subjects, although it uses implicitly the principle of facet analysis. But extensive rules have been provided throughout its schedule for classifying documents, which demand a treatment of using facet analysis and synthesis. For example:

Agriculture and Related Technologies have been divided first by crop production, then by plant injuries, diseases, pests and then by individual crops as given below:

630 Agriculture and related technologies

631 Crops and their production

632 Plant injuries, disease, pests

633 Field crops

634 Orchards, fruits, forestry

635 Garden crops

Now, a document on *Harvesting of Peaches* could either be classed in 631.55 giving preference to Harvesting or under 631.25, giving preference to Peaches. But the specific subject of the document requires a combination of the two, viz., the particular crop and harvesting. Rules given under 634.25 (Add as instructed under 633-635) precisely indicate that the two facets could be combined, drawing the subdivisions of 631 representing harvesting to arrive at 634.255 which stands for Harvesting of Peaches. In this way, throughout the schedule, rules have been provided to combine facets directly without any connecting symbol or with a connecting symbol of Zero (0). But the citation order is set by the system and is not necessarily based on any stated principle.

In addition to the set of rules prescribed at various places in the Schedules, DDC suggests a Citation Order Formula when no rule has been provided. The facets and the sequence or citation order suggested are given below:

Things

Kinds of things

Parts of things

Materials from which the Things, Kinds and Parts are made, Properties of the Things, Kinds, Parts, Materials Processes within the Things, Kinds, Parts, Materials Operations upon the Things, Kinds, Parts or Material Agents performing such Operations. This is given as Rule 4 under 8.55 Citation Order in the Editor's Introduction on page 57 (DDC 19th ed. Volume 1, Introduction, Table).The rule says: "Apply the Citation Order Formula which will generally prove to be reasonable and helpful".

3. FACET SEQUENCE IN UNIVERSAL DECIMAL CLASSIFICATION (UDC)

UDC has many more facet features than DDC. Although there is no specific citation order or facet sequence given in UDC, either in its introduction or anywhere in the Schedules of classes, a Citation Order has been recommended by Jack Mills in his Guide to Universal Decimal Classification which is as given below:

Things, Kinds, Parts;

Materials;

Properties;

Processes;

Operations;

Agent.

The Common and Special Auxiliaries with their specific facet indicators provide full scope to apply facet synthesis wherever necessary.

Particularly the relation signs Colon (:), the Square Brackets [] and the Double Colon (::) facilitate combination of facets.

For example, for classifying a document "Virus diseases and Indoor Plants", the schedule provides separate places for "virus diseases" and "indoor plants", as 635.91 and 632.38. But they can be combined by the relation sign colon (:) to get a class number as 635.91:632.38. This can be reversed as 632.38:635.91, making "virus diseases" the first facet and "indoor plants" the second, if a library prefers this sequence. But if a Double Colon (::) is used for the combination, the reversing device would not be allowed.

Square Brackets [ ] as a facet combinatory is used to indicate a particular chosen order of facets.

For example: Indoor Anemones (Anemones are kind of Indoor Plants) get the class number 635.91:582.675.1 (582.675.1 standing for anemones). But if a library wants together everything on particular plants together, under the general, heading, "Horticulture", it might change the above number to 635.91 [582.675.1] to make the main facet the individual plant (in this case Anemones) with "indoor" as a secondary facet.

This principle is known as Flexibility in Facet Citation. This is acclaimed as a strength but it could also be viewed as an undesirable feature if libraries using UDC chose different facet sequences.

The Special Auxiliaries also give scope for facet combinations. There are three types of special auxiliaries which are using facet indicators (Hyphen (-) Point Zero (0) and the Apostrophe ('). The Hyphen and Point Zero are used to introduce a facet peculiar to a given basic class.

Examples:

62.31	Reciprocating Valve Gear Parts
820.31	English Novels
621.3.066	Electrical Switch Mechanism
66.066	Clarification, etc., Chemical Engineering

The apostrophe is at present used with a rather different meaning in Chemistry and similar subjects where it is used to indicate synthesis of material elements as well as notational.

Examples:

33.33	Sodium
546.13	Chlorine
546.33'13	Sodium Chloride

7
Phase Analysis

Q. : Write an essay on Phase Relation in Colon Classification (CC), Dewey Decimal Classification (DDC) and Universal Decimal Classification.

Or

Explain how simple, compound and complex subjects are different. Discuss with suitable examples the Phase Relation in CC, DDC and UDC.

Or

Write an essay on Phase Relation in CC and DDC.

Or

Discuss the kinds of Phase Relation in CC 7th edition.

Ans. A Basic Subject is a subject which

(a) is enumerated in the schedule of BS;

(b) cannot be expressed as the Compound Subject of any of the existing BS, i.e., a subject without any isolate idea as a component;

(c) is evolved through one full cycle of the spiral of scientific method as propounded by Dr. S.R. Ranganathan. They also exhibit different modes of formation of subjects;

(d) calls for schedules of special personality, matter and energy isolates;

(e) has some specialisation-academic and/or professional segmentation. The indicators for this are:

- existence of professional societies
- degree course
- periodical publications
- whole books on the subject

For example, Mathematics, Economics, Law

There are several varieties of BS. The correlation of modes of formation of BS to the kinds of BS is summarised as follows:

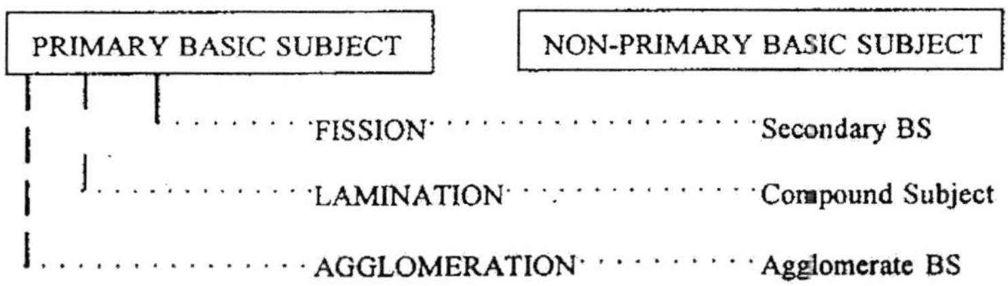

Primary Basic Subjects are the core frame for all other kinds of BS.

Compound Subject (CdS) is a subject with a BS and one or more isolate idea (IsI) as components.

e.g., Chemistry of alcohol-Chemistry (BS), alcohol (IsI)

Morphology of flowering plants-botany (BS), flowering plants (IsI), morphology (IsI).

Complex Subject (CxS) is a subject formed by a combination of two or more subjects-basic or compound.

e.g., General relation between economics and sociology

Economics for statisticians

Economics influenced by political factors

Phase Relation

The phase Relation has been devised to meet the demands of complex subjects dealing with relationship of two or more subjects. It is the assembling together of two or more of

(a) subjects (Basic or Compound)

(b) isolate ideas (in one and the same facet, or isolate ideas in one and the same array).

Assembling is done to express one or the other of possible relations between the components of the assembly. The result is a complex subject, complex isolate idea, or a complex array isolate idea, as the case may be.

Each component in the assembly, in its turn, is called a "phase".

They are called "phase I" and "phase 2" as determined by their sequence in the assemblage.

Dr. Ranganathan has divided the 'Universe of Loose Assemblage' into three kinds and thereby created three levels of phase relationship for use in Colon Classification. In the words of Ranganathan, 'Loose Assemblage is the assembling together of two or more of: 1. Subjects (Basic or compound), 2. Isolate Ideas (In one and the same facet, or facet ideas in one and the same array).'

In CC (Ed 7): A Preview, these are described in the following manner:

Loose Assemblage 1 : In this mode, two or more subjects be it simple or compound-are studied in their mutual relation.

Loose Assemblage 2 : In this mode, two or more isolates taken from one and the same schedule are brought into mutual relation.

Loose Assemblage 3 : In this mode, two or more isolates taken from one and the same array of order higher than 1 in one and the same schedule are brought into mutual relation.

Kinds of Phase Relation

The six kinds of Phase Relations have been recognised as given below with their indicator digits.

1. General
2. Bias
3. Comparison
4. Difference
5. Tool
6. Influence

The table of the indicator digits is shown below:

Inter-Array	*Inter-Facet*	*Inter-Subject*	*Kind of Phase relation*
t	j	a	General
u	k	b	Bias
v	m	c	Comparison
w	n	d	Difference
x	p	e	Tool
y	r	g	Influence

(1) General Phase Relation

It indicates more or less comprehensive relationship between two subjects or isolate ideas.

The sequence of the two subjects/isolates should be decided on the basis of the ordinal value of the class numbers of the two subjects. The subjects having class numbers of smaller ordinal value, is to be used as first phase.

(2) Bias Phase Relation

The Bias Relation between two subjects indicates that the exposition of one subject (Phase 1) is biased towards another subject specialist (Phase 2). This means that the exposition of a subject is specially attuned by the selection, arrangement, choice of illustrations, etc., of the topics as per the needs of a specialist. First phase, therefore, is termed as Biased Phase and second as Biasing Phase.

(3) Comparison Phase Relation

The term Comparison itself denotes the meaning of this phase relation i.e., comparison of one subject with another subject.

The subject or isolate whose class number is of smaller ordinal value should be the first phase. The second phase is termed as Comparison Phase.

(4) Difference Phase Relation

The term Difference Phase Relation denotes that the difference between the two subjects is expounded.

The class number/isolate number of the subject having smaller ordinal value should be the first phase. The second phase is termed as Difference Phase.

(5) Tool Phase Relation

The Tool Phase Relation denotes that the concepts of a subject (phase 2) are used as a Tool to interpret or explain or application to another subject (phase 1).

Phase 2 is denoted by the term Tool Phase.

(6) Influence Phase Relation

This Phase Relation deals with cases of documents where the influence of one or the other is expounded. Phase 1 is denoted by the term Influenced Phase and Phase 2 by the term Influencing Phase.

Types of Phase Relation

There are three types of phase relation. The relation may be between :

(i) Two or more subjects, known as *Inter-Subject Phase Relation;* or

(ii) Two or more isolates within one and the same schedule of facet isolates, known as *Intra-Facet Phase Relation;* or

(iii) Two or more isolates within one and the same array of isolates, known as *Intra-Array Phase Relation.*

(i) Inter-Subject Phase Relation

It indicates Relation between two or more subjects, which may be termed as complex subject.

Examples :

Ampersand (&) is the connecting symbol for phase relation in the 7th edition of Colon Classification.

1. General Phase Relation – Indicator a

CC6	*CC7*	*Subject*
QoaR	Q&aR	Religion and Philosophy.
IoaJ	I&aJ	Botany and Agriculture
VoaW	V&aW	Political Science and History

2. Bias Phase Relation–Indicator b

CC6	*CC7*	*Subject*
SobT15	SbT, 15	Psychology for School Teachers
Bob D	B&bD	Mathematics for Engineer
GobL	G&bL	Biology for Doctors

3. Comparison Phase Relation–Indicator c

CC6	*CC7*	*Subject*
R4ocZ	R4&cZ	Law, morality and justice–a comparative study
KocL:4	K&cL:4	Diseases of man and animals–compared

4. **Difference Phase Relation–Indicator d**

CC6	*CC7*	*Subject*
IodJ1	I&dJ,1	Difference between Horticulture and Botany
Q:353odR34	Q:353&R3,4	Difference between Faith and Rationalism

5. **Tool Phase Relation–Indicator e**

CC6	*CC7*	*Subject*
–	2&eB	Application of Mathematics to Library Science
–	D&eB	Application of Mathematics to Engineering

6. **Influencing Phase Relation–Indicator g**

CC6	*CC7*	*Subject*
Y490gA	Y,44&gA	Status of working class influenced by Scientific Develópments
YogQ	Y&gQ	Influence of Religion on Society

(ii) **Intra-Facet Phase Relation**

In intra-facet Phase relation, we see two isolate ideas of the same facet interact to form a complex subject. It is termed as Complex Isolate i.e., MC + one FC + Two Co-ordinate classes.

Examples :

1. **General Phase Relation–Indicator j**

CC6	*CC7*	*Subject*
Q20j8441	Q2&j 8441	Relations between Hindu and Sikh Religions
U.2 oj 41	U.2&j 41	Geography of India and China

2. **Bias Phase Relation–Indicator k**

CC6	*CC7*	*Subject*
X5.44Q7ok73	X5.44VX&k73	Preference of USA in the Commerce of Pakistan
T4ok68	T,18&k522	University Education for Blind

3. Comparison Phase Relation–Indicatior m

CC6	*CC7*	*Subject*
R66om8	R66&m8	Advaita and Dvaita Philosophy–a comparative study
J.2om141	J.2&m41	Agriculture in India and China–a comparative study

4. Difference Phase Relation–Indicator n

CC6	*CC7*	*Subject*
Q2on8441:4192	Q2&n8441;419	Difference between the Rituals of Hindu and Sikh religions

5. Tool Phase Relations–Indicator p

CC6	*CC7*	*Subject*
–	J;43&p25	Application of Organic Application of Manure for treating Parasites in Farms

6. Influencing Phase Relation–Indicator r

CC6	*CC7*	*Subject*
Q3or2	Q3&r2	Influence of Hinduism on Jain Religion

(iii) Intra-Array Phase Relation

Intra-array phase relation isolate ideas belonging to the same array of a facet are in a relation with each other. Such as interaction between two array isolates is termed as a Phased Array Isolate i.e. MC+ one FC + one Co-ordinate classes.

Examples :-

		CC6	CC7
1.	**General Phase Indicator-t**		
	Sense perception and tradition as source of knowledge	R211ot33	R2,11&6
2.	**Bias Phase Indicator-u**		
	A book on Saints for seekers of Salvation	Q;332ou5	Q:332&u5

3.	**Comparison Phase Indicator-v**		
	Methods of Agriculture in India and Japan–a comparative study	J.42ov4	J.42&v4
4.	**Difference Phase Indicator-w**		
	Difference between Svetambara and Digambara Religions	Q31ow2	Q31&w2
5.	**Tool Phase Indicator-x**		
	Use of Psychic Powers to control Drug Habits	S:7960x8	S;796&x8
6.	**Influencing Phase Indicator-y**		
	Male influencing Female Education	T55oy1	T,22&y1

Phase Relation Device in Other Schemes

In other schemes, the idea of Phase Relation is not used explicitly as in CC. The use of zero in DDC, the colon sign of UDC and Systematic Tables of BC are only an implicit recognition of Phase Relation Device.

(A) Dewey Decimal Classification (DDC)

It was only in DDC 13 and DDC 14 that provision for phase relation through view point division and 0001 relation (to be divided like the main divisions) were available. However, the Editors of DDC have been consistently asking classifiers to follow the guidelines given in the Introductory Part of DDC, when a work dealing with a complex subject is to be classified. Few such instructions are as follows.

(i) Class a work dealing with inter-related subjects with the subject that is being acted upon. For instance class analytical work dealing with Shakespeare's influence on Keats–With Keats;

(ii) Class the work with the subject receiving fuller treatment;

(iii) if treatment is equal, class with the subject whose number is first in the DDC schedules;

(iv) Class a work on three or more subjects in the broader subject that include all of them.

Moreover, the Seven Tables and Add Device have added faceted element, in DDC. These also help the classifier in classifying complex subjects. Following few examples testify this:

Inter-subject Phase Relation

Tool phase

020.151	Mathematical Principles applied to Library and Information Science

Bias Phase

340.2461	Law Books for Doctors
510.2462	Mathematics for Engineers

Intra-Facet Phase Relation

327.54051	Foreign Relations between India and China.
382.09054073	Trade between India and USA

(B) Universal Decimal Classification (UDC)

The Relation sign: (colon) is used in UDC to link two or more numbers denoting related concept value. This sign may also be used for phase relation of all kinds.

Examples

2:5	Religion and Science (inter-subject - general phase relation)
51:62	Mathematics for Engineers (inter-subject - bias phase relation)
22/28:294.3	Comparison between Christianity and Buddhism (intra-facet - comparison phase relation)
595.141:591.142	Difference between simple Marine Worms and Earth Worms (inter-array - difference phase relation)
7:8	Influence of Literature on Art (inter-subject - influence phase relation)
8:7	Literate through Art, a new approach (inter-subject - tool phase relation)

Examples of colon (:) for facet relation

635.91: 632.38	Virus diseases of Indoor Plants
669.14:621.791	Welding on steel
371.212:373.5	Admission to Grammar Schools
624.21:625.1	Railway Bridges

The sequence of Phase are reversible as in the case of facet relations. This is in accordance with the principle of flexibility in UDC.

Comparison between CC, DDC, and UDC.

Below are given a few examples of phase relation and their class numbers by DDC, UDC and CC which will clarity how complex subjects have been handled in CC.

Name if the Subject	*DDC*	*UDC*	*CC*
Examples of Inter-phase relation			
Relations between Philosophy and Religion	100 or? 200	1:2	Q&aR
Psychology for Teachers	150.088379	159.9:371.1	S&bT
Comparison between Philosophy and Religion	100 or ? 200	1:2	Q&eR
Difference between Philosophy and Religion	100 or ? 200	1:2	R&gQ
Influence of Religion on Philosophy	100 or ? 200	1:2	R&gQ
Examples of Intra-facet relation			
Relation between Primary and Secondary Education	372 or ? 373	327:373	T,15&j16
Epistemology for Metaphysics	121.08811	11:165	R2&k3
Comparative study of Epistemology and Metaphysics	110 or ? 121	11:165	R2&m3

Difference between Epistemology and Metaphysics	110 or ? 121	11:165	R2&m3
Influence of Logic on Ethics	170 or ? 160	17:16	R4&rl
Examples of Intra-array relation			
Relation between Import and Export Duty	336.264 or ? 338.265	339.543.3	X72,951&t5
Import Duty biased towards Export Duty	336.264 or? 336.265	339. 543.3	X72,951&u5
Comparative study of Spring	551.6 ?	551.583 ?	U2,761&v3
Difference between Undergraduate and Postgraduate Education	378.1552 or ? 378.1553	378 ?	T, 181&w2
Influence of Wind on Cyclones	551.552 or ? 551.518	551.55 ?	U2,736&y3

The worked out numbers in the above table gives a clear picture that only in CC every type of inter-disciplinary subject can be classified co-extensively. In UDC we cannot distinguish between the different types of relations because of the single connecting symbol for all relations. DDC has yet to make provision for these types of relations. At present, one can give any one number as shown in the table.

8
Common Isolates

Q. : What do you mean by 'Common Isolates'? Can 'Space isolates' and 'Time Isolates' be called Common Isolates'? Write a note on Space Isolates and Time Isolates of Colon Classification.

Or

What are Space Isolates? Compare their use in DDC, CC and UDC.

Or

What are common isolates? Explain their use in DDC, UDC and CC with the help of suitable examples.

Or

Compare the application of Common isolates in CC, DDC and UDC.

Common isolates as name indicates are those which are commonly applicable to all the classes and thus can form component of several compound subjects. According to Ranganathan, "A common isolate is an isolate idea denoted by the same isolate term and represented by the isolate number, quite irrespective of the compound subject in which it occurs, or the basic subject with which the compound subject goes". Bliss states "these are systematic not only in the ordinary sense but in that they are applicable, wholly or partly under any class, others only under certain classes or sections".

The credit of the concept of common isolates goes to Melvil Dewey, in the beginning he called them Form Divisions. They were first introduced in the second edition of DDC brought out in 1885. Since then they have undergone several changes. The name Form Division continued up to the twelfth edition of DDC published in 1922. This name was changed to Common Subdivisions in the thirteenth edition appearing in 1932. These Common Subdivisions were listed under three different categories, viz., miscellaneous common subdivisions, viewpoint and form divisions. This whole set reappeared as just Form Divisions in the fifteenth and sixteenth editions and was renamed as Standard Subdivisions in the seventeenth edition. The seventeenth edition also identified space and time isolates as common isolates and listed them as such. Until the publication of the seventeenth edition, the history schedule had been used for space isolates.

In UDC, common isolates are called Auxiliary Subdivisions. Broadly, there are two types of auxiliaries in use in UDC: common and special. Auxiliaries of Form in UDC are like the Standard Subdivisions of DDC. Space and time isolates are treated as common auxiliaries and listed separately. The use of auxiliaries in UDC is an important aspect in number building.

In the first edition of CC, there were three different schedules for Common Subdivisions of which space and time were two. The number of Common Subdivisions was small initially. It was only in the fourth edition of CC that these were recognised as Anteriorising and Posteriorising Common Subdivisions. In the fifth edition, they were named as Common Isolates. After several changes through successive editions, an exhaustive list of Common Isolates has emerged in the seventh edition of CC.

KINDS OF COMMON ISOLATES

The different kinds of common isolates include Language isolate ideas, Time isolate ideas, Space isolate ideas and Anteriorising common isolate ideas. There can also be Common Personality isolate ideas, Common Matter isolate ideas, and Common Energy isolate ideas.

It may be noted that among the manifestations of the Fundamental Categories *Energy* and *Matter*, some will be Special isolate ideas and some others will be common isolate ideas. Special Isolates are those which are special to a basic class or to a small group of basic classes in a scheme for classifications. For example the Educand Isolates in the Main Subject Education, Cultivator Isolates in Agriculture, Substance Isolates in Chemistry are all such examples of *Special Isolates*.

It means, special isolates are derived on the basis of some characteristic based on the host basic class itself, whereas common isolates represent those isolates which are commonly applicable to all special isolates. It becomes more helpful when the schemes for classification allocate to common isolates specific isolate numbers i.e., each isolate having one specific digit to represent itself wherever its need arise.

The Matter common isolate *ideas* consist of properties and values and not of materials. However, these Common Property isolates and Energy common isolate ideas too need enumeration. Further, it is found that Energy common isolate term and Matter common isolate terms are often found coalesced into a single term in the documents; one has to separate them. Also, one and the same common isolate idea is not always denoted by the same term at all times; their reduction to a single term is time-consuming.

1. Common Isolates in Colon Classification

The common isolates in CC are quite different from those in DDC. These are defined in CC as those which denote the same isolate term and are represented by the same isolate number. The several types of common isolates in CC may be as under;

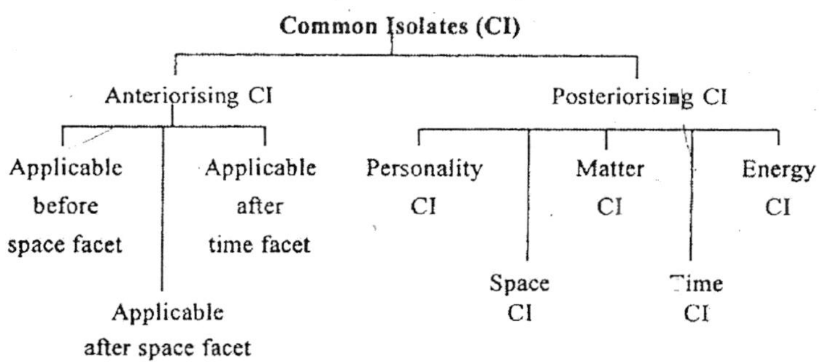

Up to the sixth edition of CC, there has been a clear distinction between anteriorising and posteriorising common isolates. Anteriorising common isolates were attached to a host number without any connecting symbol, whereas posteriorising common isolates were attached with a connecting symbol. In the seventh edition, this distinction has been removed, however, they have retained the same function, assigned to them in the earlier editions.

(A) Anteriorising Common Isolates in CC

ACIs are those which are used for documents which require to be arranged anterior to ordinary documents on the subject of concern.

The library possesses a variety of documents. Among them are the documents which are referred to as a source of preliminary reading on a particular. Subject are rightly called *'Approach Material'* It is therefore helpful to provide them anterior positions to the core reading material on the subject. These documents such as bibliography, concordance, table atlas, encyclopedia and survey etc, because of their nature have grater possibilities of being consulted by a number of user across the discipline. These are represented with the help of ACIS.

(i) **ACIs Applicable before Space Facet :** These may be attached after basic class, after personality facet, after matter facet and after energy facet.

Examples	*CC6*
Encyclopedia of Librarianship	2K
Bibliography on Economic Reforms in India	Xa44
McGraw Hill encyclopedia of Science and Technology	AK73,N

(ii) **ACIs Applicable after Space Facet :** There are only two ACIs which may be added after space facet. These are Administrative Report and Statistics.

Examples	*CC6*
Administrative Report on Women Education in Rajasthan	T55.4437.r
Population of India; 1991 Census	Y:5. 44s N 91

(iii) **ACIs Applicable after Time Facet :** The isolate are to be added only after time facet.

Examples	*CC6*
Indian, Finance Commission (1994) (Chairman K.C. Pant)	X7. 446N94t
Survey of Public Libraries in (1980)	22.446M80t4

(B) Posteriorising Common Isolates (PCI)

The (PCI) decrease the extension of the class to which these are attached. The purpose of PCI's is to sharpen the host class. These, therefore have the posterior position and documents with PCI are arranged after the general reading material on the subject.

Posteriorising common isolates are of three types, Personality, Matter and Energy common isolates. They are to be attached to the host (core) class with their respective connecting symbols, viz., comma, semi colon and colon.

(i) **Personality Common Isolates (PCI) :** PCI is used to represent institutions or organisations. It is preceded by (,), when attached to a host class. The institutional component in the number is worked out using alphabetical and chronological devices. Alphabetical device is used only in the cases when year of establishment of institutions is not known, chronological device is preceded by 9, if the institution is a national body. Given below are a few examples:

— Indian Mathematical Society founded in 1931 - B,44,g,9N31

Where,

B	-	Mathematics
44	-	India (all space isolates are added with a dot (.) as the connecting symbol)
g	-	Learned body (all lower case Roman letters represent common isolates. An element added with a comma as the connecting symbol indicates personality facet)
9N31	-	A national body is represented by 9 and the date of foundation; N31 is 1931

— Delhi University - T,18.44,t4N21

Where,

T	-	Education
T,18	-	University education. 18 from personality facet under the main class T
44	-	India
t4	-	An institution of higher education. t4 is a personality common isolate.
N21	-	Founded in 1921. Delhi University is a localised body and so 9 is not prefixed.

— Poona observatory - B9.44,f2, P

Where,

B9	-	Astronomy
44	-	India
f2	-	Observational institution (f2 is a personality common isolate)
P	-	Poona (alphabetical device)

(ii) **Matter Property Common Isolates :** An exhaustive list of matter property common isolates appears for the first time in the seventh edition of CC. These isolates are to be added to the host class with the indicator; (semicolon). Given below are a few examples :

The outgoing Tamil Nadu Ministry - V4411,2;aP5

Where,

V	–	History
4411	–	Tamil Nadu
2	–	Cabinet (Ministry)
aP5	–	outgoing - Matter property common isolate.

The Intrinsic Value of Paintings - N6;a72

Where,

V	–	History
4411	–	Tamil Nadu
2	–	Cabinet (Ministry)
aP5	–	outgoing - Matter property common isolate.

The Intrinsic value of Paintings - N6;a72

Where,

N6	–	Painting
a72	–	Intrinsic value

(iii) **Energy Common Isolates (CEI) :** The Common Energy Isolates are to be attached to the host class with the connecting symbol: (colon). Some of the energy common isolates are:

ab	-	establish, inaugurate	ed	-	mixing
af3	-	differentiate	eg	-	cleaning
ak	-	compensate	ev	-	washing

aD2	-	infiltrate	e3	-	boiling
aR	-	investigation, research	fZ6	-	preserving
aR2	-	observing	p2	-	describing
aT	-	evaluation	pR4	-	printing
d1	-	designing	u1	-	surveying

A few examples are worked out below indicating the use of energy common isolates.

— Observing Solar Eclipse – BX,3;57:aR2

Where,

BX	-	Astronomy
3	-	Sun
57	-	Eclipse
aR2	-	Observation-energy common isolate

— Research on the Ulcer of the Intestine - L,25;474:aR

Where,

L	-	Medicine
25	-	Intestine
4	-	Disease
74	-	Ulcer
aR	-	Research - energy common isolate

— Designing Architectural Plan of Library Buildings - NA9(2);3:d1

Where,

NA	-	Architecture
9(2)	-	Library buildings
3	-	Plans
d1	-	Designing-energy common isolate

(iv) **Space and Time Common Isolate (S and T) :** The Space and Time Isolates are the manifestations of the Fundamental Categories, Time and Space. These two catergories are applicable to all the basic subjects, and therefore satisfy the definition of common isolates. The insertion of connecting symbol between the host-class number and the space and time isolate numbers secure for the resulting class number a position posterior to the host class number. These two isolates, therefore, are treated in CC as posteriorising common isolates. Some of the examples are:

— University Libraries in India - 2, J4.44

Where,

2	-	Library Science
J4	-	University Libraries
44	-	India

— Mass Communication in India in the 1980s - 4.44' N8

Where,

4	-	Mass communication
44	-	India
N8	-	1980s

In the second example, both space ad time isolates are present.

Special Isolates in Colon Classification

The special isolates belonging to a particular family of isolates such as educand isolates in education, cultivator isolates in agriculture. Substance isolates in chemistry and form isolates in literature can be used to form compound subjects going with particular subject. Each such family of isolates has a distinctive character which is commonly shared by each of its members. CC does not provide compound subjects, but provides the schedule of special isolates for each basic subject. These are given separately for basic subject.

L9A	Specials
L9B	Embryo
L9C	Child
L9D	Adolescent
L9E	Old Age
L9F	Female
J9D	Dry Farming
J9S	Soilless Farming

CC7 (1987): The CC7 has made some changes and added new schedules to common isolates which are as follows.

1. Indicator digit, " (Double inverted comma) has been introduced

for AC1. In 1968 in DRTC Seminar, it was found that to increase the hospitality in an array, all the sectors including of zone (Z-a) should be made available for array division. However, the use of isolate numbers from (Z-a) was not possible as Roman small letters with anteriorising value were used for common isolates. It was, therefore, suggested that for anteriorising value the indicator digit" (double inverted comma) should be used for ACI. This suggestion was finally accepted for implementation in 1969. This has released the Roman small letters (Sa) for use in the formation of arrays in the same manner as the Indo-Arabic numerals and the Roman capital letters;

2. The small table of Common Energy Isolates (ECI) has been extended into a comprehensive schedule;
3. In the schedule for Common Personality Isolates following new isolates have been added:

   f8 Testing organisation

   h Popularising Institution (Industrial Body in CC6)

   h5 Exhibition centre

   h6 Museum

   v2 Advisory body

   x6 Aiding body

   x7 Endowment

   y Cultural Organisations

   yx Rehabilitation Centre
4. Common Schedule for Matter Property Isolates (CMPI) is provided.

No schedule for (EMPI) was provided in CC6. Although in Prolegomena Edition 2 (1957), it was stated that 'attributes of physical, chemical or biological nature, and of nature of value may be looked upon as 'Common matter isolates'... and treated as posteriorising common isolates, similar to Common Energy Isolates.' 'Each letter in an array of order 1, may represent a group of attributes or value, which can be corelated more or less to the traditional main classes.' e.g.,

c Physical properties

cu Thermal properties

r4 Ethical value

s	Psychological value
t	Educational value

Accordingly, in CC7 an extensive schedule for Common Property Isolates has been included. The isolates enumerated in this schedule are derived on the basis of such characteristics as-Property, Differentiability, Statistical Property, Physical properties, Electrical and Electronic properties, Chemical properties, Utility Legality etc. The Schedule has been termed as pseudo-mnemonic in the sense that the numbers may be devised changing the (BS) digit from capital to small and omitting the indicator digit of the (IN) if any, e.g.

Isolate	*Class No. in (BS)*	*CMPI*
Development	G;7	g7
Meaning	P;4	p4
personality	S;4	s4

2. Common Isolates in Dewey Decimal Classification

In DDC, common isolates have undergone several changes in both nomenclature and presentation. They were spelled out by different names in different editions of DDC. The different names used so far are form divisions, common subdivisions, viewpoint numbers and standard subdivisions. From the seventeenth edition onwards, they have been called standard subdivisions.

The DDC has 7 tables of which Table 1 and 2 lists notations, which in CC terminology are referred to as common isolates.

The following are the different types of common isolates in DDC-Table-1

- 01	Philosophy and theory
- 016	Indexes
- 02	Miscellany
- 022	Illustrations and models
- 028	Techniques, procedures, apparatus, equipment, material
- 285	Data processing
- 288	Maintenance and repair
- 03	Dictionaries, encyclopaedias, concordances
- 05	Serial publications

- 06	Organisations and management
- 07	Study and teaching
- 072	Research
- 08	History and description of the subject among groups of persons
- 09	Historical and geographical treatment

A note along with Table 1 states that "the notations are never be used alone but may be used as required with any number from the schedules". It is, thus, clear that the above numbers are not used independent of the core numbers from the subject schedules. Every number in the above table is preceded by a dash which merely shows that the number never stands alone. The dash is to be omitted when it is added to a core number taken form a subject schedule.

As seen, Table 1 (SS) consists of various forms such as synopsis, outlines serial publications, tabulated and related material etc. It also contains modes of treatment such as theory, study and teaching, history etc. In short, in DDC the Table 1 (SS) enumerates such sub divisions which represent frequently recurring physical forms (dictionaries, periodicals) or approaches (history, research) applicable to any subject or discipline. They may be added to any number in the schedules unless there are instructions to the contrary.

As a general rule, notations from Table 1 (SS) may be added to any number in the schedules. However, the classifier should add notations from Table 1 to any number of the Schedules only before varifying the followings:

(i) If the instruction to add (SS) notation from Table 1 is given. e.g.;

350.0001-9	Standard sub-divisions; specific aspects of Public administration.

This demands to use four Zero with (SS) notation e.g.

350.0001	Theory of Public Administration.

(ii) If enumerated standard sub-divisions are used with changed meaning. e.g.;

331.01	Philosophy and Theory
.011	Rights and position of labour
.012	Satisfaction and.........Labour

370.15	Educational psychology
610.72	Research
.73	Nursing and other activities

In DDC 21 (1996) many new number have been added to make Standard Subdivisions more comprehensive. e.g.;

- 071	Education
- 0785	Computer-assisted instruction
- 09005	Serial Publications (of Historical, geographical, persons treatment)
- 0923	Collected ethnic, national groups
- 0929	Persons treatment of non-humans (such as biographics of animals)

(iii) If the historical period is already enumerated in the schedules, e,g,; is 800 and 900.

(iv) If the extended and modified standard sub-divisions are enumerated. e.g.; under 342-347 Law of specific jurisdictions-026 - 0269.

Examples :

020.904	Library and Information Science in 20th century
020.151	Mathematical Principles used in Library Science
	(the class number is constructed using Add Device given under-015)
570.72054	Research on Life Sciences in India

(this class number has been constructed (i) by removing one zero from 570 as it becomes three digited by adding (SS) notation –072 and (ii) the areas notation–54 is added as per instruction given under–072).

A common isolate for space also can be added to a class number. Table 2 Areas enumerates geographical division–physiographic features, orientation divisions, zones, socio-economic regions and ancient and modern worlds. These divisions may be used with the divisions enumerated in the Schedules either through –09 (SS) or through Add Device. –09 (SS) provides autonomy to classifier in the use of (SS) notations.

Examples :

382.094105	Trade between UK and Asian countries
027.05	General Libraries in Asia
364.91732054	Crimes in the Cities of India
331.40954	Women Workers in India

Here, after 0, country numbers are added directly from Table 2.

Special Isolate in DDC

Table 3 to 7 list notation are representing special isolates of DDC.

Table3: Subdivisions for arts, for individual literature, for special literary forms.

"Regularly occurring topics applicable to any literature" are represented by notations in this table. This notations may be added to individual literature in 810-890 and also to special subdivision of SS.

Table 4: Subdivision of Individual Languages and Language families.

"Regularly occurring topics applicable to any language" are denoted by notation in this table. This notation may be added to individual language in 420-490.

Table5 : Racial, Ethnic and National Group

Specific racial, ethnic or national groups are denoted by notation in this table. These are applied to other notations from schedules by means of add notes.

Table 6: Languages

This is a table of notations "designating specific languages. These notations are applied to other notations in the schedules and tables by means of 'add notes'.

Table 7: Group of Persons

"Persons by specific occupational and other classes" are denoted by notation in this table. These are applied to other notation in the schedule and tables by means of "Add notes".

3. Common Isolates in Universal Decimal Classification

The most innovative feature of UDC is its auxiliary notation-the sign and sub-divisions which help to devise numbers for complex subjects. This auxiliary notation is of two kinds: the common auxiliaries and special auxiliaries.

The special auxiliaries denote recurrent characteristics that are limited to a specific subject (s). These are, therefore, enumerated with the subject or subjects to which these are applicable.

The common auxiliaries denote generally recurrent characteristics which are applicable throughout main tables of UDC. The common auxiliary sub-divisions are divided into groups:

(i) Independent auxiliary tables–Table 1 (c) to 1 (g) i.e., the auxiliaries of form, language, place, race and time. Sub-divisions of these may be added to any UDC number or may be used of their own.

(ii) Dependent auxiliary table–Tables 1 (I) to 1(K) i.e., the auxiliaries of point of view, materials and persons. The sub divisions of these are always to be added to UDC numbers.

The following diagram will explain the concept well.

Common Auxiliaries

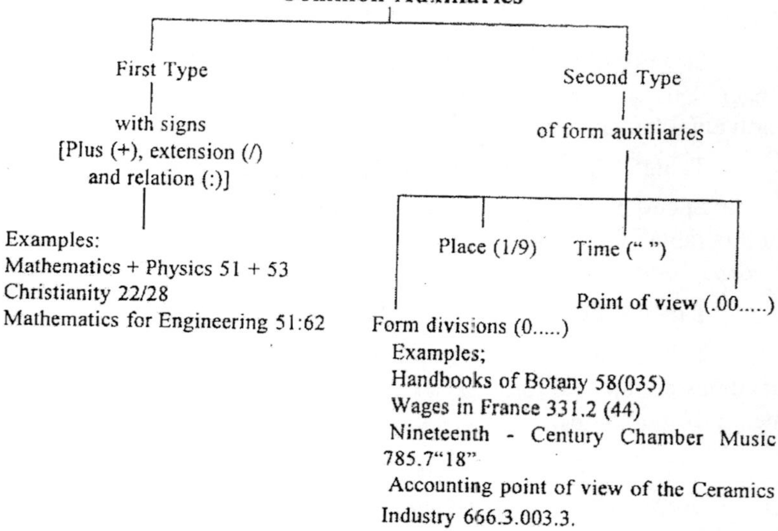

The common auxiliary of Forms in UDC are like the standard subdivisions in DDC and the anteriorising common isolates of CC.

The connecting symbols or indicator digits in UDC play a major role in the building of class numbers. As in CC, the indicator digits in

UDC reveal the type of facet used. That is the reason why in depth classification, UDC has become very popular throughout the world.

The common auxiliaries of Form are put in parentheses with a connecting symbol nought (0...). They are used more for outer forms of presentation like dictionary, journal, etc. They are also used for a few inner forms.

A space isolate in UDC is like an area number in DDC. In UDC, it is put in parentheses (1/9). As in CC, it contains a part from the political division and there is also provision for zones, orientation, physical features, etc.

A time isolate in UDC compares well with CC. There is provision to show months, days, hours and even minutes. The time isolate is encased in double inverted commas ("....").

Out of these common auxiliaries, the sub-divisions of the following auxiliaries may be termed as common isolates:

1 (d) Common Auxiliaries of Form

1 (e) Common Auxiliaries of Place

1 (g) Common Auxiliaries of Time

(i) **Common Auxiliaries of Form :** 'The common auxiliaries of Form enumerates such sub-divisions which indicate the documentary form or presentation of a subject represented by a main UDC number'. Below are given some examples:

Bibliography on International Law	341(01)
Dictionary of International Law	341(03)
Journal of International Law	341(05)
Teaching of International Law	341(07)
History of International Law	341(09)

The common auxiliaries of Form in the above examples are put in parentheses with a zero as the connecting symbol.

(ii) **Common auxiliaries of Place:** Like DDC and CC, UDC also provides a fairly exhaustive schedule of geographical isolates. This schedule covers political as well as physiographic divisions. All these are called common auxiliaries of place. Their application is simple and easily understandable. A few examples are given below. Here, the place number is always put in parentheses without any prefix.

327(540) - Foreign policy of India, where 327 is foreign policy and (540) is India.

Bilateral relations between two countries can also be shown with ease. Thus,

327 (540:41) Bilateral Relations between India and the U.K.

The number for the second country (41 U.K.) in the above case is joined with a colon.

33(540-22) - Economic conditions of rural India, where 33 is Economics, (540) is India and (-22) is Rural zone (zones or defined areas can be joined by a hyphen to another place).

(iii) **Common auxiliaries of Time:** The Time isolates in UDC are applied wherever needed. These are almost similar to those in CC. The connecting symbol for the time element in UDC is two double inverted commas ("..."). Even months, weeks, days, hours or minutes, can be represented. The minus sign (-) in the time isolate indicates periods before Christ. A few examples illustrating the use of time isolates are given below:

1988	-	"1988"
15th August 1947	-	"1947.08.15"
6th November 1987	-	"1987.11.06"
32 B.C.	-	"-0032"
6th Century	-	"05"
19th Century	-	"18"
1950$_s$ (1950-1959)	-	"195"
18th to 20th Centuries	-	"17/19"

Applying a time number is also very simple. For example, Economic conditions in India in the 19th Century: 33(540) "18" (33 - Economics, (540) - India and "18" - 19th Century).

9
Major Classification Schemes

Q. : What are the major schemes of library classification? Discuss salient features of Dewey Decimal Classification (DDC) Scheme.

Or

What are major schemes of library classification? Discuss salient features of Colon Classification.

Or

Mentioning the different schemes of library classification, discuss sailent features of Universal Decimal Classification (UDC).

Or

Explain briefly the qualities evident in the UDC, CC and DDC notation.

Or

Discuss the salient features of DDC. Explain the reason for its popularity all over the world.

Or

Make a comparative study of CC, UDC and DDC.

Or

Discuss the importance of Relative Index in DDC.

Or

What do you understand by mapping of subjects in classification scheme? Make a comparative study of the mapping of subjects in UDC and CC.

Ans. Library Classification or book classification is concerned with the arrangements of documents in the library to serve the Readers. It requires a detailed scheme of classification in which knowledge is divided into broad areas, which are further sub-divided into subjects and main classes. Each division and sub-division is represented by a system of numbers called 'Notation'.

A scheme of classification generally consists of printed schedules in such a way that the hierarchy of subjects is shown as far as possible. It has in the begining. An introduction explaining the methods and uses of the scheme followed by the table showing outlines of the main classes and main divisions and other tables like Standard Sub-Division etc.

Whatever the case may be, all the schemes of classification are grouped into :-

(i) General Schemes

(ii) Special Schemes

(i) General Schemes

A General Scheme of Classification covers all the subjects of universe of knowledge and may be used in all types of libraries. All the existing general scheme of library classification have divided the whole universe of subjects into a series of main classes, which are further sub-divided in a hierarchial manner leading to co-ordinate and subordinate classes. For example:

Literature

English literature

Hindi literature

Pubjabi literature

Poetry

Drama

Fiction

Thus, each entity (for example English Poetry) falls into a subgroup of a larger group (for example English Literature), which in turn forms part of an even larger group (for example Literature).

The Colon Classification, Dewey Decimal Scheme of Classification and Universal Decimal of Classification, are the examples of this type of classification schemes.

(ii) Special Schemes

A special scheme of classification is one which deals with a specific subject. This type of scheme of classification is useful for organizing, collection in a special library dealing with a special subject. A Special Scheme is required when the treatment of a given subject in a General Scheme is not comprehensive, for example the Library of the Institute of Fashion Technology in New Delhi will specialised in its collection on the subject. To Organize such a collection, any General Scheme will not be helpful. Therefore a Special Scheme would have to be developed. This type of Special Scheme may be an off shoot of a General Scheme i.e., it may follow the basic principles of the General Scheme but will cover the subject extensively and intensively. For example the Special Classification Scheme developed by Central Food Technology Research Institute (C.F.T.R.I), Mysore, follows the basic principles of Colon Classification scheme.

Some of the prominent special schemes are:

1. Soil Earth Science, by B.C. Vickery.
2. Classification of Social Sciences, 1961, by B.F. Kyle.
3. British Catalogue of Music Classification, by E.J. Coates.
4. Diamond Technology, by J.E.L. Farradane.
5. Organising the Arts, 1968, by Peter F. Broxis.
6. Classification of the Performing Arts, 1968, by Anthony Croghan.
7. A Classification for the Literature of Jazz, 1970, by D.W. Langridge.

Major Schemes of Classification

The main schemes of library classification in vogue are:-

1. Dewey Decimal Classification (DDC):

   -By Melvil Dewey in 1876.
2. Expensive Classification (EC):

   -By Charles A. Cutter in 1891.
3. Library of Congress Classification (LC):

   -By Library of Congress in 1904.
4. Universal Decimal Classification (UDC):

   -By Paul otlet and Henry la Fontaine in 1905.

5. Subject Classification (SC): -By James D. Brown in 1906.
6. Colon Classification (CC): -By S.R. Ranganathan in 1933.
7. Bibliographic Classification (BC): -By H.E. Bliss in 1935.
8. International Classification (IC): -By F. Rider in 1961.

Among them, DDC, CC and UDC are more prominent and are being used in majority of libraries. Each scheme is briefly discussed as below.

1. DEWEY DECIMAL CLASSIFICATION (DDC)

DDC was conceptualised by Melvil Louis Kossuth Dewey and was first published in 1876. It is now in its 21st edition. Its author Melvil Dewey (1851-1931) is veritably acknowledged as the Father of Modern Librarianship. He was born in Adam's Centre, New York on December 10, 1851 in the house of a storekeeper and shoemaker. Since his childhood, Dewey had keen interest in arranging things in a systematic way. It is told that at the age of five, he arranged his mother's larder in an orderly fashion. At the age of twenty one that is in 1872, he got a job as a Student Library Assistant at Amerest College. In 1873, he conceived the idea of formulating a scheme of classification, and in the same year, he put forward his plan for rearranging the collection in that library in a more systematic order. He was promoted to the post of the Assistant College Librarian after his graduation in 1874. In 1876, the scheme was published anonymously under the title 'A classification and subject index for cataloguing and arranging the books and pamphlets of a Library'. He became the pioneer in the fields of library classification and with him begain the new era of the history of library classification. He was the founding member of American Library Association (1876), was the guiding spirit in starting the Library Journal (1876) and edited it till 1880. He founded first Library School (1887), played an important role in establishing Library Association, London; the Reader and writer's company and the Library Bureau to supply the library stationary and other euipments. Although at the age of 80 he breathed his last on December 26, 9131, but his work still enliven the library science community in and outside America.

The first edition of DDC published in 1876, consisted of only 44 pages, of which twelve pages were devoted to introduction, twelve pages as table or schedule and eighteen pages for index. Dewey used Arabic numerals for its notation. The Dewey's Scheme for Classification was criticised by the Librarians at that time. A second greatly enlarged edited version of DDC brought out in 1985, consisted of 314 pages. Not withstanding its ever mounting criticism the popularity of the scheme was always on the rise during the course of its 21 edition.

Plan and Structure of Scheme

Melvil Dewey designed the Decimal Classification Scheme at a time when the fixed location system was becoming increasingly dysfunctional due to gradual increase in published material. The basic requirement was of a scheme which could solve the problems of haphazard arrangement of documents. Dewey had practical experienced with this vexed problem when he was as assistant in the Amherst College Library. He visited more than 50 American Libraries, read hundred of books and pamphlets to find the solution. However, it was on a Sunday morning during church service that the solution of this vexed problem flashed in his mind, when he decided to use the simplest Indo-Arabic numerals as decimals.

The structure of the DDC appears to be based on Knowledge Classification by Bacon and Harris. The following table shows the outlines of these three systems:

Bacon	*Harris*	*Dewey*
History (Memory)	Science	General work
	Philosophy	Philosophy
	Religion	
	Social & Political	Social Sciences
	Science	Linguistics, Sciences
	Natural Science	Useful Arts
	Useful Arts	(Technology)
Poesy (Imagination)	Art	Fine Art
	Fine Arts	
	Pure Fiction, Literary	Literature
	Miscellany	
Philosophy (Reason)	History	History
	Grography and	Geography and
	Travel	Travel
	Biography	Biography

It appears that the Dewey followed a reverse arrangements of subjects as given by Bacon.

Conceptual Framework

DDC is the hierarchical scheme which proceeds from general to specific. The basic plan of the scheme is to divide the whole universe of knowledge into ten main divisions, each of which is again divided into ten subdivision. Further each of these subdivisions are divided into ten sections. These divisions are known as first summary, second summary and third summary. The first division of knowledge is as follows:-

0.0 Generalities

0.1 Philosophy and Psychology

0.2 Religion

0.3 Social sciences

0.4 Language

0.5 Natural Sciences and Mathematics

0.6 Technology (Applied sciences)

0.7 The arts

0.8 Literature and Rhetoric

0.9 Geography and History

In practice, the first zero and the decimal point are taken as implied and the numbers are written simply as 1,2,3,4,5,....9.

Main class 0 Generalities enumerates such subjects which deal with whole universe of knowledge, such as Bibliography, Library and Information Science and subjects indicating point views such as News media, journalism. Main classes 1-9 are related to major disciplines or group of related subjects.

This principle is also followed while subdividing the main classes, or their divisions and subdivisions. 0 in general is used for general works. e.g. 300 = General Works on Social Sciences, 330, General works on Economics.

The three summaries (Vol. I DDC 19 and Vol. II DDC 20) provide a clear map as to how the universe of knowledge is divided and subdivided.

Auxillary Tables

Auxillary tables provide an important basis for preparing numbers and lead to uniform meanings of number when used in various contexts. A document, which is a source of knowledge, always has some physical form. Melvil Dewey in the second edition of the scheme published in 1885 introduced the concept of 'Form Divisions', to be used for the divisions of a subject based on the characteristics of documents either in accordance with the point of view of the author i.e., Bibliographical. Philosophical, Theoretical, Historical or in accordance with the form of thought content in documents. i.e., Digest, Mannual, Monograph, Dictionary, Periodical or Manual. The 'Form divisions' could be attached to any class number according to the instructions provided therein. The system of 'Form Division' remained in use upto 12th edition. The 13th edition consisted of 5 "Auxiliary Schedules". The 14th edition had 4 tables. In the 15th edition, the traditional 9 From Divisions, i.e., 01-09 were annexed alongwith tables. Without any detailed subdivisions, they were about 70 divisions was replaced by 'Standard subdivision' in the 17th editions, alongwith new area table in volume 2 (Index). The 18th. 19th and 20th editions consist of 7 auxillary tables.

Table 1 is for Standard Subdivisions

Table 2 is for Areas

Table 3 is for Subdivisions of Individual Literature

Table 4 is for Subdivisions of Individual Languages

Table 5 is for Racial, Ethenic, National Groups

Table 6 is for Languages and

Table 7 is for Persons

Of these seven tables, the Areas table occupies most number of pages in the volume. Currently, the four most commonly used tables are Standard subdivisions, Geographical subdivisions, Individual literatures and Individual languages. The Notations from these tables are never used independently, but always in combinations with the main numbers.

Table 1,2,5 and 7 can be used as required with any appropriate number from the schedules. They are applicable to the entire range of class numbers 000 to 999. Notations from Table 1, Standard Subdivisions, can be added directly to any number from the schedules or with the introduction of additional zeroes, if the zero is not reserved for general works and a notation beginning with a zero (or 00, or 000 as the case may be) has been used for special purposes.

The notations from Tables 2, 5 and 7 may be used as required either directly when so instructed, or with the interposition of appropriate standard subdivision such as 09 for areas, 089 for racial, ethnic and national groups and 088 for persons.

The notations for Table 6, languages, also have applicability throughout the schedules, but their use is restricted to only those numbers from the schedules and other tables wherein the classifier is specifically instructed.

The notations of Tables 3 and 4 are applicable only to their respective main classes, literature and languages. The notations of Table 3 can be used as required with the base numbers of individual literatures identified by an asterisk (*) under 810-890. Similarly, notations of Table 4 may be used as required with the base numbers for individual languages identified by an asterisk (*) under 420-490.

These tables have greatly enhanced the potential for details in DDC.

Relative Index

In DDC 1 (1876) the index was termed as Subject Index. However, in the Subject Index, class numbers for many such subjects were also given which were not enumerated in the Tables.

Example: *Index*

Alcoholic liquors 178,615,663 (In main table only 663 is available)

Needle work 646, 793 (only in Index)

Dewey in the Preface of this Edition stated "The Alphabetical Subject Index is designed to guide, both in numbering and in finding the books........ Most names of countries, towns, animals plants, minerals, diseases have been ommitted, the aim being to furnish an Index of Subjects on which books are written, and not a Gazetteer or a Dictionary of the nouns in the language."

In DDC 2 (1885), the subject Index was renamed as Relative Index. The Relative Index is the most important feature of DDC, more important than the classification itself. It supplements the classification in the scheme by bringing together those related aspects of a subject, which are scattered throughout the scheme due to classification by discipline followed by DDC. While the schedules group subjects by discipline and scatter the various aspects of one and the same subject according to the context, the Relative Index collocates these aspects under the subject term at one place.

The index to the nineteenth edition retains the same pattern as in the eighteenth edition. Many of the cross-references have been deleted and replaced by numbers. More synonyms have been added. To a certain extent DDC has taken a step backwards by making the index almost a substitute for the schedules.

The index is very detailed in giving, under each subject, the numbers in which it may be classed according to the discipline or aspect or point of view treated in a given document. See for example, the following sample from the index of the nineteenth edition. It has collected all aspects of the subject copper.

Copper	
Age	
archaeology	930.15
Arts	
decorative	739.511
other aspects see Metals arts	
Chemistry	
inorganic	546.652
organic	547.056 52
technology	661.065 2
organic	661.895
soc. & icon. aspects see Secondary industries	
compounds	
chemistry *see* Copper chemistry	
plant nutrition *see* Trace elements	
plant nutrition	
construction	
architecture	721.044 73
s.a. Spec. kinds of bldgs.	
building	693.73

materials	
building	693.83
engineering	620.182
foundations	624.153 82
naval design	623.818 22
shipbuilding	623.820 7
structures	624.182 2
s.a. Other spec. uses	
metallography	669.953
metallurgy	669.3
physical & chemical	669.963
soc. & econ. aspects see	
Secondary industries	
mineral aspects	
economic geology	553.43
mineralogy	549.23
mining	
technology	622.343
prospecting	622.184 3
s.a. spec. minerals	
pharmacology	
misc. aspects see Pharmacology	615.265 2
Products	
arts see Cooper arts	
mf. tech.	673.3
other aspects see	
Nonferrous metals	
Products	
roofing	
bldg. construction	695
soaps	
chem. tech.	668.125

The Relative Index also provides see also references. The numbers enumerated in 7 Tables and Schedules may also be located only through Index.

Notation in DDC

Indo-Arabic numerals 0-9 form the basis of DDC's ...... and are used decimally. A DDC class number is not less than three digits.

However, the decimal is not used in the beginning of the number. In this way the full notation for the main class 3 is 300. So the acutal notation representing main classes is as under:-

000 500
100 600
200 700
300 800
400 900

Each of the above main class/division has been divided into ten subdivisons. i.e. 100 divisions. known as second summary

The digits 1 to 9 are used as subclasses of the main division. And the digit 0 (Zero) is used for the general works throughout the main classes. Thus 500 is pure science in general, while 510 is Mathematics, and 520 represents Astronomy and Allied Sciences.

The second summary consist of 100 divisions. The full subdivisions of the Main class 3 is as follows:-

300 350
310 360
320 370
330 380
340 390

Here, 300 represents general works on Social Sciences. 310 Statistics. 330 Economics and so on.

The second division is further divided into 10 sections, making 1000 sections of main classes in all. This is known as the third summary. The method of division is the same as the earlier two summaries, e.g.

330 Economics
331 Labour Economics
332 Financial Economics

333	Land Economics
334	Cooperatives
335	Socialism and Related Systems
336	Public Finance
337	International Economics
338	production
339	Macro Economics and Related Topics

The process of division remains in continuation to any required extent. A point is used after first three digits to give relief to the eye and aid the memory:-

336	Public Finance
336.1	Nontax revenues
336.2	Taxation
339.24	Income Tax
336.242	Personal Income Tax

(i) Sometimes spans of numbers are used to express subjects. They are shown in the schedule as centered entries, so called because they appear with numbers, headings and ..centered on the page instead of with numbers in the usual number column. For example the span 541-547 represents Chemistry.

(ii) The sub-divisions of a discipline of topic are not always subordinated to the notation..... discipline or topic. This is resorted to because of the availability of spare notation and a desire to shorter notation. For example, 574 denote biology and its sub-divisions. ...... sciences and Zoological sciences are classed at 580 and 590 respectively rather than at 574.

Sailent Features of the scheme

Since 1876, this scheme did not look back, and its popularity grew day by day throughout the world. The statement can be justified by the fact that DDC has been translated into many languages, such as Chinese, Spanish, Danish, Turkish, Japanesse. Hindi, Portuguese. Sinhalese. etc. Dewey introduced the idea of using notation for the subjects in his scheme and applying the notation to the book, and not to the shelves. Certain features forming the basics of its present form can still be recognised as follows:-

(i) **Universal Scheme :** A distinctive feature of the DDC is that its classes reflect all the areas of specialized knowledge developed in modern society. These specialised areas are loosely put together in the main classes in the scheme, although in this way the principle of collocation, i.e. bringing of related subjects in close proximity is sometimes violated.

(ii) **Relative Location :** In this scheme, Dewey introduced the idea of 'relative location' as opposed to fixed location. In those days, books were identified by their location on the shelves. A certain number of shelves and a block of accession numbers were allocated to each subject in a library. Each book bearing only the accession number would be placed on a particular shelf earmarked for it according to its subject. The books were, thus, identified by their exact position, room, bay, tier, shelf and place on the shelf. These shelf marks were given to books. Once allocated, the shelf mark denoted the permanent home of a book in the library.

This arrangement was not satisfactory. He introduced the principle of relative location. For this purpose he made use of decimal notation consisting of Arabic numerals for the subjects and assigning that notation to the books on the basis of thought content, and not on the basis of the shelves. In this way, a new book on a given subject may be but in between the existing sequence at the required position, directed by the notation assigned to that book and there is no need to put the book at the end of the sequence as was the practice in fixed location.

(iii) **Decimal notation :** The decimal notation used in DDC refers to the principle of dividing each class into sub-divisions and each of these sub-divisions into another sub-divisions and so on. This feature in DDC equippeed it with a tremendous capacity for expansion to accommodate minute sub-divisions without the necessity of relocation. The first edition of DDC stopped with the division at the third place, though it continued, as suggested by Dewey, to a fourth or fifth place, if necessary, in the catalogue. The pure simplicity of notation soon won popularity for the scheme.

In the process the universe of subjects is divided into ten main classes each of which is again divided into ten divisions. Again, each division is further divided into ten sections. At each stage of division, a given number is sub-divided decimally.

A detailed account of Decimal fraction device is given as under-

531 (Mechanics)	532 (Mechanics of fluids)	533 (Mechanics of gas)	534 (Sound and related vibrations)
.5321 (Mechanics of liquied)	.5322 (Hydrostatics)	.5325 (Hydrodynamics)	.5327 (Transport phenomena)

(iv) **Minute Division :** The first edition of DDC consisted of only 42 pages and at that time it was criticised for its being too broad in its subdivision. The 20th edition consists of 2884 pages in four volumes. This growth suggests the enormous number of subdivisions which are possible and useful for minute classification. Dewey emphasized for the need of minute division as "the advantage of close classing is unquestioned if the user knows just what it is".

(v) **Mnemonic Quality :** The mnemonic quality has been explicit in the notation of DDC since its first edition in which one and the same digits were used throughout the schedule to enumerate similar concepts. The mnemonic quality has gradually increased with every new edition of DDC. The similar concepts or subjects enumerated in both Schedules and Table are also assigned one and the same numbers.

Examples:

Schedules	*Table 2*	*Table 6*
940	–4	Europe
950	–5	Asia
420	English	language –21
430	German	language –31
820	English	literature
830	German	literature

This way DDC fulfills the demands of Scheduled mnemonics.

(vi) **Hospitality:** Hospitality in DDC is secured through: (a) Decimal Fraction Device; (b) Gap Device; and (c) Other device.

(a) **Decimal Fraction Device.** The Decimal Fraction Device is the basic device which enables to accommodate newly emerging subjects in DDC. However, this device provides infinite hospitality in chain only, therefore, DDC may accommodate new basic classes or coordinate classes or their sub-divisions only in chain. DDC has utilised this device to accommodate new sub-divisions in the following manner:

571	Biology
574.8	Tissue, Cellular, Molecular Biology
574.87	Cytology (Cell Biology)
574.873	Protoplasm
574.8732	Nucleus
574.873 22	Chromosomes
574.873 223	Transcription and Translation

However, DDC Editorial Board has visualised that the process of accommodating classes in chain would soon reach to its culmination. So, when feasible help of Add Device is taken rather than enumeration.

(b) **Gap Device.** Another device used in DDC to interpolate new classes is Gap Device. Some of the numbers which are left unused or created through relocations or optionals are utilised as and when necessary to accommodate new subjects. A glaring example is the use of 044 to 066 in DDC 20 to accommodate a complete schedule for Computer Science, which was published by the DDC Editorial Board in 1985. This became possible as the class number by 044 to 066 were left unused upto DDC 19.

(c) **Other Device.** To provide hospitality in array the attempt is made through other Device. In DDC where more than 9 coordinate classes need to be accommodated, the problem is generally obviated by grouping remaining coordinate classes under 9 as others. Although there is no logical basis for this grouping. So it is purely on the flair and choice of DDC Editors whom to accommodate in 1-8 and who are to be bundled under 9. This process, however has made coordinate classes look like subordinate class. For example:

490	Other languages
491	East Indo-European and Celtic languages
492	Afro-Asiatic languages
493	Non-semitic Afto-Asiatic languages
494	Ural-Alaic,..... Dravidian languages

(vii) **Brevity and Simplicity:** The reason for the world wide application of DDC is mainly due to its simple and shorter notation. However, this quality of DDC has greatly been affected by the gradual increase in the use of Add device, the auxiliary tables both common and special and the demand of growing subjects.

(viii) **Syntheticity :** The quality of synthesis in DDC has been present since its inception. The process of synthesis however, explicitely started in DDC 2 with the introduction of Divide like device. There is constant effort of the Editors of DDC to provide a co-extensive class numbers to the growing micro literature. Consequently the synthetic elements in DDC is also increasing.

DDC Editors have thereby made a beautitul combination of enumeration and synthesis and have converted DDC in an Enumerative-synthetic Classification system. The main sources to provide synthetic elements to DDC are:

(a) the Standard subdivisions Table 1 through which the Common isolates, the Space Facet and Time Facet may be used freely with any class number enumerated in the Schedules.

(b) Table 2 Areas, 5 Racial, Ethnic, National Groups and Table 7 Group of Persons, the numbers of which may also be used freely with enumerated class numbers of Schedules through instructions given in the Schedules or through -880 (Table 7) -089 (Table 5) and -09 (Table 2) of Table 1.

(c) Add Device–This device permits to add either from the Schedules or from Tables. The subject Device of Ranganathan is used in a restricted way in providing co-extensive class numbers on the basis of the enumerated class numbers.

(ix) **Detailed specification :** The relative location, combined with decimal notation, made it easier to specify more detailed sub-divisions. Before Dewey introduced the idea of relative location, the number of subject groups into which the books in a library could be arranged was severely limited. Once the idea of moving books at any point to accommodate additions was accepted, it became possible to specify more detailed sub-divisions. Dewey listed nearly one thousand subjects in his first edition. The DDC 19th edition, lists 21, 504 classes (other than auxiliary tables) with provisions for greater synthesis and is still considered to minute enough. By and large, the development of DDC has been one of steady expansions with provision for increasing the amount of detail.

(ix) **Revison** : This is the one of the most important features which has contributed to the durability of DDC has been its sustained programme of revision and updating. Revisions usually take the following forms:

(a) Relocations

(b) Expansion

(c) Complete Revision (Phoenix Schedule)

(a) Relocations: Relocations are used in DDC to make adjustments in the schedules for accommodating new subjects or shifting of such subjects which differs from the old number in respect other than length. e.g. relocation of cocaine from 362.293 (Ed 19) to 362.298 (ED 20).

(b) Expansions: Expansions are used to indicate further sub-division of a class in the Schedules or Tables. The method of expansion has been accomplished by (a) further extending the existing class numbers; (b) using Add instruction; and (c) with the help of 04 General special concepts, where such new concepts need to be enumerated.

(c) Complete Revision (Phoenix schedule): This is a completely new development of a schedule for a specific disciplines to bring DDC update. Certain schedules, which are out of date and require drastic changes, are replaced with entirely new classifications. The earlier schedules of some one or two major disciplines are destroyed and new schedules are completely recast and their arrangement is remoulded in each of the recent editions of DDC since the sixteenth edition. These new schedules rising out of the ashes of the destroyed old schedules are called phoenix schedules. The policy of integrity of numbers is dispensed with and the entire schedule for a certain discipline or topic is reconstituted without regard to the previous divisions. In recent editions, the following schedules have been given the Phoenix treatment.

546	Inorganic chemistry and 547 Organic chemistry in the 16th edition.
130	Pseudopsychology, Parapsychology (occultism) and 150 Psychology in the 17th edition.
340	Law and 510 Mathematics in the 18th edition.
301–307	Sociology, 324 Political process and- 41 and -42 Area notations for Great Britain.

Developments in DDC

As stated earlier, DDC 1st edition was comprised of only 42 pages which was published in 1876. Since then, DDC has gone through a phases for developments. Until the publication of the 16th editions of Dewey Decimal Classification (DDC) in 1958, different editions were published at infrequent intervals. The 16th edition was edited by Benjamin Custer who set the pattern of a seven-year cycle. In this edition, as attempt was made to reconcile the conflicting aims of integrity of notation and provision of new topics. The 17th edition was published in 1965 in two volumes, viz., V.1. Table; V.2. Area Table and the Relative Index. This edition showed a trend towards more synthesis than earlier editions. The main thrust of the 17th edition was to remove certain anomalies that have crept in between the use of form divisions with zero and division of subjects with the help of zero.

(a) 18th and 19th Editions

The 18th edition published in 1976 was in 3 volumes, viz., V.I. Tables; V.2. Schedules and V.3. Index. For the first time five more auxiliary tables viz., T3. Subdivisions of Individual Literatures. T4. subdivision of Individual Languages. T5. Racial, Ethnic and National Groups, T6. Languages, and T7. Persons were added. These were in addition to the existing T1. Standard Subdivisions and T2. Areas. The 19th edition was published in 1979 in 3 volumes. The policy that was initiated in the 17th edition was also carried out in this edition. The important features we can notice in this edition are: 1. A diagram showing how hierarchical classification proceeds from the general to the specific in DDC; 2. A practical guide to the use of classifications; and 3. A very detailed step-by-step instructions for building numbers in the main class 800 Literature.

(b) 20th and 21st Editions

The 20th edition was published in 1989 in 4 volumes and edited by John P Comaromi et al: V.I. Introduction and Table; V.2. Schedules (000-500), V.3. Schedules (600-900) and V. 4. Relative Index and Manual. The main objectives of this edition are: user convenience, clear instructions, more explanations, greater accessibility through expanded summaries and elimination of duplicate provisions for classifying single subjects.

The 21st edition was published in 1996 in 4 volumes and edited by Joan S. Mitchell et al. The thrust of this volume is users' convenience, which includes; 1. More information located strategically to guide the classifier; 2. Numerous captions have been rewritten to eliminate vague headings; 3,. 'Example' and 'Contain notes' were replaced with 'including notes'; 4. The relative index has more entries than the index to the 20th edition; 5. Expanded manual; and 6. Special attention has been given to reduction of U.S. and Christian bias.

(c) Computerisation of DDC

In July 1988 Forest Press, hitherto the publishers of DDC, became a division of Online Computer Library Center (OCLC). With this change DDC joined the computer generation. Forest Press has been the publisher of DDC since 1911, when Melvil Dewey first used the name as imprint. Until 1988, Forest Press was a part of Lake Placid Educational Foundation, also founded by Dewey. Edition 19 of DDC had been printed from the computer tape in 1979. The following years witnessed the emergence of a sophisticated computer-based editorial support system and database used to produce DDC 20 and 21 editions. DDC 21 appeared in two formats: 1. In print; and 2. Dewey for Windows, a Microsoft Windows TM-based version (released in August 1996) (CD version). Dewey home page contains current information on the Dewey Decimal Classification. It is available on World Wide Web at URL: HTTp://www.oclc.org/ fp/.

Merits and Demerits

The merits of scheme which contribute for it viability and success are :

(i) Its pragmatic or realistic development conjoined with an a posterior molding of a philosophic design, notably purification of the concept of hierarchical subject relationships.

(ii) Its adaptability for use In libraries of various sized and kinds because of its hierarchically expressive notation which permits varying degree of inclusiveness and exclusiveness within its decimal structure.

(iii) Its adaptability both for conventional (manual) shelf or classed catalogue analysis and also through its meaningful notation, for retrieval mechanisation and computerised systems.

(iv) Its thrust towards international perspective both in depth of analysis and its adaptability of application.

(v) Its endorsenent and encouragement of translations.

(vi) Its use by central bibliographic services and the subsequent availability of classification numbers for specific titles.

(vii) The use of mnemonies for common subdivisions, languages, geochemical divisions, literary and language forms and subjects themselves.

(viii) A large amount of scientific detail obtained from specialists or experts.

(xi) The content attention paid to its revision; and,

(x) The very elaborate and systematic relative index.

Demerits

The only demerit of the scheme in that it supports well the western countries and less intention is paid to other countries. As for example in 200.Religion, 220–280 Class Numbers have been retained for the Christianity while other religions of the world are kept in 290. This is some what biased towards westernism. However, this is some what has been removed by reduction of Class Numbers for Christianity in online version.

Use of DDC

Though DDC was criticsed often, it was adopted by libraries rapidly and widely both at home and abroad, Surveys of the use of DDC prove this fact. Its use was so substantial even by 1901 that in that year the American Library Association's Catalog Section voted unanimously that DDC numbers should appear on the ensuing Library of Congress printed catalogue cards. Hence, due to mounting pressures from the profession, an office was established in the Library of Congress in 1930 for assigning DDC numbers to the titles catalogued by the library. Following the LC example, H.W. Wilson Company's Weekly and American Book Publishing Record, and later British National Bibliography's Catalogue Cards and Bibliographies, started providing DDC numbers to specific titles.

As far as India is concerned DDC was introduced in Punjab University Library in 1915 by its Librarian Asa Don Dickinson. Since then most of Indian Libraries are using this and presently in more than 50 percent of the libraries it forms the base of classification schemes.

COLON CLASSIFICATION SCHEME (CC)

Shiyali Ramamrita Ranganathan, a mathematician turned Librarian and the Father of Library Science in India, was the founder of Colon Classification (CC). In 1924 when he was appointed as Librarian of Madras University, one of the conditions of appointment was that he should spend sometime to study library science in England, where he keenly observed the practice followed in more than a hundred libraries. Dissatisfied by DDC and UDC, he began to formulate his own ideas on the subject. One evening, he saw the demonstration of working a Maccano set in Selfridge's Department Store, London, he observed that, by combining a dozen of slotted strips, wheals, nuts and bolts, a number of toys could be made. The idea at once struck to Ranganathan, he thought that the elements constituting a subject could be grouped into few faqcets, which may be combined together by the help of nuts and bolts for which he used a (:) colon. Hence, the scheme later developed by him was called 'Colon Classification'.

By the middle of 1925, few schedules of CC were prepared. After some years of experimentation in Madras University Library, he published the first edition of Colon Classification in 1933. The first edition developed from 1924-1932 was largely based on flair of the author and testing and experimenting of the schedules as well reactions of the users. The main features of this scheme were.

(i) CC introduced the element of notational flexibility which the then existing schemes were lacking by introducing mixed base of Roman capitals and Indo-Arabic numerals for enumerating main classes and their subdivision; Roman smalls for common isolates; : (colon) symbol as a facet indicator and 0 (zero) for phase relation;

(ii) No readymade class numbers were enumerated but class numbers were to be constructed by the combination of appropriate isolate numbers from a set of schedules given for each subject according to a prescribed facet formula. Although the sequence of the facets in the facet formula was largely based on flair and did not have deep roots;

(iii) The technique of faceted classification was introduced by Colon Device. The indicator: (colon) was used to separate different facet numbers. On the basis of this indicator scheme was named as Colon Classification;

(iv) The Bias number Device was used to implement the Phase Relation Device. Upto CC2, only one type of phase relation, that is Bias Phase relation was recognised. For example: BOD Mathematics for Engineers

(v) Separate schedules for common sub-divisions, geographical divisions, chronological divisions and language divisions were provided;

(vi) Octave Notation device was used to secure hospitality in Array;

(vii) Introduced a new method of constructing Book Numbers.

Till its 3rd edition, no changes were made in the scheme. After a lapse of eleven years the third edition of Colon Classification appeared in 1950 without any major modifications. There were, however, a few changes in terminology. The findings of research at Delhi culminated in a dynamic theory of library classification. A major finding was that in any subject there could be only five ingredients. This gave rise to the Postulate of Five Fundamental Categories, which were stated as Personality, Matter, Energy, Space and Time (PMEST). The postulate further stated that these five fundamental categories fall in the sequence of P M E S T. Each fundamental category was assigned an indicator digit (connecting symbol) as shown below:

Fundamental Category	*Indicator Digit*
Personality	, (comma)
Matter	; (semi-colon)
Energy	: (colon)
Space	. (dot)
Time	. (dot)

The indicator digit for *Time* was later changed to a single inverted comma ('). The ordinal value of the connecting symbols was also determined. These findings were included in the fourth edition of Colon Classification (1952) and the second edition of *Prolegomena to Library Classification*, published in 1957.

The fifth edition appeared in the year 1957. The fifth edition had made several changes both in the rules and also in the schedules. Many Greek letters were introduced in the fourth edition to expand the base of the main classes. These were found to be irritants and were replaced in the sixth edition by empty and emptying digits. Some changes were also effected in a few main classes. In addition, the second level of *Space* and *Time* acts was introduced. Meanwhile, the sixth edition of Colon Classification was published in 1960. At about this time, Ranganathan had shifted to Bangalore. A new centre, Documentation Research and Training Centre (DRTC), was established by the Indian Statistical Institute with Ranganathan as its honorary professor. At DRTC, Ranganathan was assisted by a team of researchers. DRTC brought out several special schedules of classification based on the new research findings.

In 1963, a reprint of the sixth edition was published with a few corrections and amendments. At that time an announcement was made that the seventh edition would be brought out incorporating all the new findings. Unfortunately, Ranganathan passes away in 1972 and the work was delayed. The long awaited seventh edition of Colon Classification with substantial changes from the earlier editions appeared in 1987, without an Index.

The 6th edition of Colon published in 1960, is most popular among all the editions and is followed in a number of libraries in India and abroad.

Basic Plan and Structure

The sixth edition divided into three parts as under:

First Part: Its first part contains rules for Classification, Devices used and the meanings of different words.

Second Part: This part has Schedules, Common Isolates, Geographical Division, Language Division and Time Division. Besides, Index is also given.

Third Part : In this part, the schedules on Classical and Sacred Books with ready made numbers are provided.

Main Classes

The number of main classes in this scheme is much than the classes of other schemes in vogue. Dr. Ranganathan has divided the whole universe of Knowledge into four zones. The symbols used for each zone also determined for the classes included in the zones. The main classes can be better understood by the following table.

(Zone)	(Main Classes)	(Notation)
(First Zone)	– Generalia Approach – Main Classes – Generalia Main Classes	Roman Small Alphabets
(Second Zone)	– Recently recognised Main Classes	(Arabic Numberals)
(Third Zone)	– Proper Main Classes	Roman capital Alphabets
(Fourth Zone)	(Newly *emerging Methodologies* and techniques)	Packeted Notation)

In this scheme, main classes are arranged from Abstract to Concreteness. In all four zones, the subjects are divided as follows.

First Zone:

Bibliography	a
Encyclopaedia	k
Periodical	m
Serial	n
Biography	w
Miscellaneous Collection	x

Second Zone:

Universe of Knowledge	1
Library Science	2
Book-Science	3
Journalism	4

Third Zone :

Natural Science	A
Mathematical Science	AZ
Mathematics	B

Physical Science	BZ
Physics	C
Engineering	D
Chemistry	E
Technology	F
Biology	G
Geology	H
Mining	HX
Botany	I
Agriculture	J
Zoology	K
Animal Husbandry	KX
Medicine	L
Pharmacognosy	LX
Usèful Arts	M
Humanities & Social Sciences	MZ
Humanities	MZA
Spiritual Experience & Mysticism	Δ
Fine Arts	N
Literature & Language	NZ
Literature	O
Linguistics	P
Religion	Q
Philosophy	R
Psychology	S
Social Sciences	SZ
Education	T
Geography	U
History	V
Political Science	W
Economics	X
Sociology	Y

Social Work YZ

Law Z

Fourth Zone :

Criticism Technique (g)

Conference Technique (p)

Administrative Report Technique (r)

In each Main Class, following points are most important.

1. The name of Main Class along with its Class Number for e.g., B for Mathematics.
2. Facet Formula, on the basis of which one can know the facets to be used along with Main Class. For example,

   2(P) ; (M) : (E) (2P)

   That is, this class will include Personality, Matter and Energy. As the Space and Time Facets can be used with any Main Class, hence the formula for these facets is not given under main class.
3. Facets.
4. Schedules, in which subjects for each Class and Sub-class are given.

Five Fundamental Categories

There are five fundamental categories (FC), viz., personality [P], matter [M], Energy [E], space [S], and Time [T], PMEST for short. As these categories are to be determined on certain features in which Personality indentifies at last so each in discusses in reverse order.

Time and Space: These two have the usual meaning known to any body. A century, a decade, a year, a month, a day, an hour are all indicators of time. If the subject is stated as Economic conditions of India in the 19th century, one can identify the time element in it. In some subjects, it may bot be stated explicitly, e.g., Economic condition during the reign of Akbar. In this example, the fundamental category time is concealed, but still identifiable.

In the same way, it is fairly simple to locate the space element in a subject. In the above title, Economic conditions of India in the 19th Century, one can find the space facet, i.e., India. Space is indicated by terms like continent, country, city, village, etc. All these come under the facet space.

Energy: The next fundamental category is Energy. Energy refers to some type of action. In the subject medicine, Diagnosis or Treatment falls under the facet Energy. It shows action. In agriculture, ploughing is Energy, in education teaching is Energy, and in sociology relief work is Energy and so on.

Matter: There is a major change in he seventh edition of CC in the case of the fundamental category matter. Up to the sixth edition, Matter was present only in a few main classes. There is a complete reversal in the seventh edition. In certain cases, what was considered Energy now forms part of the Matter facet. Besides, the fundamental category Matter has undergone some other changes. It is distinguished as Matter Property [MP], Matter Material [MM] and Matter Method [MM].

It is only Matter property, which has almost replaced the fundamental category Energy. To explain matter with a concrete example, in the class medicine, anatomy, physiology and diseases are viewed as manifestations of matter property. Similarly, in the main class agriculture, soil, manure, propagation, etc. are treated as manifestations of matter property. In the main class fine arts, under the class drawing, pencil drawing, ink drawing, and cartoon drawing are considered as a manifestation of matter method. In technology, product, and in biology substance are manifestation of matter material.

Hence, in a given subject, it is not difficult to recognise the fundamental categories of Time, Space, Energy and Matter.

Personality: The fundamental category Personality has evaded definition. Ranganathan found a way out to recognise personality by the method of residue, i.e., when it cannot be any other fundamental category it is assigned to personality. However, experience in the design of depth schedules suggests that it is possible to identify a core concept in compound subjects going with a basic subject, such as, 'Human Body' in Medicine. Such a core concept is deemed to be a manifestation of 'Personality'.

Rounds and Levels

Having identified five fundamental categories, it was found that some of them manifest themselves more than once in a subject, for example personality, matter and energy. This phenomenon was handled by the introduction of the postulates of rounds and levels. Take, for instance, a subject like Treatment of Brain Tumour by Radium Therapy. In this, we have the fundamental categories brain [P], tumour [M], treatment [E], and radium therapy [E]. Energy (E), thus, repeats itself. Such repetition of any of the three (P, M and E) fundamental categories is called round of fundamental category. These rounds are indicated as [1P1], [2P1], [1E], [2E], [1M1], [2M1] and so on.

Postulates of Facet Sequence

After five fundamental categories, their founds and levels, the next question that arises is in what order these are to be arranged. For this, Ranganathan has given five postulates followed by some principles along with them.

(i) **Postulate of first facet:** In any compound subject, the first facet should be the basic facet. It simply means that there should be a basic class or main class even if it is not stated explicitly in the title of the document. For example, if we take treatment of cancer as our subject, the basic facet is not stated. But, by implication, the basic facet in this case is medicine.

(ii) **Postulate of concreteness :** The five fundamental categories apper in the sequence of P M E S T only. This means they appear in the order of their decreasing concreteness. To explain this with an example, let us take a subject like Prevention of Fungus Diseases in Oranges in Nagpur. Here, apart from supplying the basic facet we have to find out other fundamental categories and arranged them in the sequence of PMEST. Obviously, agriculture is the basic facet and the other fundamental categories are oranges [P], prevention [E], fungus diseases [M], and Nagpur [S]. To put them in order, according to the postulate, it will be.

(Basis facet)	[P]	[M]	[E]	[S]
Agriculture	Oranges	Fungus Diseases	Prevention	Nagpur

(iii) **Postulate of facet sequence within a round:** In a compound subject, if any P, M and E occur in any round, they should be arranged in the order of P, M, E. For example, Preparation of Soil for growing Grapes has agriculture as the basic facet, preparation as the energy facet, soil as the matter facet and grapes as the personality facet. As per the postulate, the sequence of the facets will be:

Agriculture (BF), Grapes [P], Soil [M], and Preparation [E]. This postulate is known as the postulate of facet sequence within a round.

(iv) **Postulate of facet sequence within the last round:** The fourth postulate states that in the last round of facets of a compounds subject, in which each of the fundamental categories other than energy may occur, and occur only once, the sequence of facets should be P,M, S and T. Take, for instance, a title like A study of the emotions of Adults in 20th century in USA. Here the basic facet is psychology and the other facets are emotions (matter), adults (personality), 20th century (time) and USA (space). In this, there is no manifestation of energy. Hence, as stated in the postulate, the sequence should be:

Psychology (BF), adults [P], Emotions [M], USA [S], 20th century [T].

(v) **Postulate of level cluster:** The last postulate for the sequence of facets states that different levels of the same fundamental category within a round should be kept together. Take an example like Succession Rights of Minors in Hindu Law. In this, the facets, succession, minor and Hindu law are all manifestations of personality. When arranged, they will be Law (BF), Hindu law [1P1], Minor [1P2], and Succession [IP3].

Common Isolates

There are five types of isolates used in scheme. These are:

1. Anteriorising Common Isolates
   a. Anteriorising Common Isolate (Applicable only before Space Facet)
   b. Anteriorising Common Isolate (Applicable only after Space Facet)
   c. Anteriorising Common Isolate (Applicable only after Time Facet)
2. Posteriorising Common Isolates
   a. Posteriorising Energy Common Isolates
   b. Posteriorising Matter Common Isolates
   c. Posteriorising Personality Common Isolates

3. Time Isolate
4. Space Isolate
5. Language Isolate

Devices used

For classifying Classes and micro-classification, the following devices are used in the scheme:

1. Geographical Device
2. Chronological Device
3. Subject Device
4. Alphabetical Device

These devices are used to sharpen an existing isolate in array. The new subjects can also be accommodated using these devices.

1. **Chronological Device:** The purpose of this device is to sharpen a facet number. It can sharpen an isolate or form a new isolate. This is done by employing a chronological number from the schedule of time isolates. All numbers for authors in the class Literature are derived through this device. It is impracticable to enumerate all authors. The chronological device has, however, taken care of such a contingency. To give an example, the number for Rabindranath Tagore is O, 157, 1M61. Here, M61 stands for 1861, the year of birth of Rabindranath Tagore. This device has been used in several main classes like library science, mathematics, medicine, fine arts, psychology, education, economics, etc. This device can be used wherever warranted. The basic class of systems is derived through the chronological device.
2. **Geographical Device:** The purpose of all these devices, as stated earlier, is to form or to sharpen an isolate number in a schedule. Employing a geographical number from the schedule of space isolates is another mechanism of doing this. It has been used in library science, fine arts, religion, linguistics, history and in several other classes. The formation of an isolate using this device is as follows:

   152=d4437 means Rajasthani Hindi, where

   152 is Hindi

   = is the connecting symbol

d is the symbol for dialect

4437 is Rajasthan from the schedule of space isolates.

3. **Subject Device :** Subject device is used to form or sharpen a facet by adding to it (facet) another class number from elsewhere in the scheme. This device has been used in several main classes. The part of the number derived by the subject device should be enclosed in parenthesis (circular brackets).

   For example:

   Medical College Library is 2,J3 (L)

   In the above example, in library science, 2,J3 represents college libraries to which is added (L) from the main class L Medicine to derive medical college library by subject device.

4. **Alphabetical Device :** Alphabetical device is also used to form or sharpen an isolate number. The device is used taking the first or the first two or three letters of the names of persons, or objects, or products widely accepted as such. The device can be used wherever warranted. The following are some examples where the device is used:

O,157,3M61,G	Gora, a novel by Rabindranath Tagore Here, G stands for Gora
O,157,3M61, H+W	Home and the world, a novel by Tagore. Here, the initial letters of the two words in the title are connected, using the plus sign (+). (H for Home and W for World).

Phase Relation

Phase analysis is a useful concept developed by the Colon Classification, for the universe of knowledge, which is growing continuously and infinitely, as a result of interdisciplinary researches. A subject can be studied in relation to other subjects. This relationship between two or more distinct subjects is called phase relation and the analysis of any specific subject into various phases is called 'Phase analysis'. In a two phased subject, the subject which is the primary subject of exposition is called first phase and the subject which is the primary subject of exposition of the first phase is called second phase. In phase relation, original subject is studied by linking with other subjects from rest of the general classification. Thus, phase relation is linking together different classes. This is achieved by the process of assembling together of two or more basic subjects or compounds subjects. This mode of formation of subject shows relation of a subject with another subject or its subdivisions. Each component in the loose assemble is called a "phase" which indicates relations.

Dr. Ranganathan has described following types of Phase Relation:

1. Inter-Subject Phase Relation
2. Intra-Facet Phase Relation
3. Intra Array Phase Relation

Each of them is further sub-divided into five types viz.,

1. General
2. Bias
3. Comparison
4. Difference and
5. Influence

The levels and kinds of phase relations can better be understood as following:

Levels of Phase Relations	*Kinds of Phase relation*					
	General	*Bias*	*Comparison*	*Difference*	*Tool*	*Influencing*
Inter subject phase relation	a	b	c	d	e	f
Intra-facet phase relation	j	k	m	n	p	r
Intra-Array phase relation	t	u	v	w	x	y

The connecting symbol used to connect two subjects or show relation in between to subject is 0 (zero).

Notation

This scheme has used mixed notation. It consists of :

1. Indo-Arabic numerals, 1-9

2. Roman alphabet – both capitals and lower case, A to Z and a to z.
3. Parentheses ()
4. Indicator digits

The following table gives the details o the indicator digits used in the 7th edition of CC.

Digit/ symbol	*Name of the indicator digit*	*Role of the indicator digit*
*	Asterisk	indicates agglomerating and interpolation
←	Backward arrow	indicates backward range
"	Double inverted comma	indicates common isolates
&	Ampersand	indicates phase relation
'	Single inverted comma	indicates time facet
.	Dot	indicates space facet
:	Colon	indicates energy facet
;	Semi-colon	indicates matter facet
,	Comma	indicates personality facet
-	Hyphen	indicates speciator of kind 1
=	Equal sign	indicates speciator of kind 2
+	Plus sign	and, addition
→	Forward arrow	Indicates forward range

For the arrangement of the class numbers, all the notations and digits used in the scheme have been given values, and, in the ascending sequence, they stand in the following order:

) & ' . ; : , - = → a to z 01 to 9 A to Z

*(asterisk), + (plus), "(double inverted comma) and ← (backward arrow) have anteriorising value.

Besides this, the various tables and schedules for Book Numbers and Collection Numbers are also provided.

Systems and Special

Up to the sixth edition of CC, systems and specials were enumerated along with the concerned main classes. In the seventh edition, they have been listed in the schedule of basic subjects. However, they have been separately defined.

Systems: The term *system basic subjects* denotes a division of main class expounded after a school of thought. A school of thought is a group, or succession of persons devoted to some cause or philosophy. The class number for a system is derived by the chronological device. Some examples of system facets are:

B6-M8	Hyperbolic geometry, where B6 is geometry and M8 means the 1880s. The number stands for a system of geometry expounded in the 1880s.
L-B	Ayurveda. B is 999 to 1000 BC – a system of medicine that came into being prior to 1000 BC.
S-N14	Individualistic psychology. It means a school of psychology that came into being in 1914.
X-N1	Communism. The number stands for a system of economics that came into being in the 1910s.

Specials: The term *special basic subject* denotes a division of a main class in which the subject of study is restricted in some special manner. The class number of specials are derived by enumeration. Some of the examples of special basic subject are:

G-9Up	–	Marine biology
J-9B	–	Dry farming
L-9C	–	Child medicine
S-9XX	–	Industrial psychology

Index

In the sixth edition of the scheme, Index is provided from page number 126 to 172 in alphabetical order. The Index to Geographical Division, Botany and Life Sciences are provided along with the schedules in its second part. These Indexed are arranged in alphabetical orders. The Index is not of relative type but is of special type. Besides, the Indexes to Classics and Sacred Books are provided.

Salient Features of the Scheme

The most important features of the schemes are summarized below:

1. **Analytico-Synthetic Scheme:** This is Analytico-Synthetic Scheme, in which the ready-made numbers like that of DDC are not given but they are to be synthesized. Firstly, the Title is analyzed, then their facets are identified and the numbers from the schedules are collected and added as per the formula given with the main class. The whole process of analyzing a subject completes in nine steps.
2. **Five Fundamentals Categories:** This classification scheme is based on Five Fundamental Categories. The subject are analyzed on the basis of these fundamental categories and a fix-sequence is obtained for the subjects described under each main class.
3. **Round and Levels:** This scheme is also related with the Round and Levels. The Round means the appearance of a facet more than once in a category. similarly. The apearande of a facet more than once with in a facet is known as Level.
4. **Mixed Notation :** As stated earlier, this scheme is represented by mixed notation i.e., more than two types of the symbols are used in the scheme. This scheme is made by using 10 Indo-Arabic Numerals, 26 Roman Capital Letters, 23 Small Roman Létters, Greek Symbol Delta (Δ), Small Bracket (), Punctuation Mark and Forward and Backward Arrows, etc.
5. **Mnemonics:** The provision of mnemonics is also made in the scheme for the better use by the Classifier. The same symbols etc. are used denoting similar thought contents. The provision of mnemonics helps a classifier in getting autonomy and independency in deriving the class numbers.
6. **System and Specials :** The provisions of System and Specials is also made in the scheme, which is not seen in the other schemes of the library classification. System means is to traditional origin and evolution of an ideology. Similarly, Specials are used to classify a subject in micro-level based on the characteristics of the object.

7. **Devices:** Using various devices of the scheme, depth class may be provided to a document. The devices helps a Classifier to get autonomy. The following devices are used in the scheme.
   (i) Chronological Device
   (ii) Subjects Device
   (iii) Geographical Device
   (iv) Alphabetical Device
   (v) Super-imposition Device
   (vi) Mnemonics and
   (vii) Favoured Category Device
8. **Phase Relation :** In this classification scheme, the provision of showing the relation between two subjects is given by using Phase Relations. A table is given showing various types of the relations along with their symbols used. With the help of these symbols, the relation between two subjects can be established. Mainly, there are three types of the relation found:
   (i) Intra Subject Phase Relation.
   (ii) Intra Facet Relation and.
   (iii) Intra Array Phase Relation.
9. **Common Isolates :** The various isolates given in the scheme, may be used with any of the main class. Two types of Common Isolates are found in the scheme viz., Anteriorising Common Isolates and Posteriorising Common Isolates. The detailed tables are provided for use of these isolates in the scheme.
10. A ready-made schedule is provided for the class numbers for Classic Books and Sacred Books.
11. Hospitality in array and chain is provided well.
12. This scheme provides complete autonomy to the Classifier to classify a document to its micro-level.
13. This classification scheme is fully un-biased and unfavoured scheme.
14. The formula for Book Numbers and the Collection Numbers is provided in the scheme. Moreover, the Book Number is treated as a part of the Class Number in this scheme.

Drawbacks

The major drawback of CC is that there exists no machinery to keep up the revision work as in the case of DDC and UDC. The guidance provided in the recently published seventh edition is not enough and lacks clarity at places. It calls for a manual with numerous examples to explain the application of various rules. And above all, it is far from simple, the virtue most cherished by the users.

Developments in CC

The 7th edition of CC was published in 1987. It was proposed to be brought out in 3 volumes, viz., V.1 Schedules for Classification; V.2 and 3. Index and Worked-out Examples. But only V.1 Schedules for Classification was bought out in 1987. The other two volumes have not seen the light of day.

In this edition, in addition to existing indicator digits in the 6th edition (1960), a few more indicator digits, viz., & (ampersand), + (plus) = (equals), *(asterisk) and " (double inverted comma) have been added. The fundamental category Matter [M] has been transformed into Matter Method [MM], Matter property (MP) and Matter Material (MMt). This edition also provided for environmental divisions (chapter DD). The schedules of Basic Subjects have been greatly expanded. It also provides for Common Matter Property solates. The schedules for Language, Time and Space have been greatly expanded.

The major changer which occur in 7th edition, are:

(a) The number of Main Subjects/Basic Subjects has been increased in edition 7. This has been done in several ways:

   (i) Some old Main Subjects and some new Main Subjects have been divided into canonical divisions, e,g., 3 Book Science, 9 Research Technique.

   (ii) In some subjects, [1P1] isolates have been treated as canonical division, e.g., Engineering, Technology, Geography, Economics.

   (iii) In "X Economics", some of the [E] isolates have been changed into canonical divisions.

   (iv) A new kind of formation of subjects -- agglomeration (Subject Bundles) -- has been added as Canonical Division.

   (v) Systems have been changed into Basic Subjects.

(vi) Specials have been changed into Basic Subjects.

(vii) Environmental Device has been provided to indicate environment treatment of a Basic Subject, as a kind of specials.

(viii) Compound Basic Subjects --- using the System part, Specials part, and Canonical Division part as its components.

(b) The indicator Digit "(double inverted comma) is used to indicate an "Anteriorsing Isolate", instead of Roman Small letters as was done in edition 6.

(c) Edition 7 includes Common Fundamental Category Isolates -- for [E], [MP], and [P].

(d) New indicator digit "&" (ampersand) is used in place of old indicator digit "0" (zero) for Phase Relation.

(e) Change of some [E] isolates into [MP] isolates, e.g., B23 Theory of Equation, C7 Magnetism, J Agriculture, JX forestry, KX Animal Husbandry, etc. (All [E] Isolates).

(f) Change of [E] cum [2P] isolates into MP Isolates e.g., 2 Library Science, C3 Sound, G Biology, L Medicine, P Linguistics, Y Sociology, etc.

(g) Change of [2E] isolates into [1E] Isolates, e.g., J Agriculture.

(h) Breaking of [2E] cum [3P] Isolates into [E] Isolates and [2P] Isolates (Currently) [P] isolates are treated as spectators).

(i) Change of Facet Structure -- a facet formula is in a sense meaningless; it is an anachronism.

(j) Indicator Digit ","(comma) should be inserted before Level 1 of [P] facet in any Round in any subject.

These changes would involve a little amount of correction work as far as the documents already classified by edition 6. Perhaps the Principle of Osmosis can be applied in the context of reclassification.

Computerisation of CC

The developments in Case Western Reserve University, Ohio, indicate the influence of facet analysis. Dr. Fugman (ISKO,Germany) used facet analysis in his chemical analysis system. Facet analysis is also used for shelving purposes in on-line information search. Syracuse University, New York, was using PMEST in their computer-generated indexes.

In India, DRTC in 1967 wrote some computer programmes based on facet analysis and tried to experiment with the use of CC in computers to construct class numbers. CC was also used in computer programming for SDI services and for chain indexing and cyclic indexing. The Western Ontario (Canada) School of Library and Information Science used CC Schedules for developing a thesaurus. In 1968, DRTC initiated experiments to determine the feasibility of using general purpose computers in a document-finding system based on a classified catalogue system using a freely-faceted version of CC.

UNIVERSAL DECIMAL CLASSIFICATION (UDC)

The UDC was developed in 1895 by Paul Outlet and Henri Fontaine taking the DDC as its base. Their efforts resulted in the publication of a scheme called Manuel du Repertoire Universel Bibliographique, an almost-faceted scheme which involved adopting the almost-enumerative classification into one which allows synthesis. It is a bibliographic classification available in three versions:

Full edition	2,21,000 terms
Medium edition	70,000 (30% of the full edition)
Abridged edition	20,000 (10% of the full edition)

English edition is published by the British Standards Institution as BS:1000. The first edition of UDC, called, Handbook to the Universal Bibliographic Repertory, came out in 1904. So far as many as six editions have been published. The latest sixth edition known as UDC: International Medium Edition is in two parts. Part one dealing with systematic tables and schedules was published in 1985 and part two Index was published in 1988.

Basic Plan and Stricture

The UDC scheme which was initially based on DDC 5 (1884) was transformed in a universal general classification scheme by interpolating and adding auxiliary tables, signs and symbols. The main objective of the designer of DDC was to provide a method for shelf arrangement, whereas UDC was designed to classify all the information published in micro and macro literature.

There are two kinds of tables in UDC, which contain the total classification: the main tables and the auxiliary tables. The main tables are also called schedules and represent the enumerative aspect of UDC. The auxiliary tables give the analytico-synthetic character to the scheme.

(i) Main Tables

UDC, like DDC, regards the whole field of human knowledge as unity, i.e., one, which is divided into ten broadest classes denoted by decimal fractions. These ten broad classes are:

0	Generalities. Science and Knowledge, Organisation, Information, etc.
1	Philosophy, Psychology
2	Religion. Theology
3	Social Science, Economics, Law, Government..., etc.
4	Vacant
5	Mathematics and Natural Sciences
6	Applied Sciences, Medicine, Technology
7	The arts. Recreation, Entertainment, Sport
8	Language, Linguistics, Literature
9	Geography, Biography, History

For the sake of convenience, the initial decimal point is omitted. So 0 is just 0 and 1 is just 1 and so on. Class 4 was cancelled in 1963 to make room for future development and the original subject linguistics (class 4) was merged with class 8 in literature.

The main numbers and their sub-divisions are divided by continuous extension of the decimal fractions, on the principle of proceeding from general to particular in the following manner:

3	Social sciences
30	Sociology
31	Statistics
34	Law, Jurisprudence
340	Law in general
340.1	Types and forms of law
5.5.5	Legal relationship

The practice of DDC to use a dot after every third digit has been retained in UDC also. However, it has been clearly stated in the

Introduction that 'a point has been introduced between the third and fourth digits, but it is not a decimal point; it is merely punctuation for ease of readings.'

(ii) Auxiliary Tables

The auxiliary tables have alienated UDC from DDC, moulded it into a faceted scheme and provided a powerful synthetic apparatus. The introduction of an auxiliary apparatus of connection and relation signs, lacking in the original Dewey system, has made the UDC really universal, in the sense that it permits almost any desired combination and modification of basic numbers to denote the most complex subject.

UDC has developed two kind of auxiliaries: common and special. These auxiliaries are considered UDC's most innovative and influential feature. It is with the help of these auxiliary notations that compound numbers are constructed. A compound number is always constructed by synthesizing elements from more than one place in the tables. For example, we saw two numbers in our discussion on the class, *Generalities.* They are:

1.1	Encyclopaedia Britannica
02(031)	Encyclopaedia of Librarianship

The 030.1 is a simple number taken from one place from the *Generalities* table whereas 02 (031) is a compound number, as the two elements 02 *Librarianship* and (031) encyclopaedia are taken from two separate tables, viz., *Generalities* and *Common auxiliaries.* This second number represents synthesis.

(A) Common Auxiliaries : The Common Auxiliaries are applicable throughout the Main Tables and provide means of expressing interreations between subjects. These help in eliminating repetition of one and the same concept in the main tables. These auxiliaries denote recurring concepts such as language, form, place and time. The common auxiliaries may be divided into two types on the basis of the use of symbols:

- The signs
- The sub-divisions

(a) The signs : The symbols or indicators which help to relate or link two UDC numbers either from main tables or from auxiliary tables are termed as auxiliary *signs.* These are just connecting symbols and do not represent any idea or concept. Such auxiliary signs are: the plus, the stroke, the colon, the square brackets and the double colons.

(*a*) *The Plus sign* + (To add non-consecutive numbers)

The plus sign may be used to connect two or more separated (non-consecutive) UDC numbers especially when these denote commonly associated concepts or the same broad subject in different aspects, for which no single number exists.

Examples:

Main Tables

622 + 669	Mining and Metallurgy
Auxiliary Table	
(42 + 540)	United Kingdom and India
(540 + 510 + 520)	India, China and Japan

(*b*) *The stroke sign/* (to add Consecutive numbers)

When a document covers a broad subject or range of concepts for which numbers in UDC are enumerated consecutively, then the extension sign '/' (stroke) may be used to connect the first and the last numbers from the sequence of the consecutive numbers.

Examples :

Main Tables

624/628	Civil Engineering
which is equivalent to	624+625+626+627+628
Auxiliary Table time	
15/19	Sixteenth to twentieth century
which is equivalent to	1500+1600+1700+1800+1900

(*c*) *Relation sign:* (colon sign) (indicates relations)

Colon sign is the most important sign among all other common auxiliary signs. Colon sign may be used to indicate all types of *relationships* between two subjects.

However, it cannot differentiate the type of relationships as is possible in Colon Classification. It means when UDC numbers are linked by colon sign, it merely indicates that these subjects are related to each other in some way and are treated as of equal significance.

Examples :

Main Table

22/28 : 294.3	Influence of Buddhism on Christianity

635.5 : 632.38 Viral diseases of Salad Plants

Auxiliary Table Space

33 (540 : 549) Economic Development in India and Pakistan –a comparative study

The numbers may be *reversed* as per demands of the library, e.g.

294.3 : 22/28 632.38 : 635.5

33 (549 : 540)

This helps the library to prepare multiple entries for one and the same document to facilitate users service.

(d) *Square Brackets [ ] :* In abridged English edition 1961, the sign [] (square brackets) is used 'when the relationship involves a subordinate concept for which no separate entry in required by reversal, square brackets, or (()) on typewriters, may be used in place of the colon, e.g. 620.174 [669.14] Material testing – bend tests [for steel].

With the help of intercalation device this sign also allowed alternative groupings e.g.

620.1 [669.14] 74

However, in *International Medium Edition,* 1985. 'Square brackets [] may be used as an algebraic *sub-grouping device* when two or more main UDC members are linked by a plus sign or colon to denote a complex subject which is as a whole related to another by colon, or modified by a common or special auxiliary e.g.

[622+669] (485) : 31	Statistics of
or	or Mining and
31 : [622+669] (485)	Metallurgy in Sweden

It means

(i) if the class number for a complex subject is to be devised by connecting various UDC numbers by colon or plus sign, e.g.

63+66 (544.6) Agriculture and Chemical industries in Rajasthan

(ii) and this number is to be added to another number by colon, e.g.

33:61+66(544.6) Statistics of Agriculture and Chemical Industries in Rajasthan

(iii) to make the meaning of the numbers of subordinate concepts devised by plus symbol more specific and indicative, may be kept within square brackets e.g.

31 : [61 + 66] (544.6)

(e) *Double Colon :* In the IME 1985 the sign :: (double colon) has also been introduced which is used to *fix the order* of component numbers in a compound number, especially when UDC is used in a computer based mechanical information system. However, when double colon is used reversing or cycling of entries is not permitted as is in single colon sign, e.g.

641.3 : 631.26 (026) Or 631.26 : 641.3 (026)

In double Colon the position of concepts as expressed in thought content is retained, which is not possible if reversed entries are allowed.

The sub-divisions

The common auxiliary sub-divisions consist of numberic tables in which concepts are enumerated and arranged hierarchically as is in the main tables. Each auxiliary sub-divisions have their own distinct symbols which are their identifiers. These symbols are prefixed to the number, or they enclose the number once in the scheme in order that they may be taken out and attached where they are required. The common auxiliary subdivisions, thus, facilitate synthesis and create mnemonics. The symbols that are associated with them can be taken as facet indicators, e.g. parenthesis indicating the space facet and quotation marks revealing the time facet.

There are two groups of the common auxiliary sub-divisions: the independent and the dependent auxiliary tables.

The Common auxiliary tables of language form place, race and time are treated as independent auxiliary tables. The sub-divisions of these auxiliary tables may be affixed to any UDC number or may be used independently to constitute the whole number of a document. This is because of their symbols, which is either prefixed to or enclose the number. These independent common auxiliary sub-divisions may be under stand as:

	As independent	As dependent	
Language-	=30 German language	622=30	documents in German about Mining

Form (0...)	(043.2)54 Theses in Chemistry with other Theses	54(043.2)	Theses in Chemistry kept along with other Chemistry Books
Place (1/9)	(73)339.5.053 USA, Trade Balance (area studies)	339.5.053(73)	Economics
Race (=...)	(=97)39 North American Folklore (under race)	39(=97)	Folklore
Time "..."	"18"785.7 19th Century Chamber Music (under century)	785.7"18"	Music

Dependent Common Auxiliary Subdivisions

The subdivisions of dependent auxiliary tables are always added to main UDC numbers. Such tables are 1 (i) Common auxiliaries of Point of view; 1 (k) –03 and 1(k)-05 auxiliaries of Materials and of Persons and Personal characterisitics-tables added in IME 1985.

In IME 1985, the classifier has been advised to reduce full name to a standard length abbreviation, as it would be convenient both to him and the use.

Table 1(i) Common Auxiliaries of Point of View

Symbol.00 (point nought)

The sub-division of Common auxiliaries of point of view helps to indicate the specific point of view from which the thought content of the document may be considered. These are added to main UDC numbers and are never used alone. It has been advised to use point of view numbers only when expression of the point of view facet is needed to achieve a satisfactory filing order, e.g.

666.3003.3 Accounting point of view of ceramics industry.

Table 1(k-03) Common Auxiliaries of Materials

Symbol-03 (hyphen nought 3)

This table is a new addition in IME 1985. The subdivisions of this table denote the materials or the constituents of which objects or products are made. These are applicable to the main UDC numbers when the material aspect is secondary to the subject. However, these sub-divisions are specifically required by most of the subjects enumerated in the main classes 66/67 chemical technology and various other industries dealing with manufacturing and processing.

Composite materials may be denoted by apostrophe combination, in which the apostrophe replaces –03 in the second and subsequent component number, e.g.

–036.674	Polyester and Glass Fibre
–037.52	Artificial Mineral Fibres, Glass Fibres
–036.674'752	Polyester and Glass Fibres.

Table 1(k) –05 Common Auxiliaries of Persons and Personal Characteristics

Symbol – 05 (hyphen nought five)

For – 05 persons a special auxiliary table is provided in the main class 3 Social Sciences in AbE1961. This table consists of hardly 13 sub-divisions. In IME 1985, a Common Auxiliaries of Persons and Personal Characteristics has been added and all the sub-divisions of AbE 1961 have been included in this common auxiliary table, in which the sub-divisions for persons and personal characteristics are extensively provided for. A small table of abridged edition has been transformed in a useful common auxiliary table.

Examples :

294.5-05 Hindus

347.96-055.2 Female Lawyers

(B) Special Auxiliaries

Unlike the common auxiliary sub-divisions which represent subordinate ideas recurring in every discipline and subjects, the special auxiliary sub-divisions are limited in their scope and are used to denote recurrent concepts in that part of the main table for which the table is designed and scheduled. The common auxiliaries sub-divisions may be added to any main UDC number or even to another auxiliary table numbers, without any change in its meaning, that is, the same idea same number is used. Whereas special auxiliary table, as its name indicates enumerates sub-divisions which are specialized and limited in their scope as their use is restricted to a particular main class or to a specific section of the main table for which these are specifically designed. The following three indicators are used for special auxiliaries:

(i) – (hyphen)

(ii) .0 (point nought); and

(iii) ‘ (apostrophe)

The hypen series: -1/-9 serving to indicate elements, components, properties and other details of the subject denoted by the main number to which they apply. For example, the series 62-1/-9, applicable throughout 62/69, denotes engineering and mechanical details.

The point-nought series: .01/.09 denoting aspect studies, activities, processes, operations, plant and equipment. For example, 3.07/.8 means authorities and personnel in authorities.

The apostrophe series : ‘1/9’, unlike the hyphen and point-nought series, these are synthetic and integrative in function and denote compound subjects. They are at places fully listed, but elsewhere are derived through the UDC’s device of parallel division. For example.

329,17’23’12 Nationalist-Republican-Liberal parties
(synthesis of 329,17,329.23 and 329.12)

Special auxiliaries may be used singly, or in combination with other auxiliaries:

329.052 Opposition parties

And

320.053.52 Opposition splinter parties

Alphabetical Subject Index

The second part of UDC (1985) i.e., an alphabetic subject index was published in 1988. It is a computer generated index, produced by permutation of terms, taken from Part I Systematic Tables. The arrangement is word-by-word. As the croos references were completely eliminated from the index a large number of synonymous terms were included therein. One example is given below:

Lighters 629,123,15,662.58

Cigar and cigarette 662.592

Electric 662.593

Flint 662.592

Pocket 662.59

Using solar heat 662.591

Sailent Feature of the scheme

The sailent teathres of UDC may be summarized as follows:

(i) **Notation :** The UDC notation consists of the following sets of symbols:

(a) The ten Indo-Arabic numberals: 0, 1 to 9

(b) The Roman alphabets both capital and lower case.

(c) Punctuation marks like point, semi-colon, colon and inverted commas.

(d) Mathematical signs; the plus and the equals.

(e) Besides these, it includes parentheses, square brackets, the stroke and the apostrophe.

The use of different signs and symbols have added following qualities to the notation of UDC

(i) Use of mixed notation has helped UDC in alienating itself from DDC;

(ii) It has given the UDC a faceted structure;

(iii) Besides, the decimal fraction device which provides hospitality in chain, the auxiliary apparatus, the parallel division device and final digit device have increased the capacity of UDC to provide hospitality to subjects for which no class numbers are enumerated in UDC;

(iv) Flexibility in notation has been achieved by the use of distinct signs and symbols and the intercalation device which permits some of the auxiliaries to be affixed at any part of the UDC number;

(v) Mnemonic quality has also been provided by the auxiliary tables and parallel divisions;

(vi) Moreover, the library can choose a citation order useful to the library. The suggested filing order is not mandatory.

However, two main defects created in the notation of UDC are:

(i) extensive use of synthesis results in long numbers;

(ii) Uniqueness of class numbers not possible as UDC allows alternative call number.

(ii) **Hospitality :** As the UDC notation consists of numbers, which are taken as decimal fractions, it can accommodate emerging new ideas, where appropriate, *ad infinitum*. This is so in the case of not only main numbers but auxiliaries as well. The notation is, thus, hospitable and capable of reaching the required level of detail. Since it is hierarchic, moving from the general to the particular, it expresses the order of classes. For example:

6	Technology
62	Engineering
621	Mechanical Engineering.... Electrical Engineering, Machinery
621.3	Electrical engineering
621.39	Telecommunication, Telecontrol
621.396	Radiocommunication Apparatus and Methods (Radio).
621.396.7	Radio Stations

At any place in this hierarchic chain any new concept can be accommodated without disturbing the order of existing concepts. The division on the basis of decreasing extension clearly expresses the order of classes in the hierarchy.

(iii) **Facetisation and Synthesis:** Every recurrent category is a facet and the best example of facetisation is presented by its tables of common auxiliaries. The UDC's citation order for facets is flexible to a great extent. It also uses a device called intercalation to change, as required, the citation order of facets with a view to create a more helpful sequence. The UDC is, therefore, a faceted classification.

It is also a highly synthetic scheme. Ordinarily, every faceted scheme is synthetic in structure. However, in addition to facetisation in the form of common auxiliary subdivisions, UDC also contains a number or other synthetic devices such as:

1. The use of signs (+ , / ; ; [], ::) to connect two or more numbers.
2. The use of the apostrophe (') in special auxiliaries.
3. The facility to combine, in a single number, two special auxiliaries.

In short, if the main tables of UDC display its hierarchical enumerative character, the auxiliary tables represent its faceted and synthetic structure.

(iv) **Intercalation :** Intercalation is the use of the auxiliary as an infix, Generally, an auxiliary is prefixed or suffixed to a main number. In UDC, it can also be infixed to interrupt a main number. This, at time, becomes necessary to provide an alternative approach. For example:

622	Mining
622(410)	Mining in Britain
622.333	Mining of Coal
622.333(410)	Mining of Coal in Britain
622.34	Mining of Metal Ores
622.33 (410)	Mining of Metal Ores in Britain

In the above arrangement, the books about mining in Britain get scattered throughout the class Mining. Ideally, if required, all books on British mining should be brought together. It is possible to bring them together, if the auxiliary number for space in the above case in used as an infix and allowed to interrupt the main number as follows:

622

622(410)

622(410).333

622(410).34

(v) **Mnemonics :** The common auxiliary sub-divisions and the parallel division are two principle mnemonic devices used in UDC. Besides, the parallel division also, is a mnemonic feature of UDC. It consists in the use of the same notation to denote a given concept in more than one place. It is called parallel division, signalled in the tables by the sub-divide sign =. This sign indicates that the number preceding it has to be divided as the number following it. This will result in an analogous array with the same concepts expressed by the same sequence of digits. For example:

611.21/.26 Respiratory system ≅ 616.21/.26 Respiratory system

under anatomy	under pathology
611.21 Nose, sinus	616.21 Nose, sinus
.22 Larynx (voice box)	.22 Larynx (voice box)

.23 Trachea (wind pipe)	.23 Trachea (wind pipe)
.24 Lungs	.24 Lungs
.25 Pleurae	.25 Pleurae
.26 Diaphragm	.26 Diaphragm

In this case, the subdivision of 616 are the source numbers from which digits have been taken and added to the target numbers under 611 expressing the same concepts.

(vi) **Filing Order :** The filing order of UDC symbols is based on a progression from the general to the particular. Thus, a common auxiliary used as an independent number is filed before a main number. This is followed by a compound number having the plus sign or the stroke in it, as it is broader in meaning than a simple number. Next, the simple numbers are filed in the order of increasing length. The length indicates specificity (due to an auxiliary) or particularity (due to hierarchical division). The filing order of UDC notation is given on page xi of the International Medium Edition – English Text (BS 1000M: 1985) which is reproduced here.

Table: Filling Order

Symbol	Example
Independent Auxiliaries	
=	=30 German language
(0...)	(0.035.22) Microfilmed Documents
(1/9)	(430) Germany
(=...)	(=1.410) British Nationals
" "	"18" Nineteenth Century
+	622.341.1+669. 1 Iron-ore Mining and Ferrous Metallurgy
	622.341. 1/2 Mining of Iron Ores and Manganese Ores
simple number	622.341.1 Iron-ore Mining
Auxiliaries as Suffixes	622.341.1:338.124.4 Economic Crises in Iron-ore Mining
	(may be reversed to from 338.124.4:622.341.1)

: :	622.341.1: :338.124.4 Economic Crises in Iron-ore Mining (may not be reversed)
=	622.341.1=30 Documents in German about Iron-ore Mining
(0...)	622.341.1(0.035.22) Microfilmed Documents about Iron-ore Mining
(1/9)	622.341.1(430) Iron-ore Mining in Germany
(=...)	622.341.1(=1.366) Iron-ore Mining among the Ancient British
"..."	622.341.1 "18" Iron-ore Mining in the Nineteenth Century
*	622.341.1*Fe_2O_3 Mining of Red Haematite (Fe_2O_3)
A/Z	622.341.1GOE Named Iron ores: Goethite
.00	622.341.1.002.67 By-products of Iron-ore Mining
-0	622.341.1-057.2 Manual Workers in Iron-ore Mining
-1/-9	622.341.1-78 Protective Devices and Measures in Iron-ore Mining
.0	622.341.1.03 Geological Character of Iron-ore Deposits
'	622.341.1'17 Waste, Residues from Iron-ore Mining
Next simple number	622.341.11 Magnetite–haematite Ores

(vii) Gap Devices : The UDC notation is decimal and can accommodate emerging new concepts wherever necessary. In addition to this in-built provision, UDC has resorted to what is called gap device. These gaps in the notation are meant for accommodating a large number of subdivisions and are left where future expansion is envisaged. We find the following vacant numbers in the notation:

142 – 159.8 in Philosophy and Psychology

365 – 367	in Social welfare
375	in Education
4	the class Philology transferred to 8 Literature
538.1 – 538.8	in Physics
544 – 545	in Chemistry

This is how UDC has provided for future expansion.

Developments in UDC

Universal Decimal Classification (UDC) was developed on the basis of Decimal Classification and was first published in 1905 entitled Classification Decimal Universally. The scheme is revised and updated from time to time by the International Federation for Information and Documentation (FID). In addition, to a demand from several quarters for comprehensive short editions in English, abridged editions are being brought out by the British Standards Institution (BSI), the official agency. The abridged edition BS 1000A was first published in 1948. The second abridged edition with radical revision was brought out in 1957. The third abridged edition was brought out in 1961.

(i) IME 1985 and 1993

The International Medium Edition (IME) was published with more extensive division to replace abridged English editions. The IME, English Text comprises of two parts, Part I – Systematic Tables published in 1985 and Part II – Alphabetical Subject Index published in 1988. This edition contains about a third of the material in the full editions brought out English, French and German. In addition to various signs and symbols already provided in Abridged English Edition (AEE), two more new symbols: → (the arrow) meaning "see also", e.g.,. 159.9 Psychology → (301. 151;591.51; 621.821; 616.89, and ≅ (parallel division) meaning "subdivision as" have been introduced.

e.g. 611.3 Digestive system. Alimentary Canal

611.3 ≅ (616.3, e.g., 611.31 Oral Cavity)

Another IME in English was published in 1993 in two parts. The digit 4 used for Linguistics has been frozen and the Linguistics divisions have been shifted to class 8.

(ii) UDC in Computer-Based Information Retrieval Systems

It was suggested as far as back as 1934 that UDC was suitable for 'mechanical sorting'. The Royal Society's Scientific Information

Conference held in 1948 noted the need to explore the potentialities of UDC in mechanised retrieval. The research programmes carried out in the USA, Britain, Germany, Denmark and Switzerland in the sixties helped UDC to be usable as an indexing language for computerised control and processing of information in the fields of knowledge. The most significant research work in this respect was the American Institute of Physics UDC Project under Freeman and Atherton. Other experiments carried out during the late sixties in using UDC for special mechanical applications include, the indexing of Geo-Science Abstracts and the maintenance of user profiles in the metallurgic fields.

(iii) UDC and UNISIST

FID thought of making UDC a 'Roof Scheme' under which it could be hung the relevant special classifications, thesauri or descriptor lists as well as the more detailed UDC divisions themselves for those who prefer a homogeneous UDC-based system. The concept received encouragement in the efforts to make UDC adopted as the switching language for UNISIST (United Nations World Science Information System), a joint project of ICSU/UNESCO. An ASLIB study for UNISIST stated that UDC was found 'least unsatisfactory' of the major existing schemes.

(iv) Computerisation of UDC

UDC has been used advantageously working for more than three decades, in computerised bibliographical and abstracting services not only for the production of subject indexes but also for information retrieval and SDI. In the forefront of UDC mechanisation has been Rigby who, as early as 1964, showed in the Conference at Elsinore the printouts of *Meteorological and Geoastrophysical Titles* that had started the use of the computer for author and subject indexing. A more comprehensive survey on the use of computers with the UDC was compiled by Rigby with the description of more than sixty experimental or operational systems in fifteen countries and four international projects.

Merits and Demerits of UDC

Since the beginning of UDC, attempts have been made to adopt the scheme to universal needs in pursuance of its initial objective of establishing and maintaining a universal bibliography. The main merits of the scheme are:

(i) Since UDC is a general scheme of classification, it covers the whole field of human knowledge. The process of dividing a class into ten subclasses is carried to the required degree of specificity. The required degree of detail is achieved with the help of common and special auxiliaries. The resultant subject description is of utmost precision.

(ii) Its notation consists of numerals and signs, which are understood internationally. The decimal notation allows maximum hospitality for the admission of new terms.

(iii) Like CC, the UDC is an analytico-synthetic classification because of the use of a auxiliary apparatus of connection.

(iv) It is extremely flexible, i.e., adjustments to local needs can be made with relative ease. This is because the citation order in any given class often allows several alternative treatments.

(v) It is ideally suited to special libraries, as its full edition contains subject schedules of minute description. Special subject editions are also separately available. The medium edition can take care of almost all subjects.

(vi) It forms a carefully organised and comprehensive vocabulary of terms in its index for indexing and retrieval. It may be used as a thesaurus.

(vii) It is amenable to computerisation.

(viii) The users are able to participate in its revision.

But together with merits, there are also some demerits in the scheme, which include.

(i) The notation often tends to be long and appears clumsy. As a result, its use on the shelves becomes difficult.

(ii) User participation in revision has created unevenness in the scheme at places. It also delays revision of schedules until they become out of date.

(iii) The revision involves publication of several different editions and their different language versions for which FID finds its funds inadequate.

However, the merits of UDC easily outweigh the demerits in it.

10
Devices in CC, DDC and UDC

Q.: Discuss with examples the various devices for synthesis in Dewey Decimal Classification?

Or

What is Geographical Device? Explain the use of devices in Colon Classification, Universal Decimal classification and Dewey Decimal Classification with examples.

Write short notes on the following:

- Super-imposition Device

- Devices in CC, DDC and UDC

- Alphabetical Device

- Chronological Device

Ans. The constantly growing Universe of Subjects *vis-à-vis* the demands of the five laws of library science require certain amount of autonomy to classifier in every scheme for classification, be it a enumerative scheme or an analytico-synthetic scheme. The classifier has to face the challenges of such new subjects which demand either the formation of new isolates or need sharpening of an existing idea within a class in a scheme to make them co-extensive. This is possible when the classificationist incorporates in his scheme such provisions which provide autonomy to classifier to handle such situations. The devices enable the classifier to meet the situation without waiting for guidance from the classificationist.

These are the components used for forming or sharpening a facet in an analytico-synthetic classification and/or sharpening a subject in an enumerative classification. Based on the characteristic used for this purpose, they are called as chronological device, georgraphical device, etc., These devices are used by classification systems wherever helpful and possible and are applicable both in the idea plane as well as in the notational plane.

The devices make possible:

(i) to avoid enumeration and shorten the length of the schedules;

(ii) to provide autonomy to classifier; and

(iii) to secure automatic conformity to the canons of consistent sequence, helpful sequence, scheduled mnemonics, hospitality in array and hospitality in chain.

Types of Devices

The following devices are used in classification systems for forming or sharpening a facet or a subject:

1. Chronological Device (CD)
2. Geographical Device (GD)
3. Subject Device (SD)
4. Alphabetical Device (AD)
5. Enumeration Device (ED)
6. Classic Device (CD)
7. Super-imposition Device (SID)

1. Chronological Device

(i) **Idea Plane :** "In the idea plane, the CD is the device for forming or sharpening the focal ideas in a schedule of isolates or of system basic divisions-chronological characteristic when their individualization admits of being made to depend conveniently and helpfully on their respective epochs of origin, or birth, or first investigation, or discovery, or initiation, or occurrence, or any other epoch that may be definitely associated with it in any manner, or any reason".

(ii) **Notational Plane :** "In the notational plane, the CD is the device of implementing the CD of the idea plane by using a chronological number for forming isolate or sharpening of isolate number".

In CC, the Chronological Device is employed to classify the followings:

(i) Authors in Literature
(ii) Artificial Languages
(iii) Religious Sects
(iv) Systems Basic Subjects
(v) Styles in Fine Arts
(vi) Several of the Anteriorising and Personality Common Isolates
(vii) Several other places in the schedules

(iii) Chronological Number: The Chronological number should be worked out to the first, or the first two, or the first three digits of the year forming the epoch as specified in the respective rules in Colon Classification. If there is no specific rule, then the following convention may be followed:

(i) For the first isolate in an array, whose epochs falls within a century, the first digit alone should be used.
(ii) Among the other isolates calling for the same first digit, for the first two digits should be used. The second digit will be an Indo-Arabic numeral;
(iii) Among the other isolates calling for the same first two digits, for the first isolate, whose epoch falls within the same year (or decade), the first three digits should be used. The second and third digits will be Indo-Arabic numerals;
(iv) For each of the other isolates calling for the same first three digits, some vacant neighbouring years are to be used;
(v) If no neighbouring year is vacant to make the application of above convenient, the digit 1,2, etc. respectively may be added after the three digited number.

Examples : Special forms and functions in Mathematics:

CC6	*CC7*	
B239M	B2,39M	Abelian Equation
B392L	B3,92L	Hyperbolic Function

Author Number in Literature:

CC6	*CC7*	
0152,3M80	0,152.3M80	Prem Chand

Systems Basic Subject:

CC6	*CC7*	
LB	L-B	Ayurveda
XM2	X-M2	Socialism

UDC is not using (CD) for sharpening a subject or concept. However, with the help of *Intercalation Device* a subject or concept with chronological characteristic may be interpolated at the appropriate place in the class number for the subject. This is because Intercalation Device permits that the time numbers enumerated in the Common Auxiliaries of Time may be intercalated at any appropriate place in the class number of the subject for desired groupings.

Examples :

785,7 "18"	Chambers Music in 19th Century
785 "18"7	19th Century Chamber Music

(iv) **System Basic Division :** "The CD is used in the formation of a system basic division, for example."

In the 7th edition of Colon Classification Systems occur in the schedules of Main Classes: B Mathematics, C Physics, E Chemistry, L Medicine, R Philosophy, S Psychology, T Education and X Economics. Apart from this one may see the use of CD for the author number in the Main Class 'O Literature'. In the schedule for Space Isolates, certain divisions are also got by CD. Chronological device has also been used in the Language Isolate Sehedule and in the main Class 'N' Fine Arts'. In the case of Anteriorsing common isolates CD has been used to sharpen the isolates in [P2].

Some examples form the 7th edition of CC are given below illustrating the use of CD.

S-M	Experimental Psychology
CV "m44, N71	Indian Journal of Space Physics
O,157,1M61,1	Gitanjali By Rabindranath Tagore
CN48	Common Wealth
No-(44,J)	Moghul Painting

(2) **Geographical Device**

(i) **Idea Plane :** "In the Idea Plane, the GD is the device for forming or sharpening the focal ideas in any schedule of isolates or of some special basic divisions on the basis of the geographical characteristic, when their individualization admits of being made to depend conveniently and helpfully on their respective geographical areas of origin, or prevalence, or habitation, or any other places that may be definitely associated with them in any manner or for any reason".

(ii) Notational Plane : "In the Notational Plane, the GD is the device of implementing the GD of the idea plane, by using a geographical number for forming or sharpening an isolate number".

In CC, the Geographical Device is used for the individualization of:

(i) Community in History and Law;

(ii) Dialects and jargon of a language, style in Fine Arts;

(iii) Several of the anteriorising common isolates; and

(iv) Several other places in the schedules.

Examples:

CC6	CC7	
V44	V,44	Indian History
Z44,5	Z,44,5	Criminal law of India
P111,J,9D56175	P,111 = xJ = d56175	Modern Yorkshire dialect

In DDC, the geographical divisions are enumerated in Table 2 Areas, which have been used to form the community facet of subjects going with History, Law, Public Administration, regional variations in Languages and National Groups etc. either through Add Device or through enumeration.

Examples :

Through Add Device

345 Add 54 = 345.54	Criminal Law of India
427.9 Add 71 = 427.971	Dialects of Canada
Enumeration	
954	Indian History
–951	Chinese

–97	North American Native people

The (GD) has also been used in UDC.

Examples:

914	Geography of Europe (Europe as 4)
914.4	Geography of France (France as 44)
915.2	Geography of Japan (Asia as 5, Japan as 52)

The class number for a subject or concept with geographical characteristic may also be sharpened using Intercalation Device when no such sharpened class number for that subject or concept is available in the schedules.

The Common Auxiliaries of Place is provided with double indicators, which made intercalation possible and facilitates to provide a co-extensive number to a subject or concept with geographical characteristics.

Examples :

721 (540)	Architecture of Buildings in India
72 (540) 1	Indian Architectures of Buildings
726.1 (540)	Architecture of Temples in India
72 (540) "19 "6.1	20th Century Indian Architecture of Temples
72 (540) "19"1	20th Century Indian Architecture of Buildings

(3) **Subject Device**

(i) **Idea Plane :** "In the Idea Plane, the SD is the device for forming or sharpening the focal ideas in a schedule of isolates on the basis of subject-characteristic, when their individualization admits of being made to depend conveniently and helpfully on a subject in any manner or for any reason."

(ii) **Notational Plane :** 'In the notational Plane, the SD is the device of implementing the SD of the idea plane, by using a CN for forming or sharpening an isolate number. The CN so used should be enclosed in circular brackets; and it should be taken as fused and treated as if it were a single digit."

In CC, this device is employed at different stages in certain subjects. Many illustrative divisions by the SD are given in CC Schedules. Special reference may be made here, to the ethics part of the schedule, and to the "IMI Property" schedule. In some cases, it is found that the number used for the SD has been modified slightly. But, such modifications should not be freely indulged in by individual classifiers. This may be called a Quasi-Subject Device. It amounts to enumeration with due deference to the Canon of Scheduled Mnemonics".

Examples :

2,B (V;78)	National Archives Library
NA,9(2,J3)	Architecture of College Library Buildings
R4,4(T)	Ethics for Teachers
V;3(X)	State and Economics

In same cases the special components of Space Isolates are also further divided by SD.

1 = (Q7)	Muslim Countries
1 = (P,111)	English Speaking World

In DDC, the 'Add Device' shoulder the responsibility to perform the role of (SD). But there is no autonomy to the classifier in the application of Add Device. It may be used only wherein instruction to Add is provided.

Examples :

338.13	Financial Aspects
	Add to base number 338.13 the numbers following 63 in 633-638, e.g; prices of rice 338.13318
344.01	Labour (Law)
	Add to base number 344.01 the numbers following 331 in 331.1-331.8
Child Labour Law	344.01 + [331].31 = 344.0131

In UDC, the multifunctional Relation sign: (Colon) also performs the role of sharpening a subject, when sharpening is on the basis of subject characteristics and the required subject is enumerated in another place. The two class numbers enumerated in different places may be connected by using the : (Colon) symbol. For example:

32:91	Geopolitics
026:61	Medical Libraries
341.63 (540: 549)	Arbitration between India and Pakistan

If the sharpening subject does not warrant any entry under its class number to provide access to the sharpened subject, then in place of the indicator: (Colon) the [] (square brackets) may be used. For example,

620.174 : 669.14 Material Testing

620.174 [669.14] Bend Test

4. Alphabetical Device

(i) **Idea Plane :** "In the idea plane, the AD is the device for forming or sharpening the focal ideas in a schedule of isolates, on the basis of name-characteristics, provided that they have internationally accepted names and their alphabetical arrangement is as helpful as any other, if not more helpful".

(ii) **Notational Plane :** "In the notational plane, the AD is the device of implementing the AD of the idea plane, by using the first, or the first two, or the first three, etc. initial letters of the internationally accepted name, for forming or sharpening an isolate number. But, the letter "J" should be used in the place of the letter "I"; and the letter "P" in place of the letter "O".

For example:

Othello (English Drama by Shakespeare) O,111,2J64,P.

Here in this class number letter O is replaced by letter P.

(iii) **Names of Isolates with the Same First Three Letters :** "If more than one IN is made of the same three letters, in the case of the second, third, etc., of such isolates, the digits 1,2, etc., may be added respectively after the three said letters "

(iv) **Alphabetical Number for Multinomial Terms :** "In applying AD to a binomial name-that is, a name with two words –AD should be applied to each component word and two AD components should be connected by the indicator digit "+" (plus).

Examples taken from the names of dramas of Shakespeare:

M+V	Merchant of Venice
T+S	Taming of the Shrew
TW+N	Twelfth Night

For the names having the same initial letter, the first letter alone may be used for the most favoured entity – that is, the entity which has the greatest literary warrant, or which is the first on which a book arrives.

The first two letters are to be used if the name of another entity has the same two initial letters as the one already selected for two-letter representation. The number of letters used may be further increased to the necessary extent".

In CC, upto 6th edition, Alphabetical Device was used as a last resort. Ranganathan specifically stated that "this device is to be used in cases where no other method of sub-division gives a more helpful sequence." According upto CC6 this device is used for the individualization of:

(i) *Works of literary and classical authors*: If the year of birth of a modern author (say born after 1800) cannot be found by any means; the century of birth may be guessed; and the century digit should be used as the first digit of the Author (IN). The later digits of it may be got by (AD).

Examples :

O152,INC	Poems of Chin Mun
O142,3MD	Russian Novelist Dostoyevsky

(ii) *Brands of a Machine*

Examples :

D5125	Bicycle
D5125A	Atlas cycle
D5125H	Hero cycle

(iii) *Strains of Cultivators, Viruses and Bacteria:*

Examples :

J381	Rice
J381B	Basmati Rice
J381 P	Permal Rice

(iv) *Brands of Car :*

Examples :

D5133	Car
D5133M	Maruti Car 800CC
D5133MA	Maruti Car 1000 CC
D5133 MAR	Maruti Van

(v) Fauna of Vindhya :

Example :

K : 12.44 g7. V. Mountains

In CC7, there is no restriction in the use of (AD), where in it is stated that the (AD) can be used without any restriction in any Array of order 1 or when the (AD) number succeeds an Empty digit. In CC7 the free use of (AD), is clearly indicated in the following examples:

Space Isolates	*CC6*	*CC7*
Cambridge	56117	56 = OC
London	56124	56 = OL

Besides, in CC7 the rule for multi-nominal terms is as follows:

'In applying (AD)' to a binominal name-that is, a name with two words, (AD) should be applied to each component word and two (AD) components should be connected by the indicator digit '+' (plus).'

Examples :

O111,2J64, M + V Merchant of Venice of William Shakespeare

O111,2J64, TW + N Twelfth Night of William Shakespeare

As for as DDC, in concerned, it as a rule does not prescribe Alphabetical Device. However, implicitly (AD) has been recognized in DDC since long. A note 'to use alphabet or chronology for final-sub-divisions' was included in DDC 2 and also in DDC 12 to 14. The editor's note in DDC 16 it is clearly stated that although the DC is a classification based on figures used decimally it may be modified and supplemented by letters of the alphabet used in several ways and for a variety of purposes. Few examples from DDC 20, 1989 using (AD). are :

005.133	Specific Programming Languages Arrange alphabetically by name e.g. COBOL
005.262	In Specific Programming Languages Arranging alphabetically by Name, e.g., FORTRAN
005.265	Specific Computers

Arrange alphabetically by name of computer, e.g. Kaypro II

Similar instructions are given under 005.362; 005.365; 005.369; 005.7565.

Besides, such specific instructions, the use of alphabets as optional numbers is gradually increasing in DDC from edition 16 onwards.

In UDC, alphabetical Device may be used either through Common Auxiliary Table 1 (h). Further specification by non-UDC notations or through specific instruction given under different class numbers.

Examples:

(UDC Medium Ed 1985)

Common Auxiliaries of Place:

(436B)	Burgenland
(436K)	Karnten
(436T)	Tirol
(519.3 A/Z)	Provinces of North Korea

Main Classes:

230.2	The Great Schools of Theology Details by A/Z
82...A/Z	Works of Specific Authors
929 A/Z	Biographies of Individuals

(5) **Enumeration Device**

(i) **Idea Plane :** "In the idea plane, the ED is the device of forming focal ideas in any array of a schedule by their enumeration in a sequence preferred on the basis of the canon of seminal mnemonics, or some principle for helpful sequence."

(ii) **Notational Plane :** "In the notational Plane, the ED is the device of implementing the ED of the idea plane, by using numbers of the base of the notational system, either continuously or with gaps, for forming isolate numbers in any array of a schedule."

The Enumeration Device is the device which is used by all types of schemes for classification. The only difference being the frequency of its use. For example:

(a) In an Enumeratic Classification, (ED) is the only device used in all arrays, such as in Rider's International Classification;

(b) In an Almost-Enumerative Classification (ED) is used in most of the arrays, such as in DDC and LCC;

(c) In a Almost-Faceted Analytico – Synthetic Classification, (ED) is used less frequently than in others, such as in UDC and Colon Classification.

The device is to be used when (CD) or (AD) can not be conveniently applied to certain divisions. The device is used successfully in CC. For example. (CC6)

	Physics		*Chemistry*		*Medicine*
C9A	Specials	E9A	Specials	L9A	Specials
C9B1	Molecular Ray	E9G	Biochemistry	L9B	Embryo
C9B2	Atom			L9C	Child
C9B3	Nuclear			L9D	Adolescent

Besides, some schedules based on ED often forms the basis for scheduled mnemonics.

(6) Classic Devic

(i) In Idea Plane: 'In Idea Plane the Classic Device brings together all the editions and translations of:

(a) A classic;

(b) Each of its commentaries, next to it;

(c) Each of the sub-commentaries of every commentary, next to it; and so on.'

(ii) Notational Plane : In the Notational Plane, Classic Device is used in the following manner;

(a) The Classic is assigned the class number on the basis of its thought content. This class number is termed as ultimate class. Ultimate class is the class of smallest extension, admitted by the scheme for classification, into which it can be placed;

(b) After this ultimate class [ACI] digit x is added;

(c) The digit x is further amplified by [PI] i.e., Author Facet and [P2] i.e., Work Facet;

(d) The indicator digit"," (comma) need not be inserted before the Author Facet, e.g.,

Ultimate class x [P1], [P2]

In Prolegomena Edition 3 as well as in CC6 and CC7 detailed rules are given for the application of Classic Device. However, it is only in CC 6 thats Part 3 enumerates readymade class numbers for classics in different subject, which may possibly form part of later volumes of CC 7.

Both DDC and UDC also use Enumeration Device to provide class numbers for Classics.

Examples :

	CC	DDC	UDC
Plato	R7x571	184	141.131
Patanjali Yogsutra	R634x1,1	181.452	294.527

(7) Super-Imposition Device

This is connecting two or more isolate ideas belonging to the same Universe of Isolate Ideas and is used when an isolate is not scheduled in a facet but can be regarded as the mutual denudation of two of the scheduled isolates. The Number of an Superimposed Isolate Idea (S11) is got by the Superimposition Device (SID).'

Rules for the sequence of isolates were also specifically provided. Following are the rules as given in CC6 (1963) under 05863 to 05865.

(i) The constituent isolate which occurs earlier in the schedules should normally form the first number of a (S11). For example,

Y15	Women
Y31	Rural
Y15-31	Rural Women

(iii) If the number got by above rule is unintelligible and the using of the constituent isolate, which occurs later in the schedule as the first number, will yield an intelligible and a more helpful isolate number, it must be made the first number. For example,

T4	University education
T55	Female education
T4-55	University Female Education

This class number constructed on the basis of Rule 1 is unintelligible because all documents having this number would be arranged near the documents on University education in general, but it is more helpful if all the documents on University Education of Women are grouped under women education. So the Rule-2 should be followed. For example, T55-4.

(iv) If both the sequences of the constituent isolate give intelligible isolate numbers and yield different meanings, the sequence should be determined by the meaning sought, to be represented. For example,

British Territory in Malaysia

435	Malaysia
56	Great Britain

According to Rule 1, the class number would be : 435-56 i.e., British Territory in Malaysia. According to Rule 2 it would be:

56-435

This would mean Malaysian Territory in Great Britain.

Here both the combinations are intelligible, but indicate two different meaning. Therefore the class number to be constructed would depend on what to thought content of the document represents. Here in, Rule 3 is to be followed.

11

Book Classification: Book Number, Diversification of Collections and Collection Numbers

Q. : Explain the parts of a Call Number. Illustrate your answer in the context of relevant Canons of Book Classification of Ranganathan, i.e., Canon of Collection Number, Canon of Book Number and Canon of Distinctiveness.

Or

What is importance of Book Number in Library Classification? Describe the system of Book Number as devised by Dr. Ranganathan.

Or

Write notes on the following:

(a) Book Number.

(b) Collection Number.

Ans. : The call number of a book is the artificial name which is assigned to it on the basis of its thought content and physical features. According to Ranganathan 'The call number of a book unit is the symbol used to fix its position relatively to other books, it individualizes the book and may be used by the readers in calling for a book".

The call number is designed by the classifier on the basis of the following features of the book:

(i) the specific subject in which the book is written–that is its class number;

(ii) the other physical features of the book–its language, number of volumes, year of publication–that is its book number;

(iii) to these two components one more part is added by the library on the basis of its gross body, to individualise the various types of library collections, such as reare book collection, out of print collection, textbooks, periodicals, etc.–that is its collection numbers.

It means:

Class Number + Book Number + Collection Number combined together is called the Call Number of a book.

Purpose of the call number.

A call number may be helpful in following of ways:

(i) when a user asks for a book which is in a library, it must be located immediately, even though the library may have miles of shelves full of books;

(ii) when a book is returned to a library, its correct place on the shelves must be immediately determinable so that it can be replaced ready for the next user;

(iii) when a new book is added to a library it must find its proper place among the other books on the same subject;

(iv) when the first book on a new subject arrives in a library, it must find a place among the books on such other already existing subjects as are related to it, and in the degree of its relation to them.

Components of Call Number

As stated earlier, a call number consisted of (A) Class number (B) Book number and (C) Collection Number.

(A) Class number

The class number of a book is a translation of the name of its specific subject into the artificial language of ordinal numbers. This means for constructing the class number of a document the classifier has:

1. To decide what is the specific subject of a document before tranlating it into artificial language. According to Ranganathan 'The specific subject of a book is that divisior of knowledge

whose extension and intension are equal to those of its thought content. Therefore the specific subject of a document may be:

(i) of wider extension-covering one of the branches of universe of knowledge, or one main subject or two or more main subjects etc.;

(ii) of lesser extension–covering only subdivisions of main subjects; etc.

(iii) it may be a simple subject dealing with one main or basic class or five fundamental categories; or it may be a complicated subject covering one main subject, common isolates or phase relations, etc.

2. To determine the specific subject of the document. This may be determined on the basis of:

(i) title of a book if it is more or less expressive, e.g., Textbook on Constitutional Law of India, or Principles of Library Classification.

(ii) the contents and introduction as well as author's note about the book;

(iii) even then if the subject is not clear then the classifier has to go through the thought content of the book;

(iv) or he may have to take the help of the subject expert, if all the above steps fail in determining the specific subject.

3. To translate this specific subject into an artificial language of ordinal numbers on the basis some scheme for classification, after determining the specific subject of the document.

The specific subject of a document so translated is termed as ultimate class of document.

(B) Book Number

Book Number is that of library classification which clears the path for use of the book or a documents. When many documents are written on one and the same specific subject, resulting in the same ultimate class number for all these documents, then to make this ultimate class number of each document unique and distinct for their discrete arrangement on shelves some other factors of the document are used. This function is allotted to Book Number. The Book Number is, therefore, devised on the basis of the outerpart or the physical features of the documents. A document may, get its individual name only when Book Number is used along with the class number. If the class number is name of the book, Book Number is the identifier, which makes a document identifiable and distinct among all other documents having the same ultimate class number and the same form.

According to Ranganathan, the book number "of a book is an ordinal number used to fix its position relatively to the other books in the same ultimate class." In other words, the book number of a book individualizes it among the books having the same class number.

Methods of Assigning Book Number

The specific need for Book Number started the day when the first scheme for classification–DDC came into existence To fulfil this necessary demand various methods for Book Numbers have been devised by librarians and library science scholars. Some of the important methods of assigning Book Number are as follows:

1. **Use of Name of the Author as Book Number**

(i) **Cutter Author Marks:** Cutter Author Mark is a universally approved method used for Book Numbers. This method is fully explained at the end of Cutter's Expansive classification: First Six Schemes. The Author Marks were also published separately on folding cards in 1880, and was designated as "Alphabetical Order Table". The Author marks were limited to two figure numbers. Cutter later expanded this table in three figure table. The table is divided into three sequence (1) the consonents (2) the vowels, and (3) the alphabets.

When the author's name starts with a consonant, the first letter of the author's name and two digits are represented as book number. In case of the vowels and S are concerned, the first two letters of the author's name and one digit is used to convert into book number. Below are given few examples:

Consonents

Beard	N34
Holmes	H73
Huxley	H78
Lowell	L95
Macaulay	M11

Vowels and S

Abbot	Ab2
Anne	An7
Edwards	Ed9
Smith	Sm5
Swain	Sw1
Upton	Up1

Cutter's book numbering system was later revised by Kate. E. Sanborn and known as Cutter – Sanborn Three Figure Author Table.

The revised version gives three digits for majority of the alphabets except in the case of S, Q, X, Y, Z and vowels. They are fitted with either one or two digits.

An example taken from the table is given below:

Grab	751	Homb	Yoa	71	Zo
Grabh	752	Home	Yob	72	Zoc
			Yod	73	Zoel
Grabs	753	Homes	Yoe	74	Zogr
Grrad	754	Homod	Yog	75	Zoll
Grradi	755	Honc	Yoi	76	Zoner
Grae	756	Hone	Yok	77	Zori
Graess	757	Honey	Yol	78	Zorr
Graff	758	Honk	Yom	79	Zou

The numbers in the centre are applicable to the letters appearing on both sides of the numbers. For example, the call number for Homer's Illiad will be 881 H752. In case any two books get the same number they can be further individualised by adding the first letter of the title of the book.

(ii) **Author Number:** Melvil Dewey in the Introduction of DDC 12, (1927) has stated that 'Invention of translation system by which a name is represented by its initial, with remaining letters translated into numbers, e.g., Freeman F85, has led most libraries to arrange books under each class alphabetically by author.'

(iii) **Merrill Book Number :** An attempt was also made by William

Stetson Merrill, Librarian of the Newsberry Library, Chicago in 1912. to provide an approximate alphabetical arrangement by divising a table limited to 100 places.

Examples :

10	A	21	D	96	Wats
02	Agre	22	Day	97	Wha
03	Als	23	Dickey	98	Wit
10	Bix	30	Fit	99	X-Z

(iv) **Jast Book Number :** L. Stanley Jast devised his author table in 1900. He has described this table in Library World Volume 3.

Examples :

(i) Two letters if only one author, e.g.,

Jo	Johnson

(ii) If or more authors having the same first two words in name, then use also Indo-Arabic numbers, e.g.,

Jo	Johnson
Jol	Johari

This number depends on the arrival of the book in the library and not on the alphabets in author's name.

(iii) The author number to two or more works of one and the same author may be assigned in the following manner:

Premchand–Gaban	Pre. G
Premchand–Godan	Pre. G1

However, the Author Mark fails to individualize when a library has:

(a) different copies of the same book;

(b) different editions of the same book; and,

(c) different volumes of multivolumed books.

2. Year of Publication as Book Number :-

(i) Biscoe Date Table

Biscoe Date Table devised by W.S. Biscoe in 1885 is the first table for Book Numbers based on year of publication.

Examples :

A	BC
B	1 to 999 AD
C	1000 to 1499 AD
D	1500 to 1599 AD
E	1600 to 1699 AD
.	
.	
.	
R	1910 - 1919 AD
S	1920 - 1929 AD
T	1930 - 1939 AD
U	1940 - 1949 AD
V	1950 to 1959 AD
W	1960 to 1979 AD
X	1970 to 1979 AD
Y	1980 to 1989 AD
Z	1990 to 1999 AD

On the basis of this table the book number may be constructed in the following manner:

Year of publication	Book Number
534 BC	A534
320 AD	B320
1655	E55

More than two books on the same specific subject in one and same year:

Library classification	1959	V9
Library classification	1959	V9a

(ii) **Rider's Book Number :** Fermont Rider also proposed a modification in the Biscoe Date Table, i.e., after the decade number from Biscoe Table, the first letter of the surname of the author may be added.

3. Book Number in CC

Ranganathan, of all classificationists, realized fully the need for the design and development of a good book numbering system. This can be seen form the fact that he prescribed a comprehensive facet formula for book number in CC. Rangathan's canon of book number states that "A scheme for book classification should include a scheme for book numbers in order to individualize the documents having the same subject as their ultimate class and to mechanize their preferred arrangement among themselves." His facet formula for book number is comprehensive, but all the facets are rarely required to use in one and the same document.

The Facet formula is:

(L) (F) (Y) (A) (V) – (S); (C) ; (EVN)

L–Language of the document

F–Form of the document

Y–Year of publication of the document

A–Accession part of the year of publication

V–Volume number of the document

S–Supplement number of the volume number

C–Copy number of the document

EVN–Evaluation/Attachment number

L–Language number : The language number is obtained by translating the name of the language in which the document is written into an ordinal number in accordance with the schedule of language isolates . The language number may be omitted in the following cases:

(i) when language of the document (other than that of O Literature) is the favoured language of the library. Favoured language in general is the language of the country, or it may be the language in which the library has the largest number of documents, as in the case of India, English language is the favoured language.

(ii) in O Literature, if the language of the book is the same as language of the literature;

(iii) in Periodical publications, as the class number includes the number of its country of publication, therefore, there is no need of language Facet.

Following are two examples of book number with the language facet present in it:

	CN	*BN*
Respiratory diseases (written in Spanish)	L, 4;4	123
Hindu law (written in Hindi)	Z. (Q.2)	152

F–Form Number: The second facet is for the form in which the document is published. For example, picture form or in code form or paintings. The form number is devised by translating the form of exposition as is enumerated in chapters CC (CC7) and 03 (CC6). Further, the form number is not applicable to books in basic subject O Literature. as the form is already represented in the class number in literature (1P2).

Following are two examples of book number with the form facet present in it.

	CN	*BN*
A Discussion on Lung Tuberculosis	L45;421	p3
Lectures of Colon Classification	2;5N3	p1

As majority of books are published in prose form, so it is taken as favoured form. The rule is that the form number need not be written in the Book Number if a book is in prose.

Y–Year of Publication: Year in which the document has been published is indicated by year number. Year number is devised by translating the year of publication of document in accordance to the Time Schedule provided in chapter DH (CC7) and chapter 3 (CC6).

Ordinarily the year number consists of three digits, as in the following two examples:

	CN	*BN*
Colon Classification published in 1987	2;5N3	N87
Prolegomena to Library Classification published in 1967	2;5	N67

In the case of periodicals, the year printed on the cover should be reckoned for the year number, and not the year in which that volume has been brought out. Very often the periodicals are behind schedule.

A– Accession facet: *It is possible for two or more books having* the same class number to get the same book number consisting of the first three facets, namely, language facet form facet and year facet. In such cases, the books have to be arranged in the sequence of their accession in the library. The accession number to be added after the year number of the second book onwards.

Examples :

Specific Subject	*Year of publication*
Library Science	1969
First book	N69
Second book	N691
Third book	N692

V–Volume Number: All such books which are published in many volumes, need to be arranged in juxtaposition, for this purpose Volume Number is indicated in the Book Number. A multi-volume book, by definition, has to satisfy one or more of the following conditions:

— The set bears a common title and has a common index.

— In the context of the subject treatment, all volumes put together constitute a single work.

— The set has inclusive pagination, i.e., a single sequence of pagination is continued through all volumes. This may not hold good in all cases.

All the volumes of a multi-volume work may not be published at once; they may be published over a period of several years. In that case, the year of publication will vary with the volume. If, therefore, the book number for each volume is framed in isolation of other volumes, the work is likely to be scattered. To avoid this undesirable scatter of the set, the publication date of the first volume of the set is taken as the year of publication of the whole set and the book number is framed accordingly. Further, the rule for a multi-volume book states that..... the volumes of the set are to be individualized by putting a dot (.) after the year number or the accession facet of the book number, as the case may be, and putting the number of the volume after the dot in Indo-Arabic numeral." If the volume number in book number consists of more than one digit, it is read as an integer, and not as a decimal fraction.

Example :

Specific subject	*Year of Publication*	*Book Number*
Indian History in 3 Volumes		
Volume 1	1959	N59.1
Volume 2	1960	N59.2
Volume 3	1962	N59.3

S–Supplement number : Class number and the year of publication of a supplementary volume would be the same as that of original volume to bring them together. The supplement number of the supplementary volume is followed by indicator - (hyphen).

Example :

The following two book numbers with the supplement present in the second one:

	CN	*BN*
Catalogue Code, Volume 2 (1964)	2;6A	N64.2
Supplement to Volume 2	2;6A	N64.2-1

The terminal 1 in the second case is the supplement number.

C–Copy number : In many libraries, more particularly in academic libraries, two or more copies of a book are purchased. A good example of acquisition in multiple copies is the textbook collection of a university or college library. In the case of multiple copies of a book, the book number of the second and subsequent copies of it consists of the book number of the first copy followed by a semi-colon (;) and thereafter by the numerals 1,2 etc., respectively. For example,

Colon Classification Edition 6

5 Copies	qN60	Frist Copy
	qN60;1	Second Copy
	qN60;2	Third Copy and so on.

It means copy number would be assigned from second copy onwards.

Different Editions: However, if these copies of the same book are published in the form of different editions in different years. The library may find it helpful if all the editions of a book are kept together in succession. The Book Number for these editions would be:

	Year of Publication	*Book Number*
Original book	1959	N59
Second edition	1962	N59; N62
Third edition	1970	N59; N70

EVN–Evaluation Number, Attached Number: There are many important books which may not deemed to be a classic. To such work facet formula prescribed for classics is not applicable, and therefore, are classed as an ordinary books. If another book is written on such a work, then it would be helpful to keep both the works together. The original book or Hostbook is termed a Pseudo Classic and the second book on it as Attached book or Associated book. The following rules have to be followed while constructing the book number for this second book or attached book:

(i) The Attached Book should consists the book number of the Hostbook. It should be followed by:

(a) the digit pair 'y' in case of a version for practical work;

(b) by 'g' if it is an evaluation or review. The number thus added is denoted as Attachment Number.

(ii) *A–Accession facet of the attached number:* If more than one book have been written on the Hostbook/Pseudo classic, then the digits 1, 2, 3, is to be added in the following manner:

MO	Host book (1900)
MO:g	First commentary/evaluation published in 1920
MO:1	Second commentary (1925)
MO:g2	Third commentary (1940)

(C) Collection Number

A Collection number may be defined as the mark added to the class number-cum-book number of a book to indicate the collection in which that book is placed in the library.

In a library, different collections can be formed on the basis of the physical form of the holdings, or their age, or the type of service required. Following are some collections, one meets with in libraries:

By physical form

(i) Film rolls

(ii) Film strips

(iii) Microfiches
(iv) Transparencies
(v) Discs
(vi) Speaking books
(vii) Braille books

By size and age

(i) Pamphlets
(ii) Giant folio
(iii) Miniature books
(iv) Scrolls
(v) Books containing plates on loaded paper
(vi) Books in danger of destruction
(vii) Rare books
(viii) Incunabula
(ix) Manuscripts

By type of service

(i) Reading room collection
(ii) Departmental collections
(iii) Textbook collection
(iv) Topical collection
(v) Periodical collection
(vi) Reference collection
(vii) Language collections

Collections can also be categorized into permanent collections (Reading room and departmental collections), quasi-permanent collections (textbook collection and certain departmental collections) and temporary collections (topical collections that by their very purpose and nature are strictly temporary; collections arranged for seminars and short-term course whose utility ends with the end of the event).

Canon of Collection Number

Canon of collection number directs that 'A Scheme for Book classification may be provided with a schedule of Collection number to individualize the various collections of special documents to be formed on the basis of the peculiarities of their gross bodies, or their rarity, or service exigency to facilitate use by users. The collection number based on physical peculiarity may be use in bibliographies also'.

The collection Number is constructed by adding to the Class Number and Book Number, the symbol used to indicate the specific collection. However, the following scheme for collection number has been suggested in CC (7th Edn.) for use in organising collections likely to exist in libraries:

Collection	**Collection Number/Mark**
Undersize	underline call number
Oversize	overline call number
Non-open access	underline and overline call number
Worn-out	encircle call number
Reading room	rr
Secondary	se
Tertiary	te
Periodicals	pe
Physics department	DC
Law department	ZD

How to differentiate the collection of a library; what symbols are to be used for indicating the different types of collection depend mainly on the Maintenance Section of the library. The symbols may be used on the basis of scheme for classification used for classifying the documents of library, if it has such provision.

12

Latest Developments in Library Classification

Q. : Write an essay on recent developments in the field of library classification.

or

Q. : Write short notes on:

— **Broad System of Ordering (BSO)**

— **Automatic Classification**

Ans. Library classification has been defined as the process of ordering embodied knowledge and its surrogates available in various formats. It facilitates access to knowledge enabling libraries to provide services to its users. The library classification has evolved with changing times. Factors that have led to these evolvement are the changes in:

- Knowledge;
- User needs; and
- Information Technology

Knowledge was studied and existed earlier as disciplines which could be easily distinguished . It is growing exponentially, now available as multifocal, multidimensional knowledge where no clear line of demarcations are visible. User needs and requirements have changed due to increasing awareness, demacratisation of education, increasing information dependence, accountability and competition exisiting not only at the levels of individuals but also nations. Technology is also a pervading factor, affecting other factors also. Information technology has attached the processing power, storage capacities and formats as well as modes of transmission of knowledge and information. These changes in knowledge, user needs and information technology have widened the scope of library services. Widening the scope of library services requires the processes to be sharpened and library classification is one such process.

During the past few decades, not only individuals but many organisations, societies and research groups have carried on various research activities to give a new direction to library classification and to transform it into an effective tool not only for shelf arrangement but also knowledge organisation. The major once are discussed below.

1. Library Research Circle (LRC)

This was founded in Delhi by Dr. S.R. Ranganathan in 1951. This circle used to meet on Sunday at Ranganathan's residence to pursue research on various aspects of classification, especially relating to Colon Classification. Its members concentrated on fundamental categories, indicator digits, rounds and levels of manifestation, zone analysis and on requirements for depth classification. The work entitles Depth Classification, published by the Indian Library Association, 1953, provides ample testimony to the contributions made by members of LRC. Its activities withered away from 1954.

2. FID/CR

On the initiative of Ranganathan, FID formed a Committee on Classification Theory in 1950. Later in 1961, it was renamed as the Committee on Classification Research (FID/CA). This committee has been stimulating classification research. The activities of FID/CA are communicated through a serial publication entitled FID/CA Newsletter, published four times a year listing classification research projects in progress. It has so far organised six international conferences.

3. Classification Research Group (CRG)

This Group was formed in London in 1952. The early work of members of CRG is reflected in Sayer's Memorial Volume (London, Library Association, 1961). CRG as a whole published a brief outline of its views on faceted classification in 1953 and later issued a memorandum entitled, 'the need for faceted classification as the basis of all methods of information retrieval' in 1955. From 1952 to 1960 members of CRG turned their attention to the design of special schemes of library classification. CRG was to the opinion that no general classification existed which was suitable for computer retrieval. Therefore, it was decided to develop a general classification scheme in association with the MARC Project for an automated retrieval system.

Since the 1970s, CRG has been actively engaged in the following areas:

1. Revision of Bibliographic Classification of H.E. Bliss, by J. Mills;
2. Formulation of Broad System of Ordering (BSO);
3. Classification Scheme on LIS; and
4. PRECIS.

4. Documentation Research and Training Centre (DRTC)

The DRTC came into existence due to earnest efforts of Professor P.C. Mahalanobis, Founder and Director of Indian Statistical Institute, and a member of Planning Commission, has a vision of establishing a progressive, modern industrial society of India. To accelerate the process of industrial growth and development he visualised the need of having a documentation centre for training the future librarians and documentation personnel to cater the needs of specialist, scientists and technologists. It was Dr. Ranganathan who turned Proof. Mahalanobis's vision into a reality, when in 1962 DRTC was founded under the overall guidance, supervision and direction of Ranganathan, at Bangolare with following objectives :

(i) to offer course of training in documentation and information science;

(ii) to provide continuing education for documentalists and information scientists;

(iii) to promote and to cunduct continuing research in library science, documentation and information science;

(iv) to provide consultancy and advisory service in the design and development of library and information systems, services and techniques; and

(v) to publish monographs, reports periodicals in documenation and information science.

It actively promoted different levels of research in library classification. These are:

1. Development research to develop depth schedules;
2. Fundamental research to develop postulates and principles; and
3. Systematic testing of depth schedules developed by faculty and alumni of DRTC.

It has been organising annual seminars on thrust areas of Library Classification and Information Science, conducting short term courses and workshops. It is bringing out, in collaborating with Sarada Ranganathan Endowment for Library Science, a Quarterly journal "Library Science With Slant to Documentation and Information Studies" since 1964.

5. International Society for Knowledge Organisation (ISKO)

The International Society for Knowledge Organisation (ISKO) was founded on July 22, 1989 with the 'the purpose of functioning both on a national and international level as a connecting link between any and all institutions concerned with conceptual questions pertaining to the organisation and processing of knowledge. It aims to contribute to an intensified and accelerated exchange of experience, thereby helping to fill a widespread need for clarification and expansion of existing knowledge in the field.'

A Draft Charter of proposed ISKO was prepared by I. Dahlberg and R. Fugmann of Germany. It was discussed and approved by the group of German and Non-German members present on 22 July 1989, which also elected Dr. I. Dahlberg as President of ISKO. In 1996 Prof. Hanne Albrechtsen has succeeded Dr. Dahlberg as ISKO President.

The principal aim of this society is "to promote research, development and application of all methods for organisation of knowledge in general and in particular fields, by integrating especially the conceptual approaches of classification research and artificial intelligence. The society stresses philosophical, psychological and systematic approaches for conceptual objects." The society provides personal contact and opportunities to the worldwide community of colleagues who devote themselves to the creation, expansion, revision and application of tools for the organisation of knowledge according to the conceptual point of view. The society has already organised four international ISKO conferences. The society is also bringing out a quarterly journal entitled "*Knowledge Organisation*", formerly known as *International Classification*. This is devoted to concept theory, classification, indexing and knowledge representation.

6. Broad System of ordering (BSO)

The Computer technology has also made remarkable impact on library and information systems and services. In the management of effective and expeditious library services, many library operations since then have been computerised. However, in classificatory discipline its use is still in the nascent stage. Various on going experiments together with extensive and serious discussions and deliberations at national and international level are taking place to find out the extent of use and application of computer technology and other mechanical aids in library classification. The efforts of International Study Conferences on Classification Research in this regard may help in the application and use of computer technology in the discipline of library classification. The UNESCO, FID and other similar organisations have acknowledged the importance and utility of computer technology in library classification.

With the aim of developing a network of information systems in 1971 Unesco and International Council of Scientific Unions (ICSU) jointly set up a Central Committee to undertake a feasibility study of World Science Information System (UNISIST). The programme was launched on the basis of the recommendations made by the first intergovernmental conference held in 1971. The said report consists of a chapter on technical developments where it suggested that a standard list of broad subject headings might be useful to locate and transfer large blocks of information rather than specific document data.

ASLIB was requested to examine whether existing classification schemes would serve the purpose, but ASLIB committee felt that non of the schemes were suitable. Therefore, UNISIST has come to the conclusion that a completely new scheme should be developed as a Standard Reference Code (SRC), which later came to be known as BSO.

FID/CCC (International Federation for Information and Documentation/Central Classification Committee) has been working on the feasibility of transferring UDC as a 'roof scheme' for other classification systems before in entered into a contract with UNESCO on the development of BSO in 1971-72. But at the FID conference held in 1972 at Budapest, Hungary, it was decided to enlarge the size of the FID/CCC panel formed in 1971 to serve as a working group called "FID/SRC" for the purpose of preparing a Standard Reference Code (SRC) which could serve as the BSO as desired by UNESCO. Thus a small committee known as FID/BSO was constituted to develop the proposed new scheme. After two and a half years of study, the Committee presented a draft scheme called BSO, which consisted nearly two thousand subject fields in a brief hierarchical order but without a notation. FID published the "BSO-Broad system of Ordering: Schedule and Index" in 1978.

The Broad System of Ordering has been developed to serve as a switching mechanism between different classification schemes, indexing languages and thesauri in the process of information transfer. In other words it is an exchange information language in the form of 'coarse classification'. It is a general classification scheme with faceted structure. The subjects are arranged in three levels. In the first level–main classes are listed; the second level covers specific subject fields; and the third enumerates subject field divisions, covering the whole universe of knowledge in about 4000 combinable terms.

Notation : Indo-Arabic numerals are used as base of BSO. Other symbols such as Roman capitals and ISO 3166 codes are also used to individualize the countries. Two connecting symbols – (dash) and , (comma) are used to combine the different numbers enumerated in BSO schedules. For this specific rules are provided.

The notational pattern followed is–three digits (millesimal) for main subject Field; two digits (centesimal) for subsequent divisions., (comma) is used as connecting symbol. e.g.,

543,52 Feudal system.

975,70 Religions of Iranian Origin

Facet Structure : The basic facet pattern of BSO is as follows:

(i) tools or equipment for carrying out operations.

(ii) Operations (i.e., purposive activities by people).

(iii) Processes, interaction.

(iv) Parts, subsystems, objects of action, or study.

(v) Objects of action or study, product or total systems.

Common Facets :

In addition to this facet pattern which is provided in particular subject fields, the common facets–Time, Place and optional facets are also used.

Time and Space Facets : –01 is used to indicate Time Facet and –02 for Space Facet. These can never be used as independent number. These are applicable to every subject fields except 510 History, 520 Areas Studies, 544 to 546 where Time and Space are specially scheduled facets.

The outline of the Time Facet is as follows:

–012 Prehistoric times

–013	Ancient times (C 3000 BC to 500 AD)
–014	Medieval times (C 500 AD to 1500 AD)
–015	Modern times (C 1500 AD to 1920 AD)
–016	Recent times (C 1920 AD onwards)
–017	Future times

Dates in its usual form may be added to time number.

Schedule of Space Facet along with instructions is given. For example :

–021 Geographical areas of units (expand like 521)

Examples :

–021,30 National units of territories.

–021,60 Local units of areas.

Names of places are arranged alphabetically with their IS 03166 codes and these are to be designated throughout the BSO by these two letter codes added after a comma to –026.

Examples

–026, AF	Afghanistan
–026, AT	Austria
–026, BD	Bangladesh
–026, IN	India

Optional Facets : Optional facets are like Form Divisions of general classification schemes, used for designating the type of organisation for information sources, e.g.,

156,30–026, JP Japanese Press Index

Multidisciplinary Subjects: Provision has also been made at 088 for organizing information sources dealing with wide multidisciplinary spectrum of subjects. The Principle of Unique Definition is being used for individualizing of every separate entry or phenomena, which need to be individualized. This is done with the help of 088 :

For example

345,46	Insects, Zoological aspects
088,345, 46	Insects, all or many aspects

BSO Manual : The Development, Rationale and Use of the Broad System of Ordering. The Hague, 1979.

It discusses in depth the issues and problems concerning the practical application of BSO, giving a specimen file of 750 directory entries of specialised organisations and secondary information services.

An expanded version of the Broad System of Ordering (BSO) is now available on computer disk. BSO is useful as as aid in formulating and modifying search strategies, as a tool for subject cataloguing as an adjunct to other methods of subject retrieval.

The copyright to BSO has been handed over to former FID/BSO panel, which has formed a BSO Panel Ltd., which is a non-profit distribution company.

7. Automatic Classification

Automatic Classification simply means–classification by machine without human intervention. It implies that the classes of terms that may be useful for the purpose of retrieval are formed on the basis of the documents in which these terms appear.

'It is achieved by a consideration of the natural language from the text of each document and an examination of the frequency with which particular words are used. The computer can lists words according to their frequency of occurrence and be programmed to select, as terms for an index, all words with give minimum frequency. Some words may be of especial value because they appear in an auto's summary or conclusions, in the opening sentences of paragraphs or in abstract. This is an important factor in selection which can and must be acknowledged. If categories for the classification are pre-defined, it may be possible to use a small but representative sample of documents known to belong to a particular category, to make a statistical assessement of the frequency of the most-used terms in these and to determine from this to which category other documents belong–that is, new document can be 'classes' by counting the frequency of the chosen terms within them.' Smart (Salton's Magical Automated Retrieval Technique) is an example of automated classification system designed by G. Salton. K. Spark Jones is another name to whose credit goes the theory of clustering or clumps.

In SMART, System each document is represented by a set of concept numbers. A concept number represents keywords which have been reduced to a standard form by the control of synonyms and of word forms. The set of concept numbers for document is called a vector. When a request for documents on a subject is made, the request is presented to the computer as an enquiry vector–a set of keyword numbers produced in the same way as the concept vectors. The computer must then compare the enquiry vector against the concept vectors held in its memory, to select those which most nearly match. In SMART, the searcher has the whole series of processing options open to him. He can choose to search on the basis of word match, word stem match, concept group match and phrase match etc., or any combinations of these options.

But according to Jones "Computer have encouraged statistical rather than conceptual approaches to classification. There is a real difference between automatic and manual classification in that the computer can be more exhaustive than the human classifier." He further observed that the prospects of automatic classification for library purposes are not very bright. Appropriate methods and applications of classification have not yet been established.

8. Expert Systems (ES)

Another area where computer can be used for classification, is Artificial Intelligence (AI). It is an area concerned with enabling computers to do things in which humans are better equipped to do presently. AI is defined as "the part of computer science that is concerned with designing intelligent computer system, that is, system that exhibits the characteristics we associate with intelligence in human behaviour understanding language, learning, reasoning, solving problems and so on". ES is a branch of AI that is concerned with designing intelligent consultant or advisor in the area of interest helping to take decisions or solve problems. ESs have been designed in the field of library classification also. Some such examples include 'MedSORT' for classification and retrieval of serial literature at National Library of Medicine, Bethesda, USA; Herba Medica' for classifying literature on medicinal plants. Another such system was designed for aeronautics at National Aeronautical laboratory, Bangalore. The point to be noted here is that all ESs are advisory in nature, leaving the final decision to be taken by the indexer. Thus it acts as an aid to the indexer in classifying documents.

9. Classification and Online Systems

Classification can be used in online systems for organising and retrieving knowledge. It helps to overcome the limitations of notation in classification. The problem of assigning a unique no:ation can be overcome by assigning alternative notation to knowledge units to cater to varying user needs. Physical collection of material and assigning class umbers from different schemes is also possible in online systems. This helps to avail advantages of different systems and also to carry out comparative study of different schemes.

Use of hierarchical systems of classification also helps in logical subject display and searching, similarly browsing is also facilitated then systematic display of entries. Serialising is made more effective by providing call numbers alongwith verbal headings. It also helps to contextualize vague terms when hierarchical organisation is provided, use of DDC, UDC and LC has been reported in a number of online systems.

10. Classification and Internet

Internet provides a platform for creating and distributing information universally. It has brought in vast changes in the process of information generation, distribution and access. It is characterized by huge amount of information which is growing very fast. Access to this information is made available through search engines and web directories. A characteristic of this information is that its recall and precision is not very high. It has been experienced that a novice doing a search may not be able to retrieve information of his choice even with persistence search. Library and Information Professionals are attempting to organize information on the web by using traditional library classification methods for retrieval of information contained on networks. The advantages of adopting library classification schemes are:

(a) Enhanced subject search facilities;

(b) Possibility of offering multilingual access;

(c) Interoperability with other services; and

(d) Facility for partitioning of large databases.

Moreover, if the Internet service provider uses an existing and popular classification scheme, it has better chances of being up-to-date as it is revised at regular intervals and is popular with users.

A list of Internet sites that use library classification systems or subject headings can be found in:

<URL: http://www.iastate.edu~CYBERSTACKS/CTW.html

Some of the Internet sites, which are using library classification schemes for the organisation of resources, are listed below:

Sites Using DDC

CyberDewey: A catalogue for the World Wide Web. David A. Mundie (Pittsburgh, Penn.) <URL: http:/ivory.lm.com/~mundie/DDHC/CyberDewey.html>

Canadian Informations by Subject. Ottawa: National Library of Canada. <URL:http://www.nlc-bnc.ca/caninfo/esub.html>

PICK: Quality Internet Resources in Library and Information Science. Aberystwyth: University of Wales Aberystwyth, Thomas Parry Library. <URL: http://www.aber.ac.uk/~tplwww/e.pick.html>

Net first. Dublin, Ohio: OCRL.

Sites Using UDC

BUBL Subject Tree aims to give a comprehensive coverage of UK Internet resources in all subject areas. BUBL Information Service is a national service for the higher education community funded by the Joint Information Systems Committee (JISC), UK.

NISS Directory of Networked Resources is a selective service, which covers all subject areas. It uses UDC in some detail and browsing through NISS involves working through UDC hierarchies with the numbers displayed on the screen above each section.

OMNI (Organising Medical Networked Information) is a selective subject service that catalogues resourees relating to medicine. It usually uses UDC to create browsable searches. However they also use a subject-based classification scheme to create separate browsing sections.

As it is highly time-consuming and expensive to manually classify the millions of documents available on the Internet, a number of research projects are examining the procedure to be adopted for converting the subject terms (collected from searching a database) into classified notation. For example, while the Nordic WAIS/WWW Project (Lund) and Project Gerhard (Oldenburg, used UDC for the conversion, OCLC's Project Scorpion adopted DDC. A number of projects, which are exploring the possibility of neural networks and automatic conversion between classification schemes, are also in progress.

Concluding it can be said, though majority of library and information science professionals feel that library Classification has no relevance today in the age of electronic documents and online access to them. But it has been seen that library classification finds application everywhere including online systems ad organizing and retrieving information on the web. Individuals and organizations like CRG, FID, ISKO (International Society for knowledge Organization) have been engaged in pursuing and engaging research in the area to adopt it to the changing scenario.

13
Miscellaneous

Q. : Write short notes on followings.

(1) Bibliographic Classification

(2) Library of Congress Classification

(3) Systems and Specials

(4) Zone Analysis

Ans:

(1) Bibliographic Classification (BC)

Bibliographic Classification (BC) was designed during 1940-53 by H.E. Bliss (1870-1955), Librarian of City College, New York. He devoted all his life to the study of classification. When published finally in 1953, it had many commendable features, but it was not used much. The second edition known as BC-2 prepared in UK by J. Mills is one of the most scientific general classification schemes and a good model of a faceted classification. It is published by Butterworths, London.

Main Classes and Notation

A	Philosophy, Mathematics, etc.	Q	Social Welfare
B/G	Physics, Natural Sciences	R	Political Science
H	Man, Anthropology	S	Law
I	Psychology	T	Economics
J	Education	U	Technology
K	Social Sciences	V	Fine Arts
L/O	History	W	Language & Literature
P	Religion (Alternative Z)	Z	Religion (Alternative P)

In addition, there are six auxiliary tables for the synthesis of numbers:

1. Common Subdivisions
4. Languages

2.	Persons	5.	Ethnic Groups
3.	Places	6.	Periods of Time

Notation

Its notation is commendable and is balanced in complexity. It is reasonably mixed, simple, brief but very effective. It is retroactive, that is, can be combined backwardly:

JK	Curriculum
JN	Secondary Education
JNK	Secondary School Curriculum

Only some parts of the systems have been published, others are in progress. Work has been slow due to lack of manpower and money.

Special Features

1. Its order of main classes is well planned. It is based upon what Bliss called "Scientific and Educational Consensus".
2. Alternative places for some of the main classes have been given to suit local conditions. For example, religion can either be placed at P or at Z. Similarly, economic history can either be placed with general history or with economics.

Use

It is still not very popular. About 90 libraries in UK, Australia and Africa are using it. Being technically a modern and superior classification, it has a bright future.

(2) Library of Congress Classification (LC)

The LC is a purely enumerative classification which consists of 21 classes in 29 parts and 45 volumes and is the bulkiest of all the systems. It is based upon literary warrant. The main Features are :

(i) LC Classification is devised from the comparison of the then exiting schemes, and is based primarily on Cutter's Expansive Classification and the basic character of its collections and its probable use;

(ii) LC Classification is a practical scheme as designed to comply with the needs of collection and users of the library;

(iii) It is purely enumerative classification scheme, in which even common isolates and geographical divisions are enumerated;

(iv) The system has no theoretical foundation, as is clear from the statement of Herbert Putnam 'The system devised has not sought to follow strictly the scientific order of subjects. It has sought rather convenient sequences of the various groups, considering them as groups not books, not as groups of mere subject.' Commenting on LC classification defending the scheme on the grounds of theoretical as well as empirical virtues, Immorths, states 'If LC Classification is to continue to prosper in the future a justification of its theoretical base is most significant.' He further writes 'Although LC does not meet all the requirements of the theory of classification, and classification scheme construction, it is clear that it does have some sound theoretical principles with which to face the future and in many instances is superior to either the Decimal Classification or the Universal Decimal Classification.'

(v) The procedure used to design the scheme has been to make first the provisional schedules for individual classes and then develop the minute details using the collection of the library. The use of the Principle of Literacy Warrant is quite clear and reflects the period i.e., late nineteenth and early twentieth century, in which the schedules were designed. However, the schedules which have been revised, new areas also get place in then.

(vi) Alphabetical Device is used excessively. For example:

J	Political Science
JC	Theory of State
JC51	General works
JC53	Special topics A-Z e.g., Plebiscite
JC75	Special subjects A-Z
JC79	Local A-Z

The device has created unhelpful sequence.

The order of the main classes in LC classification is as follows:

A	General works	P	Language and Literature, Literary History
B	Philosophy		
B1	Religion		
C-F	History	Q	Science
G	Geography	R	Medicine

H	Social Science	S	Agriculture, Plant,
HB	Economics		Animal Husbandry
HM	Sociology	T	Technology
J	Political Science	U	Military Science
K	Law	V	Naval Science
L	Education	Z	Bibliography
M	Music		Library Science
N	Fine Arts		

The alphabets I, O, W, X, Y are still vacant. Further divisions are again denoted by alphabets:

Q	Science	QC	Physics
QA	Mathematics	QD	Chemistry
QB	Astronomy		

Further subdivisions are by numerals:

QD

142-142	Analytical Chemistry
197-197	Inorganic Chemistry
244-44	Organic Chemistry

It makes frequent use of alphabetical mnemonics for further subdivisions:

QD171	Metals
QD172	By Group A/2
QD172.M4	Magnesium Group
QD172.P8	Platinum Group
QD182.R2	Rare Earth Metals

The alphabets and numerals M4, P8 and R2 have come from the simplified Cutter Table for author marks. Sometimes the year of publication is also included in the class numbers. For example:

The Economic Way of Thinking by Paul T Helyne

HB 171.5.H46 1990

Class numbers, which are call numbers, are lengthy.

Hospitality

Gap Device is primarily used to provide hospitality to new subjects. if no gaps exists a decimal point is used for further sub-divisions. Alphabetical device is also used frequently to provide hospitality, even in places where its use may result in an unhelpful sequence.

Index

There is no general Index in LC. Each schedule contains its own full index and is relative in so far that class is concerned. The list of LC Subject Headings used for the dictionary catalogues of the Library of Congres may be used as a substitute for general Index. However, two general indexes were issued in 1974 by the Canadian Library Association.

Uses

It is one of the big three classification systems-the other two being the DDC and UDC and is being used in the largest library of the World-the Library of Congress (USA) which has about 10 crore documents. 60% of the research libraries, and 50% of the college libraries are using this system in USA. It is also used in some big libraries in Africa, Asia and Europe. LC class numbers are available on CIP data, MARC record, and are used by other centralized agencies. It is also being used in online catalogues.

Demerits

(i) It is a bulky scheme and suitable for shelf arrangement only.

(ii) It is a mark and park system.

(iii) Being enumerative, it is difficult to accommodate new subjects at proper places.

(iv) Only device used by the scheme is the gap device for hospitality.

(3) Systems and specials

The concept of systems and specials proved useful in the theory of knowledge classification. ·One finds them in all structures of knowledge. They are also available in all schemes of classification. According to Ranganathan, the terms Schools of thought or Systems indicate that a particular subject has been viewed from different approaches. The number of systems will be equal to the number of approaches and under each approach the whole range of the subject is treated. Thus under different subjects, the entire area can be examined from point of view of established schools of thought or systems.

System which has the highest literary warrant at a particular point of time is called 'Favoured System. For example in Medicine, Allopathy is considered as the favoured system. Similarly in other subjects/ Disciplines, one system in each subject is a favoured system, and this favoured system is identified with the Basic itself, for example, in Medicine, Allopathy is noted by the main class 'L' itself. The result is that documents on favoured system, say, Allopathy, precede the books on the other systems in their arrangement. However, in CC7, all the systems have be individualized, for example, 'Allopathy' has been treated as a separate system, under Compound subject L-K.

In CC6, according to Dr. S.R. Ranganathan:

(i) The system level should precede all the levels of the personality facet.

(ii) If in a class number both system and personality appear, a comma should be used before personality isolate number.

(iii) If in a class number both special and personality appear, a comma should be used before personality isolate number.

(iv) If in a class number, system, special and personality appear, (a) the sequence of the three will be first system, then special and the third will be personality, (b) a comma should be used before special, and also before personality isolate number.

Examples:

CC7	CC6	
L,2	L 2	Human Digestive System
L-9C	L9C	Child Medicine
L9S2	L9C,2	Digestive System of Child
L-L	LL	Homoeopathy Medicine
L-L-9C,2	LL,9C,2	Digestive System of Child according to Homoeopathic Medicine.

All the system isolates excluding the favoured system, in a Main Subject are created by using (CD).

The *Specials* of a basic class are those isolates under which the entire subject is viewed from the point of view of the field of specialization. In such subjects, special condition prevails, e.g., Child Medicine, Low Temperature Physics etc. and under these specials people do their specialization. Dr. Ranganathan analysed that the specials signify restriction on the field of exposition of a subject to a particular range. Each special covers the entire area of the Basic Class.

In other words, in a subject there may be different degrees of specialization restricted to certain areas. The whole subject is oriented towards that restricted area only. These restricted areas are nothing but specials.

Examples :

(i) In agriculture specials are:

Dry Farming; and Soiless Farming

CC6	*CC7*	
J9D	J-9B	Dry Farming
J9S	J-9C	Soilless Farming

Here the characteristic used is mode of farming.

(ii) In main class Medicine, specials have been demarcated on the basis of age, sex and environment.

Specials are : Embryo, Child, Old age....etc.

CC6	*CC7*	
L9B	L-9B	Embryo
L9C	L-9C	Child
L9E	L-9E	Old Age

If in a Class Number, both special and personality facet appear, special will come first and personality will be attached with special with a connecting symbol comma.

Example :

L9C,2 Digestive System of Child

(4) Zone Analysis

Zone is a portion of an array in which all the array isolates are formed by one and the same device. Zone analysis is an important concept which provides for great hospitality in any order of arrays. It may be the order of main classes, isolates, sub-isolates or any further lower order. The concept is dependent on the use of mixed notation. A particular type of notation is used for respective type of ideas. Ranganathan recognized four types of isolates and for each type of isolate, different type of digit is used.

(i) For Enumerative Common Isolates – lower cases alphabets a-z are used.

(ii) For Enumerative Special Isolates – Arabic numbers 1-8 are used.

(iii) For Devised Special Isolates – Capital alphabets A-Z are used.

(iv) For Devised Common Isolates – Numbers in brackets () are used.

According to this concept any order of array can be divided into four zones. Each zone has the provision of hospitality in it. These four zones can be found in a facet and even in isolates. The concept of zone analysis proves in full the necessity of mixed notation. It helps in full individualization of any isolate idea. Each zone has the provision of hospitality in it. Therefore, total potency of hospitality through zones is much higher. It can handle the dynamic and infinite growth of knowledge in a suitable manner. Ranganathan formulated an analytico–synthetic scheme of classification and has divided whole universe of subjects into four zones.

Zone – I : In first zone General Approach main class (e.g., Generalia, Bibliography, Gandhiana, Year book etc.) and Generalia Main Class (eg. Indology, Gandhiana, Nehruana etc.) have been kept. These are represented by roman small alphabets.

Zone-II : In second zone, recently recognized main classes, have been kept for eg. Universe of knowledge, Library Science, Journalism etc. These are represented by Arabic Numerals.

Zone-III : In this zone, proper main classes are kept. These are represented by Roman Capital Alphabets eg. Mathematics, Physics, Chemistry etc.

Zone-IV : It includes newly emerging methodologies and techniques, for eg. Evaluation Technique, Conference Technique etc. These are represented by Packeted Notation.

So it can be said, zone analaysis occupies a very important place in the classification of knowledge for documents.

Is It Police?

Confessions of a Top Cop

VK Singh, IPS

Manas Publications
(We Convert Fighters into Writers)
New Delhi-110002 (INDIA)

MANAS PUBLICATIONS

(We convert Fighters into Writers)

(Publishers, Library Suppliers, Importers & Exporters)
4402/5-A, Ansari Road (Opp. HDFC Bank)
Darya Ganj, New Delhi-110 002 (India)
Off: ☎ 011-23260783, 23265523, Res: 011-23842660
Fax: 011-23272766
E-mail: manaspublications@gmail.com
manaspublications@yahoo.com
Website: www.manaspublications.in

2nd Impression 2014 (FP-2013)

ISBN: 978-81-7049-431-7
₹ 595/-

Designed at
Manas Publications

Printed in India at
RK Print Services, Delhi
and published by Mrs Suman Lata for
Manas Publications, 4402/5-A,
Ansari Road, (Opp HDFC Bank),
Darya Ganj, New Delhi-110 002 (INDIA)

Contents

Dedicated to

My father

and

all victims of Police inaction and reaction

'*Satyamev Jayate*' is more a romantic phrase and less a reality. It doesn't happen at its own but you have to make it happen at tremendous cost – a frightening proposition.

VK Singh

Acknowledgements

I have noticed that all big authors preface their books with acknowledgements. I am not such a celebrity that acknowledgee will feel obliged. To the contrary, they may frown at me for referring to their names in such a pedestrian book. However, I will do my job and they will do their own. I have taken twenty-three years of time and all sorts of experiences to write this book. Naturally, I deserve to write acknowledgements.

I am thankful to my father, Late Shri Madhav Prasad Singh, who took immense care of a motherless child like me in my boyhood. He was a man of character and believed in simple living and high-thinking. His belief never allowed him to earn more than simple living and his high-thinking put him through such trials and sufferings that others gave his example to deter anybody from simple living and high-thinking. He was fearless, spiritual and has been my ideal. Naturally, this book would not have come into print has he not suffered himself and conditioned me to suffer in legacy. My brother Rabindra Nath Singh and Arvind Kumar Singh, senior officers, deserve my deep gratitude for always exhorting me to be a writer. They have unduly very high opinion of my writing skills. They were very happy when I got into IPS, though greatly disappointed when l could not get Bihar cadre. They have always guided me and worked as steel frame to shield me from all thoughts of going insane in police. They have undergone mental trauma along with me in their young age and thus were comrades–in-sufferings due to inaction of 'Police'. They have also supported me financially and emotionally to continue my studies. I would not have been there where I am now without their support. Both of them are fully convinced that police are the most wretched lot and thus double my agony. My sisters Santi Singh and Kanti Singh offered all bribes to God and pledged all types of '*mannat*' to see me through the gates of UPSC examinations. They have continuously showered sisterly love on me throughout and kept me strong through all bouts of depressions and frustrations. It is different issue that they themselves felt disappointed and deprived when they found '*tehsildars*' and police inspectors more prosperous than me. They feel mighty cheesed off when somebody comments that they have the best of the world because their brother is an IPS officer. Now, they are totally disillusioned of their fanciful and wishful idea of an IPS officer. However, I can't forget them for their unstinted support in keeping me steady at the time of crisis. Their pep talks and experiences have given me an insight into police functioning. I must profusely thank my elder sister-in-law Late Rama Singh who took unbelievable care of me as student and proved all theories wrong about sisters-in-law, who chuck out their brothers-in-law (*devars*) and sisters-in-law (*nanads*). She died of cancer when I was fighting the dreaded gangs of Bihar. She never gave me this guilt feeling of not paying back in cash or kind for all her services and love which she gave me when I needed it most. I ask apologies from her for failing her miserably. She used to be awake nights after nights when I was preparing for my graduation, post-graduation and civil services exams but never asked or expected anything. When the world is so selfish, she took extreme care not to hurt me where it hurts the most i.e., the feeling of worthlessness. How can I leave my younger sister-in-law Abha Singh without acknowledging her contribution to my career as a Police Officer? She always took my side when not-so-subtle hints were thrown at me for making money and always compared unfavourably with all sorts of 'rich' officers. Many a time, she was shouted down by elders for spoiling me and supporting me in a mission which leads only to doom, frustration and pauperism. She did not leave my side, and encouraged me to be what I wanted to be. I express my deep regrets to my family as I could not keep them happy but still they extend warming hands and heart.

My teachers Surendra Singh, Mahendra Pratap Singh, Ram Ekbal Singh and Sadanand Dwivedi contributed their bit to shaping of my thoughts. I am quite indebted to them.

And finally but a large 'thank you' to Vasundhara Singh, my wife, who thinks that she has obliged me by marrying me. She also enriches my memories from time to time that she got offers from many reputed families and prospective bridegrooms for marriage but she had shown her favour to this lowly and truly. She is good in cooking, a great home-maker, a fashion designer, an affectionate mother and a master packer. Given the number of my transfers and her experiences in packing, I think she should have started a 'Movers & Packers' company. Whenever I got a new transfer order, I used to avoid her depressing eyes and sullen face. One incident I vividly remember which happened in Patna. God damned posting of heading Special Task Force, Bihar catapulted me into the vortex of fighting politico criminals Mafiosi reinforced with concrete of casteist bureaucracy.

To my misfortune a news item appeared in *Hindustan–a Hindi Daily* on the front page with my smiling photograph that I held politicians and bureaucrats including Chief Secretary and Home Secretary responsible for the rot in Bihar. I also dubbed the politicians and officers corrupt. The hell broke loose. My security was withdrawn. I was asked to vacate the Government quarters overnight. I was relieved and somebody took the charge, at lightning speed at the dead of night. My requests for retention of quarters for two months were rejected. And I got secret news from PWD authorities that Chief Secretary was planning to humiliate me by throwing my household articles and members of the family out on road with the help of police.

At that time, KAH Subramanayam was the Chief Secretary as well as Advisor to the Governor of Bihar. I was too shocked to react at this humiliation and inhuman behaviour of the powers-that-be. But my wife reacted at lightning speed with clenched teeth, sad face and very swift hands. With two small children looking bewildered by her side, she packed whole household items in flat six hours by 3.00 am. She is a lover of art and felt pained at her art-objects being thrown away while packing. She always mocks at me and says that person like me should not marry because 'such people want to change the world' and thus can't maintain a family. I protest to this accusation but am always brushed aside. I learnt my lesson that you have to have a gritty wife and a wealthy father–in-law if you want to have a decent life in police.

She perhaps didn't deserve a policeman as husband because he can provide broken promises, soured wishes and shattered dreams.

How can I forget the ruling parties of Andhra Pradesh and not thank them who tossed me from one place to the other and made me learn valuable lessons of life. But for their giving me lessons in life and resultant poignant experiences this book would not have been possible.

My special thanks to police heroes at the national level like JF Rebeiro, KPS Gill, Kiran Bedi etc and at the state level like KS Vyas, HJ Dora and MV Bhaskara Rao. HJ Dora, DGP (retd) thought me a thoroughly useless officer. To his disappointment, I remained useless. He warned me not to take Government (read him) lightly and weak and it was their mercy that I was still in the service. I am highly obliged to him for allowing me to run away from the state with job in hand. "Their successful careers" taught me and motivated me "not to be like them". 'Bullets are not the replies to bullets'. If you don't follow laws, ultimately it is policemen and police organisation that bear the brunt. It is the Press which makes you big but does not bring in changes to the life of policemen and commoners. The state heroes were so close to chief political executives that they decided the fate of police. It is debatable whether the destiny of police they decided was the best for the people. I decided not to follow these role models. If you want to have a career, you have to follow such role models. If you want to have stand, you have to forget career.

Policemen are robots manoeuvred by career police officers, seasoned politicians and wily vested interests but I express thanks to Raghuvansh Singh, Police constable of Bihar Police, Tirupati Raju, Junior Commando of Grey Hounds, Hyderabad and other thousands who sacrificed their life at duty fighting gang lords by ignoring their own families. I don't know what inspired them to lay down their life for this dysfunctional system. I salute these policemen who, I don't know, why they are so much committed to their duty without any rewards. I wanted to be like them. Police will be really different had we taken those unsung soldiers without career as our heroes. I acknowledge my heartfelt thanks to these martyrs whose sacrifices have gone waste and compelled me to write this book.

Preface

I am not a writer. Before this, I have not written any either. But circumstances compelled me to become a policeman and a writer. When my saintly father who believed in non-violence and who did not allow even a snake to be killed, was sent to jail for a charge of murder that was a natural death converted into a homicide obviously with police help, I felt molten lava going through my spine. I decided to be a police officer to change the rut.

Now, I am a crestfallen police officer. You might have read many accounts of brilliantly successful police officers but now you get an opportunity to read the rumblings of a failed one. I failed because I don't find any change in police even now than when I joined twenty-three years back with a fire and zeal to change it. Some people feel that it has further degenerated. I can only assure you that

I have tried with all seriousness and commitment to add some sheen to this behemoth but I could not succeed. I could not pass in my test of changing it. I don't grudge the Government and organisation. They have given me everything what they give to a policeman. All medals, commendations and promotions. But I am unhappy because my mission remained unfulfilled. I feel, I represent a whole range of such failed police officers who had joined police not only as a means of livelihood but with a mission in heart and dream in eyes. Such police officers came from a modest background and have seen the failures of police in their childhood. Some have faced the trauma of police action and inaction. They also saw immense possibilities of service and future of the society in this organisation. I am one of those unfortunate ones who could not repay the debt to his father by failing to effect any change in this unfair police system.

A decision to join police is a suicide. Suicide of peace, idealism, convictions and family life. Sanity will become a casualty if you are really an idealist in police. You might have seen *Ardhasatya* movie. It is not quite off the truth. I don't know I am sane or insane. My colleagues can only give a certificate or you can. Had I been sane, I would have left police long back.

These chapters are writings on poignant experiences of my living through hell in police. I would have either rebelled or left police but perhaps I am not that brave. My mission is failing, my idealism is falling through but I still cling to it. Perhaps the helplessness and incapability of earning a livelihood.

If someone wants a service as a profession, police service is the best. But I have experienced limitless anguish, disappointment and pangs of failure. You join it. May be you succeed in changing what I could not because change in police lock, stock and barrel is the aspiration of crying millions of India. This book is an ode to all those police officers who tried to break their heads against wall but could not change the system and eventually find themselves at the receiving end: who wanted to change the rules of game for police but felt dwarfed by multitude of vested interests who were simply too powerful.

We have hundreds of police officers, highly decorated and greatly appreciated. The irony is that police service is one of the most despised ones despite innumerable successful professionals within its fold. And these successful professionals can't disown the failure of the organisation. If they do, what will you say? And about masses. Perhaps they are too dazed to say something.

VK Singh, IPS

CHAPTER 1

Why did I Join Police?

I had had an IAS officer in my vicinity. He had a very cute son, a very small one roughly about five years old. I used to see him every evening. The only striking thing was he used to march in full police uniform and never took it off till he went to sleep or when disrobed by his mother. His, however, is not a solitary case. All the children get fascinated by the police. But I was not one among such children. I had no such fascination for police dress in my childhood. I remember I fancied to become a civil engineer but by the time I started scouting for job, the engineers had lost charm. Those were not the heavy software days with tons of money.

If you are afraid of something you want to acquire that status because it gives you kick. As a small child student, you wish to become a teacher or if your flights of fancies go higher, an headmaster. I was not afraid of a policeman in my childhood though I was born in a village. My uncle was a sub-inspector of police, a direct recruit of 1942. He became a sub-inspector when only four persons had passed SSC from our area, roughly a conglomeration of 50 villages. Since he was a policeman, and we used to stay with him at his places of posting, I lost the fear of a policeman. I had heard a story that my great-grand maternal uncle had hid himself in an earthen pot of grains for two days when he got a news that a constable was to visit his village. Such stories would stir a child's mind to become a policeman. But this was not so with me.

As a child I had seen flurry of activities in the police stations whenever a senior police officer visited the police station. Virtually the police station used to shake and there were shock-waves felt in the homes of the police officers also when there was inspection by senior police officers. The police officers lost sleep and with them their wives and adult children. Though I was very small I also felt the seismic waves of such inspections. We were asked not to venture out of our houses. That time I used to think that I should become a senior police officer once I grew up. But the craving was not so strong because as a child I bothered more about playmates and our games.

As earthquakes change the course of a river, a shocking incident changed my thinking and my life. I learnt about uselessness and total worthless and ineffective ways of police when I was about twelve or thirteen year old boy through a heart-wrenching incident.

My father was a very pious, honest and selfless gentleman of helping nature. He was a teacher of a higher secondary school and used to take care of joint property. He was a believer in truth, non-violence and Gandhian ideals. He wore khadi dress and Gandhi topi all through his life. He was such a stickler that he never used oil, perfume or any such luxury items after death of my mother (when I was only about three) and kept his head ever-tonsured. He was so non-violent that he never allowed anybody to kill even snakes and scorpions. He commanded tremendous respect in the villages and in the school. He was fiercely impartial, fair and rule-minded. He was called far and wide for arbitration (*panchayatis*) between scabbling parties in the villages. The courts used to receive very few cases from our area because of his efforts. He was selfless to the eccentric level and used to check the students of the school 10-km away from our home on foot or bicycle because there were no roads, whether they were studying or not when he did not teach me any time in his life nor he asked to observe studies. Ironically the school never asked him to do this nor paid him anything for this. No teacher except him did this job of self-appointed monitor. He had inflated sense of justice and fair play. The school in which he worked was managed by a private managing committee but was supervised by District Education Officer in some matters. He had recurrent differences with the managing committee of the school because he felt that the scholarship to the students was not granted fairly and the managing committee appointed worthless teachers to the school that jeopardised the future of the students. Naturally the managing committee dismissed him from the service. There were disturbances in the school and violence was reported by the students against his dismissal. The Regional Director of school education in subsequent proceedings reinstated him with glowing remarks. "The teacher could not bear the remarks of his superiors fired with his extreme ideals of honesty and fair play. There are no serious charges against him. Hence, he is reinstated into service". But he was not willing to go back to the service because he had started the work of service to the people through "*Tappa Vikash Samiti*" – a social organisation. The *samiti* did not receive any donation and ran on his own meagre income or the membership fee of few members. He spent his day and night in the social service. He was totally apolitical and religious. If somebody asks me who is your ideal it becomes a difficult poser to me. I am greatly influenced by Netaji Subhash Chandra Bose and Swami Vivekananda although I have not seen these personalities. However, I have seen my father and wonder how could he maintain such a selfless and unblemished character in this bad world. Once he went to take bath in the river Ganga. A certain beggar, a half-naked one asked him for alms. He gave him his all clothes and jug for water he carried and came back in a towel traversing the busy roads of Patna on foot half-naked himself. As we know, bad world is not for good ones.

There was a family in the nearby village. They were a joint family with a notorious reputation of many charge-sheeted dacoits and criminals in the family. They had the reputation of using force and intimidation to cow down their adversaries. They also used to forcibly occupy private and government land. My father was called to such a *panchayat* for resolution of dispute between a weakling and this family over a land issue. The helpless person had appealed to everybody in the area to intercede and do justice but nobody dared to talk to those toughies. My father, as was his wont, agreed. As was expected they refused to listen to reason and challenged the person to do whatever he wanted to do. My father expressed helplessness and advised to approach police. The aggrieved person went to the police. The notorious family having almost 50 adult members, went wild and resolved to set the records straight. They felt that the 'pigmy' might not have dared to go to police had my father not advised him or taken up his cause.

They planned a big conspiracy that was unheard of. One of their elders about 65 years of age died a natural death due to cold and rains since he was watching fields on a rainy day. They planned for a cremation and people were also informed to that effect. Subsequently, they changed their mind, went to the police station and filed a case of murder by strangulation and named five persons. They also planted witnesses. At that time, my father was in school teaching moral values to the children, but the witnesses claimed to have seen him on the scene of crime. He was very sure that it would all be exposed because truth was on his side but just the reverse happened to my utter shock and disbelief. I was told by somebody that if you are a vegetarian, it doesn't mean that tiger will not eat you out. The doctor gave the medical opinion that this was a case of strangulation and the police found it to be true in their investigation. The whole world including police knew that it was a false case but 'evidence' is everything what matters. My father was arrested and I was shocked to death. I am afraid of God and destiny but I have no faith that good deeds always lead to good results. The whole world came crashing down. A child who lost his mother in infancy, saw a great injustice being meted out to his pious and innocent father by the 'great' criminal justice system. I have very little faith in previous birth because there is no way it can be proved. Even if it is there, it is of no use to me because there is no continuity and no remembrance. What is the fun in being punished for something which I have not done but, some 'imagined' soul whom I don't know and I have no visible but spiritual connection did it in previous birth. I lost faith in police system and God. I wanted to be a police officer to get out of this mess and do something to change this unfair and worthless system, which has destroyed millions of lives and happy families.

The 'notorious' family forcibly encroached upon our land, ploughed and took away our crops. We again dutifully reported to the police. They registered a case but nothing came out of it. I could know what a big farce the whole police system was. They conveniently washed their hands off telling that it was related to civil dispute. They knew it was forcible and illegal but the system had taught them to act like this.

Some happenings going around you also fashion your attitude. As a village boy, I had no much exposure to government though I was not mortally afraid of police as other village boys would be. The reason was that I had lived my early years with my uncle who was a sub-inspector of police and thus experienced policing and lived in towns also. A sub-inspector of police came to our village police station as in-charge. His prescription to all ills of law and order and good policing was thrashing the people-innocent or otherwise either at the police station or on the roads. People were damn scared to be seen on the village roads even at the dusk because of him. My elder brother whose service mate was our Superintendent of Police that time met him and gently nudged this issue to his notice. The Superintendent of Police was abrasive and appreciative of that SI's actions. This was my first occasion of having insight into police thought process and unique ways of earning money. I mulled upon this idea that perhaps the IPS officers were the real cause of all police ills. Later on, it was confirmed when horrendous things happened to my father and subsequently when I joined police and found how the IPS officers have failed the expectations of people and the country. The sub-inspector of police started getting money without asking and that also disproportionate to his rank and the going rate because people were frightened of beating. I am not sure whether Superintendent of Police was also a party to it or not. I took a resolve that by any chance if I became a police officer, I will not do this and change this style of policing. The world knows that I have put in more than 22 years and not a bit of change in the style of policing took place even in Andhra Pradesh. Needless to say that my years went waste and I had been a miserable failure.

There was a very good man Manohar Singh of my neighbouring village. He was a ranker SI. He had gone through some law and order problems in his place of posting. A crowd provoked by the budding Maoist movement leaders attacked the police party. As usual the police party led by the SI opened fire and killed seven people. A murder case was registered against the police party and the whole police party was suspended. Manohar Singh was dazed and downcast. This gave the third dose of thought to me that it was not necessary to do bad things to get suspended. It is always other than professional policing that determines the career and future of a police officer. The senior police officers buckle under the pressure of the political groups who are themselves propelled by electoral compulsions than common good. I made a commitment to myself that I wouldn't allow punishment to anybody in any circumstances who had done his professional job.

A host of such factors rocked my mind and impelled me to become a police officer. Policing was not mere a means of livelihood but a mission and passion to me because I wanted to pay debt back to my father and all the hapless souls who were victimised by police's omission and commission. It was a great commitment indeed!

CHAPTER 2

Broken Wings and Shattered Dreams

It is more than 22 years since I joined police as an Indian Police Service Officer. Destiny has been very kind to me but I did not know that it wanted to give a 'taste of police' to me. Lord Krishna in *Bhagvad Gita* had said "Everything runs according to Him. You are just a means. You know that you are doing it but it is not so. It is He who conducts the show". Now I am depressed, heartbroken and a failed police officer. I have lost my goal. The tides of police times have blurred my vision. My mission has broken wings. Career is tattered and reputation fragmented. I am very sure that a large section of police fraternity take me as insane person. Most of them must be laughing behind my back because a sizeable segment chuckles with derisive tinge "So VK! We are not getting your love letters". I feel vacuum in my life. I really got panicked. When everybody feels that something is amiss with me, it must be so. I had seen film *Ardhsatya*. Om Puri had all the kicks of police life to go insane.

One thing was clear; I tried my best to be clean in my conscience and true to myself. I never made 'new year promises' to indulge in double speak and double action. I did not want to be 'practical'. Police is like a crystal clear water in which even the tiniest stone gets detected and the system tries all means to eject. It permits soluble non-resistant compliant ingredients. A senior officer told me that there is nothing like purging of system and playing good Samaritan in police. Rules of game are very clear – either you play according to the set rules or get ejected. Missionaries are not allowed here. I learnt it hard way like in certain English clubs "Indians and dogs were not allowed". I felt the police system never took me as one of it.

If somebody thinks that honest and hardworking officers are not favoured with plum-postings, it is wrong. Virtually the system always prefers honest, committed and hardworking officer but they should be practical and careerist. The government is not happy with those who are not pragmatic and careerist. High ideals and morals are big no no. If you want to be a nationalist and idealist, you should have taken birth 50 years before to join freedom movement but not now. Since you are misfit now, it is your fault but not the fault of the system.

I have never seen such uneducated, uncivilised, indisciplined and barbaric organisation like police. It pinches me the most because police has tremendous potentials to serve the people. But the stalwarts of police have systematically dehumanised it and stonewall all attempts to reform it.

Once I was posted as Principal, Police Training College which was an Addl SP rank post. I was already DIG. I was fully convinced that I had done a good job in my previous anti-Naxalite assignment of Greyhounds. It was a record-breaking performance in all adverse circumstances in the field of anti-Naxal operations. I went to DGP to request that this post no way justified my rank as well as performance. Even if he did not think me suitable for any post, I should not be punished. He adopted Buddha like posture and said with anguished expression with a tinge of reproach, annoyance and frown all rolled together "there is something seriously wrong with you. I don't know what will happen to the department if officers like you grow senior and occupy some senior positions. I shudder at mere imagination". I was dead sure by then that I was not a sensible person. When a successful DGP who superseded eight of his seniors had this opinion about me, he must be correct. It is a different issue that he gave gallantry medals to those who never were present in action and denied to those whom even Maoists acknowledged as one of the wreckers of their armed squads in fields all because those officers didn't accept his theory of policing.

I have got one grudge against my father, my village and my upbringing. They conditioned me in such a fashion that feeling of casteism could not be ingrained in my personality. Subsequently, I learnt that lofty ideals, latitudinarianism and constitutionalism are meant for books and fools. Smart guys don't practise it. One Member of Parliament in Andhra Pradesh asked me to give proportional representation in postings to his caste, to be more precise, his nephew. I managed to be polite and told that I give postings on the basis of performance. This was good for department, the people and the MP also because anyway it was his Government and he will get good name for better policing. He really got furious and breathed fire and brimstone. He launched broadsides at me "Don't teach morals. The Chief Minister, the Ministers, the Director General of Police, the Chief Secretary all are selected on the basis of caste. If you say you don't believe in caste, so what? It is your problem. Our community should also get its share. Don't give me the crap of secularism and casteless society". I didn't do the transfer. And he retaliated by levelling all sorts of allegations right from financial corruption to several rendezvous and boozing at all stops to the Director General of Police and the Chief Minister. It is a different issue that I am a teetotaller and always default on house loan payments due to financial difficulties. The MP, however, has shown me the reality TV of life. Caste, lobbies, political support, practical wisdom are the ladder to success. Don't crib if you are incompetent to do all this. Accept your fate and incompetency.

If you commit a grave sin in your past birth, you get a cadre other than your own. If you commit *maha* grave sin, you land up in a cadre where your castemen have no significant presence and you are deprived of backing by any powerful group. Caste is a sure shot ladder to success in Indian democracy and bureaucracy. Now, there is naturality and spontaneity in the 'favicol bond' of caste and career. If you don't have the right caste tag, you have to be Colonel Sleeman to have a normal career. All posts which have public interface, are to be donned by right-caste people. Service-orientation, commitment, honesty etc etc are not the qualifying factors. If you have all these, it is good for you. But these are not the eligibility conditions for a successful career.

Policemen are great status-quoists. Naturally, it will be so because we kill all initiative, discourage all change-mongers and put great value on figures and statistics that can be fudged. Our culture, our people and our society have appreciably imbibed the principles of patience, forbearance and pardon. They are ready to bear with any kind of injustice, gross misrule and chaotic administration with great patience and fortitude. They view the good and bad elements in police with great equanimity. Naturally, I grew conscious of my uselessness and valuelessness. It was slowly turning into an identity-crisis for me. More the urge for change inside, more the pain, anguish, restlessness and feeling of void in career. You become a time-marker, you will be the most successful. Patience pays!!

If you are a policeman and want to survive you must be a smart lawbreaker. By smart means a lawbreaker who can't be caught. The world is a stage, where everybody is a player. In criminal justice system there are great players. Police feel that without breaking the law, you can't maintain law and order because there are no appropriate laws to deal with abnormal situations. The legislature which is euphemistically called so, otherwise it is the ruling party, does not frame stringent laws because it is afraid of losing votes; and judiciary which tries to fit in all situations within the written code, catch police by ears whenever they are caught breaking laws. What a comic situation! The whole nation knows including legislature, judiciary, intelligentsia and the Press that police break laws to contain terrorism, extremism, mafiosi, great crimes and petty offences but everybody poses as if they are not seeing it. Now a policeman is between the horns of dilemma. If you don't break the law and fail to produce results, you are inefficient and if you break the law and produce results, you may be caught on wrongfoot. Thus policing became a cat and mouse game. I was a total misfit in this game. I was doomed to fail. Ropes of career and my mission to change police were sticking out of my hands.

I always lived hand to mouth. And my subordinates and some of the colleagues always faulted me for this. Nothing moves without money. Even to secure a non-bailable warrant notice to surrender in a court, you have to pay money. Members of my family, friends and relatives felt pity on me because I could not keep pace with standards of SIs. Three rank below officers were living a king-size life and I travelled second class ordinary very often with my family. But you get negative marks for all such idiosyncrasies. I have also realised that running the system is more important than running it well. Fools like me don't understand this. Many a time now I plan in my dreams to become a businessman to get rid of my poverty. I think of various ideas of leaving the job and fighting the poverty. It leads to serious bouts of depression as neither I could change police nor I could reduce my insolvent status. To top it all, remarks were being asked to explain charges of corruption on anonymous petitions filed by faceless petitioners. I was wondering why could such anonymous petitions not be lodged against 'rich' police officers. Police system is a morass. More you angle for change, more you sink deep. Once I wrote to one of such allegations in an anonymous petition that it is below my dignity to reply to any allegations of corruption. Naturally it angered the bosses no end. It is different issue that the bosses had no problems with 'seasoned' policemen. Was it worth joining police? I have mulled over this question. So far I have not been able to answer this.

People have very high expectations from police, particularly those who are in distress. I had a very troubled childhood as to police experiences. Some serious differences cropped up between my uncle's and our families. Minor violence also broke out. As our uncle had a bigger family, naturally they forced us out of our legal possessions. They also attacked us and our father. We got the wrong end of the stick because physically we were quite weak. I along with my brother approached Superintendent of Police and the SHO. The Superintendent of Police beautifully wrote a 'n/a' on my petition. I was 15 then. I could not understand what is this n/a. Perhaps the SHO knew what does 'n/a' mean and used the petition with 'n/a' embossed by Superintendent of Police as tissue paper. Our uncle started ploughing all our land illegally. We complained to the police. The police came, saw and returned. There was an old man in the village. He reproachfully blurted out that police would not do anything unless they were given *dakshina*. We were so depressed and helpless. But this mattered little to police.

When I look back, I feel, I was so naïve to feel depressed because police all over India is insensitive, barbaric, uncouth and corrupt. Whenever I hear the word 'Good governance' or *Sushashan*, I feel, it is a joke of the millennium.

I learnt, people suffer both ways – due to omission or commission of the police.

I promised to myself that were I a police officer, I would change the police come what may. It was my desire to be a policeman because in my eyes police were panacea to all ills particularly in an illiterate and undeveloped society like ours. A child's mind is impressionable mind.

Things started going southward as I earned spurs in police department. Good governance is one thing which, I think, is the last priority. We don't want to do right things right. While inspecting a police station as young Asst Superintendent of Police, I met the professional confessor of crimes, who vied to confess crimes for money. I had been on the worst of terms with all Government departments. Nobody wants perfection. It is painful and boring. Let the things take its own course. Whenever I wanted to change the things, the whole world conspired to see that things went wrong for me. I was impatient itching and shimmering to do something but the system found that I was good for nothing. It is also foolishness to take myself the paragon of virtues. Lord Krishna has told that nothing happens because of a person. It was all divine will. But I lost peace because I was not a great believer. I had doubt in myself, my belief system and my values.

Slowly, I started getting radical and rebellious in my thinking. Actually why should one become honest, truthful, sincere and committed? In *Mahabharata* even the Pandavas were the losers because Draupadi was dishonoured in full public view. They spent twelve years of very hard life and ultimately lost all relatives and army except the five brothers in the war. Arjuna lost his dear son Abhimanyu even. Did the truth really triumph? What did Pandavas gain? Who knows what happens after death? An honest policeman who bears pain all his service, years of pauperism, bad career, deprivation of worldly pleasures and final failure of doing nothing, is a virtual wreck. If he maintains his sanity that is a great achievement. Who cares for his zeal for changes in the system?

I used to be very inspired in my early career with great names of police but I saw an advertisement '*Hamam mein sabhi nange hain*'! Was it the real portrayal of great police officers' real life? Those who are good can't succeed in career and those who succeed in career should forget about stand. If you have a career, you can't have stand.

I had heard and also watched in movies that police medals were not awarded to the real bravehearts but to those who managed. I laughed it off as totally unreal and imaginative. How could it be? Who will tolerate it? Media, senior police officers and government will not tolerate it. But I was shocked out of wits when it occurred so many times in Andhra Pradesh. I had participated in one encounter which was very fierce that led to many casualties to the Naxalite ranks. The Press spoke so highly of me but the Director General of Police in his wisdom recommended the name of a person who was not there at the scene but supposedly was instrumental in collecting information. The successor Director General of Police wanted to correct the wrong by recommending my name later. The Government of India in its wisdom thought that the second recommendation of single name for Gallantry medal must be a pull candidate and rejected my name for the medal. Subsequently, I kept on requesting for justice but I was asked to keep my mouth shut. It was a different issue that the same Director General of Police was found fault with for recommending names of officers for Gallantry medals who were on leave on the day of encounter and had nothing to do with the bravery. Most surprisingly the Government of India awarded them the Gallantry medals and did not take any action despite disclosure of this 'ungallant act'. After this I developed repulsion towards any medal. Somehow, I thought God was great that I was not awarded Gallantry medal otherwise I would have become unjustifiably a laughing stock.

In Bihar, a news item appeared in my name that I conducted a Press Conference and blamed the officers and politicians for looting the State. I denied the allegation that I conducted any such Press Conference though it is true that there is no casteist in Bihar but all are selfish gentlemen who have exploited their own caste brethren. I had served Bihar taking personal risks. When I had served in Bihar jungles in the beginning of my career and killed Chhangur Dusadh, a dreaded dacoit in an encounter, the dacoits retaliated by killing my two brothers-in-law, one of them my own sister's husband in his youth. When it came to rewards, we were told that we were just probationers and should not crave for bigger things. The then SP and ASP claimed the bravery awards. The only bravery they showed was coming after 16 hours of beginning of encounter. By that time the dreaded dacoit had holed himself in a corner surrounded by our team. We had collected information; we took the risk of facing hail of bullets in the dead of the night; we cornered the head of the gang who was proclaimed to be the most dreaded dacoit of the plains of the decade by BBC with Rs 50,000/- reward on his head in 1980. But we were not given any credit or reward but a *badakhana*. When second time I served in Bihar, the Government of Bihar 'rewarded' me by recommending for suspension for the Press item which I had denied. All vested interests, lobbies, few IAS officers, politicians and criminals wanted my head. The Government of India ordered my suspension and sent it to the Government of Andhra Pradesh for implementation. This was the reward for achieving record breaking performance for neutralising scores of criminal dons, kidnapping gangs and PWG Naxalites. It was the then DGP and Chief Minister of Andhra Pradesh who were taken aghast at this injustice and saved me from this ignominy.

I had never had anything good in me, but I was trying to be good. I feel guilty for my wife who bore with me all this pain. I am very sure had she not been afraid of social stigma, she would have left me. I have heard of many wives of some 'honest fools' who deserted them creating real mid- life crisis. Who understands their pain that they gave their life for good of the millions — helpless, hapless and uncared?

I have seen only humiliation and failures. What is the basis of personnel management in police? As I said the greatest tragedy of anybody's career is when he is not allotted to his native State or to a cadre where his castemen were in majority. In Indian governance many things are determined by God but not by your efforts. Your career can be predicted by your attitude, caste, ability to lobby and having no principles for life. *Mahabharata* teaches us not to stand on principles. Karna practised *dharma* of friendship and *danam*. And he was doomed. Bhishma served his family all life and he was rewarded by his death on the bed of arrows. The police job is also a *Mahabharata*. I am turning pessimist. A new theory is pervading my whole being. My friend jocularly used to say "I have a principle that I keep no principles". People speak brutal truth in lighter vein.

Almost all Director Generals of Police found me a misfit of a police officer. In my face they told that I was not practical but God knows what were the reasons. Nobody explained it to me. I told one Director General of Police "Sir, my performance is better than anyone else". He told, "performance and excellence is not everything". This is democracy. I could not understand the theme behind his statement.

I look back and brood upon my failed life. The people continue to suffer, the system creaks under its own weight, my desire, enthusiasm and commitment could yield nothing; people politicians, seniors and subordinates were equally unhappy. Nothing could change in police but I was a changed man. Terrorism, extremism, maoism, goondaism, corruption, fraud etc etc all exist not because we are not able to uproot them but because we don't want. We prefer 'we, ourselves and ours' more than the people, society and the nation. Let the sleeping Lion lie is our motto.

When I have virtually collapsed in mind and body and see 'great' police officers cringing for career at the cost of people's and national interests, I think was it worth joining the police! Someone said labours are destined to work and royals are to enjoy. All the honest, committed and sincere ones work for the system to keep it afloat and the smart and unprincipled ones enjoy the fruits without any sweat or plucking of hair. This is policing!

Chapter 3

Suns and Darkness

I met a brilliant police officer who was professionally upright and sound career-wise but squeaked like a mice when bosses asked something which was illegal. I have also read books of many committed officers who were individually tremendous but collectively useless. It was a revelation to me that officers who were thought good for nothing, had tremendous ideas for policing and had so much fire in them. But it was all a big zero in total. The police department as such is a court of Dhritarashtra. Duryodhana disrobed Draupadi, sent rightful partners-to-throne Pandvas to incognito and brought the whole population to ruins. It is a more puzzling and anguishing fact that conscientious, courageous, moralist and valiant generals like Bhisma Pitamah, Karna, Dronacharya, Salya etc did not utter a single word when all these happened. These people could sacrifice anything and were no cowards by any standard. Police generals have shown the same character. When something illegal takes place, these generals look sideways. The life and hard works of all such officers go waste because their goodness, sincerity, commitment and sacrifice don't split a hair of the unfair system. These officers are not courageous enough or lack broad vision, I don't have idea. I can only say that the life of such officers is peaceful and smooth and going great gun on shining path of career. Simultaneously, police system is running down the hill.

When I expressed my desire to join police, one of my college friends first expressed surprise. His surprise gave way to curiosity. "More is the darkness, more is the light needed" he finally said in resignation. I felt high. He took me a light. Full of ideas and enthusiasm I entered the portals of police with firm desire to set the things right. I was under the impression that I would be the only lamp or at least one of the few. People will really rejoice at my timely entry into a much-maligned arena of police brutality to reform it!

But I was shocked to find that there was no dearth of lamps in butt-of-the boot police department. It was the merchants of darkness who had snuffed the life out of all these lamps. Lamps either grew pale over time, or flickered agonisingly or died out. They were not able to fight out the thickness of organised darkness. They had no courage to catch the bull by horns but were sidestepping the issues. It was a peculiar situation in police. Many suns were peacefully co-existing with the darkness. I don't know whether I should feel pity or take solace out of this paradoxical situation. Police have got such a bad name. It has become symbol of all vices. We don't find anybody having good words for police. Just opposite we have police officers who are highly committed, honest in action and thought, examples of integrity, full of ideas and intellect, hard working and ready to sacrifice life and comforts.

Many police officers have been found wanting in their duties to family because of over dedication to job. Police have made many more sacrifices than any organisation or community, military included. Its topmost officers have also led from the front and were cut down in their primes. They don't question the motives and intentions, risk-contents and safety–measures of the orders handed-out. They are willing suicidal squad presumably in the interest of public, which everyone knows is not always the motto behind the orders handed out by powers-that-be.

Then what is the cause of darkness? The malaise is deep and wide. Certain people reason that the nature of job of a policeman is negative because it hands out only punishment and no rewards to dole out. If this be the reason, why are certain strict police officers popular? Why do people come on to roads to stage protest against perceived unjust transfer of a policeman? Why don't all the bureaucrats and development authorities get good name? (It is a different issue that recently certain street-smart bureaucrats have managed the local Press and impressed the Press-barons to get favourable brand-image. The age of advertising is changing the whole rules of game). Normally, good police officers get good name and bad officers get bad name. It is not true that all officers will-get bad name.

More confounding is the presence of very good officers in the equally very bad environs of police. It is the lack of guts, intention and will on the part of these 'suns' of police to vanquish the darkness. The police is very traditional, change-resistant and conservative department that believes in full status-quo. It discourages new ideas, initiative and progressiveness very jealously. Routine-maintenance is its sole aim. Though the Police Act 1861 is not that strong to instill and sustain this retrogressive spirit over such a long time, the sub-culture of police and the interests of ruling elite become a great bulwark against any change.

The sub-culture doesn't only protect itself but hits back against those who whisper need of changes. The hard hit is painful and highly demoralising. It is, therefore, a common spectacle that committed pro-changers find themselves on margin. If you push hard, the system ejects you out of itself. The price paid for advice of change is enormous in emotional, physical and professional terms. Pro-changers are called idealists who are misfit in this harsh-realistic police world. The system has insulated itself admirably through a fool-proof defence mechanism. There will be a spontaneous general antipathy among police–colleagues against all pro-changers. Status-quoists feel that this is the only way of running police. The system allows hard-working and honest police officers and gives lot of recognition and public acclaim if they conform to the basic framework. It is not that all good and hardworking officers are run down. But they shouldn't question the basic concept, thinking, methodology and style of policing. The police welcome cosmetic changes because it gives it credibility and public acceptability. It also has to wear badge of pacing with the modern changes and taking progressive steps to serve the masses. Changes have to be greeted and incorporated till these changes don't scratch beyond the surface. This is the reason that the police could retain all its virtues and vices over decades. As this system was devised by colonialists, it has more vices for commoners than virtues.

Mahabharata episodes are enacted everyday in police. There were honest, conscientious, brave and courageous moralists in the court of Dhritrashtra. They were ready to lay down their lives for *dharma*. But for obvious lack of situational guts and courage, to call spade a spade, allowed incident like derobing of a family–lady Draupadi. What could be worse comment than this on the character of all warriors and moralists present at the time! Perhaps it was the urge of self-preservation and self-perpetuation that immobilised the courtiers. They all perished subsequently because they could not muster the courage to oppose what was palpably wrong.

The suns of police department abound in individual merits. They have abandon courage, limitless energy for hard work, willingness to sacrifice their self but they blindfold themselves to all acts of injustice meted out inside and outside the department. Their virtues go waste because it is of no use either to the department or to the people or most of the times to themselves. They believe in cleaning their stable and thus satisfy their conscience. They earn good name for this 'positional' honesty and hard work; and love basking in this glory. Sometimes this glory may be limited and sometimes it may be all encompassing like winning Magsaysay Awards. Profuse encomiums are showered on them. These 'suns' feel highly satisfied that they have done their duty to their conscience, society and the nation. This is the easiest way to satisfy oneself; think oneself a shade different from run-of-the mill type persons and earn glory. But does this help the people or the department any bit?

Dishonesty continues; poor persons languish in jails; false cases are booked at the behest of the mighty; the laws are bent to subserve the political masters and the police look to be meant more for moneyed people. Only commoners have rightly no faith and love for police and they take it more as an enemy. They think that there would have been better justice and fairplay in the world if police were abolished. At least natural justice would have taken course and none would have been there to protect the powerful lobbies and syndicates, politicians and capitalists, landlords and exploiters. Unfortunately, the honest and hard-working policemen protect the dishonest and depraved, arrogant and powerful exploiting classes in the name of duty and rule of law. The suns of police department never took it to be their duty to question the simple rules of injustice.

These meritorious police officers have comfortably put on blinkers. They don't want to see bad in the world because it pricks their conscience. They also know that fighting the system will be very painful and trying experience. It may sometimes lead to being snuffed out unsung, unheard and unmourned. They take pleasure that they did wonderful job by clearing and purging their areas. They forget the holistic approach to the system. Curing a heart of its problems will not revive a patient dying of cancer. Cancer has to be acknowledged and fought. It is wasteful exercise to purify a room if the whole area is polluted. It is not being wise and sagacious to clean the stream down the hill when it is getting foul water upstream. They have to take courage to cut the root of the evils—not the branches. They can't see the problems from narrow perspective. The 'suns' have mostly demurred from fighting the system. It seems to be only a losing position to them and they don't like to be losing.

Another, dangerous aspect to this whole scenario is that the public-acclaimed, decorated, conscientious officers feel pricked and tricked if some other lowly colleagues take up the issue of change in police. They don't like that someone else should hog the limelight, which is their due. Unknowingly they become jealous of all such attempts. It gives them the feeling of weakness and incompleteness and that it is not they but someone else who is raising the issues what they should have raised, hurts them. This feeling of lack of fulfillment sets them against any pro-changer. They apply all means to running such pro-changers down. Unwittingly they become a party to the murky deals. They help the system in silencing these discordant voices. They are more than willing if someone wants to use their merit, skill, hardwork and goodness to fight the 'good'. These 'suns' become quite myopic if the circumstances suit them. They don't want to analyse the background of malaise and the character of rebels. They are careerist and obsessed with individual image. They are happy only with this fact that the diseased system has acknowledged their worth in putting down the voices that have raised concerns at the system's injustice. They don't want to see wrong or right of their actions. They got their opportunity to show their skills of policing and golden worth. They want fame, glory and comforts of the post all at a time in exchange of their life-time honesty and hard work. They have neither time nor will to analyse the justifiability of their action or the pitfalls of the system. Medals come pouring in; seats come tumbling down and he gets larger than life image. He is least concerned with the systemic maladies and fallacies. He says that it is not his duty to see whether system is good or bad, whether his actions are ultimately helping people but the task at hand given by the system is all he is concerned with. He has got the ability to do it well with all his commitment and efficiency. He is hero of the masses and 'suns' of the police department. The people adore them and edify them. They become demi-gods by serving the corrupt system which they should have demolished for the good of the people and the system.

These 'suns' turn philosophical when they don't get seats of importance. They pass subtle remarks; throw glances of dissatisfaction and frustration; express disquiet at the decline in the values and system but are wise enough to refrain from raising cacophony. They don't want to annoy the system but in another vein want to earn public respectability and sympathy for facing persecution for their goodness. The police would be used, misused and abused. Small fries will be sacrificed. Injustices will report agalore. People will cry for relief from any quarter. The devils will have free field. These 'suns' at this opportune moment will become philosophical and meditative. They are speechless and motionless at the sight of agony and sufferings of the people. They are like conscientious courtiers of Duryodhan who don't open mouth for fear of invisibles; for fear of backlash of the system. They allow the injustice, devilry, mischief, exploitation and everything. They confine to themselves and their table. It suits their conscience and theory of self-perpetuation and self-preservation. They are practical, worldly-wise and pragmatic. Anyway when the time comes they may squeeze out of the system their due i.e. recognition of their worth, glory, publicity. If they try to fight the devils, the devils in the system may devour them. They will not be alive to earn the glory, awards, posts and comforts. They are more concerned about self-satisfaction, self-righteousness and self-preservation. They are least concerned about the system and its maladies and people and their sufferings.

This is coming down from the generations. The succeeding suns learn all these ropes from the preceding 'suns'.

Once I asked a very senior officer why the things are not changing and why are all quiet. He quipped an answer that all great persons in the past could not reform the system so far and none can do it in future. Better to confine to our bread and butter and forget all these eccentricities. One officer was very vocal in denunciation of the system and perpetuators. Most of us believed his sincerity and rallied behind him. Feeble attempts were made to question the contradictions and injustices meted out by State. Expectedly the system hit back and some of the followers got hurt. The leader expressed concern and squeaked that it was one thing to talk about changes and incongruities in the system and quite another to make serious attempts to change it. Needless to inform that there was pin drop silence in all quarters and the hurt followers were left licking their wounds. The system remained unchallenged and unchanged. The 'sun' continued getting glory and glorious posts agalore. He kept on decrying the system and confining himself to his seat to purge the whole system. The system was angry and the leader was wise enough not to hurt it further. The 'unwise' rebels of the followers got the stick and fell battered and bruised.

The system likes idealists and moralists but in the shelves, not in the field. If some idealists go far, he is pushed further to be out of the system. If someone is idealist within the tolerable limits, he is decorated in shelves to be shown to others. Only roughs and toughs continue in the mainstream to continue the darkness. Alongwith these toughies, flourish these suns, the crowns of police who somehow hang on to earn awards and glory. The hardcore idealists anyway wilt and fadeout but the 'suns' withstand with their tactical blow hot blow cold policy which keeps closer to powers that be and 'respectable' to the masses.

The 'suns' thus survive and darkness continues. This has become a symbiotic relationship. The darkness uses the 'suns' when it suits them and then leaves them sulking. The suns are also happy that they are getting their due off and on and are willing to share the dias with the darkness. So goes the story of "suns and darkness in police with continuing gloom in the lives of miserables". Long live the suns! The system is dead!!

CHAPTER 4

Community Policing vs Community Service

A young beautiful girl came to a police station in Kurnool district of Andhra Pradesh with a boy and claimed that she is in love and so had married the boy but the parents did not accept it. She wanted the police to counsel their parents. The boy's parents disowned him whereas the girl's parents were weeping bitterly out of shame. Police found themselves helpless because both were adult and legally there were no provisions to intervene. Naturally the police refused to intervene. The couple refused to budge from the police station on the ground that where they should go if police didn't do anything. This dilemma is very common in Indian setting.

In another case it was far more peculiar. A missing child was brought to a police station of an interior district. The police tried to find out his moorings but failed. In the process, he laid his responsibility of bringing him up on Police Station. The boy refused to be sent to any charity home. The police station staff sent him to a nearby school to keep him engaged. A subscription (*chanda*) was fixed on every policeman for his expenses. All attempts by successive policemen to dislodge him from police station failed because it used to be poignant emotional scenes. People felt that police was very cruel in dislodging the boy from the police station. Anyway they were earning lot of dirty money, could they not sustain a boy!

Between such dilemmas, the concept of community policing in India came without knocking and whispering and without the realisation that police were already in the field of community service. There is nothing new about community service.

Community policing is in fashion now. New fashions attract flocks and cheap imitation. It is happening with community policing now in India. People who have neither will nor imagination nor commitment take to community policing for media hype and instant public attention. Community policing is generally confused with community services. Any community policing without the general aim of community services is a gimmick, an aberration. Unfortunately, all efforts at community policing in India have mostly been public relations exercise and are devoid of spirit and essence of the concept. Community policing is a concept, an ideology and should not be confused with methodology and procedure of policing. In India as third degree method or scientific methods of investigation is a process and a method, community policing is also practised in the same vein. So, the community policing in India has not caught up and has been a flop.

Many police officers have started experiments with community policing at different times with individual style. Some such flashy individual efforts have been adopted by the concerned governments also. Friends of Police in Tamil Nadu, Cops in Chandigarh, Peace Committees in Delhi and Maitri Sanghams in Andhra Pradesh are results of individual efforts of community policing. Most of these concepts have mainly taken birth out of individual ambitions of getting name and fame. Some have succeeded and some have failed. But almost all these concepts lacked basic ingredients of the idea. Community policing means empowerment of people and sharing the power with the people. All Indian Governments have been loath to sharing power and control with people. So, any concept which assumed potentials to gain ground and empower the people was cut off mid-way through and the officer who tried an original concept was dumped. But such efforts at community policing that brought headlines temporarily without touching the core issues were encouraged by the police top–brass and the government. Cosmetic approach to community policing suits the police department and the governments because it is generally not empowerment of people but exercise in media-management, individual glory and public relations. A department which is much maligned and lampooned badly needs image-building exercise and so encouraged by the regressive governments also.

The people respond very positively and enthusiastically to all public-relations exercise or so-called community policing. Policing has been a forbidden area to them. They generally accept any new idea with open arms. So, all the peace committees and all the *'gram rakshak dals'* have been instant success. The Traffic warden concept has given many awards to many police officers. Actually, the concept of homeguards was also a type of community policing which is ultimately reduced to being a wing of police. I have seen many peace committees, many "Friends of Police" and many "*Praja Sanghams*" meeting its grave without any whine and whimper.

The initial euphoria created by all such *Praja Sanghams* peter out because these have no inner strength to sustain. A police officer who takes over an independent charge, is in great anxiety to prove himself. All of a sudden overnight he becomes champion of people. He talks of joint responsibility of police and people to the society and the role of police in social change. The media laps it up and starts giving wide coverage. Committees are formed and office-bearers are chosen. Flashy identity cards come out. Euphoria is generated and the people start doting over the officer. The people surge forward and brace themselves up for greater role and power sharing. Hereafter the '*messiah*' police officer starts backtracking. He is not able to withstand the upsurge in expectations of people. He loses steam for two reasons. First, because he was never a *messiah* and never believed in community policing and people empowerment. Secondly, he might have been asked to restrain himself by the police bosses or the government as all such new concepts lead to imbalance in power-structure. Unfortunately, if a naïve police officer really desired to do something in the field of community policing and people's empowerment and persisted with his efforts despite advice of restraint, he is dropped like hot bricks.

Sometimes such ideas were invited for political mileage also. And this is the most dangerous application of community policing.

As explained, community policing is a species of community services. Community policing is not only sharing the burden of police because they lack manpower and infrastructure or improving relations between people and police but it is aimed at tapping the potentials of police for community service. Community policing gives a platform for both people and police to join together to serve the community. The police have a bigger role in the scheme of things and it can't be confined only to managing traffic or watching the neighbourhood. The people can't only be asked to form peace committees in times of communal disturbances or faction-fights or form gram *raksha dals* to help police check the dacoity menace. It is much more than that.

Unfortunately, neither the Indian courts nor Indian Government have understood the concept of community policing and both have been singing in different tunes. When in western countries the police officers are taught the art of mediation skill, surprisingly the Hyderabad High Court passed judgment declaring all mediation by police as infringement upon judicial domain. This much for the commitment to community policing in India! When the concept of community policing marches ahead, the people start asserting. The government and the police department become restless. They don't know how to handle this assertiveness and growing cooperation of people. And so they bury the concept as well as the officer who moots it. This is the reason that no community policing has thrived anywhere in India and all the police of different states have been giving lip-service to this concept or using this as a means of image-refurbishing exercise.

Community policing is not an end but a means to the well-being of the community. It enables the police to serve the community well. Unfortunately the service-role of police in India has not been recognised at all. There is lot of confusion about the exact role of police in laws and in the mind of people and government. Police is supposed to be confined to law and order maintenance and prevention and detection of crime. This has been the basis of great dilemma and confusion.

In the real life the police play a much bigger and comprehensive role that is not recognised by the law and the government but recognised and accepted by the society. Law and order problems and recurrence of crime are inter-linked with socio-economic, political and cultural issues. Any agency which sees these problems in isolation, will fail to tackle these issues. So, without the consent of the law and the government, the police have been dabbling in such issues that sometimes lead to lot of legal confusion.

However, it is an accepted fact that there is no social service agency like police that works for 24 hours a day all the 365 days in a year. In most of the areas in India the police stations work more like a panchayat than a police station. Whenever this functioning of police has been neglected, the policing becomes ineffective, infamous and dysfunctional. The community services may be divided into following heads depending upon the capability of the local police.

1. Provide the service themselves.
2. Taking others' help in providing the service.
3. Refer the matter to other agency.

As in medicine, any ailment that has not got a speciality department, goes to general medicine. Likewise in society any problem that can't be attended by any social service agency or government department, is attended by the police. If the earmarked agency is not functioning at odd hours it again comes to the police officers to attend to these problems. Sometimes people question the credentials of a police officer to handle such intricate wide variety of problems. But it is less important than the urgent need to tackle such problems that can't be immediately referred to specialised agency. The police can't allow it go out of control in the absence of appropriate agency. The opinion of some people taking objection to police interference in wide-ranging socio-economic problems is based on the general distrust of the police and dynamics of Indian society. By the very fact of age-old coexistence of people and police and impracticality of devising an all-encompassing acceptable-to-all mechanism to meet the legal, social, emotional and psychological needs of society, we can't wish away the vital role of police in the life of a commoner. We have to strengthen this umbilical cord instead of snapping at it. The sections of society that want to bar all police intervention in all social matters, don't comprehend that if such exigencies are not met by police, these will not be handled at all leading to added miseries of the society. Indian courts are laden with lakhs of cases that are crying for disposal. Lok Adalats are mainly running on police piggy back. It is the police officers who go to the parties, convince them through ingenious skills and bring them to Lok Adalat for compromise. If this all-important ground-work and persuasion and mediation skills of police are not used for Lok Adalat, the very concept of Lok Adalat would have been long dead. If police had to do all these ground work, then why is this hypocrisy and noise about undue intervention of police in non-police matters.

Whether the courts, the government agencies and other social-service organisations accept it or not, they who work maximum 48 hours a week, leave 120 hours for the police to service the community. Given this equation, police in all probability handle 75 per cent of the social services. When people need immediate help, they approach the police regardless of jurisdiction or area of concern. The relationship of police and people has been age-old and emotional and can't be snapped by written or unwritten laws. Wherever police refuse to intervene on the plea of law or jurisdiction, the people murmur, curse and find fault with the police for being shirker. It is because the people in crisis don't know the finer nuances of law and they want immediate help from available agency. Since it is only the police that is round-the-clock available, they approach. It will be better for the government to recognise this role of police and streamline it through framing of laws.

My experiences at police stations have shown that more than 80 per cent of the problems that come to police, are socio-economic problems and have nothing to do with primary role of police i.e. maintenance of law and order and prevention and detection of crime. While working in coastal belt of Andhra Pradesh, it was seen that problems like husband-wife quarrels, sons not taking care of parents or ill-treating them, partition of property among the brothers, boys and girls in love running away from homes and approaching police for convincing their parents to agree to their marriage etc cut into major chunk of the time of police. It was always like fair-sight at the police station. People come all the way along with large number of villagers to the police for mediation and settlement of issues. I don't see any court of law or government can stop this social process without derailing the very social life. Moreover, it is not possible for any government to substitute police with any agency because of inherent legal powers and faith of people in police to solve such matters.

When I was posted to Telangana areas it was economic help and employment that was asked of us. They also wanted us to urge different governmental agencies to move faster in solving their problems. In one case, an educated youth wanted psychological counselling from us because he was very afraid of any government official particularly police. In one case, a person wanted to commit suicide if the police did not arrange loan from the bank to repay his loan. He was a teacher who was ready to give undertaking to pay back the loan but none was willing to help him. Many destitute ladies wanted some means of livelihood. In another case, a young lady had intimacy with her consent with a man and got pregnant but the boy was not ready to accept her in marriage. She wanted police to convince the boy not to jilt her.

There were innumerable instances of such cases where no laws or no agency would help them or were willing to help them. They had neither money nor patience to approach any other agency including court because of urgency of matters. Once while with District judge in one of the sittings of District Legal Services Authority Act, the District judge commented in good faith that society will go haywire if the police don't use their good offices. The district judge requested the police to settle one issue of child-custody through mediation because it was turning into a very emotive and sensitive issue. Mind it, he was requesting this despite brutal, corrupt and bad image of police. If we have, by chance, a good and sensible police, how great will be the happiness of people.

The police deal with human lives and property. They also deal with very tricky situations in life and can refuse their role in such problems only to the grave detriment of common people. Once a Medical Superintendent of District Hospital, Medak informed me that he wanted help for a poor patient. The Hospital Ambulance was out of service since long for want of budget and the poor patient wanted immediate shift to Hyderabad for better treatment. As it was dead of the night the patient's relatives were not able to find any vehicle. In another instance Superintendent wanted immediate blood for transfusion for a particular group that was not available in town. The police immediately arranged a vehicle and blood of the required group in both cases. A police expert has commented that to say that the police should not perform social welfare and social service functions because they are not trained social workers is like saying that the general practitioner should not treat a heart patient in emergency situation because cardiologist is not available. By the very nature of their jobs, police officers are in part social workers. People who suggest otherwise are naive to the realities of the societal needs and police role.

Some police agencies in New York City, Dayton and Ohio have trained their officers in applied psychology, family sociology and crisis intervention theory and practice to intervene in domestic disputes. The New York City police do the preliminary counselling and bringing of truce between the parties in domestic dispute and refer it to professional social service agencies. Unfortunately in India, there are no standard social service agencies to intervene in all such social and domestic disputes. Earlier caste-guilds and village elders used to do it. But now all these social groups were replaced by various courts. These courts have neither skill nor time nor infrastructure and manpower nor training nor mandate to intervene in all such silly domestic disputes. So, it is the police in India who unofficially take care of all such domestic and social disputes. If we deny this service to people from police, there will be further chaos in society. The confusion prevails because we feel shy to recognise this role of police in India.

In India where illiteracy is very high, the police can work as nodal centre or information centre to all the services provided by the government. The government provides many services and many developmental schemes but people don't know about them and are denied the benefits. The police can be the best nodal centre for referral job to various departments because they work all the twenty-four hours. For example, many lunatics, old uncared people, poor people suffering from incurable diseases, unemployed youth, budding sports child, new entrepreneurs, AIDS patients etc can be referred to right places by the police. Given a mandate and a little bit training the police can cure half the ills of society and improve its own image.

The people can make people's councils (as made in Medak Dist of Andhra Pradesh) that may relate the police to the community in a positive way and serve to bring together all those agencies that help the people. The concept propounded by Medak police is one of the best community-service attempts and the people's council of a village could be an umbrella organisation to provide all basic services to the villages and promote them on socio-economic and developmental path. This role can be played by gram panchayats also but most of the gram panchayats have no universal acceptance because they are constituted out of electoral contests leaving bitter taste in the mouth of rivals. People's councils can be organised and recognised by the government as self-help groups. Theoretically, the council was to include all unanimously selected people from village, to be changed every year, if the people want and guide the village in right direction in all fields with the policeman acting as a catalyst or facilitator. Such people's council facilitates communication between the government and people and serves as an important source for service to the people.

The vast resources and the influence of the police can thus be positively tapped. The police have much better communication system and infrastructure that can be of great help in Indian context, a country with very poor infrastructure. Virtually, there is an urgent need to use all policemen as a social worker in a country like India which is so vast and so numerically unmanageable that it is almost impossible to provide basic education, health, sports, grievance redressal agencies for many years to come. The Medak experiments has shown in its limited time that the police machinery can be an effective answer to all these problems without putting in anything extra in terms of men or material by the Government.

The most important result of these people's council will be in the form of check on human rights violations, improvement in prevention and detection of crime, better maintenance of law and order and check on police corruption. All these things will be possible because of familiarity and friendship that will develop between police and people in people's council meetings.

Many of states' police have tried their hands at such councils whenever they feel like improving their image or the people cry for better behaviour from the police. These councils aimed at solving police problems, assembled people and policemen and spoke for good police-public relations, took out relationship-promotion rallies, organised police-people's dialogues, seminars in school, conducted random medical camps and water-shelters and left at that. All such efforts were exposed as sham because people felt that they are being roped in for jobs, which are basically a policeman's or a government job. They never felt that the policemen are really their helpers. Secondly, all such Committees or *Sanghams* dared not cross the barrier of traditional police job and professed to confine themselves to legal police job like watch and ward, information-gathering etc. Naturally people lost enthusiasm very fast and felt used. Thirdly, all these committees are not natural development of the policing. Generally either this is out of a need to improve battered image of the police because of some immediate causes or a temporary fad of senior police officers or the government who imposed this concept on them. Naturally, the very commitment, spirit and mission is missing in these attempts. Police continues with their age old habits of ill-behaviour, corruption and brutality. As is natural, both things can't go together. After sometime all such Committees and *Sanghams* have met their natural burial before they could really take-off.

In India there is all the more need of police working as catalyst for social change. Our constitution-makers have enacted many social legislations with lofty ideas and fond hopes of reforming the decadent society. Nothing could bear fruits. Laws alone can't change the society. They have not planned any such agency to put their ideas into practice. They have rightly not done so. Any agency which has not to do much on daily basis with the people will not be able to convince the people for any good change. Police interact with the people on daily basis. People, as it happens in a feudal and illiterate society, look to a powerful and easily available agency for guidance and help. There is nothing wrong in it till the whole culture and social-economic milieu changes. Even Britain, the mother of parliamentary democracy, continue with their anachronistic monarchy and take false pride in it. Indians reposing much faith in police because of their aura and influence has historical background. We should not shy away from police on ground of liberalism, anti-uniform ideologies and abstract principles of justice. On the other hand, we can exploit this relationship for betterment of our society and the police. Both can improve themselves by bringing a little change in their role. With the developing society the police may also adapt and tune in with the new world. When the society fully develops, the dependence on police will naturally come down.

Police have to make community services as a part of their role. They have to work as a catalyst and agent of social change. They can't confine themselves to their legal role of arrest and patrolling and aspire good image. All efforts at community policing (Indian style!) are bound to fail and is a waste of time, money and energy. Community Policing has to keep community services at the centre of its efforts.

It is better to understand it sooner because if not today after twenty years the Indian people and police will realise it but by that time it will be too late. People and the society have to suffer till we understand this ground-reality and need for change.

CHAPTER 5

Service or Disservice!

I think I had been repeating the theme. Repeating is a sign of intellectualism. Plagiarism is supposedly genius stuff. Again the next paragraphs repackage the dilemma, dichotomy and in-built character of hatred towards police. You might have read hundreds of such stories that vividly depict the horrid stories of police functioning. CID of police that is a specialised organisation for investigation is supposedly the cold-storage of sensational cases. In Bihar and Andhra Pradesh there used to be much pressure by influential accused persons for take-over of cases by CID. Once as a green horn Addl SP, I booked a case against a notorious firm for charging four times the price of a motor vehicle parts. Messages were flashed to all the districts to stop payments and start inquiries into the quantum of fraud. The firm incurred heavy loss. Subsequently, they started business by changing the name of the firms because the earlier one was blacklisted. The firm however pulled the string and got the case transferred to CID. The Addl DG, CID was furious with me for raking up such issues. Subsequently, the CID referred the case without examining me and despite full evidence available. I was issued so many show causes. I was lucky not to get charge memo because our officers showed mercy on me. Our Addl. DGP, CID rose to the glorious height of being DGP.

Wholesale transfers of police officers at the time of elections, is a common sight. The whole world including all captains of democracy knows why it was done. Wise men, however, never speak. Bofors case, Hawala case, Taj Corridor case and Shibu Soren case are all such instances that go abegging explanations.

The word police is anti-people in nature, so is at least in India. It can serve the human needs most but is everywhere disjointed and did more harm than good. The concept of police is evolved for the good of the people and betterment of the society. But the history is a witness to it that the powers-that-be have used it as coercive organ of the state and misused it rather than used. There is common perception that people will enjoy more freedom and greater peace if there was no police at all.

Time has solidified the coercive nature of policing instead of protective one because it suited the rulers. Never the good of the people has been taken into consideration by the rulers or systems of anytime. Self-preservation is the prime motive whatever the man or system may be. The desire of authority over others is the basic instinct of human beings. This desire may take different sublime forms of religious or temporal authority. As police is the greatest weapon to fulfill this desire of dominance over others, it has never been allowed to act free, how-so-much, loud professions of commitment and idealism might have been made. In the so-called liberal era when the competition to exercise authority over others has become cut-throat, the machinery and process to do it has also become complicated. All commissions on police have borne no fruits because of this basic clash of their recommendations with interests of ruling elite.

There will be more liberalism in the absence of police. Experiences of the people have shown that police and laws have put fetters only on law-abiding citizens. Only they are harassed, incarcerated and shot because they obey the laws and recognise the police. The laws and the police become ineffective (willfully or by design or due to systemic failures!) in the case of outlaws because they are out of bounds and break it and bend at their will. This explains the fact that even in a land like Punjab few cases have been convicted under TADA. Even if somebody was sentenced, it came much after the need for it ceased. Terrorism was curbed when the police also ignored bounds of laws as reflected in numerous petitions of human rights violations. The people are the natural scapegoat of the so-called outlaws and the protector of laws. It is strange that the security system meant for securing the people nibble at them bit by bit by making them defenceless through laws and procedures. I have visited many jails. Almost 90 per cent of the inmates are weak, poor and penniless who could not defend themselves in the court because of lack of purse. Those who have organised many mass killings, conspiracy, treason and fraud of astronomical dimensions never fall in the net of laws. Even the statistics of lock-up deaths shows that it is the poor and petty thieves who lose their lives. This is the proverbial justice of our system! Let us suppose a situation where there is no police. Naturally if a powerful well-connected man hits somebody, the man himself or by forming a group of his own will hit back. The powerful and influential man will be therefore afraid to hit anybody. However, in the present system if the powerful man hits, you go to the police and court. He manages to prolong the case in the court and ultimately acquittal through money, good lawyers and good influence. He can purchase or terrorise your witnesses or you may not get even a single witness against the powerful man. Sometimes if the dice is loaded too much against the powerful man the government can withdraw the case itself in public interest. What a peculiar form of justice! You have been hit; the Government as your protector fights out in the court and again withdraws it in public interest without asking you. But if you want to take revenge by yourself the police first give security at the cost of public exchequer to the powerful man because there is a threat to him from you. If, by chance, you succeed in hitting, you will be languishing in the jails because you have no money to hire good lawyers or no influence to force the government to withdraw the case in public interest. Thus natural imbalance is created in favour of rich and against a helpless commoner. The poor is always at the receiving end because of this so-called 'protective service'.

The natural balance is disturbed because of flawed police system. In the olden days when the police presence was little, people formed village squads and faced all criminal elements effectively and maintained the socio-legal fabric. There was peace everywhere. The state entered with police and its laws promising that it would protect the people and they should surrender the right of self-protection to the state. The state obviously created police for this purpose but surreptitiously used it for other purposes and more often than not against the people. The people were deceived. It is like a lady placing her honour to the trust of a protector who himself ravished her modesty. They are like those farmers who leased the land on share-basis and were dispossessed by them. Now when the outlaws have access to everything and every means of destruction, the common people have to get license even for big knife. When the criminals are making open mockery of the courts and the legal system, the houses of people are being attached and confiscated for not attending the court the hundredth time. When the criminals do not get punishment even after lengthy-procedure and heavy expenses, the plaintiff and the witnesses are chopped off for deposing before the court sometimes even in the court premises, by criminals/accused themselves.

The police have given a false sense of security and hope. The people have been made to believe that they are being insulated against vandalism and threat by an elaborate network but to his horror the common man finds in hour of crisis the protective hand missing or sometimes colluding with ravaging forces. Had the people been aware that the police is not meant for them, and they have to fend for themselves, they would be ready for such eventuality. This theory is vindicated by the fact that in all communally-scarred areas people arm themselves to teeth and a balance of power is maintained and less damage is reported from the area. Since both the groups are ready for contingent attack, the theory of deterrence works and none of the parties dares to take the initiative. Just the reverse, wherever people have been nudged into smugness and slumber by police force, spine-chilling hoary details of human destruction have been reported. This all happens because the police is not geared up and resourced to face all such exigencies. The rulers use it every time according to their purposes even to the sacrifice of people.

Vast sums are being spent to create elite forces to protect certain VIPs, some of whom are not even holy ones. Given the trips, visits, meetings, *dharnas* and number of VIP protectees, there is hardly any policeman left to the common man's localities. This is the reason that police reach the scene late and are not visible at any time of crisis. Thousands of policemen who are paid by public exchequer are of no service to the people because they are simply not available for common man. As recently the common man might have come to know that all the VIPs, who are protected, are not really threatened but they want black commandos in tow and a vast string of policemen at their houses as status symbol. If half of these policemen are spared the common man can get enough policemen to man their traffic points and beats.

The police in the present shape believes in aloofness, roughness and alienation harping at the same time on good public relations. Virtually people never figured in their scheme of things. Though the rulers may give lip-service to people's interest, the police even don't show these pretensions. It is neither responsible nor accountable nor sympathetic to the people. The people, this is why, get raw deal at the hands of police.

There is no voice to the silent masses – no organised outfit to fight for its interest. Vociferous groups grab the limelight and redressal mechanism to the complete exclusion of the common populace. The system impersonally represents vast amorphous multitude of people whereas organised, interested or outlawed groups are represented by various organisations with different names. Sometimes they masquerade as champions of human rights and civil liberties, democrats, liberals and so on and so forth. None of these groups fight for the people. Sometimes they take up stray cases for limelight, publicity and specific purposes. Most of the times they serve in the cloak of different names under their different parent organisations. Either draconian laws like TADA is imposed or repealed; in both cases, certain vested groups influence the course of action. All such actions in the name of people have nothing to do with the interests of the people. In all cases, either in police action against so-called anti-socials or reprisals by mafia, the people have been the sufferers. This is the tragedy of the history of common people.

People, left to themselves, will have no law and order problems. Law and order problems don't crop up themselves. A background is assiduously prepared or seeds are very recklessly sown for such problems. The powers-that-be who are engaged in exploitation know that at the end their actions will end in serious law and order problems but they sadistically ignore it. Petty selfish gains are more urgent to them than the common human disaster. When the law and order goes disorderly, the same rulers start counter-action. In both the processes there will be huge loss of lives and property. Surprisingly, those who create law and order problems and afterwards try to contain it, always do it in the name of popular interests but always they are the gainers and people the sufferers. If there is no police, no vested groups will have legal and sacrosanct powers of exploiting in the name of people's interest with all immunity.

If we read the account of Jagmohan in his work "My Frozen Turbulence", we can imagine what is the root cause of J&K problem. A simple man knows now that Punjab problem which devoured thousands of young lives was created by omissions and commissions and machinations of selfish forces. The common masses had very little to do with it. The police and the military were used like scapegoats that further worsened the situation. The real issues were sidetracked and the secondary (by-product) issue of law and order problem became the core issue. The powers-that-be, the supercops got good name for tackling secondary issues and the Press and media got scoops for them. But the real core issues that afflicted common people that led to dissatisfaction and unrest were never redressed. The people got the bullet and baton and the vested powers got bouquets, glory and fame.

Even various commissions in all its avatars have fought shy to go beyond certain point in reforming the police. All of them have recognised the coercive nature of the police as their primary work. These commissions having limited terms of reference, limited vision and being the representatives of vested groups couldn't look beyond the ultimate necessity of protecting the interests of their class. As they don't encounter common people's problems like corruption, red-tapism, socio-economic breakdown, near total absence of redressal machinery at grass-root level, they couldn't conceive of any other role for the police. They perhaps didn't want to dilute the rough and tough character of police lest they become the leaders of 'progressive forces'. The police have been insulated from the sorrows and happiness of common people. So despite being one of the oppressed masses, they don't take themselves to be one. People want the police to share their sorrows and ease their burden of life, but the police look at themselves as a separate class. It doesn't feel the pulse of the people because it has been fed on diet of suspicion and distrust. It is not allowed to act in good faith or for social purposes. The commissions of police never envisaged the social welfare-oriented and cultural role of the police because it does not serve the purpose of ruling and powerful elite of the society.

Corruption is in abundance but the regulating authority i.e. police is fettered. It is like a dog which is let upon whom the owner wants to be attacked. The government reserves the right of deciding who should be prosecuted for corruption or who should not. People are interested in corruption-free society but police here also do only selective jobs at the bidding of ruling elite. Therefore, corruption very much stays and the people suffer.

We hear many instances of corruption, rape in custody, lock-up deaths, criminal-police nexus, death of innocents in fake encounters for showing better statistics of improved performance etc. People have no count of minor aberrations like unnecessary beatings, illegal detention, harassment, abuses and indignities heaped on them by police. If we add the number of deaths in police lock-ups and in fake encounters it will be a horrifying story. The so-called traffic regulations in normal times is no less pain but if it is for a VIP entourage, it will be a veritable hell.

People are constrained to think why at all they should have police. What do they get from police? If somebody wants to give proof of his gentlemanliness, he says that he never visited police in his life as if who visit police are all not gentlemen or rather all policemen are ruffians as a company.

It is true, policemen are dying on duty but they are dying more for the problems created by scheming vested interests and not for the welfare of the people. It is the problem of police and they should ask the concerned to refrain from creating problems for them. Either it is Naxalite problem or Ulfa problem or Punjab problem or Jammu and Kashmir problem, it is more or less a creation of the system and power game and not of the people. So, why should people have such police that kills them for the problem created by others? The police have done more disservice to the people and it is time people say, enough is enough.

If police can't save the poor, can't check corruption, can't ensure safety and security to the people and can't help them in day-to-day life, then what are they meant for? Why should people pay taxes to sustain such a mammoth structure?

Some cynics pointed out that there is much peace, equality, lack of exploitation and absence of law and order problems in the area dominated by the Naxalites. People say that there is no theft, dacoity and rape by feudal lords in these 'so-called liberated areas'. If this is true, this is shameful to the police service. Sooner we recognise and reform this 'disservice' the better.

Strange are the ways of the world and so of the police. The protectors of the law are the greatest breakers of law. It is beyond common man's understanding that when laws are more observed in breach than in obedience, why they are made at all? A plethora of laws and blissfully ignorant policeman. To be a successful police officer one need not know laws; need not be highly meritorious and committed. He should know how the things work and what suits the establishment. Establishment does not mean only the government and the powerful interest groups, but also the common beliefs, biases, prejudices, romantic ideas held by people at large. The police system has not changed over time. And chances are quite bleak for any change in future. People from all sections and from all platforms cry hoarse at no-change in police colonial and imperial character. It is really surprising to hear these voices of concern. Are they really so naïve that they don't know that police will not change, that police are not meant to serve the society, that the welfare of people never crossed the mind of a policeman and police manual and that the policemen are to sub-serve the interests of the ruling elite and powerful lobbies or they cry because it suits their interests, soothes their conscience or serves their masters well.

It operates smoothly unruffled despite all the cries outside. The negativity of police is reinforced by the age-old thinking and attitude of policemen, confused expectations of people from police and articulate and well-programmed ways of ruling clique to exploit all law-enforcement agencies. Anybody, who tries to break from the rigid framework of functioning, gets sidelined.

Laws, courts, government, people, Press and policemen have confounded the situation to such a knotty mix that it defies any solution. Sometimes the question seems very valid and relevant; should the police institution be closed down? Will it really lead to worse situation than it is today? The question becomes more painful in the background that thousands of policemen are dying at the altar of duty. The breakers of law (police break law to bring in normalcy) can't get respect from the people and the laws. They might keep quiet if it suited them in exigencies like problems in Punjab, Jammu and Kashmir, Andhra Pradesh, North East but they are bound to criticise the police later. However, the criticism doesn't change the ways of police officers who call the shots. The conscientious ones are anyway declared misfit for the organisation.

CHAPTER 6

Myth of Policing

Children are damn scared of police. We ate food like mice when our family-ladies took the name of police when we as children refused to take food. Police and ghost-both are great weapons in the hands of all families to discipline the children.

Our neighbour, a captain, thought all thieves were on the rolls of police and they used to take commands or briefs from police before they went for their exploits. Once there was a theft in his house. He came to me pleading that I should tell the police to return all his property because police must be having them and are not returning.

Films and policemen are interlinked and both can't do business without each other. Police are born either to break bones or rape damsel in distress. Lock-ups are made for killing people and not for lodging criminals.

Once in Patna people were so angry with the police that all policemen riding public transport were too frightened to wear uniform and moved in civvies out of fear of public wrath. It was all because certain police officers had mistakenly killed three innocents in their pursuit of gallantry medals. This is the easiest method to get medals. Medal is the index of competitive spirit how much one could stoop too.

The police protagonists say that the image of the police has been besmirched and the public image does not match with reality. What is reality then?

Police is the most misunderstood concept and community. It has been shrouded in mystery and fear. It is mysterious because its structure, functioning, strengths and weaknesses, objectives and goals have been unduly kept secret. It is fearful because it wears on hard visage of cruelty, aloofness and expressionlessness. It has boxed itself in a shell to resist all changes with the times. The police have been asked to perform diametrically opposite roles resulting in role-conflict and dilemma among policemen and many misconceptions among people.

One of the great misconceptions about and accusations against the police is that it overlooks people and is unresponsive to the people's needs. The reality is that the whole police system is not designed for people at all. The policemen also feel apologetic about it because despite their toilings and strugglings, they always fail to come up to the people's expectations. The people blame them for their failure and cry for severe punishment. A person who is already working to the maximum stretch will only respond negatively to all words of condemnation. But seldom the police and the people realise that the fault lies elsewhere. The pro-rich orientation, rigid hierarchical structure and subservient work culture don't envisage police to help the people. Its objectives and goals are status-quoist. It has to subserve and perpetuate the system, good or bad. It is change resistant and doesn't have flexibility to adjust with the changing socio-economic political climate. Since the people don't figure in the priority list of the police as per the enactments and schemes of the powers-that-be, they are always ignored. It was alright during Britishers' time because the people had no voice and the police were supposed not to exercise their brains. They were always patted and rewarded by their immediate superiors for being alien to the people and people's cause like cry for independence. It suited both the police and the government well. Since the people had no voice and had little expectations from the police the criticism was not that strident enough though even police commission, 1902 castigated the police role. Even the Britishers realised that the police system was not people-friendly but they bore with it because of compulsions of British Raj. The police was a prop root for British Raj.

The situation changed drastically in post-Independence scenario. The expectations of people shot up. They got voice, forum and will to launch blistering attacks on police for their dubious and anti-people role. The nascent democratically-elected government was not confident enough to withstand the onslaught of the divisive fever. They also wanted the help of police for stability and continuance. Sardar Vallabhbhai Patel talked of reforms but was cut off by cruel fate.

None after Sardar Patel took this task of police reforms seriously because it was fraught with danger of losing a prop in times of crisis. At the same time it required will power, intelligence, vision and power of analysis to delve into complicated details and legal procedures. The government not very confident of its performance to match the soaring aspirations of people felt the need of coercive arm euphemistically called the 'strong arm of the Government'. The police was to be used to contain the unrest, dissatisfaction and unease among the frustrated masses. Too much expectations always lead to too many disappointments resulting in lawlessness. Unfortunately, the police again finds itself ranged against the people of independent India, craving for socio-economic independence. Many forces are working at cross purposes in the power game and all have tried to use the police for their personal gains in the power tussle. Thus the police of the British Raj which was alien, hostile, aloof and unsympathetic to the people, continued without any change. As the people of India expect much from all institutions after independence, they also expected much from the police and felt highly disappointed when they bore the brunt of police *danda* even in independent India. The poor people don't know that the police are not meant for them. It is more to protect and preserve the system (of whatever kind!) than to serve the people. If they want people's police, they have to fight for it as they are fighting for socio-economic justice. It is fruitless condemning the police.

There is another misconception that policemen should be rough and tough to be efficient and effective. He should have muscles, moustache and should look physically mighty. Even less brains will do but he should be of such physical dimensions that people should tremble at his sight. Surprisingly one Chief Minister of a state offered to reward the police officer having bar like moustache. Reality however can't be far from it. A policeman should not be rough and tough and cruel looking at all. Policing is not the function of physical quality but of mental faculty. Though some normal standards of physical fitness at the lowest level is required but at the managerial and supervisory level, it is not required at all. Had it been a truth, all wrestlers would have made the best policemen. Timur would not have been a valiant general and Rani of Jhansi the greatest one of 1857 War of Independence heroes. Truly speaking the policing is a great strain on mental faculty like patience, courage, perseverance, risk-taking attitude, sense of service and enthusiasm of an officer. Everybody can't withstand the stress and strain of a police job. It is the leadership in police which counts and it is not body but the brain which leads. A lame and blind can make the most highly successful police officer. The data show that ladies and frail-looking policemen have also provided glowing leadership to the police force.

The films have also reinforced this idea of a wrestler type policemen. The human psychology has the tendency to deduce that those having brawn have less brain. Naturally in a society the policeman occupies a lower-status of a 'Physical man'. Since the policeman has been given the role of an aggressive toughie, he plays this model which is absolutely contrary to the concept of real and welfare oriented police required for a civil and independent India. We want a police officer with right attitude, firm determination, high commitment, deep dedication, and bubbling sympathy for the people and the resoluteness to fight injustice. He needs not be rough and tough but he should be polite and firm, responsive and responsible to the people's needs. The people are not the target of police physical action but it is the evils of the society. We want not a fighting, kicking and yelling policeman but a thinking and conscientious policeman. In this age of AK-47 a wrestler is useless for any police action. We want a leader who can motivate his force with the force of his sterling character; a policeman, who can carry the people along with his amiable disposition, proper regard for morals and human values and right sense to feel the pulse of the society. And these leadership qualities and character are the reflections of mental faculty.

Police is identified with its baton. It is supposed to wield *lathi* and use force. There is general perception that law and order is maintained by strong-arm methods and police can't control crime and law and order without using baton. I remember one incident of Anantapur district. When I was inspecting Gooty circle, an SC *Sarpanch* of Gooty police station represented that it was wrong to ask the subordinate police officers not to use *lathi* in traffic maintenance, curbing of *matka,* street rowdyism and investigation of cases. He was under the impression that I had seized all these powers of local police by asking the police officers not to misbehave with people and beat them. He pleaded for these powers to be restored to police without knowing that it is not me but the law which prohibited it. People also believe or have been made to believe that baton is the only solution, a panacea of all ills.

One can't deny the efficacy of use of force in certain situations particularly when passions run high and the people act under mob-psychology. But we have to accept that use of baton is an ad hoc solution to the crisis-situation. Law and order situation arises out of a host of factors over which police have no control. The baton can give relief like palliatives but no permanent cure. It is not the baton but the image, credibility, acceptability equanimity and impartiality of the police force and police officers which subdues or ignites the situation. It is the principles of equality before law, rule of law and impartiality, which earn faith of the people. It has been seen that at the assurances of police officers of integrity and eminence the enraged crowds have melted whereas ill-reputed and partial police had to open fire to quell the mobs in same situations. People fear to foment law and order problems in case of good officer for two reasons – first they respect the integrity and credibility of police officer and don't want to put them to troubles. It is human nature and culture of our society to respect values, truth and goodness. Secondly they are afraid of their principled and unbending attitude. It is increasingly being seen that the mob-violence takes place because the mob is assured of inaction of the authority. The general amnesty for violent actions of the mob by the government in certain states have reinforced the sentiments. The more we use baton the more people become violent. To tackle a more violent mob the police have to be violent in a greater measure. It is the fear of law and legal action, which breaks the morale of a wrong doer. The use of baton makes the street rowdies a hero and the innocent persons a life-long critic of police. The use of baton may be at the most a temporary and ad hoc measure and that also in a riot-like situation. We have placed undue reliance on it.

A general argument advanced by police officers and believed by people is that the beating is necessary for prevention of crimes. Use of third degree methods has very often led to lock-up deaths thus offsetting all the good works done by the department. Without going into details I would like to say in brief that it is the greatest falsehood to believe that crime-prevention is or can be done by baton. If we analyse the lock-up deaths of any state we find that it is only the petty thieves, helpless strangers and temperamentally weak persons who die in lock-up. We seldom come across a case where a hardcore criminal has died during course of investigation. Virtually use of third degree method in the course of investigation is one method of collecting money from so-called suspects. It is also one method of settling scores. The rich have got the poor implicated and beaten black and blue. A hard core criminal and Mafia leaders are never touched. It is the poor and the deprived who get all kicks. And the vested interests nurture this false concept of efficacy of third degree methods. I am sure if the police leave killing all such victims of 'lock-up deaths' and in the process leave many undetected cases, it will win more laurels and people's goodwill without adversely affecting the crime scenario. Even with all third-degree methods, there is nothing much to write about crime detection!

People nurse another misconception that the police know about all the criminals and the thefts take place because they don't want to control it. The tragedy is that the police don't try for knowing. They are really innocent of all knowledge about crime and criminals. They are not able to control crime because they are much busy in manipulating their statistics by burking the cases, by showing false recovery and detection and by getting confession of complicated cases by professional confessors. I was shocked to find 'a so-called' criminal in Payakaraopet Police Station of Visakhapatnam District of Andhra Pradesh who used to confess all sorts of crimes for fixed rates and a dossier was being maintained against him. The situation of faking and shamming has come to such a pass that whole crime records have lost meaning and credibility and the crime-work by police has become a farce.

Another misconception that makes round is about the control of magistracy over the police. In all cases of police firings, lock-up deaths and police atrocities, a magisterial enquiry is ordered. There can't be a greater eyewash than magisterial enquiry. I have not come across even a single magisterial enquiry which indicted the police for its unwanted behaviour though hundreds of such enquiries were ordered in my tenure in Andhra Pradesh. And whenever it was done, it was to settle score with rival police officers. Virtually in all cases the police want magisterial enquiry to come out of morass. It is a perfect example of unholy alliance. The police for their part have always paid the magistracy for this favour by turning a Nelson's eye to their acts of omissions and commissions. The police have always acted as a buffer between the magistracy and the frustrated and enraged people.

This unholy alliance in administration has institutionalised the lack of accountability and responsibility. When something goes wrong the police blame the magistracy and the magistracy blames the police and thus both go scot free befooling the people in the process. It is curious to make Collector the head of law and order who neither has expertise, skill and knowledge of policing nor control over police force whereas the police heads have powers without responsibility and sometimes responsibility without powers and resources. Both wings only serve the purpose of outwitting each other in the process making law and order a casualty. There is need to separate both completely with magistracy to do only with development and police with law and order. Both of them should fend for themselves and not get a plank to work off their accountability and responsibility.

We commit a blunder by mistaking police for a force and equating its culture, discipline, training, style of functioning with military. Military has to act against enemy and so the working culture is entirely different from that of the police. Police have to serve among the people to make their life more comfortable, nice and peaceful. The attitude, temperament, training, orientation and expectation from the police place them between the horns of dilemma. They are trained as force and asked to work as a 'service'. The objective of police force according to Police Act 1861 is primarily "to maintain law and order and work for prevention and detection of crime" but on the field they are expected to act as agents of social change and arbiters of socio-economic issues. If the police leave attending to such works there will be social crisis. What Lok Adalats are trying to do today and have not succeeded reasonably are being done by the police stations throughout the length and breadth of the country without any extra remuneration or recognition since times immemorial.

Police can't maintain law and order by keeping itself aloof from socio-economic, cultural, moral and political issues. It is inseparably integrated with the life of the people and it has to take holistic approach if it wants to serve the society. The police can be a nodal centre for social change, cultural and moral safeguards and economic and developmental processes. The vast resources and network of police has been left unused and untapped. If we plough the resources of police in the development process and socio-cultural construction we can get rich dividends. This is a wrong view that we will overburden the police by this approach. Virtually the police work will be facilitated with its integration in the nation-building process. They have not to put in extra labour but in the process of policing they will do it as a byproduct. It will improve the police image and police public relations and open new vistas of public cooperation. Virtually, the oft-repeated charge of intelligence failure can be attributed to the insulation of police from its environs. If the police want to update itself it will have to open out. It has to mingle with the people in their happiness and sorrows, share their problems and troubles of all sorts. It can't wash off its hands by telling that it is not their job. Nobody is going to share anything for this stand-offish attitude of the police. For example, if we take the help of a SHO in identification of IRDP beneficiaries or allocation of fair price shop dealership or adult education, identification of need of school and hospitals in the area; we can have the knowledge of ground realities. It will also smoothen the rough edges of police public relations. The pilferage of funds, corruption at lower level in the developmental works can be checked through the wedging of this police check system. Police have got excellent communication network as well as manpower. The great damage is done only because of our British-inherited notion that police should deal with only law and order and crime. In welfare state, police should be people friendly and welfare-oriented. It should be given active role in the education, literacy programme, health, afforestation, tourism, culture, various social programmes and developmental projects at the grassroots level. The police can't function effectively and efficiently without public help, sympathy and co-operation. The people will extend co-operation only if they feel policeman is one of them and cares for them. The police and people have age-old relationship and both have immense scope to influence each other. We have done great injustice by keeping them apart by artificial barriers of wrong notions that law and order and development are two mutually exclusive things. Not using such vast infrastructure of police for social and welfare purposes is a criminal wastage of national resources. This is by-product of police routine-job and will not affect main policing job. It is a matter of attitude and orientation but not of time, men and material. The hardcore policemen resent it because they have neither vision nor sense of social obligations.

All police officers cry for lack of time and leisure. It will draw vociferous protests from the police officers if I say that this is a totally false perception. He looks so tired and burdened with all cares of the world. Whenever you approach any police officer, the officer is busy running against time. But the truth is that keeping yourself busy is one weapon to gain in respectability and show efficiency and commitment. It can't be denied that on some occasions police officers are awfully busy like festivals, law and order situations, VIP visits, in big and crowded cities and elections etc but in the greater part of the year the police officers have no work but enough time to think about themselves, their family, the social problems etc. Unfortunately, most of the police officers lack knowledge in time management or are experts in effortless time killing. Some of the police officers keep themselves busy in unnecessary details and pride themselves on being very thorough. Some start doing the job of their juniors and end up running around all the time. Sometimes police officers keep themselves unnecessarily busy lest their officers should brand them shirker. Once I heard one senior police officer decrying the other junior officer for being a shirker because he played tennis in the evening. All police officers left sports, going to library for reading and writing because these extra curricular activities may bring them the bad name of a 'shirker'. Officers remain at the wheels and covering the road distances burning costly fuel without any aim or purpose to show that they are hard-working. Daily teleconference for hours together in many city police stations is an example to cite how time is wasted and initiative is killed. If these police officers do a little bit of time management, leave all these shamming and useless time-killing and the senior officers spare them their useless meetings and perverted way of performance appraisal all police officers will have enough time to look after themselves, their family, their socio-cultural development as well as the people's problems.

Police officers love moving in jeeps or on motorcycles. It gives them kick. Looking into files, meeting the petitioners and solving their problems, developing intelligence network, investigating and expediting trial of cases don't give thrill. Chatting with citizens while sitting on motorcycles exudes cinematic appeal. Spending time with politicians, waiting hours together at the office of senior officers, cajoling the Press by wining and dining and winning over the influential persons and opinion-makers make them stable in the seat but take the most of their time. Sychophancy is in the blood of police job and it has been handed down from generations. Time is one casualty of sychophancy. The SHO of Nizamabad town once complained to me that he got no time either for food or for sleep. So hard-pressed he was for time! I asked him to work only six hours at the police station with two hours for emergency calls and leave the police station afterwards. If something happens I will take up the responsibility in writing. After two months he felt shy to complain of time constraints because people spoke of better functioning of the police station with two hours for emergency calls after his limited hours of work at police station. Nobody worked for him even. It was only the change in his style of functioning and cutting down on non-police/public functions. He was asked to be available at police station and go out only in specified hours for investigation and patrol duty except in emergency. His presence at the police station improved the routine work as well as his accessibility to people with satisfaction. Now his limited hours looked tougher to him than unproductive unlimited hours of job. Posting of constables hours before the VIP visits is a glaring example of wastage of man-hours.

There is commonality in this belief that training makes a man perfect and more suitable to the job. People think that no man can be a policeman without proper training. But it is not true of police training. Though it may sound outlandish but I am of the belief that if training is done away with for a policeman, we can have more human, and upright police officer with positive outlook. There is prevailing notion among the police officers that the training institutions are churning out cynical and unfinished products. Take either content of the training modules or training climate, modes of training or types of trainer, objectives of training or resources of the training institutions – everything points to doom. A pall of gloom and frustration, cynicism and negativism prevails over all police training institutions.

Almost all police training institutions are taken as the dumping ground of most inefficient, unwanted and frustrated elements. More often than not police officers are sent to training institutions as a way of punishment. I was also posted to PTC, Anantpur to give a shock treatment. It serves as a dustbin of refuge and rejects of police department. Such people devoid of knowledge, experience, character and temperament are asked to enrich the new cadets in the knowledge of policing and dedication to service of people. There can't be a funnier situation than this. I have seen many police training institutions and everywhere without exception the same situation prevails. Virtually, the training institutions serve as a training institution for learning all dirty tricks of police department in short time which he might have learnt over a long period in the job. The fledgling police officers' determination and spirit to serve the people and the nation get the first rude shock. One IPS officer told me "don't fool yourself and me by telling that any officer in the country is working for the nation and society". The cynicism and degradation is complete.

The people in general have harsh words in reserve for subordinate police officers though they are not so hard on senior police officers. The impression has gained ground that the ills ingrained in the police system owe to the mean-by-nature lower police functionaries. But the truth is far from it. This impression has been assiduously cultivated by the senior police officers and the government to shield their weaknesses. All dirty jobs are got done through the subordinate officers. They are not allowed to even question the most outrageous and foolish instructions in the name of discipline. But when things go wrong, everybody backs out leaving the lower functionaries to face music. Tragically the court also doesn't come to their rescue by ordering that obeying wrong commands doesn't absolve a police officer of their criminal act. But how and when should the subordinate police officer decide that this is a wrong command? Suppose there is a riotous mob of a political party. The police open fire to quell the violence under the orders of a senior police officer or magistrate. Many people are left dead. In the aftermath, the political party clamours and under pressure the government indicts the action of the police party to open fire and terms it excessive. A murder case is registered against the policemen. Now, the police constables can't take the plea that they had opened fire under the command of their superior officers. They are trapped in Catch-22 situation. If they obey, murder case is registered against them and if they don't obey, they are dismissed from the service for inaction. Anyway now nobody acts. Inaction in police is the best action.

Without denying the contribution of the senior hierarchy in police it can be said that it is unfair to hold subordinate lower functionaries responsible for the ailings. Police is a disciplined service. Its ranks still look forward to their senior for leadership. But the leaders have most of the times failed them. Either it is corruption or seeking political favours or lack of commitment and dedication or yielding to political pressures or misusing the office for personal gains or casteism, nepotism and favouritism it all has started with the senior officers and is perpetuated by them. In Bihar the casteism was started and nurtured by senior officers because they wanted to nurture an individual squad of followers to back them in all their omissions and commissions. The political subjugation of the police hierarchy started with senior officers, when they sacrificed impartiality and propriety to continue in the seat. There are numerous instances when subordinate officers have been asked by the SP and DIG to request the politicians of the area for postings. When the politicians give green signal then the SP gives posting in his district! In one district the DIG pestered me for posting a certain officer in one police station. It was my first district charge. I prevaricated and expressed my unwillingness. He then gave a lecture to me that in democratic set-up we had to listen to politicians even in matters like police administration and postings. Next time when I was being tossed from one bad posting to another without any plausible professional reasons, I sought an interview with the DGP and requested for any stable posting. He replied point blank that I was not adjusting with the politicians and my predicament was my own creation. That DG served the state for a very long time. The degeneration and deterioration is clearly perceived now. The subordinate officers have now two masters whether they like it or not. They have now understood that if the senior bosses go to the politicians for everything, why they should not contact them directly. Thus the chain of commands started cracking giving way to all anomalies creeping in. Now the situation is fast deteriorating. The senior officers, in search of in-service plum postings and post-retirement parking slots have just caved in and thrown all decency to winds. Virtually the whole police system has been used, misused and abused, pawned and pledged for selfish ends. The subordinate officers, though belatedly, have matched their seniors in this game for their bare survival. The seniors feel piqued to have been outwitted by their juniors at their own game. What a pity! Now sometimes we hear that sub-inspectors and inspectors use their connections for transfer of Superintendent of Police of a district. Given this background, the senior officers have no right to blame anyone but themselves. But subordinate officers are at a disadvantage and so draw the whole flak from Press and the people. Their misdeeds are visible and perceptible to the people because they are in direct contact with them and each and every action of theirs affects the people whereas the senior officers are distantly placed and can't be watched.

The corruption, use of third degree methods, cruelty and brutality have been forced upon the subordinate officers by the seniors. The police station officers are asked to manage the things without any resources. The various needs and functions of police stations require money which is neither provided by the government nor the police officers. The seniors don't place demands before the Government lest they should lose their seat. So, they pressurise the subordinate officers, an easy game to manage the things leading to corruption for legal works. The seniors want good statistics to show their efficiency to their political masters or their seniors. Naturally, there is undue pressure on the subordinates to manipulate figures by hushing, burking, minimising the gravity and so on and so forth. The urgency of getting quick results from the top and the people leads to use of third degree methods, implication of innocent persons and false recovery and detection. The law and order problems cropping up due to developmental anomalies or wrong decisions of the government are to be put down by the brutality of the police. The popular voice is silenced by the police though they might not individually like it.

Frankly speaking, the subordinate police officers are more loyal, humane, efficient, hardworking and sympathetic to the people's cause. The circumstances have disabled and dehumanised them. I know one incident in Bihar where one gunman of an SP got the bullet himself in his bid to save the SP in a gun-battle with Naxalites. Still the fierce loyalty and sense of duty flows underneath the hard exterior of a policeman. I have seen them responding overwhelmingly when a call of dedication to duty was given to them. They rally fast, get easily motivated and sacrifice their lives cheaper than the seniors who have larger stakes, have their eyes on bigger things than the loyalty and dedication to duty. It serves them well to blame the junior officers for the ills in the police because they are not bladgered by the Press, people and the government and it also doesn't bite their conscience. Everybody wants a whipboy. The society has got it in police and the senior police officers in their subordinates. They consciously throw the guilt-feeling onto the subordinates.

Creating a myth is always essential to produce fear and awe. Police have believed in policing by means of fear and awe. It believes in Hobbes so far as human nature is concerned. It does not value human dignity, decency, kindness and propriety. It should now burst out of its cocoon otherwise it will be an anachronistic organisation.

Instead of living in a make-believe world, we should know the reality about police and set upon to rectify them. The false notions about various aspects of police and its functioning have impeded a required change in it. The myth has to be exploded and new assumptions accepted.

CHAPTER 7

Bureaucracy and Political Interference

Once a police officer said that bureaucrats including police officers are more corrupt, more ruthless, anti-people, inaccessible, egoist and selfish than the politicians. The hell broke loose. He had to go through tough time. He was stripped of his body guards, orderlies and above all the government house within twenty-four hours. He was recommended for suspension. Politicians are simple creatures who have been made to believe that they are the most lowly creations of God. Ironically, these are the politicians who give all protection and respectability to the bureaucrats like their children and get the flak for all things going wrong. Perhaps they are very insecure – a lifespan of five years. People are fed this myth of political interference and believe it – mostly through a campaign by bureaucrats.

I have no politician in my family, not even remotely connected. But I feel sorry for them. All politicians disliked me. Perhaps it is my doing. I become very stiff, uncomfortable and restless in their presence but perhaps Stockholm syndrome goaded me to write something about them. I am again afraid of my tribe. Last time they stripped a police officer of his house, they could now strip me of dress. Without dress only Bollywood heroes look good.

In trains, buses, *chaupals,* posh drawing rooms, and slums if there is one conclusion on which there is unanimity, it is the villainous role of politicians. Everybody waxes eloquent about the damage done to the nation by the politicians. I also relished the talk. It gives smug feeling to judge someone from a higher pedestal. Once somebody asked me how do you think the politicians are solely responsible. I first laughed at his ignorance but the question kept nagging me. Yes, what are the grounds for holding the politicians solely responsible. I could not find the answer and then searched my soul. The question kept on assuming a global proportion nibbling at my conscience.

Is political interference in administration a myth, a hoax? Is this a bogey raised by the black sheep in bureaucracy to camouflage their own misdeeds? Perhaps this is a ploy to distract the attention of the masses from their own shortcomings, devilry and non-commitment to the cause of people. It is a smokescreen, a façade.

It has become a fashion now to hold politicians responsible for all the ills in the society. It is a classic example of defence mechanism adopted by everyone to absolve himself of guilt consciousness, heavy on his mind, for not playing his role in the betterment of society. And government servants are no exception to it. But the credit should go to the government servants for convincing the people that they (bureaucrats) are helpless creatures and the politicians are the real devils. They are merely being exploited by the politicians. But the contrary seems to be true with few exceptions. The politicians and bureaucracy were entrusted the task of building the nation in post-independence India. The things went haywire. Where does the buck lie?

It seems the politicians are not exploiting the bureaucracy but the bureaucrats are exploiting the politicians. They have played on the psychological insecurity and fears of the politicians. It is generally noticed that officers with not-so-clean record cry hoarsest about political interference than the honest and sincere ones. The politicians are enticed by the unscrupulous bureaucrats in the vicious trap of promised pelf and wealth. The mechanism runs like this in all patterns. A bureaucrat contacts a politician for personal favours like postings, promotions, deputations etc. on the promise of acting 'his man'. The politicians are thrilled at this opportunity as they are gripped by fear-psychosis of losing their seats and positions and as a bulwark against it, want to create more and more supporters in all walks of life, who can assure them that they would not lose their station. The politicians also want to create a committed loyal group who can serve them when they are out of power. The same unscrupulous bureaucrats throw all the norms to winds to make personal gains and blame the master politicians for anything going wrong. Virtually every thing goes wrong because of this unholy nexus as it is today. The people who are groaning due to fractured and malevolent administration believe the version of bureaucracy without knowing the game. The bureaucrats will do all illegal things happily to make the politicians personally obliged to himself. He ensures his future and position through a powerful politician and indulges in self-aggrandisement. But he is clever enough to fix the responsibility of his misdeeds on the head of politicians.

Who prevents a bureaucrat/a policeman from not allowing political interference? What does he lose in the process? Absolutely nothing. He does not lose anything but a place which is not his own. No service rules have guaranteed somebody a particular place or position. The Constitution, the service rules and the courts overly and zealously protect the government functionaries. None has so far lost his job for not complying with the wrong commands of politicians. They are over assured to be in the service for thirty years with all its concomitant security, perks and benefits. An SP is an SP wherever he goes and enjoys all the benefits. An IAS is an IAS and enjoys much more than is his due. The bureaucrats actually invite political interference to make friends with the politicians as some sort of future investment. The bureaucrat who wants to prove his loyalty to the political masters is a matter of more concern. One Superintendent of Police had to do some recruitment of constables. Certain names were given by the minister to the concerned Superintendent of Police for recruitment as constables. The SP did not only recruit them but reported to minister by quickest means the service he provided. It is now perhaps a common knowledge that all higher authorities ask for choices from their political bosses before they exercise the skills of personnel management like transfers, postings, promotions etc. These government authorities have made a mockery of personnel management. The common experience of the sincere ones in the government service is that it is more the senior officers – not all but practical and successful ones – who harass and tinker with the system than the politicians. Talking of rules and sincerity is a sure-shot license to career doom. They will harass, mentally torture and coerce their subordinates to fall in line with their schemes of individual and their masters' advancement. The politicians do not nurture bureaucrats because generally their life is short. It is the government servants who nurture the politicians. So, it is generally noticed that the unscrupulous elements in the government service flourish in all regimes and climes under all parties.

And only these elements cry hoarse about political interference. Unfortunately, neither the politicians nor the people have been able to understand the game.

When the politicians enter the portals of government, they don't have much knowledge of the executive rules and its intricacies. All the dirty tricks of the trade are told to them by the government servants. Our post-independence leaders were quite idealistic but the nature of bureaucracy remained feudal and imperialist. The politicians are no match to the bureaucrats. They are in the profession of politics. But the bureaucrats are playing politics with shield of constitutional protection and in the guise of impersonal entity.

The politicians have never been found to be totally unreasonable, sometimes they respect good officers. Once they are told that it is against rule; they don't fight but strive for transfer of such rule-minded officer. They go for more practical ones who are available in abundance and get their things done through them who take their own pound of flesh and a bit more. When we make a comparative analysis, we feel pity for the politicians. He is people's representative. He has to put forth people's representations before officers. It may sometimes be wrong but his misery lies in forwarding wrong things also to the officer otherwise he is threatened at the cost of his seat. I have heard constituency people abusing the minister in vulgar and vituperative slang when he refused to sponsor wrong requests of certain people. They also threatened not to allow him in the constituency. The stakes are very high for politicians. Today he is minister; tomorrow he will be on the roads. We will do injustice if we expect high standards of morality from them unless the society itself turns moralist. They are elected people and they reflect the brighter and darker aspects of the society. But the bureaucrats are selected ones. They are educated, well-paid, well-secured, well-trained and highly regarded.

They are the cream of the society and brain trust of the nation. What are their compulsions? Bureaucrats have been reported carrying out the wrong commands of politicians zealously and reporting back to them by which time the said politician had forgotten his request. All this promptness is to curry favour with him and misuse his offices in exploitation of people and breaking of norms in future for furtherance of self-interest.

The recent trend is much more disturbing. It is seen that officers with proven integrity and sincerity also succumb to the pressure for their continuance in the seat. So it is not only the monetary factor which weighs with the bureaucrats to fall in line with politicians but temperamental weakness, pliability and false sense of recognition for continuance in so-called plum postings also matter a lot. The people who have been shunted out for their non-compromising attitude are laughed at and called fools. The seniors brand them idealist, impractical, good for nothing and non-managing type. Such brand of successful seniors want to break the morale of all good elements in government service, which they have done successfully. This is also because if some act according to their conscience and don't bend, it pricks the conscience of pliant ones. It makes them feel uncomfortable and guilty and so they rationalise their weakness by branding non-bending types as rigid, impractical and misfit for the job. Since they are misfit, they deserve to be thrown out or marginalised. Only go-getters deserve to remain in the seat for the so-called good of the society. Most of the good officers are posted in such positions where they could get appropriate lessons. Once a DGP counselled us in all seriousness that one has to secure himself in the seat because unless he is in the seat of power he will not get opportunity to serve the society. In order to secure his seat one has to make few and little adjustments. The DGP did not elaborate upon what is this 'few and little adjustments' and who will decide its limit.

Some government officials try to rationalise their weakness and selfish motives by giving it a more acceptable and altruistic touch. They opine that unless one sticks to the post for some time he can't do good to the people. To sustain his flickering life in the seat of power he may make 'small' compromises here and there. We may call it euphemistically 'Mosaic' compromise. Perhaps, they want to befool others by cloaking their own motives and in the process betray their conscience.

Once you do something against your conscience, your commitment and self-esteem is compromised. A man without commitment and self-respect can neither do good to the society nor to himself.

The bureaucracy should be in principle, impartial, impersonal and apolitical. Unfortunately, the "age of committed bureaucracy" has come. The government officers want to have some political preferably ruling party badge. They have no compunction in pledging their soul and indulging in all impropriety to please a particular political boss for individual goal. Recently this shining path had been very successful and many have reached dizzy heights through this ladder. When such people land good assignments they call themselves smart and pragmatic. Simultaneously, they abuse the politicians for being responsible to degrade their highly benign conscience. Such officers call themselves "victims of circumstances" though enjoying the fruits of 'success' achieved through the guile of willingly becoming "victims of circumstances".

In one case a Dalit bureaucrat was found awfully corrupt and unscrupulous. The government had made up its mind to punish the officer. Once the gentleman officer got the scent of impending action, he lobbied with his caste political groups and *Sanghams*. It became a sensitive issue for the government. All the politicians of ruling and opposition kept on blaming the bureaucrat but couldn't do anything because of certain groups supporting bureaucrat on caste considerations, what the bureaucrat had very assiduously cultivated over time. The bureaucrat uses his money, caste and connections to defeat all powerful government. The Cabinet is an amorphous organisation comprising different groups and interests. The bureaucracy is a great lobby of vested interests. You touch one employee in the secretariat, the hell will break loose. You suspend one police officer for his illegal activities, the bogey of demoralisation of police force will make hue and cry.

Of late many opportunities have opened to the senior bureaucrats and police officers for personal aggrandisement. Earlier it was in-service opportunities. Now it is mainly post-service opportunities that tempt a senior bureaucrat to toe the line of the politicians. If you are in good book of the ruling party, you never retire. You rather achieve much bigger things that even career diplomats, academicians and social workers can get. All such posts like chairman of various public service commissions, governors, ambassadors, head of various enquiry committees etc that should go to academicians, diplomats and social workers are now going to pet 'committed' bureaucrats. Those who fail in their attempt to get such post-retirement benefits are far more bitter in their criticism of political interference. But these people never bothered to come out openly and decry the interference while in service because they always nursed the fond hope of landing such posts by cosying up to such politicians only sometime in future.

Bureaucracy everywhere is, with certain honourable exceptions, divided into multiple factions based on party and community considerations. They openly side with political parties and caste. Such connections have substituted merit for all practical purposes. In all such cases, it is not the politicians, who go to bureaucrats but invariably the bureaucrats who snuggle up to the politicians. Analysed in total perspective it can be safely said that a biased, corrupt and pliant bureaucracy has done far more damage to the nation than the politicians. Bureaucracy is a permanent structure, a defined system. If one can't ride a horse against its wish, how can one force a well-educated and well-protected bureaucrat to comply with the wrong commands. The bureaucracy was structured to run the administration for furtherance of people's cause of peace and progress. Now it has become goal unto itself. It is serving itself and the people find no place in the scheme of bureaucrats. Politicians became a useful tool in the hands of scheming bureaucrats. It is now a different issue that the politicians have also learned the tricks of the game and exploiting the bureaucracy to the hilt before they give them their pound of flesh. They are working as shield to the real culprits i. e. bureaucracy. The people are mistaken in their approach of choosing the real culprits. The politicians are not the cause but product of our faulty system.

The people have to take the stupendous task of disabusing the government machinery by exposing the unscrupulous. They have to be conscious, awakened and demanding of their rights. The injustice should not be mutely accepted but the concern should be voiced. Politicians are made or marred by the people but not the mighty government babus and policemen. It needs a sustained campaign from the people to put the system on rails. They should choose good politicians and strengthen their hands to fight this corrupt cancerous bureaucracy which is also one of the great causes for the miseries of the poor teeming millions of our great country. Politicians alone can't oppose them leave alone exploiting them.

CHAPTER 8

Strange Ways of Success

Success demands price. Price may be anything - blood, character, principles, self-respect, money etc. Everybody wants to be successful and so a policeman. To get success and be appreciated is the nature of a man and a policeman.

History is witness that it is not the most deserving ones who get success. It is a person who reaches right place at right time with the help of right person. Management also recognises it as skills of personal relations and networking. It will be quite atrocious if we mean by all this that all successful officers are networkers. Very committed ones sacrifice their family life, happiness and finer moments of life, but they are not necessarily successful. Some may be really brilliant to achieve success. But I have concluded after long-experiences that mostly success comes through winding lanes and nebulous ways.

Success anywhere is not simple. But strange are the ways of success for a policeman which betters even *gurus* of success management. Here ends and means have really no relation. A Mumbai police commissioner allegedly went to jail for taking slush money from a stamp-scamster of a southern state. The DGP used to behave like a doormat for any politician. He also asked all young officers to keep in touch with politicians and keep them in good humour to be successful. Let's read what success costs a policeman. People have become Director IB and CBI to bring disgrace to the departments. After bringing disgrace to the higher positions, they have become governors and ministers. The moralist unsuccessful officers are still carrying the baggage of the department.

Perhaps all police in India resort to fake detection of cases and recovery of property to boost up their statistics. Good officers have to keep their figures impressive. The Indian police beats all brothers and sisters of Scotland Yard in investigation. Our police can guarantee detection of any case. If the original thief is traceless, investigation (Sic!) may lead to imaginary thieves and anybody can be implicated by planting fabricated evidence and property. We have got stock confessors who are very poor and prefer to go to jail, than to remain outside hungry and uncared. These 'confessors' confess any crime which the police are not able to detect. Property generally comes out of the unreported cases. Most of the theft cases are burked because it speaks badly of police. The people may cry for a flurry of criminal activities but the police records show a clean and sanitised crime-environment. When the thief is caught and property is detected it is kept either for subsequent disclosure in undetected cases or for swallowing up. Mostly the cases are not registered for such subsequent recoveries and original complainants never know that their cases were detected and the property changed hands.

There are various 'successful' and ingenious methods to boost up showing by police. Burk cases, i.e. do not register the cases. Minimise the gravity of the offence by taking to technicalities; for example, a case of dacoity that is committed by five or more persons raises an alarm in police circle. Therefore, the investigating officer reduces the number of offenders to four and register it under robbery which is less grave. If you want to improve the figure of property stolen and property recovered, you have to use simple arithmetic. You underestimate the value of property stolen but inflate the property recovered. Thus the 'gap of inefficiency' is bridged by simple arithmetic jugglery. When the gap becomes unbridgeable, they 'deliberately' get a truck 'stolen' and then recover it. Automatically, the figure of recovered property zooms up and shows the police officer in bright light.

There is no bar to showing cases detected and closing investigation by recovering property of Rs 1000/- even if 10 lakh rupees worth property was stolen. At least the burden of detecting the case gets off their head. For this purpose the police officer shows scores of cases detected by putting small amount of property as recovery. If large amount of property is recovered in one case, they don't show it in that case only. They apportion the properties in different undetected cases to show them detected by implicating the so-called gang of one case in many cases. Implication and fabrication is an art which only successful officer knows. This is also rationalised by arguing that the gang would get less sentence if it was involved only in one or two cases. So, it is better to involve the same gang in scores of cases so that they could get tougher sentence. The logic is disarming but we get simply blind to the fact that the criminals of those scores of cases which were actually not detected but shown falsely detected are left off hook and remain at large. They simply go on rampage uncaught and undetected.

The thieves have become smarter. Now even if they are caught, they don't tell the name of original receiver but name anybody else who may be a genuine person. The police have neither time nor will to go deep into the case and forces the so-called 'receivers' to cough up property which they have not received from the thieves. Sometimes the property is recovered in unregistered cases also and the 'receivers' real or innocent have no guts to question the investigating officer. If he gives the property sheepishly even if he has not received, he is shown as witness otherwise he will be shown as dishonest receiver and booked for the crime of shielding the offender.

Unfortunately, almost all senior officers have turned a blind eye to this evil. Contrarily they encourage it by giving their tacit consent. If by chance something goes wrong, the senior officers reserve the right of taking action against the erring officials to save their skin as well as 'uprightness'. They pass conscientious remarks – "these bloody subordinates spoil the image of police".

Most of the police records are nothing but garbage. They enter garbage in and cull garbage out of the records. Most of the entries are fake and redundant. Senior officers religiously inspect the records but seldom remarks are passed on the sad state of affairs. The people generally believe that the police have records to keep track of the criminals. Most of the times it is not. The inspecting officer gives outstanding remarks at the end of all such inspections when virtually the inspected officers and inspecting seniors should have been hauled up for faking inspections. Some smarter officers also collect money from the officers whom they are inspecting. Success doesn't come cheap.

Detection of crime and recovery of property is much-hyped task of police. But nobody knows what happens to the recovered property. If you go to police station, you will find a large heap of different kind of properties like cycles, motor-cycles, cars, foodgrains, furniture and all conceivable kinds of marvels braving the sun and the rains. Police and the courts never bothered to give it back to the complainants. This is such a criminal waste of national wealth. The whole efforts going into the recovery of the property has no meaning for the people. In some of the cases, when I took extra interest to return the properties to the complainants they refused to take it back because either the things were of no use to them or the procedure to get the properties back through the courts was so cumbersome that it was not worth it. However, any successful officer does not waste time on all this unglamorous job. It does not get you brownie points. It is not necessary to care for people and the property to be a successful officer.

Recently, allegations against police officers sponsoring crimes and criminals have come to news. It has been generally seen that police officers in all worse affected areas of terrorism, become extremely corrupt. But the senior officers turn blind eyes to the aberrations of these corrupt but efficient police officers because they also want to be successful by claiming the successes achieved by such 'dependable officers'. This is a new way of earning money and developing links. All these ways are adopted by successful police officers and men to 'serve' the people and bring names to themselves. They flourish in their career, riches and wisdom, basking in the glory heaped upon by Press and people for their glorious achievements. To be successful one has to pay heavy price. A successful policeman pays in conscience and people's welfare as sacrifice. And the police department continues to be what it stands for, that is all hypocrisy, and serve the masters in the name of people's service.

Police stations run without money and the police vehicles run on water if we go by allocation of government budget. A police officer, who expresses concern for lack of funds, is no police officer. He should manage resources with his 'powers'. No stationery, no petrol, no furniture, no diet charges to prisoners under detention, no hospitality charges for the people who visit police station and no investigation expenses. The police work requires immense resources but the government generally lacks money to fund functioning of police stations. The police station has, however, managed to run through fund coming from invisible sources. The arrack depots, the gambling dens, the bars, the black marketeers, the victims visiting the police station, the transporters, all are some of the invisible sources of funding the police station. All senior police officers know about it but maintain discreet silence. Talking of it will bite their conscience. If your conscience raises its head in police, you have every chance of failing in your profession. A successful police officer puts blinkers and sees the corruption under his own nose and in his police station as if he does not see it. A station house officer who puts up an impressive and expensive show without asking for any financial help from the department is rated very high.

Shamming is an attribute to get an instant success and publicity. It is not necessary that you really mean the business. Meaning the business needs lot of imagination and hard work and may sometimes land you in soup. You require right mix of fact and publicity. Publicity comes through right contacts. Contacts come through doling out favours in terms of kind, cash, gestures or grovelling. One officer started 'community policing' programme 'cops' in one of the most fashionable cities. It was given all hype by widely circulated newspapers, police journals and others. When one survey-team visited the city, it found the 'cops' in tatters in the very presence of its mentor. Perhaps the mentor was now not interested in 'cops' because he had got whatever he could get out of this programme. Now it had no utility for him. Obviously there was no trace of 'cops' when he left.

Claiming the credit of somebody is a good means of instant success. Once two young under-training Dy Superintendents of Police were posted to Rohtas jungles for operation in Bihar. The jungles were far and wide. The mountains were parched, stiff and rocky without water. The sun was beating down on all heads mercilessly. The two youngs with CRPF moved round and round tattered and tired. Ultimately they got news of the 'ultimate catch'. The local police were lacking in courage because that dreaded criminal had always broken the dragnet of police by inflicting casualty on them. The youngs were quite high at the sight of success. Unmindful of risk they took decision to go ahead with whatever force was available. At 1.00 am the village was encircled and they were greeted by stacatto of gunfire. One contingent of criminals ran away in the darkness and in the melee the local sub-inspector could narrowly escape death. The force continued the seize till 3 pm next day. Reinforcements were asked for. Contrarily, the SP of the district with local ASP reached. The leadership slipped from the hands of two green horns to SP and ASP. The whole village was searched but the brigand was traceless. Actually, he had dug a trench in a house and hid himself when the police was searching the whole village. The ASP/SP questioned the wisdom and information of two youngs. But the two trainee DSPs insisted on the ultimate catch being inside the village on the basis of information. Everything went haywire and one young constable was killed in gunfire. Ultimately, the dreaded dacoit was killed. Lakhs of people went to see the 'invincible' terror of the area. It was reported world wide including BBC. However, when the rewards were distributed, the two youngs were comfortably and totally forgotten. Obviously, the SP and ASP claimed the credit.

One has to be tactful, resourceful and quick fix to get such crown of others. Such instances abound in police and cause heart burning. Allegedly many officers get promotions and rewards on the basis of their service for powerful, and not for their brave exploits and service to the people. But novices question such things. These are the routine things to happen in police and it is better to digest such instances than to belt out complaints and face barrage of charges. This was told to me by a worldly-wise top cop of Andhra Pradesh.

Freedom of expression and speech is a taboo for successful police officer. The meaning of discipline changes and it assumes all negative connotations. A person who has faith in democratic norms of voicing genuine concern for ills in the department becomes first casualty. Listening to Master's voice without batting an eye-lid is the pre-requisite for a good police officer. A 'police officer' should have no inner voice, conscience and principles. His soul's voice is the master's voice; his conscience is what masters prescribe and principles what masters say and his *dharma* is his master's wish. The master may be his own boss, the political boss or any influential person who can influence his career. Justice or injustice is myth and *maya*. Those who die, die of God's wishes and those who kill them, are also obeying the God's commands. So the police officer who alters murder cases into accidents and accidents into murder cases at the commands of the powers-that-be, are not committing any sin. The officer shouldn't protest against all these happenings because these protests may be serious impediments in one's climb-up the professional ladder. The three monkeys of Gandhiji are perfect models for a successful police officer. Don't listen to bad things. Shut your ears off all wailings of a hapless victim, if the ruling clique desires so because listening to their woes may be injurious to your health. Don't see the injustice in acts of injustices if the masters will it because it spells 'web of injustice' around you. Those who try to fight injustice, become victims of injustice first. Don't speak out even if you feel that blasphemous things are taking place. You can justify this in the name of discipline. What boss thinks, does and says is always right. These are the statutory warnings given by Gandhiji's monkeys. All who have not assimilated these wise tips, have tottered and faltered up the thorny path of police career and became mental wrecks. These are not for the sake of saying but bitter truth. If somebody says that he has climbed up the ladder without following Gandhiji's monkey models, he is a big liar.

Encounters are a big source of greatness, big and small. It is a dangerous proposition to go for genuine encounters. Always it is not possible also. Perhaps the concept of fake encounters made stage-in at this time. A brilliant police officer has to be brave, courageous and a great leader! Nothing can prove all these qualities in one stroke in a police officer as encounters.

Genuine exchanges of fire are sanctioned by law. If a police officer is attacked by some offenders, he can shoot in self-defence. If an offender charged with serious offence tries to escape, he can be shot dead. But if you apprehend some criminals by chance or by design and you want to get rid of him, the concept of encounter comes handy. It is totally against law and violates the public sense of morality. Various moralists and conscience keepers in the police justify such encounters on the ground of expediency and "moral responsibility to the society". They argue about the futility of court, long delays in legal process, lack of witnesses, high rate of acquittals, easy bails, brutality of their offences and difficulty in rearrest if they are set at large after arrest. These officers who talk so big and take such great risk in stage managing encounters, have no guts to speak in unequivocal terms to powers-that-be that without proper laws and legal supports, the problems can't be solved. If you say this, where lies your greatness? You have to solve the problem without rules, laws, infrastructure and continuing omissions and commissions of the political masters to be called great and 'successful'. In police, being successful is a strong drive for action. Ironically, all these great police officers who are great believers in encounters on the plea of "moral responsibility to society" become mice when the government cry halt to these encounters depending on political situation or hot situations. They forget their "social and moral responsibility" and start believing in total 'non-violence'. So much for their social and moral commitment! Chameleon is the best role-model for successful police officers.

Encounters or exchanges of fire have been managed in different ways. Sometimes you catch them, take to jungle and kill them by tying up with trees or asking them to run away. Since self-defence is to be proved, some crude bombs or country-made pistols are to be procured. None has time to ask how these criminals fought well-armed police with such crude weapons. All wings of civilisation keep quiet because it suits them. People's miseries reach such flash point that they are ready to accept anything to survive. The people have no gall to ask for legality of the action. The so-called intelligentsia, are also meek and time-watchers. When the Punjab problem was at its peak, nobody questioned police methods. They were afraid of public disapproval. But once the problem was over and the public forgot its trauma; they, the intellectuals, follow up with their lofty ideas, concerns for democratic methods and violations of law. It gives them respectability, name and awards. Such intellectuals also follow the "model of success of intellectuals".

Sometimes the dead bodies will be found at unknown places. Police will declare that some unknown persons have been killed by unknown persons. Evidently the investigation will never lead to these unknown killers.

Lock-up also becomes a transit point for such encounter-fodders. To give a tit for tat to the offenders/ extremists, the police show exchanges of fire in reply to any big offence committed by the extremists. The Press lap it up and the police officers hug headlines for extreme efficiency. If a political leader is killed by the armed rebels, the police officers get free licence to kill more than the quota.

Many a time now the offenders are jumping off the prisoner's vans to be dropped dead by police rifles. It goes beyond human comprehension how the notorious prisoners could jump off and run away from the hands of a police armed escorts. Mass graves of extremists/ terrorists defy all description and explanations.

Sources of intelligence lead to hideouts of such criminals/ extremists. They are lined, tempted to divulge details of their exploits on the promise of a safe life. Credulous extremists/criminals believe them to be killed later in such encounters. If a petty offender is caught with big 'fishes', he has to cost his life for being witness to the 'encounter' of dreaded criminals otherwise he may bear testimony to the actual happenings.

Surprisingly the lower cadres of police are so brainwashed and so convinced of the efficacy of the encounters that they take their leaders as weak-kneed who don't sponsor 'encounters'.

'Encounters' bring in instant fame, money, postings, promotions and security. To be entitled to an entourage of security personnel, you have to be on hit list. To be on a hit list you have to do encounters. Without security guards hanging around, you are not a policeman. People also feel pity on you. The sobriquet of 'rough and tough' tumbles out of such encounters. The system that fails in its duty to provide succour to the deprived and hapless souls, finds great saviour in such 'encounter experts'. Any revolution can't face the might of a modern state in armed face-off. The state gets readymade excuses to cover up its administrative failure. They can cry hoarse about their achievements in the field of public service and welfare by putting down these rebels or criminals who were themselves the product of failure of public service and welfare. However, people feel highly obliged to the powers who gave them relief by suppressing these scourges of the society. The people don't remember who were the causes of the genesis of these 'scourges'.

The people feel grateful to them for giving them respite from bullets and bombs. They don't afford being so ungrateful to question them for their fundamental failures. The successful police officers obviously go unquestioned and get gallantry rewards for their ungallant works.

Any idealist is an unsuitable boy for police. A pragmatist has a premium on him. One should be rough and tough. He should be a go-getter. Naturally more you beat, harass and be unreasonable, more tougher name you get and easier your path of success becomes. There are very few institutions where there is such a large gap between protestations and actions. What is taught in police training colleges just opposite one has to do in field. Anybody who takes the laws and teachings seriously is doomed for life. Definitely sometimes some good people seem to scale higher in police but definitely they had to compromise somewhere. There is a well-known cliché in police that knowledge is not power in police but power is knowledge. You have to occupy some post/rank to be all-knowledgeable. Your brain, a store-house of knowledge, is a real cause for troubles if you don't have a rank.

There are certain sayings in police which sound reasonable sometimes. Rules are made for fools. Naturally no policeman gets successful if he is rule-bound.

Conscience keeping is a dangerous hobby. Such hobbies do not help a policeman. Where presence of mind does not work, help yourself by absence of body. A policeman is not judged by his successes but by his mistakes. Non-performance is always appreciated. Marking time is the best philosophy if you want to be hundred per cent successful. You must be feeling disgusting. But truth is more disgusting.

New ideas are frowned upon. A successful police officer is always tradition-bound, change-resistant and backward looking. See the last pages and sign the next. Don't think. Thinking is an injurious habit because it leads you to analyse the anachronism in police, inconsistencies in commands and irrationalities in behaviours. Most of the police officers who fall prey to thinking habit and new ideas, land up in shelves of police department like police training institutes, computer, communication etc. The organisation is accommodating and magnanimous enough to give ample opportunity for introspection to these officers. It goes to the credit of police system like caste system of India that it has not changed a bit even after 140 years of its birth. It has guarded its sub-culture jealously by hounding out all new ideas and merchants of new theories.

Sycophancy has been the best merit of an individual since times immemorial. Police is also not an exception. The great kings used to keep courtiers to sing paeans in their praises. Very good literature has been penned by such bards in India. It is the sole merit that can take a policeman very far in career. But it is really very difficult to be sycophant in police because the competition is quite cut-throat. Success takes its toll and it is true for policeman also.

CHAPTER 9

Gory Incidents and Game of Chess

The ghastly killing of G Krishnaiah, the District Magistrate of Gopalganj, Bihar had once more pitchforked the important role of police into limelight. The list is becoming longer and longer with the martyrs making the bureaucratic history red with blood. We are slowly becoming immune; our conscience not ruffling at all such gory incidents. How painful it is to see our martyr's blood—blood of G Paradesi Naidu, KS Vyas, Krishna Prasad, Vandana Mullick, Govind Ram, Randhir Verma, G Krishnaiah, a non-ending list. The national dailies cry hoarse about failure of police. The confidence of people is shaken. Everybody in Bihar and outside is talking about breakdown of law and order, fear, panic, murder. What is left if DM is murdered in broad daylight. The IAS Officers' Association has expressed concern at the pace and level of criminalisation. Every eye turns to the police for relief which itself is looking for relief from all quarters. With the situation turning more critical and gloomy, the reforms in police become all the more important – the crying need of the time.

But the general perception about police role is not in tandem with the grave situation. The whole intelligentsia, the people, the Press and the humanitarians are ranged against the police. Even the judiciary does not grace it with its favour. When the Punjab was burning, it was the police in the thick of mayhem, murders, blasts, and bullets to retrieve the state. No human organisation dared to visit even Chandigarh, the capital of Punjab. Now all sorts of champions of human rights and laws have swarmed upon the Punjab police in droves to tear it to shreds. And many valiant police officers are cooling their heels in jails whereas those who have championed the murders of the police officers, civilians, the Pressmen, the politicians and the innocents in cold blood, have become holy cows. Chasing the Punjab police in courts, in the fora of various commissions and inquiry committees, in the public meetings and in foreign media and other platforms is their favourite pastime. The limited innocuous magisterial powers (which will basically make no difference on the ground in this highly critical situation) except some moral boost-up, given to the police by Andhra Pradesh Government on the eve of elections were shouted down because police supposedly were not to be trusted with extra powers.

The killing of G Krishnaiah, IAS, shows a very disturbing trend. The criminals were previously conspiring murders of the policemen. It always got unregistered by the people. The policemen are meant to be killed because they play with gun. But now the octopus of terrorism is spreading its tentacles. Even those are being cut off in cold blood that have nothing to do with the fight against anti-socials. Our law and order problems are entering the domain of terrorism – a highly risky game, which our police can't play with century-old laws and weapons. The situation is very complex – the social, religious, political, economic, foreign and so many other factors making it more and more terrible. We have to change our mindset towards police and the crux of the problems. The problem is not so simple as we take it to be. The police has grown weak due to various factors. It now serves more as a scapegoat than the strong arm of the government. We satisfy ourselves by clobbering the police and the government for its inefficiency and failure, laziness and uselessness. But there is no point in flogging a sick, debilitated and humiliated horse. If we want to save life of another innocent officer like G Krishnaiah, IAS and G Pardesi Naidu, IPS, we have to ponder over the issues. Histrionics and vitriolic remarks against the police and the government and heart-felt sympathy towards the departed only will not serve any purpose.

When we think of changes in police, it reminds us of National Police Commission recommendations. The recommendations are gathering dust since 32 years. When one Union Home Secretary was badgered about changes in police in the light of National Police Commission recommendations, he snapped "What's there in National Police Commission recommendations? It is better gathering dust". But the people now realise how urgent it is to take out recommendations off the can and implement it.

Autonomy to police is a major recommendation by NPC. What to speak of autonomy, today police is supposed to be a retarded child fit to be kept under tutelage of magistracy and the judiciary! The intentions and dignity of policemen have always been doubted. So, the confession before policemen is not admissible in the court. If you don't give magisterial powers, they abrogate judicial powers to themselves to meet the immediate problems being unable to bear the public condemnations. In the process they harm the society, the system and themselves too. What is so great about recognising the importance and giving responsibility and dignity to the police? The greatest Hindi novelist Premchand asserted that responsibility always reforms a man and whenever he goes astray, it guides him to the right path. Why do we think that police can only err? The judges also pass judgments like sentencing to death but we never question their wisdom. Then why do we jump at simple useless magisterial powers to the police who have to fight dreaded criminals and organised terrorist groups with AK-47 in streets. What an irony! The *lathis* are facing AK-47 and that also with tied hands by laws, distrust of the people and swords of different commissions dangling on head. Why can't we give some freedom, some moral support and some motivation so that when they die fighting our cause, they should die with some peace, dignity and pride?

We deny lawful small powers to the police but give tacit consent to execute anybody in the name of restoration of normalcy. The normal refrain is that police are already misusing powers. They will misuse much more if any further power is given. The police are also not bothered about conscience, due process of law and lawfulness. They have become the greatest violators of law and ironically that also with the tacit and quiet consent of people and the lawmakers. What a mockery of our concept of rule of law and appreciation of situation!

Our approach to police reform is quite negative and retrogressive. We want to cage them in more and more lest they should misuse powers but the misuse is growing day by day. At the same time police system fails to bear desired results because they don't get open support from the society for their unlawful forays though they are not punished even for those aberrations. This situation is neither helpful to the society nor to the police. We should have proactive approach towards police functioning.

Police of today can neither serve the democratic government nor the people nor itself because it has outlived its purpose. It was meant for the Britishers and the system should have died with the Britishers. Sardar Patel had grandiose plans for changing the system but he was snatched too early by cruel fate. The National Police Commission urgently felt that the police should be changed for the sake of society.

Police can do wonders to our lives. It can be the best friend, protector and representative of the people. It can be a great instrument of social change, communal harmony and nation building. Its orientation should be changed. We can't treat police any longer as untouchables without risking the fabric of nation and society. It is a vital part of the system and we can't derive fun and pleasure out of police bashing in our drawing rooms. It should be made to think for people, for the Constitution, for nation and for human rights.

Unfortunately, there is a hostile atmosphere for the thinking of restructuring of police department. People's representatives, courts and the Press feel that the policemen have stakes in the reforms. It is presumed that reforms will help and serve the policemen. There can be nothing so far from truth. It is like a syndrome where the victims refuse the help of a doctor knowing that he will die without the doctor's help. The reforms are more for the people and the society. It should be virtually pressed by the people. The police will gain nothing by reforms. A good police system will only help law-abiding citizens.

CHAPTER 10

Press and Police

I read newspapers. So does everybody. Perhaps some people read newspapers in toilet because those are worth tissue papers. But it is not compulsory to read newspapers in bathrooms and toilets. Some are serious ones also. Khuswant Singh writes much in newspapers mostly to add spice to the reading. People say that newspapers generally contain gory details of crime, criminals and police. The game of '*chor* and *sepahi*' is very old. It is liked by people. It sells and sells good. Sex also sells but people don't like to read it in public. You can't discuss sex but can discuss police in public. It is a good topic, current one at that.

The government servants generally read newspapers for news on transfers and postings. The politicians read it to see their photos in the corner of the eighth page. People are very gullible and Indians, my God! they take anything in print as gospel truth. Once something is printed, means finish.

I am afraid of Press. Everybody is. I wanted to analyse the role of Press and police for your benefit. So, another round of pages.

The Press has a great role in making police what it is. Police is the most favoured butt of criticism for the Press. Pages after pages, days on end are blackened with horrendous stories of police brutality, inhumanities and monstrosities. All spine-chilling stories enrich our knowledge about police behaviour. The Press are the eyes and ears of the democracy – a worthy watchdog. They are the conscience-keeper, the godown of the brains of the nation. But how could they shut their eyes, ears and mouth out to the vital police role? Their analysis touches the fringe of the police role and makes nothing more lucid than what a layman knows. The basic drive behind the police stories is hunger for news, not the urge to give a dispassionate analysis in tandem with popular expectations. The compulsion of business rules, that is to sell more, constrains them to present a celluloid picture of a policeman in print what is far divorced from ground reality.

One management expert brilliantly averred that the people, the parliament, the Press and the police are the four pillars of the democracy. One pillar is weakened and we get a lame democracy. Unfortunately, police is the weakest prop and none of us have even bothered to worry for it. Give a shove and the whole edifice comes down creaking and cracking. This most ancient institution was muddled with by the Britishers and remained ununderstood by the Indians. We have indulged in police bashing and it always made a good reading. All the prejudices towards the police were fortified by the Press because of compulsions of viewership game. The Press never rose above the layman trappings and gave a very naïve account of police role and objectives. So the image of ideal police changes as per the situations and public mood. Same action of police makes them heroes and villains on two different dates.

Like a man on the road the Press also glorified a policeman who took law into hands and achieved instant results in negative way with questionable means. They wrote big stories about all such cinematic policemen. Such policemen acting in an out of gear and imbalanced system are bound to err out of in-built complications and contradictions of the system. And people cry hoarse about the villainy of policeman. The Press also laps it up without knowing why it did appreciate the police first and why does it deprecate now for same type of action? Police bashing makes a good news. So there is no urgent need of analysis. They are not able to link the role of police to the future of the nation-development and democracy. It is high time we shun reading spicy stories of police brutality and analyse its causes and solutions. The Press can do it and they must do it otherwise they will be put in the dock tomorrow by the people for this glaring failure.

There is widespread concern over failure of law and order, growing anarchy and lawlessness. The poor people suffer in silence without knowing who is really responsible. The Press, the people, and the government accuse police and the police accuse everybody else but itself. The situation gets totally confused, the solution goes elusive and after a while the failure gets forgotten to be repeated again somewhere else. The criminal justice system is cracking under its own weight. The courts, laws and the police are failing to cope with the new challenges of organised terrorism and criminality with access to super technology. The universal human rights are being abused. The National Police Commission recommended freedom to police and in-built mechanism of checks and balances. But the law and order is the dual responsibility of the magistracy and the police, and ultimately nobody's responsibility. Why should we not make police solely responsible and accountable for law and order—why should they have a shield of magistracy, the so-called theoretical head of law and order who are torn apart between development and law and order. If something goes wrong, the magistracy blames the police for intelligence failure and the police blames the magistracy and the system for lack of independence of action. Ultimately nobody is held responsible for systemic failure and the story goes on leading to recurring agony to the people.

Lock-up deaths make sensational serials and ruffle the emotions of the people. But why do lock-up deaths occur at all and why is the third degree method resorted to? The Press should question the very method of interrogation and reeling of statistics. The Press has to explain why they applaud the Punjab police for dealing with terrorism through extra-legal methods and condemn Bihar police for blinding the criminals with the help of masses. It is because blinding is more cruel than killing or because poor masses in Bhagalpur were the victims or because the integrity of the nation and not the honour of Bhagalpur womenfolk was more important? They publish photographs of police officers who have caught a gang of dacoits with so much property and of those who brought down the number of crimes. But hardly they write about the methods of interrogation; whether this was genuine detection; whether the criminals were real or fake or caught on suspicion. How was interrogation done? What happened to the property after recovery; and what serious efforts are being made for crime control?

We see many photographs of 'hunter *walis*' or 'hunter *walas*' standing tall in the print of newspapers with all hyperboles. The Press has been fortifying the image of a tough cop who uses all methods to crack a case. They don't go into the morality or legality of the action. But if something goes wrong in the pursuit of such super cop exploits, they blame the police. The Press never realised and pointed out that lock-up deaths and use of third degree methods will vanish if the state takes up the task of compensating the loss of the victims. This is a highly wrong perceived notion that people will misuse the facility if government recoups the loss. There is always a fear of being prosecuted if the false reporting was done. Again an outer ceiling of compensation may be fixed. Unfortunately lock-up deaths occur only in cases of petty thefts and crimes but in all big scandals, thefts and smuggling, no lock-up deaths occur. Once the undue pressure for speedy detection of the cases is removed and the quality work is emphasised, the police image will shoot up. It has been experimentally proved that it is only in the mind of people and the police that rough handling of a suspect yields clues and prevents crime. In actual terms rough handling leads to very low per centage of detection. If only prevention work is done in all seriousness and no case is detected at all, I can affirm that situation will be no worse and there will not be any complaint of lock-up deaths, human rights abuses and third degree methods. The Press has to analyse this concept and throw it to national debate.

About 80 per cent of the people who are languishing in jails are poor who have not been able to pay the cost of judicial procedure and prove their innocence. They are poor, hapless and weak persons. All rich and monied people generally fight their way to freedom even after committing a crime through their money and influence. This is because of natural flaw in the system.

Rapes by policemen outrage the Press and people alike. It is natural because when the fence eats the crop, it confounds everybody. But have we ever appraised the mode of selection of the policemen, their training, the working conditions, their pay structure, their temperamental and cultural refinements, the social strata they come from, the educational qualifications etc? We have devised one system in such a manner that those who are admitted nowhere, show in an appearance here in police. How can we expect heavenly qualities from the despised lot? Even in service people are ill-paid, hard-worked and ill-treated. None has done any thing for emotional and cultural refinements of such an important part of our polity. We treat the police as dandruff when it is virtually the 'heart'. And so we are paying for it. We all cry for prevailing and ever growing malaise but don't apply ourselves to remedy it. Can a headless, respectless and a comfortless man provide us a peaceful life in face of most intelligent, organised and hard-core criminals? We still feel that for policing too much education is not required. Virtually a person who is not idealist, committed, self-respecting and moralist, cannot make a good police officer. A job seeker can't make a police officer. There is difference even between a professional law enforcer and a moralist police officer. The Press has to understand the difference before they blame police for anything.

Do we not recognise that law and order problems grow out of developmental anomalies? But how many *Dailies* have advocated a holistic approach to the law and order problems? Should we not involve a policeman in our developmental programmes so that he might better appreciate the problems. A policeman in Naxal affected area will better solve the problems if he knows how this problem cropped up and what are various governmental plans to tackle it? Its acceptability will increase and its own approach towards problems will be different if its mental horizon widens. The police are perceived as government at the grassroots level. Its approach and attitude reflects that of the government's. Should we not train and educate our policemen first who have got widest reach and influence among the vast masses so that they could become the harbingers of social change, women emancipation, human and democratic values? They can be carriers of government programmes in the nook and corner of villages. Once their acceptability and credibility increases, the government will be looked upon as a benefactor. Any organisation with a negative role is bound to attract approbation and inacceptability. The vast influence and reach of this organisation has been left untapped and were used only for negative purposes. There is immense scope to use the police services for the socio-economic emancipation of the society. The Press never has pondered over this possibility. The Press should know that our police training is outdated, the attitude is feudal; the methods are archaic; the resources are inadequate and value system is negative. This system will never bear fruits even if we make God a policeman. And with average selfish police officers, the system has become dangerous for people's existence.

Everybody harps on corruption as the most potent factor in our slow development. We always search for a scapegoat in the form of police or politician. But what role has the Press played? They just pick up one Khairnar or Seshan and create halo around them. They keep on blackening paper till they sell and afterwards dump them. This much for corruption elimination! Which agency has been given the responsibility for removing corruption? Police, primarily. What's it doing? If not doing, why it is not doing? How many times Press has delved into this? No police agency is free to take action. It has no direct access to the chief political executive either Chief Minister or the Prime Minister at the centre. It is trammelled with bureaucratic barriers, procedural wrangles and infrastructural bottlenecks. The corruption can be checked and it can be checked very effectively if the police are allowed a free hand. The free hand will be given by the government if it is enlightened by a third party convincingly. Has the Press ever thought on this issue to take it up with the people and the government that the corruption thrives not because police does not work but because it is not allowed to work. Unchain the police and remove the protections given to all corrupt gentlemen who are eating into vitals of the country. Sooner it is done the better.

Intelligence failure is now-a-days a favourite phrase with the Press. If anything happens anywhere, it can be attributed to intelligence failure. Even if something is very clear to all and everyone knows that it is going to happen today or tomorrow, the Press blames the police for intelligence failure for its happening. It is not the intelligence but the timely action which matters. No Intelligence agency can know everything. It can at the most predict the trend and the area. Sometimes if it is equipped with adequate infrastructure and luck favours, it spots the real cause and time. It is exception and not the rule. We should start taking preventive measures from the trend indicated by the police. At the same time, there is need to understand and realise the handicaps of the agency. Does the Press know whether our Intelligence agencies are able to match with the task they have been entrusted to? Should we give the role of astrologer to Intelligence agency? Is appropriate action being taken on the indication by the Intelligence agency? The Press should be realistic and analytical in their approach to police role.

Now it is not for the police but for the people that the police need be reformed. Police have made supreme sacrifices over a long period. The yearly data of policemen dying a violent death will prove it. The police martyrs unfortunately don't enjoy the benefits like military. Their martyrdom goes unheard, unsung and uncompensated. No regrets for this. But the sacrifice should be of some use to the society. It should not be laughed at. It is not the time to blindly criticise the police because we have reached a critical stage. If we further neglect the police, our society and culture will be doomed. The Press has to take up the stupendous task of police reforms. Convince the people and the nation of its urgent need. We can't dismiss police reforms and National Police Commission's recommendations as a controversy because certain people are unable to understand it. If people are to be saved, the police are to be reformed and only the Press can do it.

Have we read the laws? They are loaded against police. The Indian Evidence Act accords second grade citizenship to the police. The courts dubbed the police as '*Goondas* in Uniform'. The Press and the Media called them dunces and buffoons. So, sub-human characters have been given the most important task of dealing with life and property of the people. The police started acting like retarded and spoilt child because we gave them this role to play. They lost self-esteem. Can we not trust them? Can we not give their self-respect and confidence back to them by amending laws here and there? We have placed checks in the form of judiciary and magistrary on them. Have we placed any checks on judges who sentence a person to death and magistrates who deal with crore of rupees? Why so? Because we have presupposed that police are sub-human, inferior and wrongful characters, who are to be kept under tutelage. And they also pay back in the same coin what earns them the epithet of '*Goondas* in Uniform'. Any amount of check, any number of committees and commissions will not check police brutality unless we give them respect, status, confidence and place in the society.

Everybody talks about human rights of the accused, the villains, the gangsters. Nobody bothers about the innocent victims without voice. The maintenance of law and order and protection of weak and oppressed are taken as if these are the personal affairs of the police. They are untouchables of the society. Like untouchables they clean the dirt of the society and don't get even minimum sympathy and courtesy but to the contrary all humiliation, abuses and invectives. Much injustice has been perpetrated on this wing. The police are neither military nor civil, nor force nor service. They neither have the glory and prestige of the military and their concomitant physical comforts nor the status and vast avenues of individual advancement of the civil services. But they have always been asked to make much greater sacrifices than military and civil officers. The Press at least should appreciate the role of police and give their due.

The police have always been blamed to be very unresponsive to common people's needs. But the police have been fashioned on these principles of protecting the rich and the big. They have been neither trained nor taught the lessons in service to the people. It is just asking something else if we expect service from the police. Common people are like a red rag to the police because they have been brought up in this tradition by the Britishers. We have failed to change the system. The child is sick. We should try to cure it of its illness and give strength to it instead of bludgeoning it for non-performance. It will perform once it is reformed, renourished, reoriented for the new task of service to the people.

We don't get anything by decrying police and its role. The whole issue is to be seen in fresh light. The police reflect the culture and civilisation of the society. We just can't have a civil society without a good police system. Police is not a department, not an organisation but the government in itself. It represents the state. We can change the society with a new concept of police. Police is not meant for catching thieves and wielding of *lathi* but it can act as an agent of social change, cultural refinements and economic developments. It is not only a jargon of words but it is truth if we just change the way of looking at the police. The Press has failed in its duty to the society by not appraising the exact role of the police and advocating complete change of the police system. The police changes are not as necessary for the police as for the society.

Some of the supercops and award winning police officers who have achieved larger than life image because of Press publicity have grown at the cost of police image. They have achieved individual glory by causing incalculable damage to the police image. The Press should not be swayed by these publicity-hungry *hunterwalas* or *hunterwalis*. They are not the ideal policemen. The good police system is entirely different from the way these supercops have acted and established themselves as role models. The people will gain nothing from such supercops. The system has to improve. And the Press has a great role to play in it.

CHAPTER 11

Human Rights Organisations

One must admire the guts of human rightists. I always wonder what inspires them to take up such non-profit business. In this world of consumerism, it is really puzzling to see someone taking up the cause of others and particularly of left wing extremism. The human rightists - so they call themselves - have always been a great mystery to me. Since I am on the other side of the fence, naturally I will be picking loopholes in their actions. But it compels me to admire internally that this lot dares the whole might of the government and hostile public opinion. But why are they so ideologically stiff or challenged that they are not able to appreciate the other face of arguments or they do it as a matter of strategy or under certain compulsions? I don't know. We can only dissect and postmortem on the available evidence and materials.

When human rights organisations blast the police, there is big applause all around. Here is the ten for nine. Human rights are the most cherished possession of a civilized society. Its violations are sacrilege and blasphemy. Police can't go berserk, become irresponsible and kick left, right and center rather fire bullets like an eccentric. State terrorism can't be tolerated. Police must be reined in; draconian laws must be repealed. The enthusiasm shows off the dedication and commitment of members to human rights.

The scene changes and one finds himself down in the dumps. News about killing, maiming, torturing and cutting into pieces of suspected informants/class enemies pour in. The explosives -- the vehicles of development-- are put to diabolical use by self-styled revolutionaries and champion of underdogs. The Kakatiya Express is put on fire roasting forty-two persons alive. Yes, everybody expected fireworks from the Human Rights Organisation. Bullets were sprayed on innocent unsuspecting citizens of Punjab, Andhra Pradesh, Kashmir and Assam. It was high time for everybody to rise in revolt against the brutal desecration of human rights. Alas! It was a total anti-climax. It was total icy cold from the quarters where the most flashy fireworks were expected from. One is totally confused. What is human rights? I want to ferret out the common definition of it. The greatest tragedy is that human rights organisations believe in qualified definition of human rights. Human rights for killers who pass for revolutionaries and complete lack of mournings for those who die at their hands. Perhaps it is only the State which has to observe human rights rituals.

Every man is a human being. He has got some basic rights which should not be violated by anybody: be it the state or the extremists or the agrarian rebels. It can't be taken that state is skinned off for violation of it whereas others' deviations are glossed over and praised as aberrant revolutionary action. Human rights organisations' track record should be appraised in the light of these facts. These are formidable organisations having right connections, broad-base and wide Press coverage. Any off-the-cuff remark by an activist gets published in flashy headlines and gets registered in the mind of people. They have greater responsibilities towards the society.

The APCLC, one of the human rights organisations in Andhra Pradesh, is disturbed by the facts that during the last three years, 1992 to 1994, 496 people were killed in as many as 285 encounters. But the other side is slid over, as 979 people were tortured to death by Naxalites between 1989 and 1993. It is sickening to go into details of the methods and brutality adopted by the extremists. The landmine blasts in Nizamabad, Adilabad, Warangal and Mahaboobnagar (G Paradesi Naidu, IPS, death trap) have blown poor policeman to pieces who have nothing to do with class-struggle or whether the power comes through barrel of the gun or ballot box. The lower functionaries in police have joined police simply for bread. They can't say socialism from democracy or fascism. Perhaps they are sacrificed for a greater goal of total change of the system and ultimate class struggle! Price has to be paid for larger good of the society!

The Director General and Inspector General of Police, Andhra Pradesh, Hyderabad gave Press statement on 27-08-1994 that "It is true that about 400 extremists died in encounters in the last three years". But at the same time it has to be noted that 700 people including 145 policemen were killed by extremists. Eighty per cent of the victims belong to SC, ST and BC categories who were merely killed on suspicion.

Down under the pressure of public criticism, the Andhra Pradesh civil liberties committee accepts that all sorts of violence need be condemned but the state terrorism is more dangerous. True, but who will define where the line stops between state action and state terrorism? It is very easy to decry the things, pull any structure down but there are very few who have either intellect or patience to build any.

"The latest in the armoury of Naxalites includes claymore mines and grenade launchers". (*The Hindu* 4th September, 1994). The organisation which requires such sophisticated weapons to commit violence has no qualms about human rights, as we have assured to citizen. Preserving human rights is not only the state's duty but everybody's duty. Any terrorism is unpardonable in equal measure. We can't make it out from one terrorism to the other. It will not do, not convince either.

The major question before us is why this discrimination in attitude and approach. State terrorism is terrorism and the disaster and destruction spelled in the form of landmine blasts, bus-burning, government building destruction and killing is revolution. Why is human life deemed to be expendable material in the case of Naxalites? The APCLC had better ponder over it. Anti-establishment approach of APCLC is desirable because it requires guts to condemn the powerful state apparatus. But why does it shy off calling spade a spade? Does it work under pressure or it is an outfit of the revolutionary organisations which have done more damage to the society than they could do good even if the revolution came in?

Human rights organisations suffer from a sectional and factional approach to human rights. They don't see it in wider perspective. So their appeal doesn't move the people; their arguments are not convincing. State is like a red rag to them, which has no place in their basic philosophy. Do they want anarchic society if they don't want state and its action? If they are championing the cause of people why do the people manhandle them? I think people are not taken by their arguments of being manhandled by the policeman in plain clothes during

National Human Rights Commission sittings. If the human rights organisations want to survive (which is very essential for the health of democracy and human rights) it should start self-criticism and introspection.

Western Columnist AM Rosenthal writing in the *International Herald Tribune* has remarked that in America law and order has become equated with authoritarianism in the public mind. Rosenthal describes this development as unfortunate. Human rights organisations suffer from the same disease. They want state to be a mute spectator at any mayhem, loot and flagrant violation of human rights because they are being done by a group of people who are either revolutionaries or euphemistically called misguided youth. Bomb blasts killing hundred of innocent people can be tolerated but TADA putting the hideous criminals behind bars for more than six months can't be tolerated!!

Law and order is far more important to democracy than to any other system because they constitute the barrier against social collapse leading to despotism and anarchy. Any revolution and socio-economic change is not worth it if it spells doom instead of bringing bloom to people's life. Revolution for revolution sake can't be indulged. What Rosenthal says of American mentality about human rights and its overplaying is true for India also. The right to free speech has been construed as the right to preach lawlessness. The right to attend public places and places of amusement has become transformed into the right to practice rowdyism at these venues. Similarly, civil rights and human rights seem to have become the private domain of those who wish to tear the fabric of the society and the country. Kidnappings, killing, extortion, torture, rapes, sabotage and gory details of mayhem have become so common and acceptable to the people in ivory chamber that those who cry for relief and some peace get denounced as opponents of democracy and human rights.

This is the reason that all human rightists get awards and bouquets from foreign countries but they get boos and brickbats from the common people of India. When the whole world denounced the Bhagalpur police for blinding the dacoits who used to rape the women-folk before their men in broad daylight, the Bhagalpur people took out procession in support of policemen. It shows we have missed some links and chapters. We always ignore good of common people in our enthusiasm for lofty ideas. This is a classic case of modern concepts for medieval institutions in India. We have missed the woods for trees.

The silent poor disorganised masses have no champions. They want bread, peace and good sleep. The state since it has to go to them once in five years tries to protect their interests some time zealously and sometimes half-heartedly. The state, however, is rebuffed by such formidable organised and vocal organisations in the name of lofty and high-sounding ideals. The state is pressurised by organised and interested lobbies. It finds itself helpless to deliver even basic need of the people for peace due to hue and cry over the human rights of powerful criminals.

From all its protestations and presentations, the Human Rights Organisation has given signals as if it worked for extremist groups. So it found difficult to denounce the extremists when they blasted police personnel in large numbers or blow civilian jeeps to smithereens or maimed the husbands in full view of wives or butchered father in full view of their sons. They want to teach lessons to stooges of the state and the police. The horrendous details and mechanics of torture send chill down the spines of the bravest of the policeman. It defies logic that they who cry hoarse on a lock-up death which turns out to be suicide in all enquiries (even by the Press and the respectable citizens) magisterial and judicial, keeps enigmatic silence on such inhuman extremists' engineered torture-death. It will be good for them that they take a balanced and holistic approach. Supposedly, by taking a partial stance, they have done harm to all Human Rights Organisations because they lost credibility in the eyes of people. And the people had no choice but to believe the same state apparatus with which they are also not happy.

The front organisations of certain groups taking a fragmented, unilateral and biased view is a very dangerous trend. Taking cue from such organisations working on high ideals all terrorists groups will form an outfit of their own pleading in the name of human rights, amnesty for the most villainous of the criminals. How can one decide which group is genuinely interested in human rights and which group is not? Even the dacoits will form an organisation calling themselves revolutionaries fighting for bread. Dawood Ibrahim will call himself cultural revolutionary avenging upon one community for killing the others in riots. Who will declare that such and such organisations are fake and such are genuine because all of them think that state is a party and the real villain violating their rights to exploit and torture the common masses.

The state is facing heavy odds. The whole system is under acute strain because of highly intelligent and organised criminal groups who circumvent and give go by to all well-articulated laws. With money and muscle power and no moral, legal and social controls, they outmanoeuvre the state on many counts. The state is a vast conglomerate of disparate groups working sometimes with different motives, ideas and cross-purposes. Its main agency to bring peace in society is under clouds. The courts call police '*goondas* in uniform' and the police brand the courts 'white elephants'. The magistracy and police fight each other – the magistracy to retain their old privileges and the police to get a place under sun. The organised sharp-witted heavily-armed lawless goons derive advantage out of this and brand the state a villain when the reverse generally is true.

Human rights organisation is an organisation to be cherished, but not with its obscurantist ideas. It should aid the state in preservation of human rights by its healthy criticism. It should look for the blood of human beings but not for the brand. Any letting of human blood should be criticised in severest terms. It should give its teeth, its vocal-power, media-pull and organisational infrastructure to the people to guide the state and rein in when it goes berserk. It is not convincing that anybody who disagrees with human rightist's line of thinking is a reactionary and only their path is shining path of virtues and so imitable. They should be more open, receptive and latitudinal. It will be unfortunate if such organisations become a mouthpiece of certain groups in the name of championing human rights. If it wants to do so, it should consider changing its title.

The state is also not much interested in changing the situation. The failure of governance leads to unrest and lawlessness. Now the failure of governance, frustration and deprivation of people goes to the background and lawlessness becomes core issue. The government uses high rhetorics of determination and dare to crush the lawlessness and wins laurels. The people get confused. Since lawlessness becomes the immediate issue the people get obsessed with peace and restoration of order forgetting their deprivations of basic needs which the state was supposed to provide and its failure only was contributing to the proliferation of such armed underground revolutions. The people back the government and the police in their violation of human rights in the hope of peace. This ultimately proves dangerous to the total existence of dignified living of the citizens. But the Human rights organisations fail to expose the whole game of vested interests and draw the attention of people to the basic core issues. They spend more time in criticising the government for stringent tackling of law and order, (mostly through illegal methods) which had already been approved by the people under compulsions and necessity of circumstances. If the human rightists see the whole issue in total perspective, the people will also understand the failure of government and support the human rightists. But the myopic approach of these champions throw the people on the side of the powers-that-be whom people were not very enamoured of. The revolution and changes which would have come with the help of people, was stalled because people were turning their back to these human rightists. The sacrifice of these champions proved to be a simple waste.

Human rights organisations have the privilege of committed people as its members and they should rethink over their approach, strategy, aims and purpose.

CHAPTER 12

Supercop Strikes

I have to give a disclaimer - a disclaimer of jealousy, a disclaimer of ill-will and a disclaimer of frustration. Naturally it feels frustrated at not being so famous as our supercops. The pages of newspapers are full of exploits of theirs. The films are being screened on the life of such heroes. Magsaysay awards and Padmashree decorations are pouring galore. If I pick a hole in their aura, naturally they will feel bad and will sue me in the courts. So, this disclaimer that all characters willingly or inadvertently referred to are imaginary and it is an accident that my references resemble somebody. By the way this disclaimer is like giving evidence on oath in the court that I will speak truth and only truth in the name of *Gita*.

Supercops have become so glamorous that there is no charm in traditional policing. All the traditional pure dancing form has been replaced by fast, mixed fusion dancing. If you go by steps, you never reach the pinnacle of supercop-ship. If you have to jump the cue, show some dramatic stunts and heroics. But statutory warning is: these stunts can be performed by professionals. Professionals get highly paid. Stunts really stun the police organisation and it could not recover from all such stunts performed by supercops.

All Supercops who gained larger than life image in the police, contributed little. Many of the supercops who had time, opportunity and ability to add substantially to the system wasted time to bask in the glory coming to them in torrents. They became more selfish, egoist and individualistic. They thought more for themselves when outwardly they posed as if they were dying for nation. Such supercops got awards, rewards, posts, blitzkrieg of publicity and unending felicitations. But if we analyse dispassionately the role of such supercops, we find that many of them had a cut and dried plan to achieve the personal goal. They were more a careerist, manoeuvrers and managers than the heroes and the crusaders what people thought of them to be. They have by and large sailed along with the current; took extra care to keep the establishment in good humour and extracted maximum out of the system.

This police system continued for the last 140 years. Every person, every commission, every academician flayed it for its weaknesses. Evidentally, it is a failed system. This system can't deliver goods. The style of police functioning, attitude, approach, objectives and concepts differ from what the situation demands. The police lost thousands of lesser mortals at the altar of duty. Many police officers and men died unsung and unheard. Most of them were victims of the system and circumstances rather than of the problems.

Scores of top police officers worked and retired. Some shone and some failed to shine though they tried but almost none of them bothered to challenge the system. No one mustered courage to dent the system, which is taking heavy toll of police officers and innocent people. These supercops appear on the TV, the Press and public felicitation meetings and swear to die for the cause of people and the nation. Alas! had they really cared for the nation and the people, this outdated anti-people and powerful-friendly police might have changed.

Nobody can doubt the capabilities of supercops. They were bright police officers whom God blessed with ability and opportunity. These officers used their ability and opportunity to build up their own brand image, to get more Press coverage, to get more awards, felicitations and to perpetuate their longevity in the seat. Only the seat gives you rewards, awards, publicity and glory.

They all proved to be ruthless go-getter. They used men, material, system, media, government and people to get more results and more glory. They had no time to think of the means, the probable end-consequences, the health of the system and other partners like people, policemen, the culture and the traditions of the organisation. They tasted blood of publicity, glory and crude power. They had no time to think. They had to achieve, achieve and achieve. Perform at any cost to get more power, more publicity, and get closer to powers-that-be.

The terrorism in the Punjab was finished. There were various factors along with the police action. A popular government came in power that supported the police to the hilt. The people who always identified themselves emotionally with India, got fed up with the terrorists. The business and agriculture suffered due to police raids and searches and terrorist activities. The terrorists had no chain of command and they were inspired more by lucre and instant power and pelf than their commitment to the cause. Many splinter groups indulged in such blasphemous acts that left the people fuming and desperate. Supercops came to the scene and exploited the situation. It was a million dollar opportunity to ask for a change in the police system. The people, the government, the media, the courts and the intellectuals were fortunately sympathetic to the police cause and problems. They would have listened to the police pleadings. But no top police officer had time. They were busier in the policy of bullet for bullet, counting their achievements and seeing their photographs in the Press. The policemen of the Punjab responded to the clarion call of the nation. Some of them responded to earn more money in the guise of service to the nation. Normal chains of command broke. The police system overstretched itself to meet the situation. None had time to design the system for long term demands and plug its loopholes. The police would have cashed in on sympathy what the people had grudgingly extended because of greater evil of terrorism and asked for long-term people-friendly healthy reforms that is not coming because of politician-bureaucrat-criminal nexus.

The police over-reached their powers, violated civil rights, broke laws to restore laws and defied all regular channels in the name of abnormal situations. All questionable methods were adopted under the hush-hush directions of supercops. As is the fate of all ill-conceived armed dissent, the terrorism in the Punjab faded out.

But what did the police and people get? Police officers were prosecuted for human rights violations and the people got more bitter critic of police for their illegal and immoral activities. As nothing was done to tap the public and governmental support during the times of crisis, the system underwent more wear and tear and showed signs of cracks and exhaustion. Though certain supercops gained in stature but the police system, the police officers and the people lost much in the bargain.

The supercops should have refused the temptation to get larger than life image and asked for long-term solution. They would have asked for reforms in laws, reform in police rules and regulations and its minimum requirements. They would also have asked for steps that might soothe the feelings of the people. They should have refused to go for extra-legal police measures and stuck to their guns to abide by laws only. If the government thinks that the situation is really abnormal, it should declare the areas disturbed and frame new laws to meet such situations. At least the police would not have been blamed for mass graves and fake encounters and the people might have paid homage to the thousands of police martyrs. The simple greed of the supercops for power, of more time to stay in seat and of media-driven glory restrained them from being true to their uniform and they succumbed to the old police tricks. They gave it a sacred phrase of "call of Nation to fight the crisis". It may be a crisis for the nation but every situation is a crisis for police. They are meant to solve it through the established laws of the land and will of the people. They can't frame their own laws and run it because the powers-that-be wanted. They are accountable to the people, the constitution and the nation. They can't ignore it for short-term gains. The heroes adopted shortcut methods. They circumvented laws and commanded their officers also to do so. They ignored all legal pretensions and adopted all conceivable ways to get results. They got results, became famous but the police system got more infamous, more brutalised and more despised.

Supercops are not selfless personalities of freedom-struggle who really sacrificed themselves for the nation. Sardar Bhagat Singh was at least lucky that he got due glory for dying. There were hundreds and thousands who died for the nation unmourned. Our supercops don't want to be those unmourned martyrs. They want every pound of flesh for their drop of sweat. They want to be at right moment for right opportunities.

The politics is a game of power. They want a capable officer with his reins in their hands. The supercops fit the bill. They do their professional job and earn media glory and greater than life image but they also don't ask uncomfortable questions from the masters. They don't try to change the rules of game so that crisis could never arise and no supercops would be required in future. The system could take care of all such crisis.

Crisis situations are created out of power-game. The police and citizens become scapegoats. When the situation goes beyond levels of power game pleasures, some cop is required who is hungry to get supercop label. He is ready to be the hatchet man. Had all such supercops refused to be tools, the system might have changed. Had these supercops collectively or individually voiced their serious concern for the crumbling system, the system might have changed for better.

Generally, supercops take birth in metropolitan cities like Delhi, Mumbai, Calcutta, Chennai etc because there roam the national and international media and their reporters. The cops of Meghalaya slogging out in Jungles or fighting bare handed in Orissa against the anti-social elements can't become supercops because they have no opportunity to catch the attention of international and national media. Here comes in the need of the right place, right connection and right opportunity. One Chief Election Commissioner earlier in his career became Cabinet Secretary through political working and then contrived to be Chief Election Commissioner. The people who keep track of political developments know what he did in the early days of his Chief Election Commissionership. The public memory is short. His entire initial blatant partisan attitude was forgotten. He sensed the right opportunity and struck when it was hot and he had nothing to lose. He kept quiet and turned Nelson's eye to evils till he felt that it was inadvisable to raise voice because it would have marred his opportunities and career and ultimate 'Asian award'.

It is not necessary that all supercops are opportunist but most of them keep the establishment on right side. They will be slightly tilted towards the powers-that-be. The powers prop them up. It has therefore been generally seen that once the power changes hands these supercops also fall from the grace unless they have tremendous staying and persuasive powers. The supercops and powers have symbiotic relationship. Both mutually benefit each other. The media wants news because they are also compelled by dynamics of circulation. They have less to do with wherefrom and in what form it comes.

The supercops are generally autocrat and dictator, which generally passes for their courage, boldness and leadership qualities. But it is generally the craving for media glare and public glory that they don't want focus to be diverted from them. The boldness and leadership qualities are not in concentrating powers in his own hands and taking smallest decision but in delegating authority and decision-making power. The role of leader lies more in system building than day-to-day functioning. The system building and quiet policy-making is unglamorous in police but day-to-day routine function passes for achievements. So, the supercops never allowed second line of leadership to flourish. It is, therefore, generally seen that either the second line of leadership, opts out in frustration or wilt in course of time because of lack of systematic machinations by the leader himself.

All the supercops believe in individual loyalty. They systematically nurture people who have unflinching faith in their leadership and charismatic qualities. They don't like people who talk of system and are more loyal to laws of the land and moral values. People who project them as a super leader gets seats of power, opportunities and voice. The system in due course suffers because the individual gets more importance than the system. And individual howsoever brilliant and charismatic he may be, can't substitute the system. All individuals have flaws, whims, fancies and weaknesses. The supercops superimposed their whims on the system and sidelined all the dissent and sane voices. Naturally, the police became exclusive preserve of their blue-eyed boys. This attitude has harmed the process of the police wherever those supercops took birth. The supercops were so much obsessed with their brand image to the level of intoxication that they forgot they came out of the system and whatever they are today is because of the system support. But they want individual glory and so refuse to acknowledge the strength of the institution. On the contrary, they have systematically tried to destroy it. And so pathetic is the state of affairs in police today.

India has tradition of hero-worship and *avatar*-philosophy. We always hope that some charismatic personality will come and end all our worries. We had a long tradition of monarchy and dynastic rule. Even in democracy we have managed our own dynastic rule through elections. This gives scope, inspiration and hope to supercops to subjugate the system to individual ambitions because it gets the tacit consent and sometimes boisterous applause from the people. The people never thought that any super human being has only rocked the hopes and happiness of the people. It is only the fairly-run system and collective wisdom of the people that bring happiness to their lives. This is precisely the reason that supercops wherever they were born and prospered, left the system in ruins after them to add to the miseries of the people.

The supercops have to please their masters beyond their expectations. So they want to prove that they could do wonders within the limited resources what their predecessors could not do. Out of this strong desire they put tremendous pressure on their subordinates. The subordinate police officers lose their emotional, social, physical and family peace to satiate this thirst of 'proving-mania without resources' of the super leader. Many sacrificed their lives. Nobody asked that these lesser mortals who sacrificed their lives at the calls of supercops wouldn't have died had the system been oiled, repaired and taken care of well in time. Had all other agencies worked properly to alleviate the sufferings of the people who in disgust took to arms? Nobody allows you to ask these questions. And the super leaders neither raise these questions themselves nor allow anyone below him because it doesn't suit his schemes of becoming supercop. His subordinates die. He gives it the term of professional hazards. They join police to die. Unfortunately, these cops never tried to make it clear whether these deaths were for the country or otherwise.

Media management is one of the best qualities of these cops. They try all means to cultivate media and Press. These people give them larger-than-life image. They extol those not-so-glorious qualities. Such cops somehow manage to retain themselves somewhere in daily newspapers. This is one way of becoming great. You have to etch yourself in the mind of people. Those works which any police officer worth his salt has to do, are glorified as one of the great achievements of Indian police. Pressmen are favoured or rather bribed through various ways. One has to pay price in some way or the other to become great. As maxim goes, there is nothing like free lunch.

We never grudge anybody becoming great. But we definitely feel pained if somebody becomes great at the cost of the system. And feel more pained if somebody assumes larger-than-life frame by subverting and demolishing the due process. I always wonder if we have so many highly decorated and great supercops, why the people cry at every action of police even now? Why is Indian police still archaic, unfriendly and barbaric? Why is our training methods, working system and thinking medieval in approach?

Do our supercops really deserve the encomiums they got? Should the people not ask accounts of their sorrows and pains from them? Should they not be guilty of individual ambitions and emotional blackmail? Have they not betrayed the loyalty of their own subordinates? Have they not demolished the system for their individual glory? The nation must call them to accounts for all this.

CHAPTER 13

Police : A Riddle

How ignorant are people! A fairly educated person told me in confidence that every beggar at the road crossings with suspicious eyes is a policeman. They disguise themselves in such a fashion to collect intelligence. An army major had the impression that all the burglars get themselves registered with the police and then go for burglaries. People have colourful impressions about police. All policemen are corrupt, rough in behaviour and wrestler in real life. They should crack every case in jiffy, should not pay for any services or goods in the market and can do everything. All lower officials in police are bad people whereas senior officers only do some justice. Policemen are very busy and they don't have time for themselves or their families. People will be surprised to know that 80 per cent of the senior police officers are jobless and doing research on little items of work.

Police has a sub-culture which has different sets of rules, beliefs and traditions. Sometimes it is neither beneficial to the people nor to the policemen. But it is still being followed. Certain beliefs narrated above are reinforced without any logical reason.

Police has done much harm to society than good. It has caused much sufferings, much miseries and trauma to the poor and deprived ones whom it was meant to protect. This is true all over the world. Had police not been there physically, there would have been more peace, less injustice and lesser sufferings. The majority of human population are law-abiding and peace seeker. It is not the police in its present form but the concept of policing that has maintained equilibrium in society. Many people don't live a criminal life not because the police prevent them from doing so but because they have fear of presence of policing. They presume that if they commit crime, they will be caught – the lurking fear.

Besides this, large chunk of people are afraid of social opprobrium and religious and moral prescriptions. If people are not restrained by their intrinsic nature of peace, longing for social approval and socio-religious restrictions we would have had crimes everywhere. And our present police set-up would have either been torn asunder or connived with the criminals because of sheer enormity of problem and helplessness as people believe today.

I have seldom come across any class of people who invoke so much antipathy, so much hatred and revulsion as police. Perhaps in India the politicians can match them to some extent. Even criminals enjoy better credibility and respectability than the police. All dacoits and negative characters in movies painted as heroes draw more admiration and acceptance from the people. Many people boasted of having not visited police in their life as a certificate to their being a gentleman. If you are a gentleman by not visiting a policeman or police station what will be the situation of a policeman who visits police station every day. He has become the villain of the first order in the people's eyes.

There is no section in the society that is happy with a policeman - politicians, Press, people, academicians, bureaucrats, civilians, rich, poor all hate a policeman. He has become symbol of hatred and despise.

One lady IPS probationer was quizzed about her preference to ask help from somebody in times of distress. She named policeman as the last person to look forward to for help. She felt that a lady was more unsafe at the hands of a policeman than being alone.

Those who deal with statistics and data tell us that the people, dying in police custody during interrogation or lock-up are mostly poor, petty thieves or suspects. Even if they do commit crime, they commit it out of bare necessities. The harsh methods are not applied to people who devour thousands of crores or commit dacoity with rape in broad daylight. The policemen are a frustrated, ill-provided, despised and low self-esteem group. They are themselves used, abused and misused. They know they are being used but are unable to do anything about it.

Poor people are at the receiving end. Police organisation is more to perpetuate the rule of the strong than that of weak ones. The percentage of jail inmates indicates that most people who do not have money to get them out of jail, languish in the jails. The rich though criminals manage to bluff the police or the court with the help of money. In most of the jails, I have seen 80 per cent of the people are from poorer sections of the society. Lock-up deaths account for elimination of petty thieves, pickpockets and poor suspects. Though in police department, for long, I have not seen any hardcore dying in lock-up. People who come mainly from poor background to join police are temperamentally inimical to the poor masses. What an irony!

All policemen slog day in and day out in this belief that they are doing much service to the society. But it is not true. The police spend their time and energy to prop up the ruling clique even if they are oppressive, unconstitutional and corrupt. The *bandobust* and security duty is cutting into the time of police man-hours. Once a minister wanted a guard at his house from the police station where there were only six sparable manpower that was meant for town patrol duty. When I ordered the withdrawal of the guard, the minister raised a great hue and cry. Though I did not relent but made an arch enemy of the minister who inflicted severe damage to my career subsequently. In Puttaparthi and Tirupati of Andhra Pradesh all high dignitaries come in scores. As they are to be given security and protocol paraphernalia otherwise they get annoyed, the police here only do *bandobust* and security duty. It is just impossible to seek appointment with any senior police officer because they are always busy with high-ups and rarely have time for general people. Sometimes, I really wonder what the police do for safety and security of general people!

Prevention and detection of crime is more in the nature of statistics jugglery than preventing crime-occurrence and safety to the people. Right from the government down to the constable at the police station, they are obsessed with number of crimes. The real situation on the ground has less relevance to them. So it is generally seen that police officers who are quite unpopular with the people are taken to be very successful officers in official circles. Virtually, there is no consistency and congruity between the thinking of police bosses and aspirations of people. They have diametrically opposite views about role, scope and style of functioning of police. This is the reason that people dislike policemen from core of their heart despite supreme sacrifice by policemen all over the country.

All intelligence organisations of police which should work for safety and security of the people and strengthening of the Constitution and the system are mostly engrossed in collecting political intelligence as desired by the powers-that-be. The police thus mainly become the protector of establishment and the interests of dominant sections of the society. Unfortunately, this situation has not changed at all even in Indian Republic.

The incidents of police partiality or helplessness are not few and far between but in abundance. In Guntur District of Andhra Pradesh, there was a bomb blast on the eve of elections in a minister's house while the bombs were being manufactured. There is general perception that it was being done in the knowledge of the minister. The opposition parties and certain sections of the Press asked for CBI enquiry. When all this was going on, the then Director General and Inspector General of Police declared in the Press without even preliminary investigation that the Minister was innocent. So much so for the efficiency and impartiality of the highest dignitary of the police! I generally agree with the people that it is really difficult to get justice at the hands of police. But the policemen are also helpless.

I had been hearing cases of police inaccessibility. I got that first taste when my own batch mate, a Senior Superintendent of Police, Patna could not be contacted for two weeks despite my all-out efforts to catch him anytime in the day or night. His deputy was also equally busy with the law and order situation! When I tried to contact the Dy Inspector General of Police of Patna he told that it was a small issue and did not merit attention of a Dy Inspector General of Police. When this could happen to a Senior IPS Officer, what would be the fate of general people!

Police is such a powerful weapon as it has got vast infrastructure, fleet of vehicles, book loads of legal powers (the crude and brute power not included!) and a vast army of trained manpower. All the skilled recourses and vast manpower are manipulated to serve those who are in seats of power. Five per cent of morally depraved, corrupt and soul-sold officers have held the police to ransom. It is not correct that all police officers are dishonest, brute, partial and barbaric. Most of the police officers are really dedicated, highly committed and fairly honest but they are marginalised. They are not wanted by the establishment. Their existence is meaningless to the establishment and the department, to the people and the society and finally to themselves. The sacrifice of thousands of policemen are going in vain because the people are ultimately not getting benefited. All these sacrifices are manoeuvred in such a way that it serves only the privileged ones.

I was just calculating the cost-benefit analysis of Andhra Pradesh Police. The Andhra Pradesh police guzzles about Rs 3100 crore per year. The yearly loss of property in all types of thefts, robberies and dacoities is around Rs 500 crore or less. The areas where people get benefited through police is traffic, property loss, protection to life and in law and order disturbances. Traffic everywhere in India is in a mess. It may be the fault of traffic police or all the other wings of the government, but it is immaterial to the people. If we add the prevailing corruption in the traffic police to the traffic mess, the proposition is of colossal loss and nuisance. If we take the case of property protection, the situation gets more comic. If we have to maintain an elephant to protect a cat, it is more than unwise. One always wonders how it will be about paying the compensation for all property losses through insurance. We will be saved of the fabricated investigation of police that consumes reams of paper, years of time and tonnes of money and simultaneously leads to hundreds of lock-up deaths. At least India will have a shade better human rights record if we stop our 'ace investigators' from 'skilled investigation'.

Some people knowledgeably affirm that it is not so simple. We can't estimate the gains of police department through visibles. We have to see the enormous gains what society derives from police through invisibles like sense of security, prevention of crimes through various measures like patrolling, night-beats etc., and arrest of criminals leading to check of crimes. But we have other schools who feel that police has given more psychological insecurity to the people. A good corps of private detectives would have done a better professional job than the ill-trained policemen who are shown more as a bunch of jokers in Hindi films. Fabrication of evidence, burking of crimes and property offences, implication of innocents in false cases, and false detection and recovery of property sometimes in cases like murder and rapes are so high in Indian police that it is revolting against moral sense. It in itself becomes the sole ground for closing down the shop of police. Nobody could understand why do police burk the crime and kill the people to detect a case? Why do police sacrifice so much for so little? Policemen from top to bottom have poor quality of life. They face sometimes time constraints and sometimes approach constraints. Their sub-culture has made them sub-human to the extent that they don't know how to enjoy life. If we see the distortion of truth by high and mighty and mockery of criminal justice through fabrication of evidence under various pressures we will be fully convinced that independent India does not need police system. Lord Byron had said, "there is in fact no law or government at all and it is wonderful how well things go on without them".

Cowardice is the hallmark of police organisation. A policeman is damn afraid of the government and his senior bosses. He who lays down his life facing bullets from a criminal, surprisingly meekly surrenders to unreasonable demands or commands. They follow the dog-eat-dog policy and run down their own colleagues who have even traces of independence and sense of fairness. This trait of a policeman has been a bane of this organisation because nothing would change in its nature and structure for its lack of vision and boldness.

Police is one organisation that kills all vision and creativity in its fold. It dislikes all new approach and divergent thinking even if it is positive. Status quo is the basic *mantra* of police organisation. Engagement is more important than involvement. Activity is more important than productivity and creativity. An officer who sits in the office for fourteen hours generating paper and wasting money and time of the government is respected. Because he is not a threat to the system but directly perpetuates its theme of status quo. But anybody who wants to do rational thinking for improvement in the system is laughed off.

Police officers like any other inorganic organisation do not grow in knowledge, thinking and experience. Police is one organisation which has designed its training and system in such a manner that even an IPS officer acts like a bumpkin after ten years. His thought process is not in sync with that of a civil gentleman. Policeman is choked of all avenues of growth.

Corruption is an accepted norm in police like beating, fake encounters, political interference, burking of crimes, bad behaviour etc. senior police officers say "so and so is very corrupt but a smart policeman. He produces the results". Such smart gentlemen are ruling the roost.

People have very wrong notion about intelligence network of police. I have worked in two states and I can safely say that there is nothing like intelligence network of police. It is all trial and error and cock and bull stories. Mostly, it is the schism in the ranks of the criminals or some renegades spilling the beans. That intelligence comes to police otherwise it is all dark tunnel. We have always been hearing in newspapers that intelligence has failed and the national security is in danger. When there is no intelligence network how can it fail? But yes! The system is running because of individual brilliance not owing to organisational mechanism.

The most useless person I have seen in the department, is me. All others have been claiming brilliance, honesty, effectiveness and commitment. They lament the wrong practices, bad traditions, blacksheep in the department and take vow that they would do their level best to clean the stable within their sphere. When so much brilliance is there then why so much muck and filth in the department? I am at least not able to unravel this knot of mystery. All senior officers retire with great satisfaction and pride that they contributed their mighty-self to the service of police. But the people pray to God that police, snake and creditor should not have even a chance encounter with them.

Hard work of a policeman does not actually go in vain but in maintenance and oiling of the system. To run a machine also we need a driver, fuel and lubricants and a mechanic. Mechanic does hard work but does not create anything: only maintains. Only engineers can create things and improve the machine. Policemen are mechanics. They are doing hard work of a labour but smother all engineers. A successful police officer is generally a manager but not a leader. A leader can't progress in police career because police does not withstand a leader.

But how all this has crept into police? Long years of colonial rule or system of training or illiteracy and poverty of people who bear with brutality and idiosyncrasies of police or our nascent democracy which has so far failed in its philosophy. We, Indians are great hypocrites and so our police. We take the name of Maharana Pratap and Chatrapati Shivaji as a proof of our valour to cover the ugly face of crore of Indians who have not stood up for truth and justice, pride and dignity. Police is also no exception. Riddle is still unsolved and mystery unknotted.

CHAPTER 14

Justice to All: What Nonsense!

All that glitters is not gold. What Constitution embodies, is not always implemented. Rule of law, equality before law and equal protection of law are maxims of democracy but the unstatutory warning is: It is dangerous to take it on face value. Justice to all is a big deception and a mirage. It is music to ears and a very good ware to showcase but in practice it does not exist as a safeguard. It is like our NGOs and development projects executed by the government that sounds robust on papers but deficient and sometimes non-existent in reality. One very senior officer who was very close to the government and had been Addl Director General, Intelligence, Andhra Pradesh for long years told me that King had never been fair and so is the modern state. He was defending the government or rather warning me against future shocks, I have still to decipher. Perhaps he wanted to convey that the government was not very unfair if they did some injustice.

My family had been a bunch of law abiding citizens. They always tried to get justice through laws. It is a good lesson to all of them including me that none got justice in their life. My father who had himself been a true Gandhian and was honest to the core, used to give money to the court room staff otherwise they would never tell you dates of the next hearing. They will harass you through ever-inventing devices. My father brought this to the notice of the Magistrate also. But he only drew ridicule and derision. My father did not get justice through courts despite all evidence because the opposite party went to High Court and got all proceedings stayed. My family had no money to move Supreme Court because the worth of property did not warrant that foolhardiness. My father went into depression as his lands were encroached upon; crops were looted and he was physically assaulted innumerable times but 'rule of law' was glaringly absent. He broke down economically, emotionally and psychologically. All Gandhians nowadays meet the same fate. He had to seek psychiatric help. After my father broke down my eldest brother took up the cudgel. Taking leave from his job, he used to go to the courts early in the morning and come late in the night. His efforts also didn't fetch anything except bitterness, loss of money and despair. Ultimately our family enterprise of years of efforts of getting justice through established system bore no fruits. And this 'eternal rule' applies to all citizens living in India. You don't get justice through beautifully - crafted criminal justice system.

In my childhood, my father used to tell stories of various families which got ruined in the maze of court cases. They sold everything to get justice and retrieve their pride. They went to the grave in the fond hope of getting that 'elusive' justice. Naturally, the pride also goes with loss of money. The children of those families still live in our village devastated and destitute. They are the classic examples of ravages wrought upon by our justice system. The hope of justice is like snake's eyes – charming, magnetic, mesmerising and lethal. You are bound to doom and death if you crave for it.

I am still to get a person who got justice from the system. And even if he got it, it was of no meaning to him by the time he got it. Many also manage to get justice but through other 'ingenious ways'. It is highly dangerous to believe that - justice will be done to you if you seek it. It is so because if you are ready for the danger, it is possible that you will ward off the harm befalling. If you are wary of a danger, a person or a situation, you will fend for it and devise some emergency safeguards, but if you are rest assured that the state is the safety-net and it will save you against unlawful elements and situations, you are going to get a lesson of your life. In all probability you will not get justice and if you are unlucky enough to be ranged against a 'privileged one', you should be dead sure that you will not get justice and on the contrary invite some more injustice.

If you have money and power it is a great defence against any law in our system. We have got layers of courts to appeal endless times. Fortunately, it takes the process long years to wade through each layer of courts. In the meanwhile you have got all the time in the world to win over the witnesses, threaten them, tempt them or eliminate them. You can also try to buy the complainants. There is every chance that they might have been drained of their energy, time, money and patience to get justice and would be wise enough to settle with the 'enemy' himself. Even if you are the unluckiest person in the world and lose your case after dozens of years of fight and fool enough to not break the witnesses and sort out the complainant, you have still the chances of appealing to the President for pardon. Even if the President is a candidate of the opposition party and you have no chance, the state government will be kind enough to send you on parole or furlough or pardon sentences while serving the term. It was very amusing in Andhra Pradesh when Government of Andhra Pradesh had pardoned a politician after only a couple of years of imprisonment who had been convicted for life imprisonment by the Supreme Court. The Supreme Court had to intervene in this travesty of justice. Now it is a different issue that the Supreme Court will intervene in one in millions of cases and you will be definitely not that lucky enough. Here also the Supreme Court was approached because the complainants belonged to powerful opposite political group who also had got all the resources to approach the Supreme Court umpteen number of times. A poor person has no gall to aspire for this justice because he would have to burn all his life and resources to get this costly justice. Thus the right to justice or the right to do injustice with impunity is the exclusive preserve of the privileged ones, not for the pigmies. Stories have been heard and many a time true also that you can get murder case converted into accidents and accidents into murder cases if you have right resources and connections.

Justice delayed is justice denied. You might have read in your primary school books and so have I. Statistics reeled out by the government agencies show that about two crore cases are pending in the lower courts of India. When these cases will be listed for hearing nobody knows. This should be the basic duty of the state to liquidate all these cases on priority basis because implementation of rule of law is the basic principle of any civilised state. But the government has not bestowed its benign attention on it. The courts which had been passing landmark judgments in public interest litigations have also not compelled the government to discharge this primary duty to the citizens.

The fate of civil cases is more miserable than the criminal cases. Now the commoners have realised the futility of going to the courts for settlement of civil cases. If you have to get your house vacated from the occupation of a gritty tenant or you have to get illegal encroachments removed from your rightful land possession or you have to realise hand loans or rightful dues from a borrower, even a layman on the street will tell you that it will be futile to go to the court. You have to approach some toughies of that locality who have mushroomed all over like consultants to help you obviously for a handsome fee. Everybody in that ward has got his address though they might not be knowing location of police station and courts. So much so for citizen's faith in police, courts and rule of law.

Now even there are agents everywhere in the court to advice that there is no point in wasting your time in litigation if you want your thing done. This networking is now so set and institutionalised that at least in Metropolitan cities it has taken over the mantle of justice delivery from the formal mechanism. It has become an alternate career for *pehalwans,* thanks to our police and criminal justice system.

If some *goonda* or a bandit does not kill you and take your money, it is not because he is afraid of police or law but it is on account of his own human and benevolent qualities. Now, I have got immense faith in Locke's philosophy about humans, being kind, benevolent, affable, justice and peace-loving otherwise what will explain that these hoodlums are not unleashing a killing and raping spree; what will explain that ladies are still moving on the roads with ornaments on their person and beautiful girls are going ashopping. Everybody knows that if a toughie does something nothing would happen to him eventually. Take for example the case of Narayan Dutt Tiwari and a case of paternity against him. It is when Tiwari is not a ganglord and he is in gentlemanly manner exploiting the loopholes in laws. A toughie will just put his gun on the temple and phut. Man is gone and with him the case is finished. Police and court will close the file for lack of evidence. Definitely sometimes we see some high profile individuals going to jails mostly due to media glare and the compulsion of showing justification for the existence of this moribund system. By taking some action in Jessica Lal case and Dey murder case, do we really think that we have done justice to the crores of people? How many have this fortune of dying in Delhi and Mumbai and attracting media glare? Who has the time and resources to dig out thousands of cases buried deep in our villages and small towns which go abegging attention and justice? We may feel happy and satisfied reading all such cases in newspapers and gloat over that the rule of law prevails in India. But this false smugness and hypocrisy does not obviate the injustice done to lakhs. The blood of innocents which was spilled and could not be recompensed by punishing the guilty due to this system shines bright and ugly.

This is an age of media and mass communication. There is general tendency among our courts to act fast and tough in all those cases which are taken up by media. People don't understand why CBI increases its speed in some cases and forgets about it as per political temperature. People also fail to 'appreciate' the process, quality of evidence and standards of investigation proportionate to the weight of the people or spectrum of the political party involved. The whole nation is agog with happenings in Sohrabuddin case of Gujarat. Perhaps the people, the government, and the court know that Sohrabuddin was a notorious criminal who had gone beyond the pale of law. His killing by police has led to the ruination of as many IPS officers as have not been for the accumulated injustice to the crores of people. People of India would have been really indebted to CBI and the courts had the same alacrity been shown for the unseen and mute millions whose pleas are not heard. Why this more justice is done to some people and in some cases, is inscrutable to millions of Indians. Citizens would have felt safe had some IPS officers been jailed for killing people in their lockups. Thousands of lock-up deaths that have taken place in our country are not of Sohrabuddin like notorious criminals but of petty suspects of the thefts who do not get two square meals. The policemen who should not be punished, are punished and those who should be punished, go scot-free. The policemen of Gujarat took recourse to 'illegal' means to silence Sohrabuddin as there was no other way to silence him. The political dispensation has repealed TADA, POTA and all other laws because these came in the way of vote-politics but no substitute laws were given. Unless there is a political flavour and news-value to a case it does not get the attention what is due to it. It is not the mechanism of justice but wheels within wheels that works. Everybody knows that riots can't take place and go unabated if government, wants to subdue it. No terrorism can flourish unless political dispensation shirks from its responsibility of curbing it. The courts feel heavenly satisfied by punishing some sundry policemen. It definitely gets some media glare and false sense of doing its duty but always the cancerous cells are left untouched. In our system it is like this only.

In fits and starts we get so obsessed with ideas of civility, rule of law, natural human rights and sanctity of laws that we forget that we are throwing baby with bathwater. We are totally confused as to whom do we want to do justice - criminals or victims or criminal-victims. If the national territory and its unity is safe, then only we can talk of justice, human rights, rule of law etc. If the very integrity and fabric of the nation is torn asunder; its existence is put in peril; its citizen's life and liberty are at risk, who will be there to talk about rule of law and human rights? We have lost our goal and objectives and are confused about the whole issue. India as a young nation has not consolidated its territory and position. Our neighbours are always nipping at our borders and fomenting troubles inside. The very Constitution is under threat. It is the solemn duty of the politicians, press and intelligentsia to plug all the loopholes socially, legally, politically, economically and culturally to refuse any entry to saboteurs. Unfortunately without creating a solid framework to strengthen our internal security system and agencies, we are trumpeting our high ideals and intellectual prowess to the world. We are cutting off the same branch on which we are sitting. We are so stoned that we want to cut off our arms for being filthy than purifying it.

If you are a ganglord I can give warranty that you will not get punished. When I was in-charge of Special Task Force, Bihar, the force raided one village Ladwan in Barh sub-division of Patna district and killed eight criminals who were equipped with illegal sophisticated arms. One STF commando was also killed. The leader of the gang became honourable MLA. There was an all out effort by officer of his caste to book murder case against the STF. 'The Hon'ble MLA' enjoys the freedom and comforts of life. He is also right hand man of Nitish Kumar, the Hon'ble Chief Minister of Bihar.

When RJD was in power, the STF party raided one notorious criminal Krishnanand Ray of Munger district of Bihar. His speciality was that he had declared his area of influence as out of bounds of police. No policemen could venture into his dominion. It was not only that he was better-armed and superior in tactics and local support but he also had immense political influence. The STF did not inform any senior line officers of the district and straight away reached the local police station in the night. When they asked the local SHO to come with them, he feigned illness. When the leader of STF who was Dy SP pressurised the SHO he asked for permission to put on uniform and ran away from rear gate. Bewildered and puzzled the STF virtually bundled the local ASI along and raided the stronghold of Krishnanand Ray. The STF had had their lights out when they faced bullets raining upon them from four-corners from different villages. The forces were really panicked and the leading Dy SP was crying for reinforcement. When I contacted the local Dy IG of Munger, he found fault with me for raiding those areas. The STF leader was screaming that he had to go for massacre if he wanted to break the siege laid by goons of Krishnanand Ray and come out. I told, come what may, you have not to incur any loss of STF Jawan and avoid aimless killing. Just protect yourselves.

It was a great crisis and flush of tension and stress. We could not express the relief we felt at safe return of our forces. But it shook Krishnanand Ray and his cronies because STF had given them the taste of their own firepower. Krishnanand had to save life by fleeing away stealthily which he had never had to resort to in his chequered criminal career. All hell broke loose when the RJD supremo came to know about it. The Superintendent of Police of the district and the Dy IG of Munger got the dressing down of their life. The Superintendent of Police told me later that what enmity I had with him and of all the dists why he was bestowed upon the favours of STF raids. He requested that if I wanted to see him in the seat of Superintendent of Police, Munger I should leave him and his criminals in peace. However, I don't know why I was spared this dressing down by RJD supremo when I was the real culprit of conducting the raids. The Superintendent of Police, Munger survived but Superintendent of Police, Bettaiah and SHO of the concerned police station were not so lucky when STF raided Bettaiah and killed two members of dreaded Bhangad Yadav gang while Bhangad Yadav himself could narrowly escape through. I could not understand this policy of ruling elite. They could have reprimanded me and transferred me out. However, they did not do so but kept on terrorising the field formations and holding 'rule of law' to ransom.

The Government of Bihar has framed the most regressive Police Act which will never allow police to be accountable and progressive. I tried to meet the Chief Minister Nitish Kumar to tell him about the ground realities but I could not get audience. Subsequently I was told that senior officers in Bihar also do not get audience for months together. So I left the attempt. Holding *Praja darbar* and getting political mileage is one thing and knowing the grass-root reality and correcting it is another. It is good that many states did not implement Bihar Police Act as model as the Chief Minister wants all to follow his policies. Bihar suffered a lot in the last thirty years and still the situation of rule of law is such that you can kill dozens and still roam free. And so is the case with many other states. The issue is not one state or police or the courts. The issue is whether you have the money and brute power to buy the witnesses, kill the complainants and engage battery of lawyers. You can also pay money and delay the cases in courts for years. Justice is all yours.

Corruption has seeped into pores of all portals of Indian body-politic and society. K Balchandran, Retd Chief Justice of Supreme Court was doubted for his integrity. Many Judges of High Court are reaching the threshold of impeachment. The PF scandal of Ghaziabad rocked the judicial edifice. So far as the corruption in police is concerned less said the better. In this scenario, if justice is beyond reach of rank and file, what is so unusual about it?

In Delhi, I was interacting with a renowned publisher. I narrated him the horror story of Indian criminal justice system including my personal experiences. Nonchalantly, he told he was not shocked. But I was shocked. If this pathetic state of affairs does not shock an educated and enlightened person in Delhi, there is something amiss in the whole story of Indian democracy.

The people of Bhagalpur supported the police who blinded the criminals because they believed that all these criminals will never be punished by due process of law. The criminals had understood the limitations of law. Once you understand the limitations of law, you can violate it with impunity. The dacoits raped young brides in front of their husbands and brothers, cut the husbands into pieces bit by bit in front of their wives and threw the pieces into the Ganges. Now there was no recovery of dead body. No witnesses could muster courage to depose before the courts. No complainant could withstand the threats of death and doom. They thought it prudent enough to avoid more calamities by not angering the criminals further and did not persist with the case. Naturally, they had no faith in police, prosecution, courts and jails. Since police were in the throes of problems and the most visible pillar of the criminal justice system they drew all the flak. Unable to bear the humiliation and pressure heaped by press, politicians, people and senior officers they resorted to the "illegal" means. Clouds burst with Arun Shourie's revelations.

While I was under training in LBSNAA, Mussoorie, the memories of Bhagalpur blinding case was fresh in the mind of people. Arun Shourie had won laurels what he could get for exposing startling barbaric act of police. The whole press milched it to the maximum and the police officers involved in the blinding cases went through hell of their life. Indian intelligentsia and world consciousness were very happy that human rights were still alive in the country and the Indian courts were keeping the goddess of justice protected. But did all these brilliant minds of country do justice to helpless and hopeless Indians? Did they not pave the way for ruthless criminals to perpetuate their barbaric ways? Is it justice that the policemen who fought for people were punished and dubbed as criminals when actually the Parliament, the Legislature, the Courts, the jurists and the intelligentsia should have been punished for their failure to devise a fool-proof system to tackle all such savage dacoits and mafiosi. As per morals, commonsense and natural justice, the policemen had done the right thing which was illegal as per our 'laws' which have no spokes, no teeth and no sense. This law which can be manoeuvred and manipulated by the clever and the criminals.

There is a disconnect between the people and postulates of law. Our society is at different levels of development and acculturation. It is ancient in traditions, mediaeval in institutions and modern in concept. When we don't have basic wherewithal to implement rudiments of law, we want to adopt the lofty ideals of democracy and human rights. We are so confused about the whole western concept that the system now finds itself ranged along the criminals against the people and the victims. The Courts, Press and intelligentsia spend more time to save and sympathise with the criminals than the people whom they are supposed to protect. This is the reason that Supreme Court has spent its valuable time to protect the human rights of Sohrabuddin than the people whom Sohrabuddin killed. Long years and reams of pages were used to punish the police officers who fought and blinded the criminals of Bhagalpur. Hypocrisy is at its height in our system. The Punjab Government, the Andhra Pradesh Government and the J&K Government supported its police and turned blind eye to their 'unlawful' deeds because they fought the greater evil. Our existence as a civil society and a nation was at stake. But the courts which have to protect the laws punished these officers. Why this disconnect? Why this confusion? Why this hypocrisy? Why do we want to be advanced and modern in thinking and concepts to the extent of absurdity? Why don't we have clarity of thoughts? The rule of law can't be interpreted from confines of high walls and safe environs. Justice is not only for Delhi and Mumbai but also for Ballia and Bhagalpur. Laws have to be framed to protect the innocent victims but not to satisfy the high philosophy and modern thinking. Modern is not what send people to be guillotined by the criminals helpless and unprotected. Nobody wants to live in such hypocritic and confused system.

We have said a lot about police and courts. Let's talk about prosecution also. While working as Controller, Department of Legal Metrology (earlier Department of Weights and Measures), Andhra Pradesh, I found that the department was losing all the cases. In the police also I found that the department was losing all the cases either in the tribunals or the courts. Highly incensed at this, I wrote to the government, that the department should be allowed to engage private lawyers because I thought that government pleaders are not able to present our cases properly. The government, sent it to law department for opinion. The law department, Government of Andhra Pradesh remarked that we had systems of government pleaders created by the government. So there is nothing, we have to do about it. Secondly engaging of private lawyers will demoralise the government pleaders and this will affect their dignity. I could not understand the logic. But the government, again referred it to Advocate General for remarks. Advocate General also endorsed the remarks of law department. This is called the vicious cycle of vested interests. I wrote back that government has no business to protect the dignity of the government pleaders and save them from demoralisation at the cost of public interest. There is nothing sacrosanct about the system of government pleaders. If the system is not functioning we can very well change it. On the other hand, I was not asking for scrapping the system lock stock and barrel but I wanted a provision to engage private lawyers at the rate fixed by government, wherever the Head of the Department felt it so. But the law department and Advocate General both did not like it. They work to protect the turf for their fellow brethren. I have the unenviable distinction of seeing the courts since my childhood. The job of government pleaders barring some noble exceptions is to take money from both sides and see that the government lose the case. How come that the conviction rate is as poor as ten per cent in heineous and sensational cases? If the victims know that there is only ten per cent chances of the accused being convicted and that also at lower courts level, nobody will approach police or court. They will settle the issue at their own level. That ten per cent of conviction rate in heineous crimes goes further down by the time the case goes through its regular rigmarole of layers of courts and battery of government pleaders. It is felt that the state has made all arrangements to see that the cases failed in its march towards securing of justice. In this scenario only a fool can expect a justice.

In all criminal cases the state presents all the victims. It is so because state has the primary duty of protecting life and property of a person and maintenance of law and order. Basically this is the prime motive for formation of a state. State has a big paraphernalia for discharge of this duty, but as in most of other state concerns, this has been a major craft. The state represents the victims in the courts and it also decides whether to go in for appeal or not. As is the present status almost 80 per cent of the cases get acquitted. By the time it reaches the apex court, the percentage falls further down. The main question is why should one trust the state and allow it to represent when it is almost sure that he would not get justice. The very contract between the state and individual is in question because the state does not fulfill its promise. Had the individual been left to himself he would have represented himself in the court. At least he would have had the satisfaction of trying his best. Here he is denied justice because of state failure due to corruption, red-tapism, and inadequacies in the system and breach of trust. Then why should he believe the state at all? How 'eye for eye' system of justice was worse than the present system? Why should we spend crores of rupees on this behemoth which does not dispense with the justice?

Vote-politics has affected all organs of the state. We profess that we are the secular, socialist, democratic republic but the caste is the greatest philosophy and merit our system believes in. Even the old Hindu society doesnot decide the civic life on the basis of caste and religion as our secular polity does. Right from constitutional posts down to the appointment of peons through all grades of officers and government functionaries like judges, government pleaders, advocates, governors, ministers, members of public service commission etc are decided by caste. Even laws, rules, regulations, selection of beneficiaries and above all dispensation of justice is decided by caste and community. It also depends on your caste, religion, community and political colour whether you will get justice from the system. It is difficult to say whether we really made any stride from the days when the village elders handed out crude justice. At least the justice then was fast and transparent. Even if the caste guilds and village *sabhas* did injustice in the name of caste, they were not opaque and hypocritical about it. Now the very problem of our system is trust deficit, moral confusion and hypocrisy. They don't deliver what they profess to deliver. Goddess of justice has really become blind in India. I am also waiting for an *avtar* who will do something about it.

Baby Steps
and
Failed Attempts to Change Police

Chapter 15

Narsipatnam Experiments

Every police officer thinks he is a supercop. He sets out to design scheme of changes in the department. But his colleagues don't think so and the first important assignment of the worthy successor is to efface all changes brought about by his predecessor. This game of 'make and break' like hide and seek is going on in police since the date my memories go back. This is also the solid reason of status quo in police.

I was also charged up with zeal and mission to change the department. It all started with great conviction. It was very popular among the people because we were doing extra than what was expected from us or so the people and my comrades in reforms thought. There is a saying in India that if you do your duty, you become a great man because none does his duty though he is paid for this.

Narsipatnam was my first posting as Asst Superintendent of Police which is a sub-division of Visakhapatnam district. It was full of vast tracts of jungles and tribals who used to speak many languages including Telugu that was all Greek to me.

The end results of the Narsipatnam experiments in police was that the whole revenue department officials of Visakhapatnam district rose in procession against me for my illegal 'encroaching upon their turf'. One MRO issued a notice of contempt of court taking himself to be a 'court'. Surprisingly, the then Collector also identified his cause with them. The District and Sessions Judge backed up by all judicial officers wrote a report against me for action for perfunctory investigation. The High Court of Hyderabad wrote to the government to take action against me for marking a copy of report against JFCM to the High Court. This was all happening because the local police under my directions inspected 'fair price ration shops' and I wrote a report against a First Class Judicial Magistrate for asking a free jeep ride failing which he issued many non-bailable warrants against junior police officers for not appearing to depose evidence despite their requests to be absent for some urgent purpose. Everybody wanted to give a taste of his nuisance value.

When subsequently I carried out these experiments on a bigger scale in Medak district, a whole social welfare department pitched a tent in front of the Collectorate against me and went for *satyagraha*. They had the moral support of the local minister and the collector. The cause for all this outrage was that the Special Branch of District police had given a report about absence of hostel wardens and fudging of number of hostel inmates in government residential schools to siphon off the government funds. The *satyagrahis* demanded that the police should have no right to report against such things. The police bosses felt that I unnecessarily created ruckus, that I was not doing my duties of police and that I was craving for publicity.

Now you go through so-called experiments that ruffled the feathers of our gentleman colleagues in other areas.

In India, the police is now the last hope of society but it is everywhere in shambles. In spite of immense and intense sacrifices there is none in the whole country who talks well of police. Contradictions beset the police role.

With the onset of modernity, progressiveness and material prosperity, the natural controls of society have lost their effectiveness. The expanding society has no in-built social control over its members; the religion is interpreted in a perverted manner and adds to lawlessness; the caste-guilds exert less control on their members and lead more to inter-caste clashes and the lack of civic sense and peculiar interpretation of fundamental and human rights have led to people's flouting of governments' authority and rule of law.

Added to the vanishing natural controls, the modern life craze for materialistic gains, success and power has left no scruples in people. The result is growing chaos, restlessness, disorder and lurking fear in the mind of people. With declining social, moral, religious and judicial checks and restraints, the burden fell on the police, a machinery which was neither intended nor designed nor allowed to discharge this responsibility. The Britishers wanted police with limited role to protect their life and colonial interests. They preferred a corrupt, brutal, mechanical and efficient police force - better a mercenary which can act against its own people. The Police Act, 1861 was designed for this ultimate aim after the great lesson from "First War of Indian Independence - 1857". Naturally the police have been anti-people, apathetic, brutal and touch-me-nots. The people never figured in their scheme of things and they don't figure even now. Their parameters of successful functioning and efficient handling of the situation are totally different from what people expect from them. The independent India has larger expectations from independent Indian police which has not been able to break the mindset of the colonial past. It, hence, draws severe public criticism; and the criticism lowers down their confidence and self-esteem leading to increased need of defence mechanism and running away from ground realities that resulted in further gap between police and people.

The police experiments in public relations thus started on two suppositions.

(i) There is nothing wrong with the police and policemen. They are good people with human qualities as other citizens of India. (ii) There is something wrong with the traditions, perception and the police system. The sub-culture of police has got great influence on its members. And minor changes can produce better results.

Based on these assumptions, the Narsipatnam police in 1989-1991 and Anantapur police in 1993 started experimentation in public relations. The basic conceptual change was that the police had to work for the people and not only for the government. The policemen should not do anything which hurts the people. Secondly, the general perception among the policemen that they should be aloof from the people because it compromises their toughness and impartiality, is a wrong concept. The policing will not succeed with fear and authority but impartiality and respect for 'rule of law' and 'equality before law'. The policemen should not be rough and tough but firm and polite. He should avoid all such acts which are illegal but implicity sanctioned and appreciated by society like blinding of Bhagalpur dreaded dacoits and beating a rapist in a public place or in custody. He must avoid all temptations of playing to gallery because the people appreciate a policeman temporarily for immediate relief but decry his action thoroughly in the long run. And finally the new idea that the police is the guardian of the society, friend in need and ubiquitous helper. They can't confine themselves to crime and law and order only, since an isolationist approach to such problems is bound to fail as it has failed. Policing should be sold off like a commodity. There should be no secrecy, mysticism about it. It should be transparent to all, nothing to hide.

With all these ideas, a psychological warfare was launched. The police started making people believe that they cared for them and they were only for them. The concept of 'Reception counters' at police stations was started at Narsipatnam and continued through Nizamabad and Anantapur towns. Lady constables were asked to receive all phone calls, reply on the wireless sets and usher in the visitors. It was comfortable for the lady visitors. The courteous reception of complainants was emphasised. In many cases the police officers were reprimanded or punished for behaving discourteously. People told "don't act on our complaints but behave well". The police got the cue – "A seat and a glass of water wins half the battle".

Organisational climate and work atmosphere also count much. All police stations were asked to shed off dirt and filth around, whitewash the police station buildings, maintain good turn-out with ironed-out uniform and polished shoes, develop garden and plant trees around police stations. To a great satisfaction some of the police stations did remarkably well whereas most of them washed their shabbiness off. The Superintendent of Police camp office and the District Police office was also given a 'look beautiful' exercise.

An 'Emergency cell' was proposed where the senior officer either at Anantapur or Narsipatnam received the complaints personally at any point of time (day or night) and assured action within forty eight hours. A set of officers maintained emergency cell register and monitored the action taken thereon on wireless sets. The complainants were further informed that they had to meet once more if they were not satisfied with police action. A more senior officer was asked to re-enquire into the complaints to be doubly sure about the genuineness of the police action.

Generally in police it becomes very difficult for a commoner to catch hold of an officer since he is either busy with all sorts of meetings or out on some tours. Monday was declared a 'Grievances day' when public could meet the Superintendent of Police. All SHOs, Inspectors and Deputy Superintendent of Police were asked to stay put at their headquarters for instant clarification on wireless set or phone about any problem brought forth to the Superintendent of Police. The complainants could know the action taken by police personally and instantly on the wireless set at the emergency cell. If he was not satisfied with that action he could appeal to Superintendent of Police, to look into it personally. Even though Superintendent of Police could not see all complaints personally, psychologically the gain was tremendous. The people were feeling that there was one agency where they could go to and all the SHOs and lower functionaries are not unreliable.

For the people of far-flung areas a new scheme 'Emergency card' was introduced. In this scheme in Narsipatnam five postcards addressed to ASP Narsipatnam with 'Emergency card' embossed on them were mailed to prominent persons of the villages in the area. They were required to write and post this card to police of all hush-hush crimes against women, weaker sections, public order and tranquility. It suited those helpless people who dared not talk openly against perpetrators of crimes or had no means of seeing the police because of their being in far-off places with no conveyance. It was more suitable for a place like Narsipatnam division with vast tracts of forest and tribal areas.

Police officers were asked to register cases without caring for statistics. No complaint should go unregistered. Non-registration of cases, minimisation of gravity of crimes or of value of lost property in property offences were strictly stopped. Many officers were suspended and punished for refusing to register the case or for minimising the gravity of offences because the old habits die hard. The Superintendent of Police, Anantapur told the police officers "Don't detect the property offence but register it". If you don't detect, your successor may do but if it is not registered, it is a life given to the criminals". Police officers are shy of registering the cases because their efficiency is judged on the statistics. It was conveyed in clear terms that statistics will not be measuring rod of their efficiency.

If there is one aspect of policing which brings bad name to the police most, that is prevention and detection of crime. All dirty jobs have been done in the name of prevention and detection of crime. Wrongful detection, use of third degree methods, instances of professional confessions of crimes, harassment of innocent persons on suspicion, false detention and recovery (due to pressure from the top to detect the case), corruption, custodial deaths etc., are by-product of the police obsession with property crimes. A survey showed that in a district like Anantapur of thirty-two lakh population all small and big thefts and dacoities combined could not cross 400-mark in a year. But the people were so hostile to the police due to their alleged crime work that they attacked four police stations previously in the district in one year alone – sometimes on account of lock-up deaths in course of investigation of property offences. It is not the actual number of lock-up deaths which is alarming but the psychological fear in people that they could also meet the same fate. Therefore a blanket ban on use of questionable methods for interrogation, use of baton in all circumstances except in law and order problems (as sanctioned by law), and illegal detention in the lock-up was imposed. It is remarkable to note here that the officers in Hyderabad were given this impression that the police officers in Anantapur were sympathetic to criminals. This is the age-old stereotyped image of police that the police must beat to get truth out of a thief! But the greatest achievement of the steps was the remarkable fall in public complaints against police harassment and instances of corruption. Once a police officer complained that the people were threatening them that if they did not act swiftly, they would complain against the police officer. The people were brazen and audacious and the police officer could teach that person a right lesson but for the Superintendent of Police because Superintendent of Police listened only to these petition mongers. A clear case of misunderstanding between local police and the public. I assuaged his feeling and told that very soon the man would realise that he was being too discourteous and you were the real helper, not the Superintendent of Police. The problem of today is not that the police did not work but that the people have lost confidence and see police action with jaundiced view.

Baton has never solved law and order problems. It has acted as a road-roller for the time being and in turn generated hatred against the system. Had the 'police stick' been so effective, there would have been no law and order problems today. It is the impartiality, firmness, respect for 'Rule of law' and equality before law which brings in law and order. The hard core tribe of pickpockets in Narsipatnam who continued their profession defying all beating and cases were calmed down with action as per law. Pick-pocketing was just stopped. In Nizamabad where the dacoities were a menace and could not be tackled despite indiscriminate beating, wrongful detention for six long months and harassment, were ultimately brought down to naught through lawful means, moral policing and public cooperation. It was a great surprise that the area in Nizamabad which reported eight dacoities per month was made dacoity-free by the basic police methods and simple patrolling.

There is general complaint against the police that it works for a small minority and overlooks majority. The police started a new concept of "public security system" in which it assured to provide constable watch at everybody's house who left his house to go outside for a week. We received many appreciation letters for this scheme in Narsipatnam and Anantapur. Measures like improved traffic, drinking water centers in summer season, medical camps in interior areas with the help of primary health center doctors, adult education centers, seminars on topics concerning burning social issues brought police closer to the people. All such camps were organised with the help of sister departments. Police could only offer itself as event-managers. These are cosmetic changes which many officers and organisations do but it is relevant for police also.

A campaign to prove police a friend of the people culminated in numerous *praja-sadassus* (people's meetings) i.e. each SHO conducting four *praja-sadassus* in a month for on the spot solution of the problems. The problems which could not be solved by the SHO were to be brought by the SHO to the Superintendent of Police. Surprisingly, many such problems not related to police were also brought to our notice including a psychological case where a man had phobia of the police. Of all the problems brought to our emergency cell, 80 per cent of the problems were related to land disputes, family problems, and social problems which could not be solved by any agency and they wanted our mediation for amicable settlement. A survey of random samples of people conducted by boys of Government Junior College, Narsipatnam showed that people wanted police to take interest in all walks of people's life and solve their problems like a good Samaritan instead of standing aloof and waiting them suffer because most of the social needs of the society have no earmarked agency to tackle such problems. They highly appreciated the police for the public relations exercise. Positive and proactive approach designed for the police won the hearts of the people. The system which is so impersonal, cold and ruthless doesn't suit the police functioning.

To bolster up confidence in the people about the police that the police really meant what they said, a big advertisement was given in vernacular newspapers that whosoever reported about any corruption or irregularity committed by police will be rewarded publicly. Not to be content with this, an open debate with all eminent personalities including journalists, lawyers, politicians, doctors, businessmen and commoners was organised about police functioning where charges were traded freely and emotions flowed. In the end, it was the police which gained because we proved that we have nothing to hide but transparency. To make the gains solid and reach all the ideas out to lower rung of hierarchy a crash training course for constables and head constables was programmed and executed. It received good response from the cutting edge officers i.e. the constables.

Development and social welfare cell is a concept to tap the potentials of police organisation. It is realised that police are the highly unexploited government resources for non-conventional use. When property worth one crore rupees is lost in all sorts of crimes in one district, few crores are spent only on TA and DA of the police personnel in that district. For saving one crore rupees if we maintain a behemoth which guzzles more them ten crore rupees, it is against all principles of management and accountancy. Police has to identify with the happiness and sorrows of the people. They have to work as nodal welfare authority particularly in rural areas.

To this end, all the police officers were asked to make night halts in the villages, interact with the people of the area and note down all their problems. All these problems would be entered in a register. Subsequently, the SHO will address the concerned authorities of other departments to solve the problem. If it is not solvable at local level, the SHO would write to District Special Branch. The Development and Social Welfare Cell, District Special Branch will correspond with the District authorities to sort out the issue. The Superintendent of Police will pursue the people's problem with the highest authorities for its logical conclusion. The District Special Branch will maintain data on all the issues solved or unsolved.

People have got tremendous suspicion on police. Though policemen are not that harsh and rude as people think but people don't believe a policeman. To obviate this impression and build up confidence in police system, wide publicity was given through Press and media that anybody who proved that he was wronged by police, will be rewarded Rs 500/- for every such complaint and tough action would be initiated against that officer. Though certain complaints came to our notice and few officers were punished on the basis of those complaints but none came forward to claim the money. The complainants felt embarrassed in taking the reward money. However, the number of such complaints were in single digit but the effect was like 440 volt. We conducted press conference and openly invited the people and even the media to come up with such complaints. It was not known whether all the complainants who had not got justice from police approached us but the credibility of police went up high.

A concept of *jan maitri* was started in which the police constable was made an in-charge of one or two villages depending upon the number of villages in that police station and the strength of the police station. They were virtually eyes and ears of the department to collect all vital and non-vital information and issues. They were advised to mingle with the people and collect information on all issues of public importance. They were also warned that they would be held liable if something happened in the village and they could not keep tab on the issue. The villagers had now visible government at their doorstep.

In Medak district, District Welfare Fund was created to help the orphan, helpless and poor in education, health, marriage and other social welfare matters. The need of such fund arose after breakout of communal riots and burning of some houses by a frenzied mob. A board was also created with respectable persons to monitor this fund. The police had nothing to do with this body and they had merely advisory role. This was an idea to bring police within the sympathy zone of people. It was very surprising that people donated enthusiastically to this welfare fund. This also ensured good feelings between both communities.

An idea of mobile policing in rural areas was also started where police vans would be moving in interior areas where there was no police presence and people settle all matters including rape themselves.

Many counselling centres like youth counselling, job counselling, marriage counselling was started with the help of conscientious people.

A traffic board was also constituted to involve the people effectively. Such traffic board and counselling centres have been tried at many places but the strength of the idea is in real practice and effective participation of the people.

Generally, the stolen properties recovered and seized by the police rot in the police station. All efforts which go in detection of cases and recovery and seizure of such properties go without appreciation because the people don't get their properties back. Police pat themselves in the back for good investigation and detection of the crime but the people curse them for not getting the property back. All the police officers were asked to return the property through the orders of the court that easily comes through. The court and the people both appreciate the police efforts and the police stations are also saved from giving the look of a junkyard.

Another new wing called Victims' Cell for compensation was also conceived to help the victims of the crime claim their amount of compensation. All the governments have sanctioned many grant and schemes for the welfare of the victims like victims of accident, rape, SC/ST atrocities, fire, Naxalism and terrorism but they don't get it because either they don't have any idea of the existence of such schemes or get tired in pursuing the labyrinthine process. This Cell sees to it that all victims of true cases get their compensation. The officers were asked to enter it in case diary whether the victim got his or her compensation. Sometimes small steps earn big hearts.

To improve the basic policing we also devised a 25-point checklist and 30-point programme for improvement in policing. Going by the Press reports it looked as if things were looking up.

But as usual, the government under pressure of the local people's representatives wanted transfer and cessation of all such activities in the name of the reforms. There was a bigger surprise in store when the High Court decreed in the public interest litigation petition filed by the lawyers that the People's Council was an unconstitutional body which was interfering with judicial process. Unfortunately, the court could not appreciate that People's Council was a social organisation and it was not taking any judicial decision. It seems that government pleaders could not put the facts across to the court in a proper way. But people had impression that the government pleaders and even the courts were sympathetic to the lawyers who were losing their livelihood due to existence of People's Council. Medak District Bar Council passed a resolution against all these police efforts because they were losing civil cases – the money spinner because of increased interaction of police with the villagers.

Many were sceptical about this policy because it did not endorse the traditional policy of 'tough police'. But the greatest satisfaction was for the reason that the policy got thumping endorsement by the people both in Narsipatnam and Anantapur. Like Watson, a behaviourist, the police can also claim "Give us any trouble-torn place with hostile people; with our behaviour therapy, we can make it police-friendly in one year". The people who say that police has negative image because of their nature of job are innocent of the ways of policing.

It was a great surprise to me that people who had nothing in common with me in language, culture, caste, lifestyle etc went for flash and complete strike against my transfer in districts and sub-divisions of Andhra Pradesh.

It is a different issue that our successors saw to it that all traces of 'reforms' were erased to the last print. Baby steps of reforms in police are always smothered. It happened with me also in all my postings. All efforts realy went waste.

Chapter 16

People's Council: A Novel Concept in Police-People Partnership

The police of the third world, developing and underdeveloped countries including India attract many allegations of human rights violations and people-unfriendly approach. The third world countries need a police – based on practical experiences and ground realities suited to their conditions. Medak police once have tried to evolve people-friendly and service-oriented police system which is a good example of police-public collaboration to deliver goods.

People's Police

The experiment in Medak with new policing has been to do policing for the people, of the people and by the people. Policing by the people is an old Indian concept, which is ingrained in our culture but has disappeared over time. In ancient India caste guilds and social communities played the role of police and courts very effectively and its traces are still available in certain parts of India. We tried to re-establish it through *gram panchayat* but the spirit could not be revived because of over-politicisation of the villages. The policing by the people through People's Council in Medak has succeeded and worked as a model for present '*Maitri Sangham*' in Andhra Pradesh which is a watered-down version of People's Council.

Police Role in Socio-Economic Regeneration

Today we do policing for the sake of policing and act in isolation without keeping the people in focus. People's service and welfare should be our aim which is not being achieved because of our defective approach to problem. The police cannot improve its image unless it widens its scope, break the confines of being limited to crime and law and order and encompass the activities relating to the well-being of people. The police should also help socio-economic and cultural regeneration of the society.

The concept of People's Council was based on three postulates.

1. The police can't succeed in policing unless it shares the socio-cultural responsibilities of the people.

   It means that the police have to break their colonial mindset, should step out of so-called police limits and self-imposed professional limitations and help the people solve their socio-economic and cultural riddles. Since there is no such agency that can help the people in daily chores of their life and petty nagging problems the police have to fill up the void if they want to succeed in enlisting people's cooperation in sharing police responsibilities. The people fail to understand as to why they should help the police in their job when they are paying for their services. Once the police show interest in them they will start showing interest in police. Dale Carnegie has said that it will take years to make people show interest in you for a partnership and two days if you show interest in them.

2. The people are ready to co-operate and trust the police if police trust them.

   It has been generally seen that there is always a massive response for police call for co-operation or any new steps of improving police-public relationship. The more difficult job is to sustain the interest of the people because the police after initial euphoria goes back to its shell. They are afraid of chinks in their tough exterior.

3. The police are unnecessarily rough and tough and secretive in their behaviours.

   The very concept that the police officers particularly middle and top order should be rough and tough is misleading. More appropriate will be the theory that the rough and tough policeman scares the general people whereas it means nothing to criminals because he has chosen the path of crime and it matters little whether the policeman is tall or short, tough or polite. The fiercely-looking policeman and slaughter house look of a police station has been like a scarecrow to the people. Policing is more in the nature of mental and psychological function than physical one. Anyway if the armed disturbances take place, we have got para-military forces. So, the police should be more open, transparent, outgoing and mixing type. There is no need of being secretive because by mixing, you collect more intelligence.

People's Council/*Gram Samiti*

In every village People's Council is formed to take care of all the problems including social, educational, health, police and family problems. It was started on 12-01-1996, and attracted very good response from the people.

People's Council is an idea to revive the spirit of brotherhood, self-reliance and unity among the people through police efforts. It has been realised that no law and order and crime problems can be tackled without people's help. The increasing influence of the anti-social elements and organised vested interests on government machinery and police has further led to the need of people's help for effective policing. The potentials of the police department are like a river which is not being channelised for the people's welfare and going waste. If we channelise the centuries-old police influence on the society and people there will be revolutionary change in the concept of the police and its relations with the public and overall socio-economic reformation and regeneration.

People's Council is also a concept to change the society, to make the government schemes a success and improve the police-public relations for optimally utilising the police infrastructure and manpower for development and welfare activities. Police officers give a confused look if I say that police should see that every child should go to school, the sports is promoted in the villages and the villages maintain health and hygiene. I feel that the above are the prime duties of police because crime and lawlessness is the product of host of complex factors. People have turned cynical and they don't trust any government agency. The police job is such that without co-operation from the people, it can neither curb crime nor prevent lawlessness. But if we somehow enlist the co-operation of the people, the police job could be lightened by at least 60 per cent. Whether it is intelligence collection or information about occurrence of crime or hide-outs of criminals or traffic maintenance or crowd control or riot management, people's support is of immense value. But the police have never tried to win the hearts and minds of the people and so have miserably failed in their primary tasks. They don't understand that small gestures of kindness means a lot. Since our society is not educated and it may take minimum fifty years to make everybody literate, the influence of police over their mind is tremendous. Advice from police officers in villages is taken as government orders. This leverage of police has to be used for the improvement of the people's lot. Police should concern themselves with all public issues that are supposedly non-police issues but indirectly affect the crime scenario. It doesn't require a rocket scientist to understand that an illiterate and unemployed young man with immense frustration and enough time with empty mind is an explosive dynamo that can batter public peace. This can be tempered if we empower the people to do the police job. And People's Council or *Gram Samiti* is an attempt at that.

Every village or its hamlet will have a People's Council or *Gram Samiti*.

1) Number of members : 15 to 20 members

2) Who can be members :

1. Freedom fighters
2. Retired employees
3. Caste elders
4. *Sarpanch,* MPTC, Ex-*sarpanch* elected representatives
5. *Dwacra* Group in-charges, *Mahila Mandali* Presidents and all other lady clubs
6. Youth clubs, Nehru Yuva Kendras, Youth Associations,
7. Teachers
8. VAO as Ex-officio members
9. Voluntary organisations
10. Any social organisation or club
11. Any respectable person selected by villagers

3) Disqualification :

1. Anybody involved in any criminal case
2. Militants and sympathisers of any extremist group
3. Ill-reputed persons like smugglers, bootleggers etc.

Meetings

In villages People's Council should meet every month. They should inform about the resolution to SI. There will be one Secretary to People's Council who can be changed any time as per the wishes of the People's Council. There will be General Body Meeting once every three months. SI/ASI/HC will attend the meeting merely as an observer. It will include all the villagers. The General Body can change council members of the People's Council. Any member who does not attend three consecutive meetings will be automatically removed from the council.

Objectives

1. To check flow of arrack in the village.
2. To check social vices like gambling, prostitution, bhanamathi, harassment of women and weaker-ones etc.
3. To stop the activities of anti-social elements and check their visits to the village.
4. To form village defence squads for the protection against thieves and anti-social elements.
5. To spread adult literacy and to send all the children below ten years to schools.
6. To persuade the parents to undergo family planning.
7. To promote sports activities.
8. Tree plantation
9. Every People's Council must create one asset through *Shramadan*. Police can assist them by getting governmental help.
10. To counsel the villagers for amicable settlements in land-disputes, family disputes, petty cases and other civil disputes. All such settlement reports should have to be informed to SI. All such disputes should be settled through the consent of both the parties. Nobody should be compelled to abide by the decision of People's Council. The resolution of conflicts should be through counselling and mutual consensus. All People's Councils will act within

Legal Services Authority Act 1987 and bring all disputes to its notice. Police will not directly interfere but see that People's Council don't go beyond legal framework.

11. To observe the functioning of government offices, welfare and developmental measures including fair price shops. They should report to the higher officers and people's representatives of any lapses.
12. To maintain cleanliness in the village, help the sick persons and other health problems.
13. Any other social welfare measures suggested by the villagers.
14. Prepare a report about the problems of the village and send it to SI every month to be taken up at higher levels.

The People's Council will be helped by three wings in the village. It will have:

(i) Youth wing

(ii) Women wing

(iii) Village defence squad

Youth wing will consist of youths of the village who will shoulder the responsibility of giving dynamism to the development of village including sports promotion, cultural promotion, *sharmadan*, literacy etc.

The women wing will take care of the atrocities on women of the village which generally does not come to light. The women wing will fight against all such atrocities and try for consciousness among the women of the village. They will also try for economic self-sufficiency of the women through various voluntary organisations and government schemes.

The village defence squad will comprise of selected able-bodied persons of the village who will resist all anti-social forces including the extremists and thieves. They will make night rounds during dark fortnights and unitedly face any physical intimidation by any anti-social group till the police help reaches.

Selection of Members

Age: The People's Council members should not be below eighteen years. Education is not mandatory.

Process: A meeting in the village will be called. The villagers will be asked to select 15-20 members to the People's Council. There should be unanimous selection of the People's Council members. All communities, sex and age-groups (except children) should be represented. The role of SI will be that of a facilitator and advisor.

Duration: The elected People's Council should continue for three years. The *Sarpanch/Mukhia* and Ex-*Sarpanch*/Ex-*Mukhia* will be ex-officio-members of the People's Council. If the general body wanted, the People's Council could be dismissed any time. People's council Convener/ Secretary could be re-elected but the convener should invariably change every three years.

Maitri Sangham of AP police:

Andhra Pradesh started *Maitri Sangham* modelled on the lines of People's Council. But the *Maitri Sangham* could not wish away certain flaws because of non-changing mindset that it should confine to police job. Now there have been complaints of *Maitri Sangham* members working as police brokers. *Maitri Sangham* members are mostly dependent on police for their sustenance and the police play the big-brother role in this partnership. Nobody can play big-brother to the people. And if anybody plays, he is bound to fail. *Maitri Sangham,* though a good beginning could not imbibe the spirit of People's Council because we balked at empowering the people to a reasonable extent. Reservations in our approach make people suspicious and it fails.

The People's Council was such a roaring success that the CPI-ML (PWG) threatened all the People's Council members to desist from its meetings. In their Provincial

Committee despatches, they noted that this concept was doing great damage to CPI-ML (PWG)'s roots. The district Bar Association of Medak filed a writ petition against the People's Council and police because cases were being settled by people, among themselves with the help of people's council and the lawyers got fewer cases. With it their income also dwindled. The local politicians complained because none was going to meet them for any help and it was impacting their clout. They felt they were losing their hegemony. Surprisingly, it was naxalites and the politicians who claim to be working for people, were the greatest adversaries of peoples council. The naxalites worked overtime to threaten, beat and intimidate People's Council (later named *Gram Samiti*) members. The politicians did loud and vociferous thinking that if the police did everything, what would be their role and who would care for them.

Subsequently a meeting of People's Council members was called in 1996 at District Headquarters which was a sight to cherish. Men, women, children on various conveyances like cycles, motorcycles, rickshaws, bullock-carts, wheel-carts, jeeps, cars from far flung areas assembled to hear the police. The Press estimated the crowd to be 15,000. This was all without spending a single paise. It is to note that they were only *Gram Samiti* members. We had not called general body members or villagers to the meeting otherwise it would have run into lakhs. And this crowd for a small district like Medak was unprecedented.

But as happens in police, the man proposes and the successor disposes. The successor Superintendent of Police took the first action to discontinue all these practices to take it back to square one. And this was the grand burial of police reforms which could have been game-changer.

The People's Council is a concept that can be applied to any place with local modifications. It will give a real boost to police-public partnership in policing and grievance redressal. This will be the real reform in police that can bring about revolutionary changes in concept of administration.

Chapter 17

Integrated Approach to Training

When we were in training we were made to run like horses, ate sumptuous breakfast (everything looked sumptuous after that drill) and slept in indoor classes. Our speakers were so understanding that they lulled us into sleep through their lectures if sleep was not coming otherwise. Many miles to sleep before we pass out of this training minefield was our motto. Except fabricating some imaginative love stories between the trainees and sometimes between the faculty members there was nothing worthwhile to learn or pass time. So, we fervently hoped for end of the nightmare.

Sadism is synonymous with perfect training. Police training is sadism personified. All basic training courses are nightmares and in-service courses a pleasure trips.

Training has been such a great waste of time, money and energy. I lost my better part of originality during training. I have particular fascination for police training because it is the best way to produce rascals.

Let's talk something about training

Training makes a man perfect but police training makes a robot out of a man. A normal human being starts behaving abnormally as if he is possessed with vampire. This is not my feeling but what the people in general say. Hundred years of training could not produce policemen who could bring in genuine changes in the image of police. It carries the same cross of bad image what it bore hundred years back. Doubts have been expressed about the very need of training institution. Would it not be more useful and wise to close down all the training institutions? How does it affect the functioning of police department? The new recruits can be imparted on-the-job training, which will reduce cost of training and add to the man-days of police department. There is nothing in the training institutions that can't be taught on-the-job. Many of the departments don't impart any basic training to their executives in exclusive institutions but their officers are as efficient as the police officers who learn many more dirty tricks in their training institutions.

Less we talk about the content of the police training the better. If a commoner knows about the contents of police training, he will feel appalled to know how his tax-money is being wasted. But for paramilitary forces, no police force gets opportunity to do parade in its day-to-day activities nor it is required to do so. But more than three-fourths of training time is wasted on parade, physical endurance and other outdoor activities like *lathi* drill, horse-mounting and unarmed combat. Nobody can learn unarmed combat tricks in thirty classes. Parade is never used in normal times except 'attention' 'at ease' and 'salutations'. It will be a great fun to see policemen learning riot-control drill and *lathi* drill to face mob violence. I have never seen any of the policemen using all these techniques in controlling mob violence.

Training contents don't meet the requirements of a good policeman. Right from IPS down to constable the policeman is given a good dose of physical toughening as if they have to go for Olympics. After a reasonably longer period of physical work-out none is left with energy or motivation to grasp even a single word of academic inputs. The foundation of wrong concepts that the policeman should look fierce, rough and tough with a cruel face is laid down here with all inhuman treatment and belabouring received at the hands of trainers. Without any off-setting ennobling contents cadets lose human elements and finer nuances of a civic life. Here we get police officers of stunted mental growth. Unfortunately, the physical toughening process comes to no use because all police officers react to this excessive physical strain after training and develop allergy to all exercises leading to big belly – a readymade grist for criticism for the movies and cartoons.

Most of the training institutions have no favourable climate for training. They are starved of resources. Sometimes they are so impractical and theoretical in their approach that it can't be emulated. Once a policeman is out of training institutes, he is never back to any training course. The basic training is taken as some sort of baptism. Basically all jobs require right attitude, a little bit of commitment and dedication than the bookish knowledge. And it is more true of police service. Knowledge about laws, guns and procedures is hardware which is just useless without software of right approach, commitment and dedication. A policeman with all these qualities with a dash of commonsense will do far better than a trained graduate from such training police institutions who are not convinced of the need of their own existence.

The issue has got fixated because of some old-timers who have got great faith in these techniques and time tested training methods. Whenever the training system is blamed for the ills in the police, pat comes the reply that those who advocate for change in the system, don't suggest new system to substitute the old ones. When pressure mounts, committees like Gore Committee is formed to silence words of criticism. I am always unable to understand what has happened to us. We became slave so many times because of our rigid attitude to learn from the mistakes and adjust with the times but still we are ostrich-like. We refuse to listen to saner elements. The western society has crucified one Jesus Christ but we are crucifying 'Jesuses' daily who dare to vent saner voices. So, we are what we are today.

We are very poor in martial arts. So, invaders kept on running through India without any meaningful resistance. We should have developed our skills and military tactics, police tactics and methods but we refused to change to be overrun again and again by all sorts of foreign invaders. In the last 5000 years, we never attacked anybody but were attacked many times; vanquished and plundered.

Definitely there is something wrong with the system. If training is good, products will be good. Good products will definitely better the image of the department. We find that there is persistent decline in image and standards of policing for various reasons. We can fault the government for interference, and starving the police for fund, infrastructure, manpower, and binding it with irrational procedures. The courts can be blamed for delays in justice, their suspicious attitude towards police and liberal attitude to criminals and their indifference towards plight of a policeman; laws can be blamed for being anachronistic, liberal and defective. Society can also share its part of blame for not understanding the police and helping it in solving its problems. All these factors are beyond police pale of influence to change either the government or the court or the laws. But they definitely can try to change this society and themselves.

Today the basic principles of police training are based on perfecting the policeman and his techniques. It is unilateral in approach. It trains only the service-providers but never cared for the service-user. The consumers are the people and we never bothered to enlighten them and train them. All the good consumer companies don't only train their mechanics but the users also. The users should know how to derive maximum benefit out of the products. They should also know the precautions and dangers involved, scope of services and utilities. The police is also a service organisation. It never focused on its most important consumer – the people. They have lots of misgivings and misconceptions about police. They don't have right idea about this all-important service provider that is entrusted with the responsibility of protecting life, honour and property of a man. The present approach to police training is defective, truncated and lop-sided. It should be holistic.

As there is solution to every problem, there is solution to this problem also. Integrated approach to training is one good way-out. This concept is based on principles of seeking people's co-operation and understanding. The police training should take the people – the customers, into account. The people should also know the utility, possibilities, limitations and handicaps of police service. Out of their ignorance they presume many things. The police is meant for service to the people but is broadly caught in quagmire of government, laws, courts and statistics to the exclusion of people.

Basically, speaking, training should have two-pronged approach. It may continue enlightening the police officers as it does today with change in contents of syllabus, approach and orientation. Secondly, it should also start modules to sensitise the people about optimum utilisation of police services.

About contents, approach and orientation of police training syllabus, many committees have presented their studies and deliberations. Now there is no more need of studies but will to implement them. Once application process starts, further refinements take place in due course.

Sensitisation of people needs certain concrete steps. It may start with simple techniques of public relations. The training institutions may start essay competitions, painting competitions, music and sculpture competitions on the police themes. The people from different walks of life may be invited to participate. These events may be given wide publicity. Participation should be encouraged and certain prizes can be distributed on Republic Day or Independence Day or any specially organised functions.

The police trainees may be given opportunity to interact and have a meaningful interface with people, in their own settings. Generally interfaces are organised for trainees by inviting certain people to training institutions. This makes the whole atmosphere artificial and uncomfortable. The trainees may be left in the villages, small towns, urban wards for 15 days; and free discussions and interactions may be allowed about the expectations and apprehensions of people. Both trainees and people may have brain-storming sessions about their perceptions, presumptions, capabilities and possibilities, sensibilities and conditionalities of policing. The trainees may be allowed to stay in the village for some time and a facilitator may be provided to organise free and frank discussions. This should be incorporated in the training curriculum itself as I included in Andhra Pradesh police syllabus.

When there are no training courses running, the training institutes should try to train the customers i.e. people about police strength and weaknesses, its limitations and opportunities. The people should know how they can avail the services of the police and how much. Such workshops could be conducted in the villages and remote areas also.

Seminars and symposia may be organised in all academic institutions with trainees and students as participants. The schools and academic institutions are great disseminator of messages and information. By holding such seminars a rapport may be created between the budding opinion-makers and the police trainees. The apprehensions may be cleared in the beginning itself. The people from Press and media may be invited to all such symposia and seminars. They may also be taken to villages during interface of the trainees with the people in their own setting. The bias and prejudices of the Press may melt down by seeing all these sincere efforts at police training.

Such seminars and symposia may consequently be conducted in every village. Care has to be taken that all such seminars and symposia do not become formalities. Committed instructors only should be entrusted this task.

Specialisation is a good thing but sometimes it is dangerous. It leads to compartmentalisation of goals and thus defeat the purpose. More so it has happened in the case of police. Police has been asked to confine itself to its own items of work. This arrangement is divorced from many realities and happenings of the society. It is incapable in sharing the sorrows and happiness of the people. And so people fail to emotionally integrate with the police.

Police is in an enviable position to become instruments of social change. It can be a great psychological nurse to the society. The training should be directed toward this goal also. The emotional integration of people with police will solve most of the problems in one stroke. This can't be done unless police are trained to empathise with people in their sorrows and happiness. Any attempt by any police officer of emotional integration of police with people has yielded tremendous response. It is pity that police have failed to tap these vast opportunities.

Police training has indirectly led to emotional chasm between people and police. In police training there is nothing which teaches them to think for people. This major inconsistency of not having service component in police training should be removed. The trainees may start with their lessons on emotional integration with people.

The trainees can be taken to all spots of human sufferings and degradation. Well-documented and reasoned lectures on such sufferings can be delivered on-the-spot. They can be taken for field visits to charity hospitals, prostitutes' homes, mentally retarded shelters, old-age homes, untouchables' colonies, extremism-ravaged areas, places of natural calamities, orphanages, *devdasis* and in far-flung areas where human existence is miserable. The trainees should be allowed to interact and form their opinion. A facilitator should always be there to help form positive opinions. They can interact with voluntary organisations, human rights organisations, government departments, politicians of all hues and colours. They should be made to visit service institutions like charity hospitals, AIDS victims rehabilitation centres etc to see how the workers there serve the humanity without expecting anything in return. If they can serve the society, the policemen who are taken care of well by the government can very comfortably do it. The trainees may also have one-month community service in their curriculum.

The police trainees may discuss issues like illiteracy, population, poverty, corruption in all forms-social, political, economic and cultural – evil effects of casteism, environment, proper growth in economy, sports, harmony etc. It is not necessary that the trainees may harp only on police subjects. It is more advisable that trainees talk less about subjects when they go for interface with people in their own settings. The police issues will automatically spring up. Let the people think that the visitors are really concerned about their affairs. The police have to show that they are helpers to the society. Helping the society is their main job and maintenance of law and order and crime prevention is by-product.

It is also not necessary that police trainees may be imparted training in police institutions only. They can be given on-the-job training also. But since our police stations are not properly equipped, we may first start with training institutions as nodal centres. After sometime we can limit the role of training institutions in training in theories for a month or two. Afterwards more on-the-job training can be imparted.

Basically, the training provided by training institutions today is more redundant than relevant. The curricula look more funny and of little use. If we cut out the irrelevant portions like parade, PT, *lathi* drill etc for civil police officers and enjoin upon them training themselves in laws by self-study, 90 per cent of the job of the training institutions will be over. It is a common experience that all policemen lose their physical fitness and knowledge of laws once they leave police training institutions. It seems, the present training pattern wastes time on irrelevant things. It also cultivates negative discipline, apathy to people and inferiority among police officers.

Today training is more trainer-centric. Knowledge in the theories and laws gets precedence over actual learning. Trainees become secondary. Trainees learn very little of whatever is taught in the training institution. Besides this, the training institutes teach ideal things that can be practised in ideal institutions and ideal situations. It has very little connect with the ground situations. So, the bosses in the field tersely command all the greenhorns coming fresh from the training institutions to forget what they had learnt there because they are more a handicap than a handle. The instructors also know this and they perhaps never expect the trainees to follow whatever they teach. Once the trainees are out of institutes they see the vast gap between what they were taught in institutions and what they see on the field. At the first instance itself, they dump all the teachings of training institutions and become practical.

All police trainings ignore application. It is all mugging up business. Surprisingly even higher institutions like SVPNPA, Hyderabad also deal only with dry theoretical lessons. Trainees have no scent of the purpose and meaning of all this training. The purpose of training is not known to trainer also.

Interactive methodology as described earlier will leave deep imprint on the mind of trainees. Generally, the talk in values and ethics is frowned upon; but it will be of great use if it is given by people of conviction. We can invite people of great eminence and virtues to interact with the trainees. We should consciously avoid people who have achieved high positions through machinations and manipulations. It is a difficult choice but we have to make it. The trainees have to differentiate vices and virtues on their own by interacting with various people of great virtues. The race of careerism should be dissuaded in the budding stage itself.

Group activity should be encouraged to inculcate team work. Presently police training is so rigorous that it can produce only sadists. We drive them to the point of break-down so far as physical regimentation is concerned. We keep them deprived of all social and emotional sources. It may be necessary for paramilitary and military but certainly not for police if we want to make police a service. These things have to be kept in mind before we discard the present training syllabi and adopt the new one. Every trainee wants to get over the phase of training as fast as possible with a feeling of never to look back. This is a sad commentary on our training syllabus and institutions. They never treat it as their alma-mater to feel nostalgic and affectionate about. They have mostly negative reminiscences. This situation has to change.

However, it is very necessary that facilitator should be willing, committed and knowledgeable. As of today all police training institutions are stuffed with unwanted, unwilling and uninspired faculty members who do more harm than good to trainees. No training at all is far better than present training. We have to choose facilitators from all walks of life. They should be more social service agents than police officers. They have to emphasise more on attitude and orientation than the content of the syllabus. Knowledge can be imbibed if the man is inspired, willing and sincere. We have to create atmosphere in training institutes which is conducive.

Integrated approach to training thus involves people and trainees in equal measure. It also entails changes in content, approach and orientation of the syllabi. The environment, facilitators and methodology need modification. All this cost little money and efforts but results will be tremendous in terms of social service and peace and harmony. Can we do it? At least, so far we have not done it and there is nothing visible in the horizon for future also.

Chapter 18

Who will cry for Police?

As a policeman myself, I have to seek some explanation for such a poor image. Once I was watching TV. The reporter was interviewing wives of policemen. One lady was carrying vegetables in bags. She was in a boisterous mood to defend her husband and his service. "What will these people say? Who is not a thief? The poor policeman does not get enough even to meet the basic requirements of family. Now I am carrying this bag. Most of your viewers must be feeling that I have got it free from the market because you newspaper reporters feed such imaginative stories to the people".

Spice is the life of story. There should be a whipping boy. Unless you search for somebody as a whipping boy, you can't explain the whole situations in the story. Our films, our TV shows, our news reports add spice to their stories by sprinkling of police brutalities.

Bashing police makes a good story. When the society is crumbling someone has to be made responsible.

But like the wife of that policeman, I will also do my duty to defend police and see some points for them.

Police is a great service but it is in total disarray. We see very committed police officers and men dying in thousands for the safety of people and unity and integrity of the country. It is only the police which has lost incredibly high number of senior officers including IPS officers. But it is tragic that this is the most maligned and favoured-to-kick organisation. This is a great dilemma which every policeman finds himself in. Violence and terrorism have unfortunately come to stay in India for a host of factors – political, social, economic and cultural. Police have no control or any say in any of the factors leading to the anarchy in the society. But we call the police invariably to deal with the formidable task for which they are no way equipped. Take anything like infrastructure, resources, training, motivating factors, incentives etc. You will find police a poor match to any terrorist organisation in India. To talk about laws and courts is a sad tale. The police officers are treated like criminals as if the maintenance of law and order in the society is their personal gain. Less we talk about police infrastructure is better. Pushing the archetypal police jeep down the road, cajoling it to start or a police station running in *jhuggi–jhonpdi* is a common sight. Training is in a miserable condition. After basic training, 90 per cent of the policemen don't get a chance to feel rifle or undergo any refresher course. Even the syllabi in SVPNPA, Hyderabad, a premier institution for training of IPS, don't have input to produce humanised force to meet the expectations of vibrant aspiring Indian populace. They still feel they have to serve British India. If we count demotivating factors and disincentives, the list will be inexhaustive. Dehumanising service conditions, constant death-threat, twenty-four hour job, negative image among the people, poor stature and pay structure, the Press and media hunting like hawks, laws treating them as second-grade citizens and poor promotional avenues provide little incentives. The successive raw deal meted out to police officers by various pay commissions is a fact in issue.

The police system is a tool. It can't produce good results on its own. It depends on its user. The flaws and lacunae of the system are not its creation. If the police system is not able to deliver goods, it is not the fault of policemen. The police Act 1861 has continued despite policeman crying hoarse for its change. The National Police Commission, 1978 recommendations which is also not all pervasive and radical, are gathering dust. We continue to distrust the police system by subjugating them to magistracy and judiciary and thus forcing the system to adopt defence mechanism. There is common perception among the policemen that it is better to have a judge or magistrate as an enquiry officer in any police related crime than to have a police officer who is more ruthless. There is common feeling that police system is being deliberately kept cruel, brutal, subservient but efficient in times of need by the vested interests. The police system is ironically forced to be efficient for its survival by the vested interests so that the system may serve their ends when the need arises. It is the reason that the police who have fought terrorism in Punjab, the Naxalism in Andhra Pradesh and dacoit menace in Madhya Pradesh and Uttar Pradesh successfully are a big flop to deliver the goods for common people. It is because it is neither intended nor designed to serve the common people. It is meant for being scapegoat if something goes wrong. It is something like diarchy-responsibility without power and role. The police have no role to play in the general mechanics of administration and socio-economic-politico life of people which cause turbulence in human life but they are held responsible for all ills and lawlessness in society.

The social role of the police can be better understood if we see the fair-like sight at police station in Andhra Pradesh coastal belt. The people in hundreds don't come for any crime but for such issues which have nothing to do with police. The issues range from arranging inter-caste love-marriages through husband wife disputes to complicated social economic and political issues. And I am a witness to it that 80 per cent of the police time is consumed in working as 'social Arbiters'. Surprisingly, when there is a cry to confine police to law and order only, the all-pervasive role of police in coastal belt is highly appreciated and accepted by the people. Is it different from a role of social worker? Is it necessary to doubt every motive and every action of a policeman? Can we not take him as a good Samaritan without any string attached to his image at least in his role of a social worker? These are such aspects which have not been taken into consideration even by the National Police Commission. The society can gain a lot by recognising the socio-economic and developmental role of police. All police institutions which are held responsible for cleaning public life are subjugated to some persons or agencies who are not responsible anyway to the people or media or nation to answer for lawlessness. Naturally the situation now is like give dog a bad name and hang it whenever it suits you. The police thus is caught in vicious trap. It can't get its due, its deserved stature and dignity despite its supreme sacrifice. And this piquant situation is adding to the frustration of a policeman. A constable can't think of a promotion. He is born constable and dies a constable. A police officer actually becomes more suited to any job after braving fire of constant death-risk, demanding duties and testing public gaze. It is left to the intelligentsia to recognise the services of the police.

The police are playing many roles which it is not supposed to do as per Parent Act, i.e. Police Act 1861. All the responsibilities to keep the man's life rolling that are not attended to by any other agency, come to police automatically without sanction of law but the tacit sanction of the society. Unfortunately the elite of the society and opinion makers shy from recognising this role of police. They keep quiet till the things go fine because of police handling of all such unattended social needs but they start crying of undue police interference in unchartered areas when it doesn't suit them. This double standards and double thought of the Press and intelligentsia has put the policemen to tremendous psychological and professional strain.

The society feels coy to admit that our criminal justice system has collapsed; our laws are outdated and the systems are dysfunctional. There should be urgent and comprehensive change in our attitude and thinking towards the whole process. It is foolish to flog dead horse like police and criminal justice system. It doesn't serve any purpose. Even if God comes in place of a police officer, He will be an utter failure in our present police set-up. Certain police officers look bright and on certain occasions certain police performances look positive only because we view them in narrow perspective and in situational circumstances.

When the situation is quite depressing it is the reformed and a new vibrant police system which can save the society. The dilemma and role-conflict of a policeman is to be tackled by the society and powers-that-be. The hostility to a tool (the police system) is misplaced. It should be directed against the user (the laws and the society). The tool was designed for different type of work and different set of circumstances. We have to change it. We have to recognise the larger role of police in our fast developing life. We can't see police in isolation as a mechanical tool for checking law and order menace. When *The Hindu* writes that the policemen should be confined to "law and order" alone, they forget that this isolationist policy has failed the system. We should shed tears for policemen who die in thousands every year with this role conflict in mind and fond hope of serving the society but with the agony that the people have not recognised their services and the martyrdom of G Pardesi Naidu, Randhir Varma, Govind Ram, Vandana Mulick beckons to the people to give a fair consideration to the whole issue in total perspective and help police get fair system fair laws, and fair deal. And this demand of fair deal is only to serve the people better. Is there anyone who will cry for the police?

CHAPTER 19

Why do Experiments Fail?

As I have said earlier, police is a change-resistant organisation which drills into the mind of a policeman the natural impulse to resist change. Right from the Director General of Police down to the police constable, all frown upon any change. Cosmetic changes are appreciated but systemic changes are spurned. All of my successors saw to it that whatever I tried was thrown overboard lock, stock and barrel. Seniors passed derogatory comments, peers jeered at and the subordinates looked with all doubts and uneasiness. Working for reforms in police is like ploughing the sand.

Even if you could pass through the travails of resistance by police brethren, the powers-that-be undo it. They have installed an iron-frame. Transfer is the most potent weapon. They just nudge you out if you become a grain inconvenient. Your all reforms, hard work and assiduously executed changes come down tumbling. You are asked to be out of the loop. No reforms sustain without the nurse. The nurse is thrown out. The plants of reform die automatically.

Vested interests in the form of powerful groups, individuals, media barons, caste groups, criminal elements get offended easily because it is generally they who get hit by all such reforms. They see to it that you are liquidated. They may attack you from all sides. You are not a Bollywood hero. You are alone without moneybag to sustain yourself and your family. You are forced to fade out in oblivion.

The people, the media and all stakeholders don't identify with any of police reforms. They have adopted a policy of aloofness. That fire which is required for change, is missing. Perhaps they are waiting for last straw on the camel's back.

The reformers themselves have fat ego. They think that there is none a super intellectual like him. He goes out of sync with the time and the people. He becomes a lone ranger by his own choice and is destined to fail.

There is an old and weather beaten story: once Police Heads of Russia, China and India went to God and asked, as to when the police officers will become people-friendly. God replied to the Head of Russian Police that it would take fifty years. He similarly replied to the Chinese Head of the Police that it would take hundred years for Chinese police system to change. Similarly, the Head of Indian Police requested about expected time for Indian police to change. God had tears in his eyes. He replied with heavy voice "Child, there will be definitely a change in the Indian police but I will not be there to see it!" This is the condition of the hope of police reforms in India.

Whatever the reasons, all attempts at systemic changes have failed and are bound to fail till people of the nation realise that changes are for them and they have to force it.

Index